THE NEW JOURNALIST

The New Journalist

Roles, Skills, and Critical Thinking

Edited by

Paul Benedetti

Tim Currie

Kim Kierans

2010
EMOND MONTGOMERY PUBLICATIONS
TORONTO, CANADA

Emond Montgomery Publications Limited
60 Shaftesbury Avenue
Toronto ON M4T 1A3
http://www.emp.ca/university

Printed in Canada on recycled paper.
Reprinted December 2011.

We acknowledge the financial support of the Government of Canada through the Canada Book Fund for our publishing activities.

Acquisitions and development editor: Mike Thompson
Marketing manager: Christine Davidson
Supervising editor: Jim Lyons
Copy editor: Claudia Forgas
Proofreader: Francine Geraci
Indexer: Paula Pike
Cover designers: Stephen Cribbin & Simon Evers

Library and Archives Canada Cataloguing in Publication

The new journalist : roles, skills, and critical thinking / Paul Benedetti, Tim Currie, Kim Kierans.

Includes index.
ISBN 978-1-55239-329-1

1. Journalism. I. Benedetti, Paul II. Currie, Tim III. Kierans, Kim, 1956-

PN4731.N44 2010 070.4 C2010-900783-2

Brief Contents

PART THREE Social Media and Multimedia

PART FOUR Responsibilities

Contents

PART THREE Social Media and Multimedia

Preface

As journalism undergoes unprecedented changes, there is no shortage of opinion about what it all means, both for the practice of journalism and for society as a whole. But above all the noise, one simple fact will always remain, no matter what forms and directions journalism might take: the basic desire people have to be kept informed, to *know*.

With journalism embarking on a new path, the time seemed ideal to produce this book. But we felt a simple overview of reporting skills would not suffice; students today require a broader sense of what journalism is—its economics and ethics, its recent history and its new capabilities—and they need to bring a critical thinking mindset to the Internet-based world. We hope we've achieved our goal of offering readers a thorough and accessible introduction to this vitally important profession.

The recurring boxes are designed to draw attention to the daily working lives of journalists ("In Practice"), relevant background information ("Sidebar"), and advice on specific skills ("Tools & Tips").

Behind this book lie a couple of simple core beliefs: first, that journalism is undeniably changing in fundamental ways, and that these changes, though difficult in some respects, offer great potential to create better journalism; and second, no matter what changes technology brings, the many perennially important (and mostly "platform-neutral") journalism skills that have formed the foundation of good journalism over the years will remain no less important in the 21st century. In other words, knowing how to ask a good question will always be an essential skill, regardless of where a story appears.

The title *The New Journalist* might remind some readers of the literary "new journalism" movement of the 1960s and 1970s, but at the risk of causing any confusion, the publisher and editors decided that it should be kept for this volume, because it captured the idea of a new type of craftsperson being born. There can be no doubt that being a journalist today means something different from what it did in decades past, in terms of both practical skills and professional values. This book not only recognizes that journalists must change with the world around them, but also offers the hope that a new generation of journalists will be capable of *leading* those changes.

At the heart of journalism today is a great paradox: the industry is in the midst of uncertainty caused by the very same technologies that allow journalism to reach far broader audiences, more quickly, and with greater input, feedback, and resources than ever before. We feel strongly that journalism's future is very bright. Technology is changing journalism forever, but the core techniques of quality journalism are more important than they have ever been. We hope you'll agree that this book does a good job of straddling those two realities.

• • •

The publisher and authors wish to thank the following people for their feedback and assistance during the development of this project: Patricia Bell (University of Regina), Wade Hemsworth (*The Hamilton Spectator*), Paul Knox (Ryerson University), Wayne MacPhail (media consultant, *w8nc.com*), Mary McGuire (Carleton University), Ivor Shapiro (Ryerson University), and Lois Sweet (Carleton University). We also wish to thank the many contributors to this volume for sharing their insights and expertise.

The authors also wish to thank copy editor Claudia Forgas and supervising editor Jim Lyons, and acquisitions editor Mike Thompson for proposing this project.

Additional Resources

Several of the chapters in this book are accompanied by videos designed to assist students in understanding specific skills or concepts. Please visit the book's website, **emp.ca/newjournalist**. The website also offers an online appendix to Chapter 19, "Convergence Journalism: Audio," which presents extensive guidelines to using the free audio-editing software Audacity.

Please also visit the website for information on the ebook version of *The New Journalist*.

About the Authors

Paul Benedetti has been a professional reporter and writer for more than 25 years. He has published work in the *Globe and Mail*, *Toronto Star*, *Hamilton Spectator*, *Canadian Living*, *Homemakers*, *Reader's Digest*, and many others. He served as deputy editor of *J-Source.ca*, and teaches full time in the journalism program at the University of Western Ontario. He is the author of the book *Spin Doctors*, an in-depth investigation of the chiropractic industry in Canada.

Tim Currie is an assistant professor of journalism at the University of King's College in Halifax. He teaches online journalism and the Online Workshop, with which he publishes *UNews.ca*, a news site dedicated to Halifax's post-secondary community. He helped launch Canada's first course in online journalism at King's College in 1995.

Kim Kierans was a reporter and editor with the Canadian Broadcasting Corporation for more than 20 years, and continues to produce radio documentaries. She is vice-president of the University of King's College, where she is also a professor in the School of Journalism. She teaches courses in journalism foundations, research methods, broadcast writing, and radio documentary. She is also an adjunct faculty member in the master's journalism program at the Konrad Adenauer Asian Centre for Journalism.

Contributors

Tyler Anderson is a photographer for the *National Post* and a multimedia instructor in the Loyalist College photojournalism program.

David Beers is founding editor of *TheTyee.ca* and an instructor at the University of British Columbia Graduate School of Journalism.

David Eaves is an adjunct professor at the Centre for Digital Media, a fellow at the Centre for the Study of Democracy at Queen's University, and an adviser to the mayor of Vancouver on open government. He writes online at *Eaves.ca*.

Mike Gasher is an associate professor in the Department of Journalism at Concordia University and co-author of the textbook *Mass Communication in Canada*.

Alfred Hermida is an assistant professor at the University of British Columbia Graduate School of Journalism and a founding editor of *BBCNews.com*. He writes online at *Reportr.net*.

Shane Holladay is an instructor at the Ryerson University School of Journalism and a business analyst for *Canoe.ca*.

Mathew Ingram is a senior writer at *GigaOm.com*, a technology blog network, and was the first communities editor at the *Globe and Mail*. He writes online at *Mathew-Ingram.com*.

Dean Jobb is an associate professor of journalism at the University of King's College and author of *Media Law for Canadian Journalists*. He also edits the media law section of *J-Source.ca*.

Darryl Korell is research director with the Canadian Media Research Consortium, a research centre that includes the University of British Columbia School of Journalism, York/Ryerson Graduate Program in Communications and Culture, and the Centre d'études sur les médias at Université Laval.

Donna Logan is president of the Canadian Media Research Consortium and founding director and professor emerita at the University of British Columbia School of Journalism.

Lisa Lynch is an assistant professor in the Department of Journalism at Concordia University.

Rick MacLean is an instructor in the journalism program at Holland College.

Mary McGuire is an associate professor at the Carleton University School of Journalism who teaches multimedia and broadcast journalism, and helped create and develop the award-winning student news magazine *Capital News Online* (*CapitalNews.ca*).

Frank O'Connor is coordinator of the Loyalist College photojournalism program.

Taylor Owen is a doctoral candidate and Trudeau Scholar at the University of Oxford and a lecturer at the Trudeau Centre for Peace and Conflict Studies at the University of Toronto. He writes online at *TaylorOwen.com*.

Ivor Shapiro is an associate professor and undergraduate program director at the Ryerson University School of Journalism. He is the founding editor of *J-Source.ca*, and editor of *The Bigger Picture: Elements of Feature Writing.*

Clay Shirky is an adjunct professor in New York University's Interactive Telecommunications program and author of *Here Comes Everybody: The Power of Organizing Without Organizations*. He writes online at *Shirky.com*.

Vinita Srivastava is an assistant professor and the online stream director at the Ryerson University School of Journalism.

Kelly Toughill is director of the University of King's College School of Journalism and former deputy executive editor of the *Toronto Star*.

Fred Vallance-Jones is an assistant professor at the University of King's College School of Journalism, and winner of a National Newspaper Award for investigative reporting.

Stephen J.A. Ward is James E. Burgess Professor of Journalism Ethics and director of the Center for Journalism Ethics in the School of Journalism and Mass Communication at the University of Wisconsin—Madison.

Jennifer Wilson-Speedy is a columnist at the *Toronto Star* and the editor of *Yourhome.ca*.

Karen Zypchyn is a full-time faculty member in Grant MacEwan University's journalism program and a former journalist with CBC and CTV.

INTRODUCTION

Why Study Journalism Now?

Mary McGuire

CHAPTER OUTLINE

Wanted: Passion and Fresh Approaches

A great sense of curiosity, a passion to find and tell stories, and a love of language were once considered reason enough to study journalism. A career in the news business, after all, offered the opportunity to get paid to do what you love to do. What could be better?

These days, though, as traditional media companies fall on hard times, many wonder why anyone would choose to study journalism now.

There are many reasons to study journalism beyond the obvious one of preparing to work in the newsroom of the future. Plenty of journalism graduates put their tangible skills to good use in a variety of fields other than journalism.

Too many people, especially seasoned journalists, think too narrowly about the value of a journalism education. Recently, traditional news organizations have closed foreign bureaus, laid off reporters, and eliminated editing and production jobs, which has led some journalists to argue that journalism programs are no longer useful. Journalism schools, they say, should close.

Those critics fail to recognize that journalism is simply changing, not dying, and it needs new people with fresh approaches. They don't understand that studying journalism is about more than just learning how to write copy stories for the local newspaper or produce TV reports for the supper hour newscast. They also seem to ignore that journalism skills can be stepping stones to all kinds of opportunities outside newsrooms.

A good journalism program is not about teaching skills that are fast becoming obsolete. It's about providing students with the following:

- the skills to thrive in a changing media world
- the knowledge and understanding to help reshape journalism, which plays an essential watchdog role in any democracy

- a variety of tools and experiences that are transferable to fields such as business, law, communications, politics, and any other field that requires the ability to write, research, conduct interviews, and communicate clearly

A Time of Change—and Opportunity

It's clear that the news industry is being reshaped by new economic forces and technological change. Newspapers delivered to people's doorsteps and news broadcasts on TV at suppertime are fading in popularity. Some media jobs are disappearing as a result. At the same time, people have a healthy appetite for news, and they want it delivered online, on demand, and open for comment. In fact, while traditional media are suffering, we are simultaneously living through an information revolution: Readers have access to more journalism than could have ever been imagined, which has led some observers to suggest that we may be entering a "golden age" of journalism.

People are finding their news in new ways, in new places, and using new media. These changes are undermining the traditional business model, in which advertising dollars financed the news-gathering operations at newspapers and television stations. But while advertising dollars decline as circulation numbers and ratings drop, people still want to know what's happening in their neighbourhoods, their cities, their countries, and beyond. Similarly, people who once bought records and turntables, then cassettes and recorders, then CDs and walkmans, and now digital files and iPods have never stopped listening to music.

As new business models replace old ones and new jobs emerge, the importance of journalism remains unchanged.

The Importance of the Journalist's Role

In this world of information overload, skilled professionals are needed to help filter it all and provide context and analysis. People do value those who can sift through all the information and provide them with credible, focused information that is well produced and available online, on mobile devices, and in new ways yet to be seen. No matter how they get their news, people still want to know about the devastation caused by earthquakes, why the mayor was arrested, or which team won the hockey game they missed the night before.

Much of what students learn in journalism programs will help them produce news and information not only for today's newspapers and newscasts but also for new formats, even as they change and evolve. Journalism programs are about more than producing stories for either old delivery systems or the latest device people are using to access news. Indeed, many of the skills required to do good journalism remain the same whether news is delivered on newsprint or an iPad.

In simple terms, journalism students learn three essential things:

1. How to use and develop a sense of curiosity to find stories that others might find interesting or important or both
2. How to check stories out carefully by getting beyond just the superficial details and spin from vested interests to the facts
3. How to write, tell, or present stories clearly and in interesting and responsible ways in a variety of different media

For example, an enterprising student might wonder why she got sick after eating out at a local restaurant. She might ask around and discover that she was not alone. She might make a few phone calls to the local authorities to inquire about past reports of people getting sick there. With a few more phone calls to the right people and a little digging, she might confirm that the restaurant has a history of being cited for health violations but that health officials have no authority to do any more than impose a small fine on the restaurant—so small it's unlikely to deter that restaurant or others from future violations.

That's a story worth sharing. That's a story anyone who eats at the restaurant would want to know. Indeed, it might even lead local politicians to take some action so that health officials could impose harsher penalties to force restaurants with bad habits to clean up their kitchens.

The final story would be packaged differently, depending on whether it is to be published in a newspaper, broadcast on radio or television, or presented as a multimedia or interactive feature online. All the skills required to identify that story, track it down, call on officials who are accountable, and cut through all the details to focus on what is essential for the audience to know and understand clearly are the same today as always. They are valuable skills whether the reporter is reporting for a news magazine, a blog, or a hyperlocal news website.

Journalism Skills: Essential and Portable

While the business models that finance journalism change and the tools to deliver the news evolve, the essential skills required to find the story, check it out, and tell others about it are just as important to learn now as they were when newspapers thrived and television newscasts had big ratings.

They are also skills that travel well. For example, studying journalism helps students become better—and faster—writers. Good writers are essential to any news organization, but they are in demand elsewhere, too. High-tech firms have hired journalism graduates to help translate the language of their engineers into plain speak for employees and customers. Financial sector companies have hired journalism grads to help translate complicated financial information for people who are not accountants and just want to understand what's happening to their investments. Charitable organizations have hired journalism grads to help find and tell stories on their websites about how the funds donated are used to help improve people's lives. Politicians have hired journalists to become their speech writers. Journalists have even become novelists.

Studying journalism means learning to be editors, too. Editing, although maybe not as exciting to some as reporting, is also highly valued in many workplaces. Good editors do more than just correct grammar and spelling mistakes; they help reporters/writers say what they mean more clearly, more gracefully, and more concisely. They help make sure the information is accurate and consistent. Most important, perhaps, they save many a writer/reporter from the embarrassment and humiliation of getting things wrong.

Good editors learn to write effective headlines. Capturing the essence of a story or a message in just a few short, clear words is increasingly useful in a world where so much of what we do takes place online. When people communicate via tweets or manage their overflowing inbox by only opening those messages with clear and compelling subject lines, learning to pack a punch with few words is important.

Studying journalism also means developing good research skills. Reporters must do more than just rewrite news releases. Students learn to dig for information beyond what's in a news release or government report, using many different resources and tools. They find out the background and history of a story, check the credentials of the people involved, and make connections among the players, for example. Good research skills will continue to be an essential element in the toolkit of reporters—and other professionals—in the future.

Good journalism requires good interviewing. Much of the information in news stories comes not from news releases or online research but from speaking with people directly. Students are often surprised to discover that getting people to open up, tell their stories, and provide useful information is not nearly as easy as one might expect. Only through trial and error, with guidance and experience, do people become effective interviewers. Interviewing skills are useful at work and in life. For example, they can help you choose anything from the right director for the documentary film you want to produce to the right caregiver for your toddler.

Developing broadcast skills is also a valuable part of journalism. Learning to adapt information for print, broadcast, and online audiences, and understanding the difference between writing for print and broadcast will be a key to future success in news organizations where journalists will be expected to deliver stories in multiple platforms. This ability is also useful to almost any organization with a website or any employer who communicates with more than just words on a page. In addition, learning to present stories in front of a microphone or camera helps students build their confidence, as well as presentation and performance skills.

Journalism Programs Today: A Multimedia Mindset

Journalism programs are changing along with the news industry. They now include courses in more than just research, writing, and editing. Most teach students to produce stories using a variety of tools for multiple platforms as well. So, students learn to produce not only print stories or television reports but also stories with text, audio, video, photos, and interactive elements. They also learn about crowdsourcing and social media tools and their impact on journalism. Some programs also teach students how to use databases to help uncover revealing information that can lead to compelling and original stories that reporters on daily deadlines rarely have time to do. Many working journalists wish they had time to take courses in multimedia journalism and investigative techniques so that they could grow and change as the industry does. Instead, working journalists struggle to learn these skills on the job and on deadline or risk being seen as out of date.

Changing Skills for Changing Times

Other industries and professions, from business to engineering to computer science, are being reshaped by new economic forces and technological change. Jobs in those fields are also lost during economic downturns. But no one asks whether it makes sense to study business, engineering, or computer science. As the economy recovers and as businesses and industries reinvent themselves for future markets, well-educated people with new ideas will be needed in a wide variety of industries facing tough times today.

They will be needed in journalism, too.

Old media companies are in the midst of a major upheaval. Journalism is changing. It needs fresh ideas about how to survive and thrive, even if newspapers don't. It also needs people with an entrepreneurial spirit who might help invent new business models. What better way to generate those fresh ideas than among young people interested enough in journalism to choose it as a field of study after high school, but not yet ensconced in newsrooms where people who have always done things the same way may be resistant to change? After all, young people with innovative ideas were the force behind Google, Facebook, and Twitter. A good journalism program can inspire young people to experiment with new ways of storytelling, news gathering, and news production using all of the latest tools, software, and web-based services.

Learning More Than Simply How to Report the News

Beyond the practical courses in print, radio, television, and online journalism, journalism programs usually include courses on the role of the media in a democracy as well as media history, law, and ethics. Developing an understanding of issues related to the media helps young journalists become thoughtful, responsible journalists—and citizens—rather than just people who know only how to operate the latest video camera or editing software.

No one expects all the students who pursue undergraduate degrees in history or economics to get jobs as historians or economists. No one expects almost any of the students who take philosophy to earn a living as philosophers. Undergraduate degree students learn far more than just their subjects; they learn useful skills as researchers, writers, and critical thinkers that can be applied in many ways at many jobs. The same is true for students who pursue a journalism degree; many don't want or expect to become traditional journalists. Instead, they are interested in the media—the way other students are interested in history, economics, or philosophy—and they want to develop some practical skills that might be useful to them in any job that requires them to communicate in more than one medium.

The Benefits of Studying Journalism

Young people are told that they need to learn to be adaptable and multiskilled because they can't expect to do one thing for the rest of their lives; they are told that they must be prepared to reinvent themselves throughout their careers. So, studying journalism makes a lot of sense. Journalism students learn the same research, writing, and critical thinking skills that they would in other academic disciplines. They also learn practical communication skills in a variety of media, along with good writing, editing, research, and interviewing skills that are useful in tomorrow's newsrooms and beyond.

Those are reasons enough to study journalism these days.

Journalism has other benefits. Alexandra Bornkessel (2009), a journalism graduate and journalist turned social marketer, recently published an open letter to high school graduates, encouraging them to consider journalism. Her "40 reasons to still study journalism" include the following:

- Journalism teaches you to be a talker, and a good one.
- Journalism teaches you to learn on the fly (you will need to become an instant expert on things you know nothing about).
- Journalism makes you look at situations, problems, and issues from multiple perspectives.
- Journalism gives you an excuse to talk to someone in the know.
- Journalism changes every day (so you will never be bored).

Bornkessel's list was quickly and widely circulated online. Others jumped in with their own suggestions. One came from Jacqui Banaszynski, a Pulitzer-prize-winning journalist, trainer, educator, and the Knight Chair in Editing at the Missouri School of Journalism. She wrote: "Journalism is a license to learn and explore every day of your life. It's a passport to new worlds and a reminder to pay attention. What could be better?"

REFERENCE

Bornkessel, Alexandra. 2009. Dear May 2009 graduate, here's 40 reasons to still study journalism. SocialButterfly, June 3. http://www.fly4change.com/http:/www.fly4change/dear-may-2009-graduate-heres-40-reasons-to-still-study-journalism/791.

PART ONE
Thinking About Journalism

CHAPTER 1

New Challenges for Journalism in the 21st Century

Alfred Hermida

Introduction

The emergence and uptake of digital, networked technologies in the late 20th and early 21st centuries have resulted in the development of the Internet as a platform for the production and consumption of news. This chapter examines the challenges facing established media, which have tended to transfer their journalistic culture to digital media rather than rethink established routines and conventions. It draws from studies in new media and new literacies to suggest that new technologies, new rules, and new skill sets necessitate a new conceptual framework for journalism. The new journalist needs to understand how news and information work in a digital world rather than simply apply established norms and practices in communicating that may no longer be effective.

CHAPTER OUTLINE

Redefining the Journalist and Journalism

Journalists are grappling with the changes taking place in the profession in a media environment where even the questions of who is a journalist and what is journalism are open to interpretation (Deuze 2005). Bill Kovach and Tom Rosenstiel (2001) say the primary "purpose of journalism is to provide people with the information they need to be free and self-governing" (12). The responsibility of the journalist is to deliver the independent, reliable, accurate, and comprehensive information considered vital to the functioning of democratic societies.

However, defining who is a journalist proves far more problematic. The *Oxford English Dictionary* defines a journalist as "a person who writes for newspapers or magazines or prepares news or features to be broadcast on radio or television." This definition is less about what a journalist actually does and more about whom they work for. It reflects how the profession of journalism developed in a mass media system where there was a close relationship between journalists, publishers, and the means of production.

The 20th century was characterized by the rise and dominance of mass media in Western liberal societies. The mass media system has its roots in the 19th century, with the spread of newspapers, mass market books, magazines, and eventually film, radio, and television. The shift toward an industrialized society where people lived in large and impersonal urban centres rather than in smaller communities led to the institutionalization of communication (Parsons 1964).

In a media system designed to reach the many, the journalist emerged as the mediator between power elites and the public. There was a need for "professional observers and communicators to work full-time to access, select and filter, produce and edit news, which is then distributed via the media to network members" (Domingo et al. 2008, 329).

The definition of *journalism* and the role of the journalist are closely linked to the socio-historical development of the media. Traditionally, journalism has been attached to the media as an institution, based on the production of news by paid professionals who decide what the public needs to know, when it needs to know it, and how it will know it. The term *gatekeeper* is used to describe this journalistic role, maintained and enforced by professional norms and practices arguably to ensure the quality and objectivity of journalism (Reese and Ballinger 2001; Shoemaker 1991).

Yet advances in technology and the introduction of new media are fundamentally altering the nature of mass communication, and with it journalism. The start of the 21st century has been marked by media industries facing profound change in their structure and business models, the nature of their content, and their relationship with audiences. Journalism and the journalist as a media professional are at the centre of a transformation that is challenging norms and routines that have remained, until now, highly consistent (Schudson 2003; Tuchman 2002). Mark Deuze (2005) suggests that

> [t]he combination of mastering newsgathering and storytelling techniques in all media formats (so-called "multi-skilling"), as well as the integration of digital network technologies coupled with a rethinking of the news producer-consumer relationship tends to be seen as one of the biggest challenges facing journalism studies and education in the 21st century. (451)

The Changing Nature of Journalism

The idea of the convergence of media and technology was first proposed by Nicholas Negroponte of the Massachusetts Institute of Technology (MIT) in the late 1970s. He argued that three distinct areas—broadcast and film, print and publishing, and the computer industry—would come together by the 21st century. Another MIT political scientist, Ithiel de Sola Pool (1983), described the impact technological convergence could have on the media. He suggested that convergence was blurring the lines between distinct forms of media such as newspapers, radio, and television, given that "conversation, theater, news, and text are all increasingly delivered electronically" (27).

Convergence is more than a technological process that brings together multiple media functions. For Henry Jenkins (2001), "media convergence is an ongoing process, occurring at various intersections of media technologies, industries, content and audiences; it's not an end state" (93). He argues that this process is leading to what he calls *convergence culture*, with the flow of content across multiple media platforms, the cooperation of multiple media industries, and new behaviours by media audiences as they seek information and entertainment (Jenkins 2006).

Figure 1.1 Until 2010, this spot at a busy Toronto intersection where a planter box now stands was occupied by a long row of almost a dozen newspaper boxes. "Convergence culture" has forever changed how news and information are created, distributed, and consumed.

The Effects of Convergence, Multimedia, and Audience Participation

A discussion on the effects of convergence on journalism could easily fill several volumes. In broad terms, it has changed the creation, distribution, and consumption of content (Gordon 2003). The convergence of print, broadcast, and online operations has resulted in changes in news production practices, with journalists required to produce multimedia content for delivery on digital platforms. Journalism on the Web is characterized by the ability to combine multiple media, blending elements from print, text, and graphics with those of broadcast, sound, music, and video. The mere presence of different media in a story, however, does not by itself create a multimedia story. Multimedia storytelling involves using text, photographs, video clips, audio, graphics, and interactivity in a complementary (rather than redundant) manner, requiring journalists to make editorial judgments about the choice of medium or media.

The boundaries between print, broadcast, and online media have eroded as newsrooms explore convergence and adopt multimedia working practices. Discussing the crisis in the American newspaper industry, Leonard Downie and Michael Schudson

(2009) indicated that "many newspapers are extensively restructuring themselves to integrate their print and digital operations, creating truly multimedia news organizations in ways that should produce both more cost savings—and more engaging journalism."

Research into the merging of the old and new logics of news production suggests that cultural resistance to the transition to a multimedia newsroom exists, as journalists who previously worked in one platform, such as newspapers, are required to provide content for the Web, in text, audio, or video (Singer 1998). Studies have also indicated unease among news professionals about the pressure to use storytelling techniques in different media formats (Cawley 2008; Klinenberg 2005; Lawson-Borders 2006).

Despite these concerns, a reporter in a converged media environment is increasingly required to know how to produce a news story in more than one format. In their study of the attitudes of editors and news professionals, Edgar Huang et al. (2006) found that the two top valued skills were good writing and multimedia production. While critical thinking remained important, they concluded that "multimedia writing and production skills are equally important when it comes to delivering a thoroughly reasoned, well-told and balanced story to the public in the multitude of ways readers want to access news today" (Huang et al. 2006, 94). They concluded that journalism education could play a role in overcoming professional and institutional obstacles by training students to practise news in multiple media platforms. Journalism schools are revisiting curricula to take account of the shifting demands of the industry and the new media environment (Young and Ward 2007).

Past changes in editorial workflow and patterns of content production have affected the routines and practice of journalism, but they have not challenged the space journalists have traditionally occupied as gatekeepers of information. However, the start of the 21st century has seen the emergence of online tools that allow for broad audience participation in the creation, publication, and distribution of news content. Dan Gillmor (2004) argues that "in the past 150 years, we've essentially had two distinct means of communication: one-to-many (books, newspapers, radio and TV) and one-to-one (letters, telegraph and telephone. The Internet, for the first time, gives us many-to-many and few-to-few communications" (26). Scholars suggest that the Internet has changed the relationship between journalists and audiences from a one-way, asymmetric model of communication to a more participatory and collective system (Boczkowski 2004; Deuze 2003; Tremayne 2007).

The ability of the audience to participate in the gathering, analysis, and communication of news and information presents a fundamental challenge to the "we write, you read" dogma of modern journalism (Deuze 2003). In their influential report, *We Media*, Shayne Bowman and Chris Willis (2003) argue that the participatory potential of new media technologies means media professionals have to give up control, even though the "news media are geared up to own a story. They shape it, package it and sell it" (60). Peter Horrocks (2009) has characterized this mindset as "fortress journalism":

> [Journalists] have lived and worked in proud institutions with thick walls. Their daily knightly task has been simple: to battle journalists from other fortresses.

> But the fortresses are crumbling and courtly jousts with fellow journalists are no longer impressing the crowds. The end of fortress journalism is deeply unsettling for us and requires a profound change in the mindset and culture of journalism. (6–7)

Journalists have been resistant to relinquish their jurisdictional claim to the news, even at a time when that claim is being challenged by the emergence of the audience as content producers. Research shows that existing journalistic norms and practices have shaped audience participation opportunities in mainstream media (Hermida and Thurman 2009; Thurman and Hermida 2010) with what David Domingo et al. (2008) describe as "a general reluctance to open up most of the news production process to the active involvement of citizens" (339). By limiting the ability of the audience to exercise agency over professional publications, news professionals are maintaining the core journalistic role of gatekeeper.

Indeed, a growing body of research indicates that institutional media have sought to normalize the potential of new media, subduing them within established journalistic norms and practices (Hermida 2009; Matheson 2004, Robinson 2006; Singer 2005). Faced with challenges to newsroom routines, journalistic conventions, and professional identity, journalists have largely sought to reassert established norms and practices. John O'Sullivan and Ari Heinonen (2008) found that while journalists view the Internet as essential to their work, "the social institution called journalism is hesitant in abandoning its conventions, both at organisational and professional levels, even in the 'Age of the Net,' when overall communication patterns in society are being re-shaped" (368). (See also Chapter 2, "The Journalist and the Audience.")

Understanding New Media

Fundamental to an awareness of the causes, dynamics, and consequences of technological change on journalism is an understanding of new media. This term is routinely applied to a wide range of information and communication technologies. Rather than use a definition of new media that is limited to particular technologies or content, this chapter adopts the comprehensive framework proposed by Leah Lievrouw and Sonia Livingstone (2006). Thus, *new media* is defined as "information and communication technologies and their associated social contexts" (23). A discussion of new media should take account of the following three factors:

> The artefacts or devices used to communicate or convey information; the activities and practices in which people engage to communicate and share information; and the social arrangements or organizational forms that develop around those devices and practices. (2)

This framework provides a method to better understand the transformation of journalism. The media have been in a state of continual technological, cultural, and institutional change, from print to radio to television. The new delivery systems for the transmission of news and information, such as the Web and mobile devices, are not simply new platforms for old content. New media cover both the remaking of established news organizations as they adopt new technologies and the development of unique forms of digital media, such as blogs. New media technologies do not just offer new ways of delivering existing content. Rather, they are changing journalistic norms and practices.

In his discussion on what is new about new media, Terry Flew (2005) considers what is new in terms of the delivery of video. Satellite and cable television may be considered forms of digital media, but Flew suggests that they have not changed the viewing experience as the content available at any one time is determined by the broadcaster, rather than the viewer. He argues that these technologies contrast with the ability to download TV shows and films from the Internet. He cites the latter as an example of new media "because it changes the means of distribution and storage, and the associated business models, of these media" (2).

In the context of journalism, let's look at the impact of new media on newspapers according to Lievrouw and Livingstone's framework. The printed newspaper is a physical delivery system that provides an array of content, combined into one package. Consider the Internet as a delivery system for the newspaper. Instead of being stored, delivered, and consumed in analog format, the news is digitized into binary code. The online content might be the same as on the printed page, but the nature of the newspaper changes once it loses its physical form. The news and information it contains become atomized and fragmented. Nicholas Carr (2009) calls this the "great unbundling":

> When a newspaper moves online, the bundle falls apart. Readers don't flip through a mix of stories, advertisements and other content. They go directly to a particular story that interests them, often ignoring everything else. In many cases, they bypass the newspaper's "front page" altogether, using search engines, feed readers or headline aggregators. (153)

Together with changes in the news delivery system come changes in the practices of the public to access the news, such as being able to access specific content on demand and through a variety of devices. The cellphone, for example, has emerged as a ubiquitous device that allows us to check the news at any time from any place, as well as capture news events in photographs and video, and share them online. Unbundling is not limited to the news industry but being felt across most online media, such as music and film.

The digitization of news also has an impact at an organizational and societal level, such as in the shift to online news sources. In Canada, about 78 percent of Internet users go online for news (Zamaria and Fletcher 2008), while in the United States substantially more people regularly get news online (37 percent) than regularly watch one of the nightly network news broadcasts (29 percent). In addition to changing patterns of consumption, new ways of organizing the news emerge, such as news aggregators and search engines, as well as new forms of gathering, selecting, and disseminated the news, such as citizen journalism sites or social media services.

This brief overview of the impact of new media on journalism serves to shift the discussion away from an emphasis on technology and instead focus on how the systems, patterns, and structures that have traditionally been associated with journalism are changing.

New Media, New Journalism

Cultural, organizational, and institutional factors have shaped the adoption and implementation of new media technologies in journalism. Much of the research indicates that established media have tended not to realize the potential of new technologies. Rather, it suggests that journalism as a profession largely considers the media environment as the same as before, only now more technologized. Such thinking underestimates the consequences of what is new for the media industry and society:

> New technologies alter the structure of our interests: the things we think about. They alter the character of our symbols: the things we think with. And they alter the nature of community: the arena in which thoughts develop. (Postman 1992, 20)

This chapter draws from the research in new literacies to further the discussion on the role of the journalist in a digital media environment. Literacy has been traditionally defined as the ability to read and write. The development of information and communication technologies has given rise to the notion of computer literacy—the ability to use a computer. These ideas are focused on skills rather than the ability to understand and interpret media. A more widely accepted definition of *media literacy* is "the ability to access, analyze, evaluate and create messages across a variety of contexts" (Christ and Potter 1998, 7).

New literacies research suggests that digital technologies are fundamentally changing communication and information flows. Julie Coiro et al. (2008) argue that the speed and scale of the technological changes require scholars to consider literacies with fresh lenses. Taking such an approach seeks to address what Deuze (2008) has identified as a bias in journalism studies, which he argues "is largely informed by the standards of research, education, routines, rituals, and practices set by print journalism" (199).

Scholars argue that as new technology develops, new literacies emerge. Mastin Prinsloo (2005) suggests that while existing literacies are "print-based, paper-based and language-based, reading and writing associated with the new literacies are seen to integrate written, oral and audiovisual modalities of interactive human communication within screen-based and networked electronic systems" (1). In their attempt to define what is new about new media, Colin Lankshear and Michele Knobel (2007) distinguish between *technical* and *ethos* aspects of literacy. The technical aspects refer to digitization, which they argue represents "a quantum shift beyond typographic means of text production as well as beyond analogue forms of sound and image production" (9). The ethos aspects apply to the mindset informing a literacy practice. Lankshear and Knobel suggest that there are two mindsets: a physical-industrial mindset and a cyberspatial-post-industrial mindset (see Table 1.1).

Journalism research suggests that many journalists and news organizations have adopted the first mindset, assuming that the norms and practices that guided them in the modern industrial period continue to apply in a more technologized world. Within this paradigm, the value of journalism is based on the function of scarcity, where access to the machinery of news production and publication is an expensive commodity. The industrial view of production can be applied to the newspaper industry, based on its use of paper and the printing press. The individual person is the journalist or editor, whose authority is derived from the role of gatekeeper and affiliation

Mindset 1	Mindset 2
The world basically operates on physical/material and industrial principles and logics. The world is "centred" and hierarchical. • Value is a function of scarcity • Production is based on an "industrial" model – Products are material artifacts and commodities – Production is based on infrastructure and production units and centres (e.g., a firm or company) – Tools are mainly production tools • The individual person is the unit of production, competence, intelligence • Expertise and authority are "located" in individuals and institutions • Space is enclosed and purpose specific • Social relations of "bookspace" prevail; a stable "textual order"	The world increasingly operates on non-material (e.g., cyberspatial) and post-industrial principles and logics. The world is "decentred" and "flat." • Value is a function of dispersion • A "post-industrial" view of production – Products as enabling services – A focus on leverage and non-finite participation – Tools are increasingly tools of mediation and relationship technologies • The focus is increasingly on "collectives" as the unit of production, competence, intelligence • Expertise and authority are distributed and collective; hybrid experts • Space is open, continuous, and fluid • Social relations of emerging "digital media space" are increasingly visible; texts in change

Table 1.1 Some dimensions of variation between the mindsets

SOURCE: Lankshear, Colin, and Michele Knobel. 2007. Sampling "the new" in new literacies. In *A new literacies sampler*, ed. Colin Lankshear, Michele Knobel, Chris Bigum, and Michael Peters, 1–24. New York: Peter Lang, 11.

with a news organization. The space is the newsroom and the newspaper, which have a specific purpose and are largely closed off to the audience. Finally, the stable textual order is the fixed hierarchy of authorship maintained by the newspaper.

In contrast, the second mindset suggests that the media environment is significantly different from 30 years ago because of the development of networked, digital technologies and the new practices and social arrangements enabled by these technologies. According to Lankshear and Knobel (2007):

> The world is being changed in some quite fundamental ways as a result of people imagining and exploring new ways of doing things and new ways of being that are made possible by new tools and techniques, rather than using new technologies to do familiar things in more "technologized" ways (first mindset). (10)

In the second mindset, the machinery of news production is widely available through, for example, blogging software, so value is created by the dispersal of information. In a post-industrial view of production, the focus shifts to enabling services, such as Google, and to tools that facilitate connectivity, such as Facebook. This mindset assumes a focus on collective intelligence, seen in online tools that enable people to collaborate online. Conventional social relations associated with the roles of author/authority and expert have broken down, challenging journalistic jurisdiction over the news. The emergence of what has been labelled "citizen journalism" can be considered part of this process. In this construct, the Internet represents an open and continuous space that has no inherent stable generic order. Rather, digital media spaces allow new activities, such as remixing content, that disrupt established authorial social structures.

Lankshear and Knobel (2007) acknowledge that new literacies are more complex than a simple table can express and admit that their approach tends to polarize the mindsets. However, the table does provide a functional tool to convey the differences in the two approaches and a way to understand the scale of the changes taking place in journalism. The practice of journalism has been focused on the production of finished products by designated individuals and teams, based on individual expertise and intelligence, operating in a shared physical space. However, new literacies research suggests that the changes taking place challenge fundamental norms, conventions, and routines of journalism. One of the most fundamental changes is the ability of the audience to become an active participant in reporting and disseminating news in photographs, videos, and text, undermining the monopoly on reporting that journalists traditionally enjoyed (Bowman and Willis 2003). In terms of the profession itself, news blogs have been described as a new genre of institutionalized journalism, where the journalist is more visible and the style is more personal (Domingo and Heinonen 2008).

The new literacies privilege the following:

> Participation over publishing, distributed expertise over centralized expertise, collective intelligence over individual possessive intelligence, collaboration over individuated authorship, dispersion over scarcity, sharing over ownership, experimentation over "normalization," innovation and evolution over stability and fixity, creative-innovative rule breaking over generic purity and policing, relationship over information broadcast. (Lankshear and Knobel 2007, 21)

Conclusion

This chapter has explored existing conceptions of the role of the journalist and journalism, and sought to locate these in the research in new literacies. It has avoided placing too much emphasis on the technological tools of media today and instead explored the interplay between changing social and cultural practices enabled by technology and the function of the journalist. The struggle of journalism as a profession to adapt to change may be indicative of a lack of understanding of the nature of the shift taking place—from a physical-industrial mindset to a cyberspatial-post-industrial mindset. Seen through the lens of new literacies research, digital media are more participatory, collaborative, and distributed, and less finalized, individualized, and author-centric than previous forms of media.

However, research indicates that journalism practice is rooted in the first mindset. Deuze (2003) says that the "suggested added values and characteristics of online journalisms cannot simply be incorporated one-by-one without fundamentally changing the 'nature of the beast'—the beast being that particular newsroom culture and the professionals involved" (216). This is not simply an argument over the relevance of the traditional gatekeeping role of the journalist.

It centres on reimagining the functions and place of the journalist in a networked media ecology. Charlie Beckett (2008) argues that while news and information have never been more abundant and accessible, "journalism has never been more necessary to the functioning of our lives as individuals and societies and for the healthy functioning of global social, economic, and political relationships" (3).

Alongside the traditional, linear media system for journalism, a new framework has emerged that has eroded established definitions of producer and consumer. In the words of Jane Singer (2008), "in a networked world, there no longer is the 'journalist,' 'audience,' and 'source.' There is only 'us' " (75). According to Rosenstiel, the journalist shifts from being the gatekeeper to being an authenticator of information, a sense-maker to derive meaning, a navigator to help orient audiences, and a community leader to engage audiences (Hermida 2008).

The future role of the journalist will clearly be determined by the complex interplay between media technologies, professional practices, and societal factors. Journalism has developed as a relatively closed journalistic culture for the production of knowledge, based on a system of editorial control. Yet new media are characterized by their connected and collaborative nature. The challenge for journalism, and the journalist, is to find a place along the continuum between control and connection, and between a closed and a collaborative media culture.

DISCUSSION QUESTIONS

1. How do digital Internet technologies affect the role of the journalist?
2. How has the Internet blurred the distinction between the professional and the amateur in the field of journalism?
3. What is the value of professional journalism training when anyone can be a journalist?

SUGGESTED RESOURCES

J-Source.ca, The Canadian Journalism Project. http://www.j-source.ca.

Nieman Journalism Lab. http://www.niemanlab.org.

PBS MediaShift. http://www.pbs.org/mediashift/.

PoynterOnline. http://www.poynter.org.

Teaching Online Journalism [Mindy McAdams's blog]. http://mindymcadams.com/tojou/.

REFERENCES

Beckett, Charlie. 2008. *SuperMedia: Saving journalism so it can save the world*. Malden, MA: Wiley-Blackwell.

Boczkowski, Pablo. J. 2004. *Digitizing the news: Innovation in online newspapers*. Cambridge, MA: MIT Press.

Bowman, Shayne, and Chris Willis. 2003. *We media: How audiences are shaping the future of news and information*, ed. J.D. Lasica. Reston, VA: The Media Center at the American Press Institute. http://www.hypergene.net/wemedia/weblog.php.

Carr, Nicholas. 2009. *The big switch: Rewiring the world, from Edison to Google*. New York: W.W. Norton.

Cawley, Anthony. 2008. News production in an Irish online newsroom: Practice, process and culture. In *Making online news: The ethnography of new media production*, ed. Chris Paterson and David Domingo, 45–60. New York: Peter Lang.

Christ, William. G., and James W. Potter. 1998. Media literacy, media education, and the academy. *Journal of Communication* 48 (1): 5–15.

Coiro, Julie, Michele Knobel, Colin Lankshear, and Donald J. Leu. 2008. Introduction: Central issues in new literacies and new literacies research. In *Handbook of research on new literacies*, ed. Julie Coiro, Michele Knobel, Michele, Colin Lankshear, and Donald J. Leu, 1–21. Mahwah, NJ: Lawrence Erlbaum.

Compact Oxford English Dictionary. Journalist. http://www.askoxford.com/concise_oed/journalist?view=uk.

Deuze, Mark. 2003. The Web and its journalisms: Considering the consequences of different types of newsmedia online. *New Media and Society* 5: 203.

Deuze, Mark. 2005. What is journalism?: Professional identity and ideology of journalists reconsidered. *Journalism* 6 (4): 442–464.

Deuze, Mark. 2008. Toward a sociology of online news? In *Making online news: The ethnography of new media production*, ed. Chris Paterson and David Domingo, 199–210. New York: Peter Lang.

Domingo, David, and Ari Heinonen. 2008. Weblogs and journalism: A typology to explore the blurring boundaries. *Nordicom Review* 29 (1): 3–15.

Domingo, David, Thorsten Quandt, Ari Heinonen, Steve Paulussen, Jane B. Singer, and Marina Vujnovic. 2008. Participatory journalism practices in the media and beyond. *Journalism Practice* 326–342.

Downie, Leonard, Jr., and Michael Schudson. 2009. The reconstruction of American journalism. *Columbia Journalism Review*, October 19. http://www.cjr.org/reconstruction/the_reconstruction_of_american.php?page=all.

Flew, Terry. 2005. *New media*. 2nd ed. Oxford: Oxford University Press.

Gillmor, Dan. 2004. *We the media: Grassroots journalism by the people, for the people.* Sebastopol, CA: O'Reilly.

Gordon, Rich. 2003. The meanings and implications of convergence. In *Digital journalism: Emerging media and the changing horizons of journalism*, ed. Kevin Kawamoto, 57–74. Lanham, MD: Rowman & Littlefield Publishers.

Hermida, Alfred. 2008. The new roles for journalists in a multimedia world. Reportr.net, February 19. http://reportr.net/2008/02/19/the-new-roles-for-journalists-in-a-multimedia-world/.

Hermida, Alfred. 2009. The blogging BBC. *Journalism Practice* 3 (3): 1–17.

Hermida, Alfred, and Neil Thurman. 2009. A clash of cultures: The integration of user-generated content within professional journalistic frameworks at British newspaper websites. *Journalism Practice* 2 (3): 343–356.

Horrocks, Peter, 2009. The end of fortress journalism. In *The future of journalism*, ed. Charles Miller, 6–17. London: BBC College of Journalism. http://www.bbc.co.uk/blogs/theeditors/future_of_journalism.pdf.

Huang, Edgar, Karen Davison, Stephanie Shreve, Twila Davis, Elizabeth Bettendorf, and Anita Nair. 2006. Facing the challenges of convergence: Media professionals' concerns of working across media platforms. *Convergence* 12 (1): 83–98.

Jenkins, Henry. 2001. Convergence? I diverge. *Technology Review*, June.

Jenkins, Henry. 2006. *Convergence culture*. New York: New York University Press.

Klinenberg, Eric. 2005. Convergence: News production in a digital age. *Annals of the American Academy of Political and Social Science* 597 (1): 48–64.

Kovach, Bill, and Tom Rosenstiel. 2001. *The elements of journalism: What newspeople should know and the public should expect.* New York: Random House.

Lankshear, Colin, and Michele Knobel. 2007. Sampling "the new" in new literacies. In *A new literacies sampler*, ed. Colin Lankshear, Michele Knobel, Chris Bigum, and Michael Peters, 1–24. New York: Peter Lang.

Lawson-Borders, Gracie. 2006. *Media organizations and convergence: Case studies of media convergence pioneers.* Mahwah, NJ: Lawrence Erlbaum.

Lievrouw, Leah A. and Sonia Livingstone, eds. 2006. *Handbook of new media.* Rev. student ed. London: Sage.

Matheson, Donald. 2004. Weblogs and the epistemology of the news: Some trends in online journalism. *New Media and Society* 6: 443–469.

O'Sullivan, John, and Ari Heinonen. 2008. Old values, new media: Journalism role perceptions in a changing world. *Journalism Practice* 2 (3): 357–371.

Parsons, Talcott. 1964. Evolutionary universals. *American Sociological Review* 29: 339–357.

Pool, Ithiel de Sola. 1983. *Technologies of freedom.* Cambridge, MA: Belknap Press.

Postman, Neil. 1992. *Technopoly: The surrender of culture to technology.* New York: Vintage Books.

Prinsloo, Mastin. 2005. The new literacies as placed resources. *Perspectives in Education* 2 (4): 87–98.

Reese, Stephen, and Jane Ballinger. 2001. The roots of a sociology of news: Remembering Mr. Gates and social control in the newsroom. *Journalism and Mass Communication Quarterly* 78 (4): 641–658.

Robinson, Susan. 2006. The mission of the j-blog: Recapturing journalistic authority online. *Journalism* 7 (1): 65–83.

Schudson, Michael. 2003. *The sociology of news.* New York: W.W. Norton.

Shoemaker, Pamela J. 1991. *Gatekeeping.* Thousand Oaks, CA: Sage.

Singer, Jane B. 1998. Online journalists: Foundations for research into their changing roles. *Journal of Computer-Mediated Communication* 4 (1). http://jcmc.indiana.edu/vol4/issue1/singer.html.

Singer, Jane B. 2005. The political j-blogger: "Normalizing" a new media form to fit old norms and practices. *Journalism* 6 (2): 173–198.

Singer, Jane B. 2008. The journalist in the network. A shifting rationale for the gatekeeping role and the objectivity norm. *Trípodos* 23. http://www.tripodos.com/pdf/Singer.pdf31.pdf.

Thurman, Neil, and Alfred Hermida. 2010. Gotcha: How newsroom norms are shaping participatory journalism online. In *Web journalism: A new form of citizenship*, ed. Garrett Monaghan and Sean Tunney, 46–62. Eastbourne, UK: Sussex Academic Press.

Tremayne, Mark. 2007. Harnessing the active audience: Synthesizing blog research and lessons for the future of media. In *Blogging, citizenship and the future of media*, ed. Mark Tremayne, 261–272. New York: Routledge.

Tuchman, Gaye. 2002. The production of news. In *A handbook of media and communication research: Qualitative and quantitative methodologies*, ed. Klaus Jensen, 78–90. London and New York: Routledge.

Young, Mary Lynn, and Stephen Ward. 2007. Facing the future, burying the past: A new vocabulary for graduate journalism education in Canada. Paper presented at the World Journalism Education Congress, Singapore.

Zamaria, Charles, and Fred Fletcher. 2008. *Canada online! The Internet, media and emerging technologies: Uses, attitudes, trends and international comparisons 2007*. Toronto: Canadian Internet Project. http://www.ciponline.ca/en/docs/2008/CIP07_CANADA_ONLINE-REPORT-FINAL%20.pdf.

CHAPTER 2

The Journalist and the Audience

Mathew Ingram

CHAPTER OUTLINE

Introduction

Before the Web became an integral part of our lives, the relationship between the journalist and the audience was relatively straightforward: The journalist researched and wrote the news and turned it in to an editor who ensured that it would be published in a newspaper or magazine or be broadcast on television or radio, and at some later point it was picked up and read, watched, or listened to.

If readers or viewers had any comments to make about a story, they likely made it to an acquaintance, a co-worker, or a family member. That's because there was little or no opportunity to pass on their thoughts to the actual journalist involved in the story, let alone to interact with him or her, apart from possibly a letter to the editor or a phone call—or a call-in show, in the case of TV and radio.

In other words, the two sides of the journalistic relationship—writer and reader—have been fundamentally disconnected for decades. All of that changed, however, when the Internet arrived and media outlets began publishing stories online.

Just as the Web has allowed journalists to write and edit their work continuously, adding and changing details as a story progresses, it has lowered the barriers between the audience and the journalist and allowed the two sides to truly communicate, and even collaborate.

The implications of this shift are profound. As described and elaborated on by other writers in this book, lowering the barriers between writer and reader has also meant that the line between the two has blurred.

The rigid distinction between the journalist and the audience, in which one side delivered a specific object to the other to consume at some future time and place, has become—at its best—much more like a cooperative relationship, with information flowing in both directions. Readers provide information that changes a story, corrects errors in real time (instead of days or weeks later), and can take a report in new directions.

This changed relationship results not just in a stronger link between writer and reader, but in many cases a better journalistic outcome as well. Thanks to the Web, readers and viewers have become what veteran journalist Dan Gillmor and New York University journalism professor Jay Rosen call "the people formerly known as the audience."

The People Formerly Known as the Audience

As Rosen (2006) describes it:

> The people formerly known as the audience are those who *were* on the receiving end of a media system that ran one way, in a broadcasting pattern, with high entry fees and a few firms competing to speak very loudly while the rest of the population listened in isolation from one another—and who *today* are not in a situation like that *at all.*
>
> - Once they were your printing presses; now that humble device, the blog, has given the press to us. That's why blogs have been called little First Amendment machines. They extend freedom of the press to more actors.
> - Once it was *your* radio station, broadcasting on *your* frequency. Now that brilliant invention, podcasting, gives radio to us. And we have found more uses for it than you did.
> - Shooting, editing and distributing video once belonged to you, Big Media. Only you could afford to reach a TV audience built in your own image. Now video is coming into the user's hands, and audience-building by former members of the audience is alive and well on the Web.
> - You were once (exclusively) the editors of the news, choosing what ran on the front page. Now we can edit the news, and our choices send items to our own front pages.
> - A highly centralized media system had connected people "up" to big social agencies and centers of power but not "across" to each other. Now the horizontal flow, citizen-to-citizen, is as real and consequential as the vertical one.

The Networked Age

In a report entitled *Red Kayaks and Hidden Gold*, written for Oxford University's Reuters Institute for the Study of Journalism, former *Washington Post* columnist John Kelly (2009) argues that the relationship between a journalist and his or her audience has "fundamentally changed." If not a substitute for traditional media, he writes, the Internet provides a parallel one—"a low-cost distribution mechanism that is newspaper delivery truck, paper boy, and radio and TV transmitter all in one" (6).

For most of journalism's history, Kelly (2009) says, "users were the people at the end of the production chain: readers, viewers, listeners. News was a broadcast, from one to many. We live in the network age now, where the many can talk to the many, bypassing the one completely" (1).

In his book *We the Media*, Gillmor (2004) writes that

> Big Media … treated the news as a lecture. We told you what the news was. You bought it, or you didn't. You might write us a letter; we might print it. … It was a world that bred complacency and arrogance on our part. It was a gravy train while it lasted, but it was unsustainable. Tomorrow's news reporting and production will be more of a conversation, or a seminar. The lines will blur between producers and consumers, changing the roles of both in ways we're only beginning to grasp now. The communication network itself will be a medium for everyone's voice, not just the few who can afford to buy multimillion-dollar printing presses, launch satellites, or win the government's permission to squat on the public's airwaves. (xiii)

Not everyone likes the implications of this paradigm shift in the relationship between the reader/viewer and the journalist, however. Journalism researcher Adam Tinworth noted in a post on Twitter on May 19, 2009, that "journalists' sense of entitlement to an audience may be the most difficult challenge to overcome." By that, Tinworth says, he meant the feeling that "I've made it as a journalist. Hence, I have an audience."

Guardian editor Kevin Anderson (2009) argues that the problem is even deeper than that: "I think the institutional belief is that if we work for a major publication or broadcaster that not only do we have a de facto audience but that we *deserve* an audience. It's the height of institutional arrogance and self-importance." In the end, Anderson says, "We've taken our audiences for granted, and now we have to do a lot of hard work to earn them back."

Implications of the New Relationship Between the Audience and the Journalist

In a nutshell, what was once a one-way relationship has become two-way, or multiway—a process of give-and-take, of cooperation. "Journalists must accept that the dynamic has changed," says Kelly (2009). "They must see the public as more than an inert, monolithic audience. They must explore new, collaborative ways to tell stories. And they must do all of this on the tilting deck that is today's trade. Or profession" (2).

In a recent speech to journalists, Reuters head Tom Glocer (2006b) said:

> for the last two hundred years—let's be honest—we've been in charge. And that has made things simple. But now our readers, our viewers, our listeners are grabbing the mic, the printing press, the camera. The couch potatoes have grown legs, got off the sofa and want a slice of the action. Maybe, it's because of the ubiquity of mass media, maybe it's the rise of celebrity, maybe it's a result of mature political societies—but people now want to make their views heard.

What are some of the implications of this transformation in the relationship between the audience and the journalist? What follows are a few examples, although there are many others.

Citizen Journalism

One of the major benefits of a multiway relationship between the journalist and the audience—one whose potential has only begun to be realized—is that in some cases audience members can play a role in the beginning of the reporting process, if they happen to observe something or are present at the scene of a news event, and are able to use social media tools such as Twitter, Flickr, YouTube, Quik, Livestream, and Facebook to report and distribute details of the event.

Janis Krums, who took the first photo of US Airways Flight 1549 that had just made an emergency landing on the Hudson River in January 2009, was arguably engaged in a journalistic act when he took the photo and posted it on Twitter. His photo was seen by thousands of people within a matter of minutes (see Krums's Twitter post in Chapter 17). In Canada, a bystander named Paul Pritchard video-recorded the fatal use of a Taser on Robert Dziekanski by a number of RCMP officers at the Vancouver airport, a case that drew widespread public attention. Pritchard later received a "Citizen Journalist" award.

In Mumbai, dozens of people posted their observations on Twitter and other social networks as terrorists attacked the city in 2008. During the national elections in Iran in 2009 many "citizen journalists" posted events in real time, in addition to a video recorded by a bystander of the shooting death of protester Neda Agha-Soltan, whose murder by police forces became a rallying point for Iranian protesters and international observers (see posts on both events in Chapter 17).

At the time of the 2004 tsunami in Indonesia, Glocer (2006a) noted on his blog that "for the first 24 hours the best and the only photos and video came from tourists armed with 1.3 megapixel portable telephones, digital cameras and camcorders. And if you didn't have those pictures you weren't on the story." In a speech to journalists, Glocer (2006b) said that "the job of reporter and the job of editor will have to change. The skills that we need to blend—traditional skills with the skills of navigating the blogosphere—are not ones that we currently have. We continue to train our journalists for a time in history now long gone."

Figure 2.1 Abraham Zapruder's famous footage of the Kennedy assassination in 1963 could be considered one of the first significant examples of citizen journalism. Today, citizens' contributions to major news story coverage are a daily occurrence. (Zapruder Film © 1967, Renewed 1995. The Sixth Floor Museum at Dealey Plaza)

Citizen journalism isn't a creation of the 21st century—the famous hand-held video recorded by Abraham Zapruder of US President John F. Kennedy being shot during a motorcade in Texas was arguably the first modern example of the phenomenon. But with the explosion of "smart" cellphones with photo and video capabilities, as well as the popularity of "flip" video cameras, virtually anyone now has the ability to film such an event, and the advent of YouTube and other video-sharing sites means that images can be distributed almost instantly.

Social scientist Yochai Benkler (2007) points out in his book *The Wealth of Networks* that "the material requirements for effective information production and communication are now owned by numbers of individuals several orders of magnitude larger than the number of owners of the basic means of information production and exchange a mere two decades ago" (4).

Kelly (2009) says:

> "citizen journalism" is the term by which this phenomenon or practice is most widely known but it is by no means the only one. Other terms have entered the lexicon, among them: user-generated content, user-created content, participatory journalism, audience material, "we media," collaborative journalism, community journalism, pro-am collaboration, grassroots journalism, open-source journalism, crowd-sourced journalism, interactive journalism, networked journalism, network publishing, bridge media and "random acts of journalism." (17)

The best definition, Kelly (2009) says, comes from *We Media*, a 2003 report by Shayne Bowman and Chris Willis. "To them citizen journalism refers to the 'act of citizens playing an active role in the process of collecting, reporting, analyzing and disseminating news and information'" (17).

He adds that citizen journalism offers a number of benefits:

- It brings experts into the reporting process so that stories can be more accurate and nuanced. … Supporters of citizen journalism argue that inviting readers to contribute to reporting improves the end result.
- It makes possible the coverage of events that the mainstream media might otherwise miss. Citizens with a viewpoint or agenda that differs from that of the mainstream media can unearth news that might be overlooked.
- It can save money. By enlisting the help of unpaid volunteers, news organizations can supplement their offerings with user-generated content.
- Through blogs especially, it can influence the news agenda or "resuscitate" stories the mainstream media might have let die. … As more and more blogs link to an article, or to each other, a story can have a life beyond the traditional news cycle.
- It can demystify the journalistic process. … Now that citizens can try some forms of journalism on their own … they will inevitably understand more of the machinery.
- It can build a sense of community, increasing the understanding of, and participation in, civic life. This is the benefit that the most ardent proponents of citizen journalism hope for. (Kelly 2009, 26–28)

OffTheBus: Managed Citizen Journalism

During the Obama campaign in 2007, the Huffington Post and Jay Rosen's "NewAssignment.net" project formed a partnership aimed at using "citizen journalists" to cover the presidential campaign. The partnership was known as OffTheBus (since traditional journalists covering a campaign are described as being "on the bus"), and involved several hundred contributors reporting on events from around the United States and being edited by editors from NewAssignment.net and the Huffington Post.

Figure 2.2 Mayhill Fowler's reportage in the 2008 presidential campaign was controversial, but also symbolized the changing nature of journalism. The *Los Angeles Times* said: "Watch out for that face in the crowd. ... Mayhill Fowler embodies a media revolution that is helping to shape campaigns and national debate."

As Kelly (2009) describes it, OffTheBus gained some notoriety from two incidents involving a contributor named Mayhill Fowler, a 61-year-old from California who paid her own way around the country following candidates. In one case, she attended a fundraising event that was open to Obama supporters but closed to the press and quoted the candidate in a story, an act that generated a lot of criticism. In another incident, she spoke with former president Bill Clinton during a "meet-and-greet" event and quoted his remarks in another story, which generated criticism as well.

So why the controversy? In both cases, Ms. Fowler didn't identify herself as a journalist or say that either man would be quoted. As Kelly (2009) notes: "What was sometimes lost in the furore was the fact that both sets of remarks—Obama's and Clinton's—were newsworthy; that while Fowler may not have been a 'proper' journalist she did what one would hope a proper journalist would do: publish; and that neither the Obama nor Clinton campaigns complained about Fowler's right to do just that. The two episodes were also reminders that in the age of the citizen journalist 'off the record' was losing much of its meaning" (41).

User-Generated Content

In many ways, citizen journalism is just one aspect of a much broader phenomenon that the Web has empowered, known by some as *user-generated content*. In effect, user-generated content refers to any content that is created and/or distributed by non-professionals, such as comments on news stories, blog posts, Twitter messages, Facebook posts, Flickr photos, and wiki content.

New media entrepreneur Bronwen Clune (2009) said on her blog that "participatory media doesn't mean you letting your audience participate in the creation of news, [it's] about acknowledging that you participate in news creation along with your audience."

The BBC has even gone so far as to create a User Generated Content unit, which sits right in the middle of its multimedia online newsroom, as described by Peter Horrocks (2008) in the BBC editors' blog:

> Within the multimedia newsroom department, for which I have responsibility, we are now preparing a major physical re-organisation to accompany the structural changes. All of the key daily news teams in radio, TV and the web will be seated alongside each other next to the people who run the newsgathering. And close to the middle of that operation will be our User Generated Content unit. It will be right alongside the newsgathering teams that deploy our conventional journalistic resources. And the UGC team will be deploying and receiving our unconventional journalistic resources—information and opinion from the audience.

Crowdsourcing

In addition to the "people formerly known as the audience" actually reporting things about news events and generating content themselves, there has been an increase—again, thanks to the Web and social media—in a related phenomenon called *crowdsourcing*, in which readers are asked to help with fact-gathering or sifting through large quantities of information that might be useful for a journalistic project.

Two of the most prominent examples of crowdsourcing took place through TalkingPointsMemo.com and the *Guardian* (www.guardian.co.uk). Readers waded through the thousands of pages of documents related to the firing of US Attorneys by the Justice Department posted by Talking Points Memo, sending tips and new developments to the blog's editors. Readers also dug through the thousands of British MP expense documents posted by the *Guardian* to help find the best stories. In the case of the *Guardian*, more than 20,000 people participated in the investigation and pored over hundreds of thousands of pages of information, something that would have taken the newspaper months, if not years, to do.

Jane Hamsher (2006) of FireDogLake.com says that bloggers can act as a kind of analytical adjunct to the reporters who spend all their time chasing news stories:

> In this light bloggers serve the function of analysts. Or re-analyzers, more aptly, who attempt to contextualize as they sort through available data and look for patterns, inconsistencies and greater truths. For my money if I was trying to marry a blog with a newsroom that's where I'd start—I'm constantly amazed that with all the access to information now available the big news bureaus don't have a deeper pool of researchers to be the adjunct memories of people who spend their time in the development of external news sources.

Greater Interaction via Comments

One of the first ways in which the Web lowered the barriers to interaction between the journalist and the audience, turning it into a real-time, two-way relationship for the first time, was the introduction of commenting systems at newspapers and other media websites—allowing readers and viewers to post comments on stories after they were published. Although other newspapers were also experimenting with reader comments at the time, the first full-scale commenting system appeared at the *Globe and Mail* in Toronto in 2005, with comments available on every story published on the newspaper's website.

Allowing comments on stories is one of the easiest ways to empower readers to let you know when you (1) have gotten something wrong or (2) are missing some crucial information from a story. Not only can gaining this information improve a story—and even take it in a different direction—but responding to comments is a real way of interacting with readers directly and letting them know that their contributions are valuable.

Reading and responding to comments via other social media tools such as Twitter and Facebook produces much the same kind of relationship: The journalist gains information or perspectives that can be valuable for reporting or interpreting a story, and the reader benefits from a closer relationship with the journalist and with the media outlet doing the story.

Continuous Verification and Updating

From newspapers to television and radio, journalistic entities have a pretty embarrassing track record when it comes to admitting errors. Newspapers typically do their best not to run corrections. When they do, corrections are often at the bottom of a page that no one reads, days or even weeks after the mistake was made, and they are often so cryptically worded that it's difficult to tell what the initial error was. Why is this? Perhaps in part because traditional media spend so much time editing and rewriting and verifying the material they print or broadcast that to admit an error is to effectively admit defeat.

In a newspaper and in broadcast, correcting something after the fact is difficult and time-consuming, and the correction can never appear alongside the original. Online, however, it is a simple matter to add an update or correction to a story. As a result, online publishing via blogs and other tools has developed an ethic that stresses continuous verification and updating—as New York City University professor Jeff Jarvis (2009) says, it has turned journalism into a process rather than a product. This is not to suggest that journalists don't always do their best to report as accurately as possible the first time—far from it. What it does mean is that mistakes can be corrected more quickly and information thus becomes more accurate.

There are those who believe that admitting errors more frequently will cause the public to lose faith in the media, since they will be revealed as fallible. Another view, however, is that few intelligent readers and viewers likely see the media as omniscient or infallible to begin with, and that admitting errors more frequently might actually increase the level of trust they feel in the media. After all, someone who claims to be infallible is almost certain to be seen as untruthful (since everyone makes mistakes), while someone who admits and corrects his or her error is more likely to be seen as honest and transparent.

Gillmor (2004) says:

> It boils down to something simple: readers (or viewers or listeners) collectively know more than media professionals do. This is true by definition: they are many, and we are often just one. We need to recognize and, in the best sense of the word, use their knowledge. If we don't, our former audience will bolt when they realize they don't have to settle for half-baked coverage; they can come into the kitchen themselves. (111)

If we accept Jarvis's idea that journalism is a process, then instead of assuming that the publication of an article marks the end of a journalist's job, it should be seen instead as the beginning of something—a process that involves reader feedback and additions.

The main reason why many media outlets resist this sort of view, he says, is "journalism's myth of perfection." In a speech to journalism students, Emily Bell (2009) of the *Guardian* made a similar point, saying: "as my mum said, at the kitchen table, 'whenever I read or see something I know anything about I'm always struck by how wrong it is.' It amounts to the same thing—your readers and audience know and see more than you ever could. Find ways to let them add their knowledge. … The fact that everywhere you go now, there are witnesses, potential reporters, holders of vital information, is one of the key revolutionizing factors in telling stories."

Enhanced Civic Activism

For some advocates of social media and citizen journalism, these tools are an important democratizing force that can help society as a whole. Rosen (2009) says:

> In the age of mass media, the press was able to define the sphere of legitimate debate with relative ease because the people on the receiving end were atomized —meaning they were connected "up" to Big Media but not across to each other. But today one of the biggest factors changing our world is the falling cost for like-minded people to locate each other, share information, trade impressions and realize their number. Among the first things they may do is establish that the "sphere of legitimate debate" as defined by journalists doesn't match up with their own definition.

In the past, Rosen (2009) says, "there was nowhere for this kind of sentiment to go," but now it is collected and expressed online—and it can find an audience that can expand that sentiment and turn it into a force for change. "Journalists call this the 'echo chamber,'" says Rosen, "which is their way of downgrading it as a reliable source. But what's really happening is that the authority of the press to assume consensus, define deviance and set the terms for legitimate debate is weaker when people can connect horizontally around and about the news."

Clune (2009) says that "until recently ... news was controlled by those in charge of deciding who/what/why and when something was newsworthy. Twitter is an example of almost the exact opposite of 'control media' because journalists are not in control [of] the flow of information anymore."

Kelly (2009) says that citizen journalism

> can improve the journalism itself, by involving in the process people who actually know about, or are affected by, the issue at hand. And it can have a beneficial impact on those content-generating users. It can make them more interested in their communities, it can demystify the political process, it can excite them about the things the best journalism strives to do: explain, crusade, call to account. (2)

Glocer (2006b) calls the changes in journalism "the democratization of media," saying that "all the people we used to broadcast to are broadcasting right back at us. There has been a democratization of media. There's still a government running the infrastructure—but the citizens are making and implementing policy of their own." He says that people are "using the media to air their views on all kinds of public policy questions. Perhaps it is that they don't feel their voice is being heard at government levels, or perhaps it is that standards of living are so good that politics no longer matters? But what I see is people participating and sharing their opinion aired in a really exciting way—this is where political debate and argument is now at. It seems that media is more real to people than politics."

Social Media Policies

As more journalists embrace social media tools such as blogs, Facebook, and Twitter, the institutions that employ them have struggled with how to embrace that direct connection between the journalist and the audience, while still maintaining the standards of behaviour that most traditional media entities see as appropriate. Many outlets have written social media policies that govern the behaviour of their journalists on social networks, and more than a few clashes over the restrictions that are being placed on what some see as personal behaviour have taken place at newspapers such as the *Washington Post*. In a world of social media, the line continues to blur between what is personal and what is professional.

One of the standards that has been tested through the lowering of barriers to interaction between the journalist and the audience is the principle of objectivity. Some observers and social media advocates argue that true objectivity is impossible, and that it would be better if journalists replaced objectivity with transparency. David Weinberger (2009), co-author of the book *The Cluetrain Manifesto*, has gone so far as to say that "transparency is the new objectivity," and argues that objectivity is something that traditional media valued only because they didn't have the ability to link out to supporting sources, the way Web media do.

Journalism instructor Paul Bradshaw (2009) said in his Online Journalism Blog that the *Washington Post*'s social media policy was "aimed at preserving the *appearance* of objectivity rather than its actual existence. It focuses on what journalists are *perceived to be*, rather than what they actually *do*." He added that "transparency is hastening the demise of the already crumbling notion of journalistic objectivity; but it also represents the best hope for journalistic integrity—and ultimately, for many journalists that was what the pursuit of objectivity was about."

Bradshaw (2009) offers this advice:

> Keep your social media profiles, and make yourself available to a thousand potential sources rather than relying on the dozen in your contacts book. Link to your raw material and let people comment on the holes in your narrative. Engage with online communities if you expect them to engage with you. And stop thinking about the PR of how you look and focus on the journalism of what you do.

The Need for Greater Transparency

As the journalist develops a closer relationship with his or her audience (or the people formerly known as the audience), the dynamic becomes much more one of person to person rather than person to institution. This is a good thing. However, from an institutional point of view, the closer relationship—and the greater opportunity for a journalist to share personal opinions—could affect a journalist's and the media organization's credibility. How journalists and media organizations balance the personal with the institutional is a challenge that both will face with increasing frequency as the use of social media becomes more commonplace. Does being transparent about opinions or attitudes make up for what a media entity might see as a loss of objectivity?

In a presentation to the Inter American Press Association entitled "The Changing Relationship Between Journalists and Their Audiences," Dr. Klaus Meier (2008) said that one of the ways journalists can earn the trust of their readers/viewers is to achieve more authenticity and transparency by "learning from the Blogosphere":

- Are the sources in articles clearly identified? (linking creates checkability and hence credibility)
- Is the rationale behind the news explained, especially the editorial decisions?
- Has the journalist "a human voice"? Does he talk about "how we got the story"?
- Are all sides asked to comment? (news as conversation)

Weinberger (2009) says that instead of pursuing an almost unattainable ideal like objectivity, media should instead pursue "transparency." As he describes it: "What we used to believe because we thought the author was objective we now believe because we can see through the author's writings to the sources and values that brought her to that position. Transparency gives the reader information by which she can undo some of the unintended effects of the ever-present biases. Transparency brings us to reliability the way objectivity used to."

Weinberger (2009) argues that objectivity became the default approach because of the limitations of print, but that online transparency—via links—becomes much more possible, and more desirable:

> Transparency prospers in a linked medium, for you can literally see the connections between the final draft's claims and the ideas that informed it. Paper, on the other hand, sucks at links. You can look up the footnote, but that's an expensive, time-consuming activity more likely to result in failure than success. So, during the Age of Paper, we got used to the idea that authority comes in the form of a stop sign: You've reached a source whose reliability requires no further inquiry.

He adds: "Objectivity without transparency increasingly will look like arrogance. And then foolishness. Why should we trust what one person—with the best of intentions—insists is true when we instead could have a web of evidence, ideas, and argument? In short: Objectivity is a trust mechanism you rely on when your medium can't do links" (Weinberger 2009).

As journalism teacher Amy Gahran noted in a post on Twitter on September 27, 2009, far from establishing a journalist's credibility, "when journos pretend to have NO opinions/biases, it *undermines* their credibility."

A Renewed Community Connection

If the traditional media relationship is no longer between the journalist and the audience, then how are we to describe it? One way to think of it is as a relationship between a media outlet and the community of people interested in its content—a community that likely mimics many of the aspects of a real-world community, with some people on the fringes, some people who are die-hard members, people who come and go, and a variety of good and bad behaviour. But the relationship between a journalist and these community members is much more complex than a simple one-way journalist-to-audience connection.

In *The Elements of Journalism*, Bill Kovach and Tom Rosenstiel (2001) say: "This kind of high-tech interaction is a journalism that resembles conversation again, much like the original journalism occurring in the publick houses and coffeehouses four hundred years ago. Seen in this light, journalism's function is not fundamentally changed by the digital age. The techniques may be different, but the underlying principles are the same" (25).

Gillmor (2002) describes the principles that define the current "we media" movement:

- My readers know more than I do.
- That is not a threat, but rather an opportunity.
- We can use this together to create something between a seminar and a conversation, educating all of us.
- Interactivity and communications technology—in the form of email, weblogs, discussion boards, websites and more—make it happen.

Audience-Driven News: Good or Bad?

As the relationship between the audience and the media has evolved into one that is multidirectional and in real time, the influence that readers and viewers have over the media has changed as well. Websites can monitor in real time what readers or viewers want to see, and since advertising revenue is still their primary source of funding, page views and unique visitors are the benchmark for success. One predictable outcome is that more and more news websites have turned to the quick hit, the salacious report, or the questionable video to drive the kind of results they want to see. But should a journalistic organization always give the audience what it wants to see or hear, or should it take into account other factors?

In an op-ed piece in the *Miami Herald*, journalism professor Ed Wasserman (2009) takes issue with the idea of giving readers what they want—saying that "for journalists the hitch has always been that news, if done honestly, is routinely unwelcome and, more to the point, that it isn't just another consumer product. It's a kind of civic good. Sure, it must be bought, but if success were measured solely by marketability journalists could safely ignore vast areas of coverage that help keep leaders honest and the public conscious of significant realities. Hence, the paradox: If all you do is give the public what it thinks it wants, you aren't doing your job. But if you ignore those wishes, you won't have a job."

Wasserman (2009) goes on to say that "ultimately, people look to journalists for a special service—keeping them on top of what they need to know. They can't say exactly what that is, any more than journalists know in the morning what they'll report that day. But they trust the news source to tell them." In other words, giving people what they want isn't good enough.

However, in a response to Wasserman on the FixJournalism.com blog, journalism professor Donica Mensing (2009) argues that this view of journalism is flawed, and that a new view of what journalism is for (which she calls "reform journalism") is a better approach:

> In this version of journalism, the public is a partner with the journalist, not an ignorant mass that can't be trusted to know what it needs. Reform journalism also recognizes that journalism operates within a network of multiple publics, of differentiated audiences with overlapping interests and chaotic (for now) patterns of media use.

A New Ethic of Journalism

What if there was a new ethic of journalism that included reader interaction? John Carroll of the Knight Foundation raised that idea at a conference on the Future of News in 2009. He speculated that in the future, having some form of reader input or feedback or "user-generated content" would become the norm for most reporting, and that a story which didn't include that kind of input would seem as out of place or as flawed as one in which a person's name was spelled incorrectly, or one that didn't give names at all.

SIDEBAR

New Roles for Journalists

What is the role of a journalist in this new era? Veteran journalist Howard Owens (2008) says that journalists should play six roles:

- **The Ethical Role.** … We should deal more swiftly and transparently with ethical errors within the profession, but we should also provide teaching tools on information ethics, what ethics means and why it's important. …
- **The Guide/Filter Role.** Editors and reporters should assume some responsibility for providing their audiences with pointers to the best stuff on the web. …
- **The Understanding and Context Role.** Why should the best bloggers get to have all the fun? The best journalists should become the best bloggers. …
- **The Conversation Leader Role.** … We should provide our own insights and supplemental knowledge to any conversation we find. We should be full participants, not just the lurking overlords of top-down media.
- **The Aggregator Role.** We should aggressively gather data related to the communities we serve. We should make sure that anything that is knowable about a community we serve is findable through resources we provide. …
- **The Straight News Role.** … We must know about everything important going on in the communities that we serve, and we should strive to be the first to tell our communities about the important news of the moment.

Conclusion

Like it or not, the reality is that journalism in the age of the Web has become a multi-directional phenomenon. No longer is it something journalists do by themselves, with little or no input from readers, producing disconnected conversations and responses that they are also not a part of. Instead, it is becoming a give-and-take process between the journalist and "the people formerly known as the audience," an ongoing relationship in which each side provides something valuable. And as apprehensive as some journalists might be about this new state of affairs, there is much to like about this new relationship: It produces better journalism, it engages readers more directly—something that has crucial implications for media as a business—and it makes for better journalists. It is not something to be feared, but instead it is something to be embraced.

DISCUSSION QUESTIONS

1. Kevin Anderson of the *Guardian* is quoted above as saying "We've taken our audiences for granted, and now we have to do a lot of hard work to earn them back." What specific strategies or improvements are required for traditional media to achieve this? Do the changes brought by new media and new attitudes mean traditional media will never return to their previous dominance?
2. This chapter points out that the new relationship between the journalist and the audience is in its infancy. Try to imagine some interesting new directions this relationship could take in the coming decades. Also try to imagine what new communications technologies might evolve in the near future, and how journalism might be affected by them—whether positively or negatively.
3. Many traditional journalists have lamented the revolutionary changes happening in journalism and feel that important aspects of journalism have been lost. What sorts of arguments might a traditional journalist make in asserting that the "old" relationship of the journalist and the audience was better than the newly evolving one described in this chapter?
4. Twenty-first century journalism is sometimes described as a return to the conversations that took place in public spaces hundreds of years ago. Do you agree or disagree with that comparison?

SUGGESTED RESOURCES

Bowman, Shayne, and Chris Willis. 2003. *We media: How audiences are shaping the future of news and information*, ed. J.D. Lasica. Reston, VA: The Media Center at the American Press Institute. http://www.hypergene.net/wemedia/weblog.php.

Diakopoulos, Nick. 2008. Notions of transparency in journalism. http://www.deakondesign.com/?p=81.

Dvorkin, Lewis. 2009. Inviting the Rise of the Entrepreneurial Journalist. Nieman Reports, Fall. http://www.nieman.harvard.edu/reportsitem.aspx?id=101890.

Hollis. 2007. Futurist updates "audience as journalist" process. PRPD News for Programmers, July 25. http://prpd-news.blogspot.com/2007/07/futurist-updates-audience-as-journalist.html.

Oliver, Laura. 2009. Citizen journalism will remain part of changing news models, says report. Journalism.co.uk, September 18. http://www.journalism.co.uk/2/articles/535868.php.

REFERENCES

Anderson, Kevin. 2009. Overcoming journalists' sense of entitlement to an audience. Strange Attractor, May 19. http://strange.corante.com/2009/05/19/overcoming-journalists-sense-of-entitlement-to-an-audience.

Bell, Emily. 2009. Lecture to Falmouth. Emily Bell's Blog, May 8. http://publicserviceblog.wordpress.com/2009/05/08/lecture-to-falmouth/.

Benkler, Yochai. 2007. *The wealth of networks: How social production transforms markets and freedom*. New Haven, CT: Yale University Press.

Bradshaw, Paul. 2009. The end of objectivity. Online Journalism Blog, September 29. http://onlinejournalismblog.com/2009/09/29/the-end-of-objectivity-web-2-0-version/.

Clune, Bronwen. 2009. Journalists are the audience formerly known as the media. Bronwen Clune, November 10. http://www.bronwenclune.com/2009/11/10/journalists-are-the-audience-formerly-known-as-the-media/.

Gillmor, Dan. 2002. Journalistic pivot points. eJournal: Dan Gillmor's News and Views. March 27.

Gillmor, Dan. 2004. *We the media: Grassroots journalism by the people, for the people*. Sebastopol, CA: O'Reilly Media.

Glocer, Tom. 2006a. The two-way pipe—facing the challenge of the new content creators. Tom Glocer's Blog, October 11. http://tomglocer.com/blogs/sample_weblog/archive/2006/10/11/97.aspx.

Glocer, Tom. 2006b. We media speech. Tom Glocer's Blog, October 11. http://tomglocer.com/blogs/sample_weblog/archive/2006/10/11/98.aspx.

Hamsher, Jane. 2006. The people formerly known as the audience. The Huffington Post, January 3. http://www.huffingtonpost.com/jane-hamsher/the-people-formerly-known_b_13192.html.

Horrocks, Peter. 2008. Value of citizen journalism. BBC—The Editors, January 7. http://www.bbc.co.uk/blogs/theeditors/2008/01/value_of_citizen_journalism.html.

Jarvis, Jeff. 2009. Product v. process journalism: The myth of perfection v. beta culture. BuzzMachine, June 7. http://www.buzzmachine.com/2009/06/07/processjournalism/.

Kelly, John. 2009. *Red kayaks and hidden gold: The rise, challenges and value of citizen journalism*. Oxford, UK: Reuters Institute for the Study of Journalism, Department of Politics and International Relations, University of Oxford. http://reutersinstitute.politics.ox.ac.uk/fileadmin/documents/Publications/Red_Kayaks___Hidden_Gold.pdf.

Kovach, Bill, and Rosenstiel, Tom. 2001. *The elements of journalism: What newspeople should know and the public should expect*. New York: Three Rivers Press.

Meier, Klaus. 2008. The changing relationship between journalists and their audiences. PowerPoint presented at the Conference of the Inter American Press Association (IAPA)/Sociedad Interamericana de Prensa (SIP), Madrid. http://www.klaus-meier.net/blog/wp-content/uploads/2008/10/meier_iapa_madrid_oct_08.pdf.

Mensing, Donica. 2009. Should you ask your audience what they want? Fix Journalism, May 12. http://www.fixjournalism.com/journalists/should-you-ask-your-audience-what-they-want/.

Owens, Howard. 2008. Six roles, or job duties, of modern journalism. Howard Owens, January 26. http://www.howardowens.com/2008/six-roles-or-job-duties-of-modern-journalism/.

Rosen, Jay. 2006. The people formerly known as the audience. PressThink, June 27. http://journalism.nyu.edu/pubzone/weblogs/pressthink/2006/06/27/ppl_frmr.html.

Rosen, Jay. 2009. Audience atomization overcome: Why the Internet weakens the authority of the press. PressThink, January 12. http://journalism.nyu.edu/pubzone/weblogs/pressthink/2009/01/12/atomization.html.

Wasserman, Ed. 2009. What readers want vs. what they need. The Liberty Voice, May 13. http://www.thelibertyvoice.com/what-readers-want-vs-what-they-need/.

Weinberger, David. 2009. Transparency is the new objectivity. Joho the Blog, July 19. http://www.hyperorg.com/blogger/2009/07/19/transparency-is-the-new-objectivity/.

CHAPTER 3

Missing the Link: How the Internet Is Saving Journalism

David Eaves and Taylor Owen

Introduction

In 2008, prominent political blogger Josh Marshall (TalkingPointsMemo.com) won a prestigious George Polk Award for Legal Reporting. While recognition for his blogging comes as no surprise, the fact that the accolades originated in the hallowed halls of traditional print journalism marks a notable moment in the decade-old battle between "old" and "new" media. This battle continues to be fought, although quietly, between the print and online departments of newspapers around the world. But the divide between the "new" media of blogs and the "old" media of newspapers is largely mythical and increasingly being bridged by practitioners like Marshall. What we can learn from them is essential to the future of print journalism.

CHAPTER OUTLINE

However much newspaper editors and journalists may complain, it is clear that blogs are here to stay, and that the practice of journalism has only benefited from their proliferation. Unfortunately, despite its exponential growth, blogging continues to be misunderstood by both technophiles and technophobes. For the past decade, the former have maintained that blogs will replace traditional journalism, ushering in an era of citizen-run media. Conversely, the latter have argued that a wave of amateurs threatens the quality and integrity of journalism—and possibly even democracy. Both are wrong.

Blogging is not a substitute for journalism. If anything, this past decade shows that blogging and journalism are symbiotic and mutually beneficial. (See also Chapter 17, "Blog to the Future: Telling Digital Stories in the Post-9/11 Decade.") Admittedly, many in the newspaper industry have been loath to embrace emerging technologies. Most have been reluctant and highly conservative in adopting online strategies. As a result, few have generated sustainable revenue or successfully fought the decentralization of news content creation. And while it is one thing for an outgoing generation of media barons to misunderstand new media and what it means for their business, it is quite another to have this perspective shape the choices of a generation whose careers will be shaped by new media.

The future of traditional news institutions in a new media world is far from certain, but they can survive if they correctly identify their core competencies and are ruthlessly disciplined in shedding or altering everything else. The new media are good at many things, but not everything. Traditional media, by failing to understand and focus on their core competencies, risk losing sight of their real value. Capitalizing on their narrow, but critical, utility could provide direction to the struggling industry.

So what is going on? And what should traditional media do about it? In order to ascertain this, we will first outline seven lessons traditional newspapers can learn from new media and the Internet. Drawing on these lessons, we will then outline three principles that must frame a competitive strategy to ensure traditional media's survival. Despite fatalistic predictions, traditional media's survival is both important and possible. However, success will require substantially more dramatic changes than those prescribed by traditionalists.

Seven Lessons from New Media

1. Blogging Is a Medium, Not a Practice

All too often, those in the print media pejoratively label everything written online as "blogging" and consequently dismiss the competition as a mob of "amateurs." Unfortunately, this definition is premised on both quantitative and qualitative errors.

The quantitative problem is a miscount of the competition. The numbers (which will undoubtedly have grown by the time you read this) certainly sound impressive: Technorati reported in 2007 that it was tracking over 70 million blogs, with 120,000 created daily and 1.5 million new posts every day (about 17 posts per second). Such statistics are frequently debated, but either way, this is a tremendous amount of content. But not everyone who publishes content on a blog competes with journalists. Blogging is merely a medium, a tool that allows content to be published online easily, and at little or no cost.

Consider another medium, such as books. Hundreds of thousands of non-fiction books are written every year. Do print journalists compete against all these books? Obviously not. Some, although relatively few, are journalistic in nature. But even here it is unclear if print journalists compete against these books or if journalistic books increase interest in journalism and the print media. Like books, blogs are merely a medium. Journalism, in contrast, is a practice that some people use via the medium of blogging (or books) to disseminate. It is true that blogging may facilitate a different type of journalism (as do books), but let's not confuse the medium with the content. Blogs are just the new pen and paper; it's what's written on them that matters. And needless to say, not everyone with a blog is producing journalistic content.

2. Aggregators and Bloggers Are the New Editors

Many have correctly pointed out that generations Y and Z will become their own news "editor-aggregators." This is a critical development and an important insight, with dramatic implications: There is really no reason to believe that aggregators will respect the division between the online versions of print media and the rest of the "wild Web." As David Weinberger points out in *Everything Is Miscellaneous*, what makes the Web interesting, compelling, and democratic is that data doesn't get organized based on where it came from, but on *how interesting each individual reader believes it to be*.

This is a perfect example of how a traditional medium's model blinds it to an effective reassessment of its utility and strategy. Accepting the reality and implications of online aggregators would mean accepting that the role of newspaper editor is under threat. For many traditionalists, this challenge to the pantheon of journalism is simply too much to bear. However, competition in news aggregation is real, evolving rapidly, and transformative.

This new competition can be seen as two interrelated, but quite different Internet-based phenomena: aggregators and bloggers. Algorithm-based aggregators, such as Google News and Delicious, and human-run websites such as the Drudge Report and The Huffington Post, provide powerful alternatives to the newspaper editor. Aggregators, both human and algorithm, don't care where content is from and so can draw it from virtually anywhere. This capacity to ferret out the best content from across the Web and deposit it on your computer screen raises the question: If you could choose to read the best articles drawn from a pool of 100 authors versus a pool of 1.5 million, which would you choose? Can any editor compete?

The second threat is the very networked nature of the Internet itself. The Web's interconnectedness allows news items to spread virally as opposed to centrally. Younger readers increasingly read articles found through links from blogs. This does not mean that the news itself is written by bloggers, although that too is increasingly the case. Instead, it is their community, not the editor of the *New York Times*, that influences their reading. This is not simply a quirk of the Net. It turns out that readers like choosing their editor. And now, because the blog format allows readers to forge relationships with authors/editors, they can. Take, for example, our relationship with the prominent political blogger Andrew Sullivan (AndrewSullivan.TheAtlantic.com). While we have never met in person, we know his perspectives; we know his biases; and we have lived through his daily struggle with the Iraq War. It is this personal connection that keeps us, and his 80,000 daily readers, coming back. Who we don't know is the editor of the *New York Times*. Indeed, the top-down process of traditional media establishments is designed to prevent us from ever getting the chance to. As everyone knows, traditional media editorials are anonymous.

Consumers now have a choice. Use aggregators and a blogger community to draw content from over 1.5 million posts every day or rely on faceless editors who can choose from 50 pieces. This isn't some hypothetical world of tomorrow. Aggregators are the new editors.

3. Free Markets Are Good Fact-Checkers

One oft-repeated critique of blog journalism is that it is not subject to the same rigorous fact-checking procedures used by newspapers. Without experts, researchers, and editors, how can online content be trusted? Journalists accustomed to the structured and hierarchical nature of a newsroom probably can't imagine how the "wild Web" can yield reliable content. However, it turns out that the Internet's principal attribute—its "open source" nature—makes it a surprisingly good fact-checker.

The point is not to undervalue the utility of traditional fact-checking. There should be no doubt that the mechanisms in place in most major media outlets result in a product that is far more trustworthy and accurate than information available on the average blog. However, there are also limits to the single-source fact-checking model. As good as a 21-year-old Ivy League intern may be, he or she will never be as clever

IN PRACTICE

"Mystery Solving": Journalism in the Era of Open

David Eaves has written extensively on the emergence of the open data movement. In a March 2009 blogpost, he discussed the implications for the practice of journalism as massive amounts of information become easily accessible:

> If much of investigative journalism has been about uncovering the dirty secrets within opaque institutions, what does it do if an increasing number of institutions have fewer and fewer secrets?
>
> I suspect the ideal of good journalism will shift from being what Malcolm Gladwell calls "puzzle solving" to "mystery solving" (see *The New Yorker*, January 8, 2007). In the former you must find a critical piece of the puzzle—one that is hidden from you—in order to explain an event. This is the Woodward and Bernstein model of journalism, the current ideal. But in a transparent landscape where huge amounts of information about most organizations are being generated and shared, one critical role of the journalist will be that of mystery solving: figuring out how to analyze, synthesize and discover the mystery within the vast quantities of available information. As Gladwell recounts, this was the very type of journalism that brought down Enron. All of the pieces that led to the story that "exposed" Enron were freely, voluntarily and happily given to reporters *by Enron*.
>
> I for one would celebrate the rise of this mystery-focused style of journalism. It has been sorely needed over the past few years. Indeed, the housing bubble that led to the recent financial crisis is a perfect example of a case where we needed mystery solving, not puzzle solving, journalism. The fact that sub-prime mortgages were being sold and re-packaged was not a secret; what was lacking was enough people willing to analyze and write about this complex mystery and its dangerous implications.
>
> Interestingly, this is precisely what many blogs—alone or as part of an emergent network—already do. They take large, complex stories, break them down, and by linking back and forth to one another, create a collective analysis that slowly allows the mystery to be decoded.

SOURCE: Eaves.ca, March 17, 2009 (excerpt).

or as knowledgeable as the combined fact-checking capacity of thousands of readers. The Internet provides both the research tools to fact-check and the technological opportunity for knowledgeable readers to comment on other people's work.

Open source fact-checking works in two interconnected ways, both bottom-up. First, anyone anywhere can comment on a piece, analyzing contradictions, typos, and factual errors. In short, an online writer's audience is also her editor and fact-checker, providing feedback with which she can update and refine her work in real time. Second, good posts filter their way up though the blogosphere. In order to make it to the large blogs and aggregators, a piece must first be seen by hundreds if not thousands of readers—all of whom are evaluating, judging, and commenting. The process is brutal, ruthless, and market driven. (And bloggers soon learn that their work will never rise to the top if it consistently contains errors; credibility and reputation are critical in the blogosphere.) However, once a post starts getting picked up, its readership might reach tens if not hundreds of thousands of readers within days. In such cases, the content is generally as compelling and accurate as what can be found in any major daily. This is the world of open source fact-checking, and it may be the most undervalued attribute of new media. Together, we would argue that these two pillars of open source quality control rival the best professional fact-checkers.

Media companies need to adapt to what many software engineers have known for years—much of the best, and most reliable, content is now open source. Much like the large entrenched dinosaurs of the software world, traditional media have been hesitant to embrace the clear merits of this model. Online collaboration is significantly more than the sum of its parts. It creates, promotes, and filters content better than any one source ever could. It may appear messy to the uninitiated, but it works.

4. Newspapers Are Great Creators, Poor Distributors

Newspaper editors generally feel confident that given the opportunity, most journalists would prefer a column in a traditional daily than on an online-only forum. This confidence rests on the credibility of traditional media, which allows writers to put a recognizable brand on their work and provides them access to the marketplace and to a particular audience. But the online world is maturing, and the credibility gap is shrinking. Over time, writers will gravitate to those places that either pay the best, or more likely, ensure their work reaches the most (or the right) eyeballs. Andrew Sullivan, the aforementioned blogger, epitomizes this future. As he wrote on his blog, The Daily Dish, in 2007: "What would I rather be doing? A lucrative op-ed column or a blog that racked up 3 million page-views this month? Put it this way: no regrets."

Sullivan is merely pointing out a cold, hard fact: The distributive capacity of the printed page, or a restricted newspaper's website, is a fraction that of new media sites. Even newspapers that do share their content freely will remain burdened by their expensive print assets and won't be as financially competitive as their new media competitors. Compared with the online world, newspapers have a costly and severely limited distribution model.

For over a century, newspapers have vertically integrated content creation with content distribution. Benjamin Franklin pioneered this strategy in America's early years. As a printer he forged one of North America's first media empires, publishing content such as news stories, almanacs, and flyers—to ensure his printing presses were constantly busy, and profitable. Prior to the Internet this integration also made sense to consumers. Readers needed a channel (in this case the newspaper) that made content easy to digest. The challenge is that newspapers have performed these two functions—creation and distribution—for so long that people often conflate them, believing them to be a single activity. They are not.

It is understandable that newspapers lament the passing of this old, cozy world. But they should take heart. Distribution was always exogenous to traditional media's real value. New media may deliver content more effectively and efficiently than newspapers, but then, why would traditional media want to compete on distribution? All those resources, employees, and infrastructure can now be redirected toward what newsrooms really care about—finding, reporting, and talking about the news. If you are a newspaper that loves the news, and you are willing to let go of distribution, this is the start of a golden age.

5. Objectivity Is Condescending

Blogs do more than just report or opine. They often do both. For traditional journalists, this is anathema—and something they claim they never do.

For better or worse, many readers want more than objective facts. They want informed, intelligent commentary mixed in with their news. The print newspaper's practice of separating editorial content from objective news was never real or viable. Maintaining the illusion of objectivity requires a control over production and dissemination that is unnecessary, time-consuming, and expensive.

Generation Y is perhaps the most news-savvy generation in history. Having grown up inundated with media, its members naturally pull out and separate editorial content. This means that they don't have a problem with it being there in the first place. Indeed, this accounts, in part, for the popularity of *The Daily Show*, which regularly mocks the editorial perspective that old media pretend doesn't exist in its news pieces. Like Jon Stewart, Generation Yers simply do not accept the pretense that media are objective.

6. Nostalgia Is Not a Growth Model

Only baby boomers are nostalgic for newsprint, and catering to them is not a growth industry. Media traditionalists often cite two examples—incidental reading and ideological objectivity—to explain why physical newspapers will and should remain the main distribution channel for print media. However, the purported value of physical newsprint simply doesn't hold up to scrutiny.

Scanning the pages of a newspaper is indeed a virtue. It exposes readers to articles they might not seek out, broadening their range of news and opinion. However, this process is no different from what happens online. Links, aggregators, and email steer readers to a far broader range of articles than they could conceivably imagine by simply flipping through a newspaper. Indeed, the Internet enables this incidental reading better than newspapers.

The other oft-cited example of the value of newspapers is that they prevent readers from falling into self-selected ideological silos. The argument is that, when left to their own devices, innocent readers will gravitate toward the poles of their ideological bias.

What they need, and should pay for, is a physical entity that provides them with a limited, but "healthy," range of information.

This argument ignores the fact that many newspapers operate as ideological poles themselves. The *New York Times* clearly favours the left, whereas the *Wall Street Journal* appeals to the right. The Internet, unlike print media, provides tools to overcome these silos. Not all content delivered through an aggregator will be consistent with a reader's perspective (indeed, one can imagine a customized aggregator that specifically targets news pieces that challenge its audience; and RealClearPolitics.com provides an existing example of "mixed" aggregated content). More important, the Internet gives readers the freedom (and safety) to select content from a broader range of perspectives. The ease, speed, and anonymity of the Web stimulates exploration that the physical world prohibits. In addition, many posts are written in response to other pieces, to which they inevitably link. Neither traditional nor new media can single-handedly mediate or resolve political differences, but at least new media link the poles to one another, rather then creating isolated playgrounds where pundits can safely take shots at one another.

7. The Decline of Newspapers Is a Sign of Democracy, Not a Symptom of Its Death

A recent Columbia Journalism School panel on the future of the newspaper industry ended with a solemn and bold pronouncement: "If print newspapers disappear, it will be a fundamental threat to our democracy."

Such statements made many new media participants roll their eyes—and for good reason. Are newspapers really a precondition for democracy?

This type of irrational hyperbole discredits traditional media's claim to rational objectivity. Newspapers are not a precondition for democracy—free speech is. This is why the American Constitution and the *Canadian Charter of Rights and Freedoms* protect the latter and not the former. Free speech is also what makes the Internet important—it provides a powerful medium through which free speech can be transmitted. As we argued earlier, the Internet offers its own democratic way of filtering content, allowing what people think is important, relevant, and interesting to be aggregated and heard. It may be messy and far from perfect, but then so is democracy.

Newspapers, in contrast, are many things, but they are not democratic. They are largely hierarchical authoritarian structures designed to control and shape information. This is not to say that they don't provide a societal benefit—their content contributes to public discourse. However, how is having a few major media outlets deciding "what is news" democratic, or even necessarily good for democracy?

Far from a prerequisite, traditional media are to democracy what commercial banks are to capitalism. Are banks necessary for capitalism? No. Have they sped up its growth and made it more effective? Definitely. But could some better model emerge that performs their functions more effectively? Absolutely. Much like claiming "you'll never get by without me" rarely reignites a relationship, fear mongering and threatening your customers won't bring readers back. This approach merely demonstrates how scared old media have become of their readers, free speech, and the type of democracy that many of them want to build.

Three Strategic Principles for the Newspaper Industry

This chapter is not the first, nor will it be the last, aggressive critique of traditional media. However, unlike the work of our techno-utopian contemporaries, our criticisms should not be seen as a jubilant celebration of a dying industry. Traditional media have served society well, and with the right attitude and adjustments, could continue to do so for the foreseeable future. Based on the seven lessons outlined above, we believe that any successful initiatives will be bound by three principles: concentrate on the core, respect the long tail of news, and be open.

Principle One: Concentrate on the Core

To be successful in this new era, print media may be forced to decide whether they are content creators or distributors. For many traditional media institutions, the default choice has been distributor. Content has been outsourced to freelancers and the newswires. That is okay; distribution is a valid choice, particularly for more local newspapers. However, this choice also comes with significant risks. The newspaper medium may be relevant for another 20 years, but beyond that, what is currently a steady decline will likely turn into a cliff—and that's presuming that some cheap new portable technology isn't adopted sooner.

The more exciting possibility is for newspapers to transform themselves into "real" aggregators. As was discussed earlier, newspapers are already, in essence, news aggregators. They just limit what they aggregate to staff writers, available freelancers, and what they pull off the wires (which is pretty generic). Why not draw content from across the Web?

If, however, traditional media institutions want to become content creators only, then they must create an exit strategy from distribution. This should be welcome news. Good newspapers have always been defined by the quality of their newsroom, not the quality of their distribution network. For example, the *New York Times* is known because it provides a high baseline starting point for content—a quality guaranteed by its brand. Non-branded content can get to this level of quality, and even surpass it, but it takes time for a piece to filter up through the Internet's open source fact-checking process. In the Internet era, this is an advantage. What a newsroom can do is "elevate the starting line." It can create reliable content that is branded as fact-checked and sourced, faster than anyone else.

Bill Kovach and Tom Rosenstiel (n.d.) have remarked that "[t]his discipline of verification is what separates journalism from other modes of communication, such as propaganda, fiction or entertainment." We agree. But this only gets journalists in the game. They still have to perform once there. And this means participating in the open source evolution of content. Newsrooms should supply content that others can use or build on. Imagine a news article that a journalist manages for two or three days, posting good comments and redrafting the piece once or twice to reflect new information and corrections. This is a remarkably different model of content management, but it would likely be far more engaging. To succeed, though, traditional media will also have to both respect its readers and open up.

Principle Two: Respect the Long Tail of News

In an era of web-traffic-based measures of advertising and readership success, it must be asked, if hits are the sole metric, then why not feature soft porn on the *New York Times* website? The answer, of course, is that the *New York Times* is in the business of news, and pornography is not news. However, the line between entertainment and news is becoming increasingly blurred, an outcome in part driven by the highly flawed "most-emailed" or "most-read" article rankings that most newspapers include on their web pages. These measures assume that all Internet users are the same, and that the goal of any site is to attain traffic from anywhere. This is simply not the case. The goal of a newspaper should be to improve the quality of its traffic, not the quantity. This means, first and foremost, resisting the temptation to gain hits by adding tabloid content to its website.

A few points are important. First, quality reporting is increasingly a "long tail" business. The days in which a handful of papers and networks dominated the market are over. What does this mean? As we have discussed, readers will reach a newspaper's website through a vast number of mechanisms, including searches, recommendations, links, and so on. If the paper's article is good, they may go somewhere else on the site. But the odds are that they will return only if there is another unique piece of content on the site that attracts them. This means that online articles are competing for readers in a very different way than print articles. They want the person interested in a specific article, not the person interested in the entire paper. Luckily, there are many more people who want to read one article than would commit to reading an entire paper. The strategy for targeting them is completely different, though.

Dumbing down one's content to increase traffic will only drive these long-tail news-seeking readers away. Worse, such a strategy forces papers to compete with entertainment, gossip, and tabloid sites, which receive ten times their traffic.

Second, advertisers are increasingly concerned about the quality rather than the quantity of traffic. Again, if the sole valuation of ads on a newspaper's website is number of eyeballs, then they will lose out to the hundreds of sites that will always receive far more traffic. Competing against the Google homepage for advertising revenue is neither realistic nor an appropriate model, as the two provide entirely different services. It is the quality and specificity of the eyeballs that are newspapers' advantage in the online advertising game, and becoming a tabloid will only degrade that readership.

Third, if the goal is to attract educated readers who value quality reporting (that is, ideal newspaper customers), then a website needs gatekeepers. In the Wild West of the Internet, it is links that drive and direct traffic. Good links, from quality sites, will make or break the type of traffic any news site receives. Central to this marketplace of referrals and links are bloggers.

Principle Three: Be Open

The power of the Internet is its openness. Trying to stay isolated on the Internet requires swimming against a torrent. Why not go with the flow?

First, traditional media should keep their content free and accessible. People read what they can link to. By preventing their material from being linked to and read, traditional media are essentially pulling it off the market. To charge for online content, you need to offer something not available in the countless posts published daily, as well as the content available in free dailies and new media sites. This approach is increasingly untenable.

Second, traditional media need to become more permeable. The staff writers of the *New York Times*, while certainly talented, are not the be-all and end-all of news. Consequently, simply recreating newspapers online won't work. Web pages that interlink with others are more likely to be visited because readers will know that in addition to the base content or analysis, they will also be pointed to interesting material, both within the site and outside. Isolated news pages will invariably remain just that—cut off.

Finally, allow your readers to edit and comment. As we mentioned earlier, traditional media have a competitive advantage in elevating the starting line of content quality. However, no matter how esteemed the *New York Times* brand may be, its edge is diminished every second its content remains unedited and in isolation. The brand lets you move your starting line forward, but to maintain your lead, you'll have to let your readers participate in the content's evolution. And why not? It will keep eyeballs on the news page (and consequently the advertising), improve content, cultivate loyalty, and build community, all while leveraging an essentially free resource.

Conclusion

While the preceding discussion outlines three admittedly broad principles that we believe should guide the transformation of the traditional print news industry, it does not provide a prefab template, and for good reason.

The type of transformation necessary for survival in the new media landscape cannot be predefined. It will involve creative solutions that have yet to be developed, using technology that in many instances is on the distant horizon. This unavoidable reality reinforces the need to think about the industry in a fundamentally new and open way. The major newspaper companies must stop acting like Ford, and start behaving like Mozilla. It is only by drawing on the wisdom of crowds, both for content and distribution, that these hierarchical organizations will adapt to an interconnected world.

There should be no doubt that this transformation will require dramatic restructuring and experimentation by established companies who are not used to, or structured for, taking risk. Such risk aversion may very well prove to be the fundamental impediment to the industry's renewal. Ultimately, what makes all of this hard is not that the strategy must change (which is hard enough) but that the values embedded in many traditional media institutions need to evolve. A new operating philosophy is required.

What is encouraging is that these values aren't necessarily new to either journalism or the media industry—in fact, they are the very principles upon which North American newspapers have been founded for over 300 years. While these values have remained important, they have increasingly been offset by the business demands of a centralized and closed distribution model. The principles that we feel are required for success in the new media world (focusing on quality content, respect for readers, and openness) are not new. This stuff is in our DNA. The Internet allows us to go back to the beginning.

DISCUSSION QUESTIONS

1. In his blog, Jay Rosen talks about mainstream media as being grounded in an industrial production model. How has the production of news (as opposed to the nature of journalism) constrained the ability of journalists and editors to adapt to the Internet age?
2. Think of the three most recent "big" newsworthy stories you have heard about. From what source, or platform, did you first hear about them? What does your answer indicate for the future of news?
3. The Huffington Post is one website that includes, in addition to its central focus on "serious news," a good deal of very light content (entertainment and pop culture stories, fashion disasters, Hollywood celebrity news, and so on). Does this strategy make sense? Does it undermine the site's credibility at all, and are the "rules" different for a traditional newspaper migrating to the Internet? At what point does one cross the line into "tabloid" journalism? Or, are The Huffington Post editors merely conceding that readers of serious news are also interested in lighter entertainment, and that there's nothing contradictory about that?

SUGGESTED RESOURCES

Blogs About New Media and the Future of Journalism

Berlin Johnson, Steven [blog]. http://stevenberlinjohnson.com.

BuzzMachine [Jeff Jarvis's blog]. http://www.buzzmachine.com.

Nieman Journalism Lab at Harvard University. http://www.niemanlab.org.

PressThink [Jay Rosen's blog]. http://journalism.nyu.edu/pubzone/weblogs/pressthink/.

Project for Excellence in Journalism. http://www.journalism.org.

REFERENCES

Kovach, Bill, and Tom Rosenstiel. n.d. Principles of journalism. http://www.journalism.org/resources/principles.

Weinberger, David. 2007. *Everything is miscellaneous: The power of the new digital disorder.* New York: Henry Holt.

CHAPTER 4

Newspapers and Thinking the Unthinkable

Clay Shirky

The following blog post appeared on March 13, 2009 (at www.shirky.com/weblog) and immediately went viral, prompting widespread discussion and response. Some excerpts from selected responses to Shirky's post appear at the end of this chapter.*

CHAPTER OUTLINE

Back in 1993, the Knight-Ridder newspaper chain began investigating piracy of Dave Barry's popular column, which was published by the *Miami Herald* and syndicated widely. In the course of tracking down the sources of unlicensed distribution, they found many things, including the copying of his column to alt.fan.dave_barry on usenet; a 2000-person strong mailing list also reading pirated versions; and a teenager in the Midwest who was doing some of the copying himself, because he loved Barry's work so much he wanted everybody to be able to read it.

One of the people I was hanging around with online back then was Gordy Thompson, who managed Internet services at the *New York Times*. I remember Thompson saying something to the effect of "When a 14-year-old kid can blow up your business in his spare time, not because he hates you but because he loves you, then you got a problem." I think about that conversation a lot these days.

The problem newspapers face isn't that they didn't see the Internet coming. They not only saw it miles off, they figured out early on that they needed a plan to deal with it, and during the early '90s they came up with not just one plan but several. One was to partner with companies like America Online, a fast-growing subscription service that was less chaotic than the open Internet. Another plan

* Reprinted under a commercial Creative Commons License, and with permission of the author. Originally posted at www.shirky.com, March 13, 2009.

was to educate the public about the behaviors required of them by copyright law. New payment models such as micropayments were proposed. Alternatively, they could pursue the profit margins enjoyed by radio and TV, if they became purely ad-supported. Still another plan was to convince tech firms to make their hardware and software less capable of sharing, or to partner with the businesses running data networks to achieve the same goal. Then there was the nuclear option: sue copyright infringers directly, making an example of them.

As these ideas were articulated, there was intense debate about the merits of various scenarios. Would DRM [digital rights management] or walled gardens work better? Shouldn't we try a carrot-and-stick approach, with education *and* prosecution? And so on. In all this conversation, there was one scenario that was widely regarded as unthinkable, a scenario that didn't get much discussion in the nation's newsrooms, for the obvious reason.

The unthinkable scenario unfolded something like this: The ability to share content wouldn't shrink, it would grow. Walled gardens would prove unpopular. Digital advertising would reduce inefficiencies, and therefore profits. Dislike of micropayments would prevent widespread use. People would resist being educated to act against their own desires. Old habits of advertisers and readers would not transfer online. Even ferocious litigation would be inadequate to constrain massive, sustained law-breaking. (Prohibition redux.) Hardware and software vendors would not regard copyright holders as allies, nor would they regard customers as enemies. DRM's requirement that the attacker be allowed to decode the content would be an insuperable flaw. And, per Thompson, suing people who love something so much they want to share it would piss them off.

Revolutions create a curious inversion of perception. In ordinary times, people who do no more than describe the world around them are seen as pragmatists, while those who imagine fabulous alternative futures are viewed as radicals. The last couple of decades haven't been ordinary, however. Inside the papers, the pragmatists were the ones simply looking out the window and noticing that the real world was increasingly resembling the unthinkable scenario. These people were treated as if they were barking mad. Meanwhile the people spinning visions of popular walled gardens and enthusiastic micropayment adoption, visions unsupported by reality, were regarded not as charlatans but saviors.

When reality is labeled unthinkable, it creates a kind of sickness in an industry. Leadership becomes faith-based, while employees who have the temerity to suggest that what seems to be happening is in fact happening are herded into Innovation Departments, where they can be ignored *en masse*. This shunting aside of the realists in favor of the fabulists has different effects on different industries at different times. One of the effects on the newspapers is that many of their most passionate defenders are unable, even now, to plan for a world in which the industry they knew is visibly going away.

• • •

The curious thing about the various plans hatched in the '90s is that they were, at base, all the same plan: "Here's how we're going to preserve the old forms of organization in a world of cheap perfect copies!" The details differed, but the core assumption behind all imagined outcomes (save the unthinkable one) was that the organizational form of the newspaper, as a general-purpose vehicle for publishing a variety of news and opinion, was basically sound, and only needed a digital facelift. As a result, the conversation has degenerated into the enthusiastic grasping at straws, pursued by skeptical responses.

"The *Wall Street Journal* has a paywall, so we can too!" (Financial information is one of the few kinds of information whose recipients don't want to share.) "Micropayments work for iTunes, so they will work for us!" (Micropayments work only where the provider can avoid competitive business models.) "The *New York Times* should charge for content!" (They've tried, with QPass and later TimesSelect.) "*Cook's Illustrated* and *Consumer Reports* are doing fine on subscriptions!" (Those publications forgo ad revenues; users are paying not just for content but for unimpeachability.) "We'll form a cartel!" (… and hand a competitive advantage to every ad-supported media firm in the world.)

Round and round this goes, with the people committed to saving newspapers demanding to know "If the old model is broken, what will work in its place?" To which the answer is: Nothing. Nothing will work. There is no general model for newspapers to replace the one the Internet just broke.

With the old economics destroyed, organizational forms perfected for industrial production have to be replaced with structures optimized for digital data. It makes increasingly less sense even to talk about a publishing industry, because the core problem publishing solves—the incredible difficulty, complexity, and expense of making something available to the public—has stopped being a problem.

• • •

Elizabeth Eisenstein's magisterial treatment of Gutenberg's invention, *The Printing Press as an Agent of Change*, opens with a recounting of her research into the early history of the printing press. She was able to find many descriptions of life in the early 1400s, the era before movable type. Literacy was limited, the Catholic Church was the pan-European political force, Mass was in Latin, and the average book was the Bible. She was also able to find endless descriptions of life in the late 1500s, after Gutenberg's invention had started to

Figure 4.1 Gutenberg's invention of movable type had revolutionary consequences. Shirky: "We're collectively living through 1500, when it's easier to see what's broken than what will replace it. … Society doesn't need newspapers. What we need is journalism."

spread. Literacy was on the rise, as were books written in contemporary languages, Copernicus had published his epochal work on astronomy, and Martin Luther's use of the press to reform the Church was upending both religious and political stability.

What Eisenstein focused on, though, was how many historians ignored the transition from one era to the other. To describe the world before or after the spread of print was child's play; those dates were safely distanced from upheaval. But what was happening in 1500? The hard question Eisenstein's book asks is "How did we get from the world before the printing press to the world after it? What was the revolution *itself* like?"

Chaotic, as it turns out. The Bible was translated into local languages; was this an educational boon or the work of the devil? Erotic novels appeared, prompting the same set of questions. Copies of Aristotle and Galen circulated widely, but direct encounter with the relevant texts revealed that the two sources clashed, tarnishing faith in the Ancients. As novelty spread, old institutions seemed exhausted while new ones seemed untrustworthy; as a result, people almost literally didn't know what to think. If you can't trust Aristotle, who can you trust?

During the wrenching transition to print, experiments were only revealed in retrospect to be turning points. Aldus Manutius, the Venetian printer and publisher, invented the smaller *octavo* volume along with italic type. What seemed like a minor change—take a book and shrink it—was in retrospect a key innovation in the democratization of the printed word. As books became cheaper, more portable, and therefore more desirable, they expanded the market for all publishers, heightening the value of literacy still further.

That is what real revolutions are like. The old stuff gets broken faster than the new stuff is put in its place. The importance of any given experiment isn't apparent at the moment it appears; big changes stall, small changes spread. Even the revolutionaries can't predict what will happen. Agreements on all sides that core institutions must be protected are rendered meaningless by the very people doing the agreeing. (Luther and the Church both insisted, for years, that whatever else happened, no one was talking about a schism.) Ancient social bargains, once disrupted, can neither be mended nor quickly replaced, since any such bargain takes decades to solidify.

And so it is today. When someone demands to know how we are going to replace newspapers, they are really demanding to be told that we are not living through a revolution. They are demanding to be told that old systems won't break before new systems are in place. They are demanding to be told that ancient social bargains aren't in peril, that core institutions will be spared, that new methods of spreading information will improve previous practice rather than upending it. They are demanding to be lied to.

There are fewer and fewer people who can convincingly tell such a lie.

• • •

If you want to know why newspapers are in such trouble, the most salient fact is this: Printing presses are terrifically expensive to set up and to run. This bit of economics, normal since Gutenberg, limits competition while creating positive returns to scale for the press owner, a happy pair of economic effects that feed on each other. In a notional town with two perfectly balanced newspapers, one paper would eventually generate some small advantage—a breaking story, a key interview—at which point both advertisers and readers would come to prefer it, however slightly. That paper would in turn find it easier to capture the next dollar of advertising, at lower expense, than the competition. This would increase its dominance, which would further deepen those preferences, repeat chorus. The end result is either geographic or demographic segmentation among papers, or one paper holding a monopoly on the local mainstream audience.

For a long time, longer than anyone in the newspaper business has been alive in fact, print journalism has been intertwined with these economics. The expense of printing created an environment where Wal-Mart was willing to subsidize the Baghdad bureau. This wasn't because of any deep link between advertising and reporting, nor was it about any real desire on the part of Wal-Mart to have their marketing budget go to international correspondents. It was just an accident. Advertisers had little choice other than to have their money used that way, since they didn't really have any other vehicle for display ads.

The old difficulties and costs of printing forced everyone doing it into a similar set of organizational models; it was this similarity that made us regard *Daily Racing Form* and *L'Osservatore Romano* as being in the same business. That the relationship between advertisers, publishers, and journalists has been ratified by a century of cultural practice doesn't make it any less accidental.

The competition-deflecting effects of printing cost got destroyed by the Internet, where everyone pays for the infrastructure, and then everyone gets to use it. And when Wal-Mart, and the local Maytag dealer, and the law firm hiring a secretary, and that kid down the block selling his bike, were all able to use that infrastructure to get out of their old relationship with the publisher, they did. They'd never really signed up to fund the Baghdad bureau anyway.

• • •

Print media does much of society's heavy journalistic lifting, from flooding the zone—covering every angle of a huge story—to the daily grind of attending the City Council meeting, just in case. This coverage creates benefits even for people who aren't newspaper readers, because the work of print journalists is used by everyone from politicians to district attorneys to talk radio hosts to bloggers. The newspaper people often note that newspapers benefit society as a whole. This is true, but irrelevant to the problem at hand; "You're gonna miss us when we're gone!" has never been much of a business model. So who covers all that news if some significant fraction of the currently employed newspaper people lose their jobs?

I don't know. Nobody knows. We're collectively living through 1500, when it's easier to see what's broken than what will replace it. The Internet turns 40 this fall. Access by the general public is less than half that age. Web use, as a normal part of life for a majority of the developed world, is less than half that age. We just got here. Even the revolutionaries can't predict what will happen.

Imagine, in 1996, asking some net-savvy soul to expound on the potential of craigslist, then a year old and not yet incorporated. The answer you'd almost certainly have gotten would be extrapolation: "Mailing lists can be powerful tools," "Social effects are intertwining with digital networks," blah blah blah. What no one would have told you, could have told you, was what actually happened: craigslist became a critical piece of infrastructure. Not the idea of craigslist, or the business model, or even the software driving it. Craigslist itself spread to cover hundreds of cities and has become a part of public consciousness about what is now possible. Experiments are only revealed in retrospect to be turning points.

In craigslist's gradual shift from "interesting if minor" to "essential and transformative," there is one possible answer to the question "If the old model is broken, what will work in its place?" The answer is: Nothing will work, but everything might. Now is the time for experiments, lots and lots of experiments, each of which will seem as minor at launch as craigslist did, as Wikipedia did, as *octavo* volumes did.

Journalism has always been subsidized. Sometimes it's been Wal-Mart and the kid with the bike. Sometimes it's been Richard Mellon Scaife. Increasingly, it's you and me, donating our time. The list of models that are obviously working today, like *Consumer Reports* and NPR, like ProPublica and Wikileaks, can't be expanded to cover any general case, but then nothing is going to cover the general case.

Society doesn't need newspapers. What we need is journalism. For a century, the imperatives to strengthen journalism and to strengthen newspapers have been so tightly wound as to be indistinguishable. That's been a fine accident to have, but when that accident stops, as it is stopping before our eyes, we're going to need lots of other ways to strengthen journalism instead.

When we shift our attention from "save newspapers" to "save society," the imperative changes from "preserve the current institutions" to "do whatever works." And what works today isn't the same as what used to work.

We don't know who the Aldus Manutius of the current age is. It could be Craig Newmark or Caterina Fake. It could be Martin Nisenholtz or Emily Bell. It could be some 19-year-old kid few of us have heard of, working on something we won't recognize as vital until a decade hence. Any experiment, though, designed to provide new models for journalism is going to be an improvement over hiding from the real, especially in a year when, for many papers, the unthinkable future is already in the past.

For the next few decades, journalism will be made up of overlapping special cases. Many of these models will rely on amateurs as researchers and writers. Many of these models will rely on sponsorship or grants or endowments instead of revenues. Many of these models will rely on excitable 14-year-olds distributing the results. Many of these models will fail. No one experiment is going to replace what we are now losing with the demise of news on paper, but over time, the collection of new experiments that do work might give us the journalism we need.

Replies to Clay Shirky's Blog Post

Below are several excerpts from blogs written in the days immediately after Shirky's piece appeared. They are all reprinted here by permission of their authors.

Adrian Monck

"Clay Shirky: Wrong About Newspapers" (excerpt)

AdrianMonck.com MARCH 17, 2009

In response to Shirky's comments about paywalls at the Wall Street Journal, *Monck writes:*

The reason these papers can charge subscribers is because their readers make up a community that uses the content to orient themselves in what you might call (if you were the kind of person who liked making up these terms) the topography of professional information.

To be direct, there is a value in knowing what everyone else in your community knows in order to place a value on your own particular knowledge.

The *Wall Street Journal* and the *Financial Times* are promontories in the broad information landscape of their (still) wealthy and educated readership (although not everyone plays ball), who are willing to pay their modest fees for the privilege of reading them online, on the phone or on paper.

So the paywall content is not financial information whose recipients don't want to share. It's just good old-fashioned news and comment for finance professionals, read in the knowledge that a lot of other finance professionals will be reading it too and thus making it modestly useful in their everyday working lives.

It doesn't mean that paywalls will work for everyone. For example, in Hong Kong English-language daily the *South China Morning Post* has one, but faces free competition from the *Standard*.

But when an aggressive price-cutter like Rupert Murdoch keeps a paywall in place (for just one of his suite of news products), you know it's a model that has its niche. It's just a niche based around a professional community, not around the value of information *per se*.

So that's a different explanation to Shirky's one line dismissal. Different but important.

Charlie Beckett

"Thinking the Thinkable: Clay Shirky on the Future of Newspapers" (excerpt)

CharlieBeckett.org MARCH 20, 2009

Was Clay Shirky being trite or profound in going back to the past to argue about journalism's future? His recent article, "Newspapers and Thinking the Unthinkable" has provoked a global ripple of applause from technological optimists around the world, although there have been some voices who claim that Clay is merely thinking the already thought. Others ask what his solution is.

It is certainly a very US-centred view. Their papers were bloated and boring and due for a fall anyway. The debate between "Old" and "New" media has always been more theological in the States with entrenched positions taken on points of dubious principle. It was always a proxy for a wider cultural debate that lacked the pragmatism of, for example, the British newspaper groups.

But that does not mean that newspapers are not deeply threatened. Nor does it mean that we don't need to think about what replaces them. However, in such a fast-moving, technologically-driven market, is it possible to plan? Or are we, as Alan Rusbridger has said, taking a leap in the dark? …

… How do you plan for a world without newspapers—or even without news as we know it? I argue in *SuperMedia* that journalism as we know it has about 5 years left to make its case to society and preserve its long-term future. Despite the current economic chaos I think that much of the current media infrastructure will still be around in 2020, but it will be greatly diminished and transformed. But it would be a useful intellectual exercise to take the worst-case scenario and extrapolate it out to the realms of science fiction. What about a post-News world? …

… If there was an easy answer [to journalism's future] then I would be sitting on a private jet next to Rupert Murdoch drinking champagne as I explained it to him. But having just written a book on one way forward you will understand why I refuse to take Clay's rather fatalist approach. I guess that Clay is not a journalist and so doesn't quite feel the urgency that I do. I think there are plenty of ways forward. I argue that most of them involve much greater public participation and a shift of power from media institutions towards creating social networks of news.

Mark Morford

"Die, Newspaper, Die? The Geek Gurus All Weigh in on the End of Dead-Tree Media. Are They Wrong?" (excerpt)

***San Francisco Gate* (*San Francisco Chronicle*), www.sfgate.com/columnists/morford/** MARCH 20, 2009

The gurus are all aflutter. Shirky, Winer, Johnson et al., a smart, motley crew of big-name, big-brained tech seers and programmers and futurists have weighed in, guys you've probably never heard of unless you're a Slashdot regular or a co-founder of Digg or have a fetish for hardcore database programming. …

The grand upshot? They don't really have any idea. …

… In the howling absence of all the essential, unglamorous work newspapers now do—the fact-checking, interviewing, researching, all by experienced pros who know how to sift the human maelstrom better than anyone, and all hitched to 100+ years of hard-fought newsbrand credibility—what's the new yardstick for integrity? On what do you base your choices? Some fickle mix of personal mood, blood-alcohol level, and how many followers your given source has on Twitter? Right. …

Steven P. Johnson's notion of a new media "ecosystem" seems to come closest to understanding the challenges facing the future of journalism, insofar as he at least gives decent props to the need for professional editors and journalistic know-how. …

The truth remains: You pick up the *New York Times*, the *Washington Post*, the *San Francisco Chronicle*—or read their online products—you immediately have an anchor, some credibility and authority, not to mention a sense of place and context. In whatever you read, you know there has been, at minimum, some real editorial oversight and integrity of product borne of trained, experienced editors and writers who, believe it or not, still value accuracy and truth above all else. …

Hell, Johnson and Winer both tacitly admit to this mandatory value: Johnson made a point to immediately post an update to his Twitter feed, alerting his 202,000 followers that his and his pal Shirky's essays had both been referenced in … wait for it … a *New York Times* blog. Why did he do it? For the instant hit of big-media credibility, that's why. …

There's also a reason that saying "I read it on XYZ blog, so it must be true" still carries little weight in a serious discussion, whereas, "I read it in the *Washington Post*," gives you instant authority. Instant cred. Even today. *Especially* today. Has that authority unraveled and weakened in the wake of the Net and news-as-entertainment? Absolutely. Do we have anything better? Not yet. Not by a long shot.

All these provocateur pundits are right about one thing: something new and hopefully wonderful might emerge out of the ashes of the death of print. It is indeed a great time for experimentation, new thinking, even tentative optimism.

But it's also enormously sad and troubling. Because even if you say you still want great journalism, serious investigative reporting, and lots of news expertise, the Internet and its various pundits have all led us to believe that no one is willing to actually pay for it. And they never will be. Let's hope they're very, very wrong.

Tom Watson

"Ink-Stained Retching" (excerpt)

TomWatson.Typepad.com MARCH 15, 2009

For journalists of a certain vintage, these are the days on the digital horizon that were long-feared and yet somehow unanticipated. The newspaper world is slowly asphyxiating, starved for the oxygen of classified advertising and simultaneously kicked in the chest by a massive recession that is hastening the tombstones in the graveyard of newsprint. …

Crowdsourcing journalism is all the rage, but the idea of its widespread ascendancy and competence is the exclusive province of either deranged optimists or ideological cyberlibertarians; the vast populace will never produce great journalism—or even sufficient journalism of the kind that has nurtured our republic—any more than it will perform surgery on a widespread amateur basis, or turn out competent oil paintings by the millions.

Yes, occasionally brilliant exceptions will appear; the tools available for creating and disseminating great stories will be put to good use by people with the talent for reporting and telling those stories. But the journalistic print edifice will not be replaced. …

The Internet has been a destructive force for many business models, but none threatens the basis of the republic as much as the digital knife busily sawing at the fraying Achilles tendon of American newspapers. As an editorial in the *Spokane Review* (rather plaintively) asked:

> So as newspapers die, it's worth considering the effects on society. Who will tell the people what their institutions are doing? Who will ferret out the corruption? Who will fend off the legal challenges to public information? If no viable alternative emerges, what does that mean for our representative democracy?

Author and NYU professor Clay Shirky wrote a grim and all-too-accurate assessment of journalism's dire strait, a piece that really places no blame but captures well the doomsday formula now unfolding. …

Last year at the Personal Democracy Forum, NYU professor and media critic Jay Rosen gave a talk about the rise of semi-pro journalism that took in some of the still-arrogant attitude of "old journalism" and its resistance to going the way of the dinosaur. He adapted the talk for his blog:

> We are early in the rise of semi-pro journalism, but well into the decline of an older way of life within the tribe of professional journalists. I call them a tribe because they share a culture and a sense of destiny, and because they think they own the press—that it's theirs somehow because they dominate the practice.
>
> The First Amendment says to all Americans: you have a right to publish what you know, to say what you think. That right used to be abstractly held. Now it is concretely held because the power to publish has been distributed to the

> population at large. Projects that cause people to exercise their right to a free press strengthen the press, whether or not these projects strengthen the professional journalist's "hold" on the press.

That hold is slipping every day. Yet some of Rosen's set piece, his construction of the central tension in the story, now seems quaint, only nine months later. The attitude of recalcitrant old print journalists doesn't matter any more in this season of shuttered newsrooms. It's not about old journalists versus the rising amateurs. It's about the disappearance of one of the carrying beams of our democracy and what, if anything, will replace it—and the loss of that "everyday truth."

Micah L. Sifry

"Three Modest Proposals for Online Journalism's Future" (excerpt)

TechPresident.com/Blog/Micah_L_Sifry MARCH 16, 2009

If you follow me on Twitter, you probably noticed that I spent my lunch hour at the Open Society Institute today for a talk on "The Future of News" by Paul Steiger, the longtime managing editor of the *Wall Street Journal*, who is the head of ProPublica, an "independent, non-profit newsroom that produces investigative journalism in the public interest." It was a mostly gloomy session, framed by the news that 11,000 professional journalists have lost their jobs in the last two years, and all the bad news currently coming out of the newspaper industry.

You also probably know, if you follow me on Twitter, that I was gnashing my teeth for much of the time, frustrated by several questions from audience members who wanted to focus on shoring up the failed business model for today's dying newspapers (mostly by charging for content) instead of figuring out what comes next and how we insure that intelligent, inquisitive and informed reporting and analysis continues to enrich our society. Almost no one in the room seemed cognizant of the arguments being made by thinkers like Clay Shirky and Steven Johnson, either about the inevitable death of print newspapers or the vibrant rise of a rich online ecology of topical, and often deeply investigative, journalism.

In fairness to Steiger, I should note that he personally seems well aware that, as he said at one point, the horses are already out and attempts to slam the barn door shut would probably not work. He also spoke optimistically about emerging forms of online media, and more than once expressed hope that crowdsourcing, as practiced by OfftheBus … , could be a viable model for pro-am collaboration.

I left the lunch a bit depressed, but as I thought things over on my subway ride back to the Personal Democracy Forum office, a few ideas began to coalesce in my head about how we could perhaps foster a stronger ecology of investigative journalism in the new online environment. So, instead of beating a dead horse (to mangle my metaphors), here are three ideas for projects that could help sustain investigative journalism however it is practiced going forward:

1. In an Age of Mass Participation, Make News Easier to Make Together

We need better tools for mass collaboration. …

2. In an Age of Data, We Need Easier to Use Visualization Tools

Earlier today, my colleague Nancy Scola tweeted at the start of her SXSW talk on White House 2.0 and open government that "Data is the new 'plastics.'" …

But how to make sense of all this data? I think we need easier-to-use tools, and that some targeted investment in fostering better tools might produce a huge payoff. Blogging took off because free tools like Blogger made it so you didn't have to know how to write .html code to publish a web page. Videosharing took off because YouTube made posting video online as simple as attaching a file to an email. But data visualization is still too hard. …

3. In an Age of Mass Information, Make It Easier to Find and Share Investigative Reporting

Steven Johnson's hyperlocal media site Outside.in currently tracks news, views, and conversations in 11,860 towns and neighborhoods. If you search on the words "political scandal" you get more than 3,000 results. …

Does anyone have any idea how many stories, blog posts and videos are published every day that shed light on local, state or national corruption? What about corporate crime? …

[M]aybe some smart information hackers can pull together some algorithms to scour the web and help us see the hidden patterns to what old and new media outlets together are publishing online. … If we want more investigative coverage, we need to develop better filters to help us zero in on the good stuff and also find hidden patterns in seemingly disconnected stories. Plus, better filters might eventually channel more traffic toward producers of good investigative journalism, and thus prop up whatever business model they may be employing.

DISCUSSION QUESTIONS

1. Adrian Monck talks about papers making up "a community that uses the content to organize themselves." He's referring to professional financial information, but can you think of any "communities" you are a part of, in the sense of a group of people accessing the same electronic information? Do you pay for it? If it's currently free, would you pay for it if a paywall were introduced?
2. Charlie Beckett says that many newspapers, particularly American ones, were "bloated and boring and due for a fall." Do you find paper-based newspapers boring? How often do you read them?
3. Tom Watson calls newspapers "one of the carrying beams of our democracy." Do you believe Internet-based news sources can play a similar role in our society? Why or why not?

CHAPTER 5

From the Business of Journalism to Journalism as Business: 1990 to the Present

Mike Gasher

CHAPTER OUTLINE

Introduction

A significant shift in the business of journalism over the last two decades has been the passing of the entrepreneurial torch from the owners and managers of mainstream news organizations to journalists themselves. If there has always been considerable tension in journalism between the public-service ethos and the commercial imperative, North America's principal news producers have shifted the balance dramatically by increasingly treating journalism as a business like any other; journalists are mere content producers, news is less an essential public service than just another commodity for sale, communities are simply target markets, and news audiences are consumers. Corporate journalism confronted the new challenges of the 1990s by looking backward rather than forward, reverting to the time-tested strategies of monopoly capitalism—merger, acquisition, cost reduction—with little apparent regard for the qualitative impact these would have on the journalism franchise. These manoeuvres have backfired to such an extent that it is common today to speak of not only a structural crisis in the commercial, mainstream news industry but also an existential crisis in journalism itself.

This transformation occurred at the same time as the practice of journalism was exploding with exciting new means of gathering the news (computer-assisted reporting, the Internet), with new methods of disseminating the news (all-news radio and television channels, digitization, mobile and wireless technology, the World Wide Web), and with new ways of thinking about how to tell stories and engage and involve people who were previously treated merely as audiences. For example, civic journalism sought to re-engage people in the public life of their communities by treating news audiences as active citizens; peace journalism borrowed conflict-resolution techniques to promote peaceful solutions to crises typically presented as divisive and futile; narrative journalism employed literary techniques to render news stories more compelling; crowdsourcing allowed journalists to tap into the information resources of the general public; and citizen journalism put the tools of journalism and access to news media in the hands of ordinary citizens. The real leaders were not corporate news organizations, which have responded slowly, cautiously, even defensively, to these new possibilities, but journalists themselves, most of them working outside the corporate umbrella, demonstrating to the mainstream what journalism in the 21st century could be.

The result has been a stark divide between conservative mainstream media managers (who have a short-term focus on the three Rs of ratings, readership, and revenues, and a reluctance to invest in innovative new ideas about journalism) and front-line journalism workers (who maintain their belief in public service, citizenship, and democracy and have taken up most enthusiastically new, often experimental, journalism forms, providing leadership in the transformation of the practice). The news industry appears to have borrowed from the old music industry playbook, by which the major recording companies let the independent labels do the research and development, only signing on to new sounds once they start to attract a following. The significant difference in journalism is that no one yet has a viable business model: Corporate journalism is bleeding audiences, advertisers, and newsroom staff, and the independent innovators haven't figured out yet how to make a living from the journalism of the future.

The Business of Journalism

The conventional business model was best described by communications scholar Dallas Smythe (1977), who noted that the commercial mass media make their money, not by selling the media product itself, but by selling audiences to advertisers. News organizations, that is, function economically by putting together a package of news content—a newspaper, a TV newscast—that is intended for a specific audience market, and selling access to that audience to advertisers who are interested in pitching their products and services to those specific audience members. The media serve the economy by generating audiences and thereby creating advertising markets.

Media industries are unique economically because they participate in two markets at the same time: the audience market and the advertising market (Picard 1989). What news media try to do is marry their content package—which comprises editorial *and* advertising content—to an audience that will be interested in both. This is easiest to understand through the example of special-interest magazines. Fashion magazines such as *Vogue* or *Flare* provide news and comment about the fashion world side by side with advertising for clothing and cosmetics; their readers are as interested in the advertisements as they are in the articles. The same formula works with general-interest news media; advertisers place their advertisements where they think they will have the most impact (for example, automakers and car dealers advertise in the automotive section of the newspaper). News organizations compile detailed demographic profiles of their audiences, serving as matchmakers for their advertising clients.

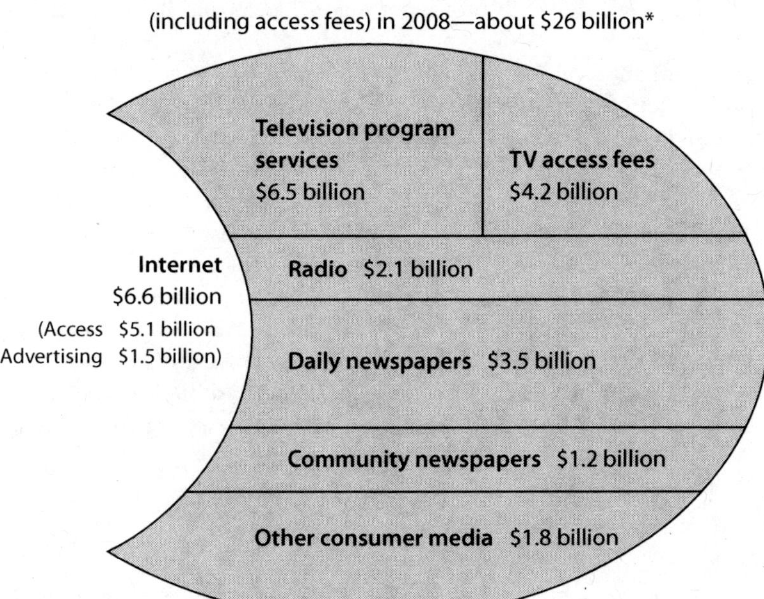

Figure 5.1 Estimated total media revenues in Canada, 2008. Traditional media are being hit hard by declines in advertising revenues (due in part to new online tools such as craigslist), and while the Internet continues to expand its advertising reach, ad revenues for online media are still a small fraction of what they have been for traditional media, as this figure shows.

SOURCE: Canadian Media Research Consortium/Communications Management Inc. 2009. *The state of the media in Canada*. © Communications Management Inc.

Advertising accounts for the lion's share of commercial news organizations' revenues. Conventional radio and television, and most online news sites, cost nothing to access and are therefore completely dependent on advertising to make money. Newspapers and magazines typically charge a subscription or single-purchase fee, but advertising accounts for between 60 and 80 percent of their revenues. Figure 5.1 shows estimated total media revenues in Canada in 2008.

There are exceptions, of course, because not all news organizations treat journalism as a business. The CBC, for example, is a public broadcaster whose principal mandate is public service rather than profit. CBC Radio is commercial-free. Nevertheless, the CBC participates in the economy and needs to generate revenue to fulfill its mandate. In the fiscal year 2008–9, the $1.07 billion the CBC received from the federal government accounted for just under 60 percent of its revenues and would not have been enough to cover its operating costs. The CBC earned $356 million (19.8 percent of revenues) from television advertising and another $367 million (20.4 percent of revenues) from other sources (CBC 2009). CBC TV's need for advertising dollars explains its interest in broadcasting *Wheel of Fortune*, *Jeopardy*, Hollywood movies, and NHL hockey, even if such programming detracts from its distinctiveness as a public broadcaster.

The predominant economic model has significant implications for news organizations, and for journalism. If commercial news organizations are dependent on advertising for their economic survival, they have to generate not only significant audiences but also audiences composed of the right people: people who are most attractive to advertisers. This means that the news media do not serve the general public, but instead their marketable audiences. While most mainstream news organizations continue to provide at least some coverage of the events and institutions that engage us as citizens—politics, foreign affairs, economics, culture—a great deal more are devoted to topics that sell and speak to us as consumers: sports, popular entertainment, celebrity culture, investing, and lifestyle. Some topics, such as poverty (see sidebar "Ignoring Poverty"), are largely excluded because they are deemed of little interest or relevance to the audiences that commercial news organizations serve.

SIDEBAR

Ignoring Poverty

Each year during the Christmas holiday season, media organizations across Canada stage events to raise money for charity. In Montreal, on a mid-December weekday, news reporters and media personalities from all of the city's major media outlets stand in the cold at busy intersections collecting money and non-perishable food items for the needy from motorists and passersby. This event is called *la grande guignolée des médias*, and it generates considerable feel-good news coverage.

It prompted a different reaction in 2009, however. In an article published in the newspaper *Le Devoir* the day after *la grande guignolée*, Stéphane Baillargeon (2009) wondered why this was the only day the news media paid attention to poverty. Citing the 2009 *Canadian News Review* by the Montreal press review organization Influence Communication (2009), Baillargeon noted that the problem of poverty in Quebec earns as much media coverage as 2.2 Montreal Canadiens' hockey games, and most of that coverage comes the week of *la grande guignolée*.

But the amount of coverage wasn't the only problem. So was the type of coverage. Baillargeon spoke to Université de Montréal researcher Pascale Dufour, who pointed out that the news reportage defined poverty as a problem that could be solved through charity rather than through public policy.

There can be many reasons why particular events or social problems do *not* receive significant news coverage. But the economics of news production may be one of them; the poor are not an attractive audience for advertisers.

The strict separation of the business and editorial sides of the news industry used to be a central feature of journalism culture, and a point of pride among journalists who fiercely guard their independence. This separation has been eroded dramatically in recent years. There was a time when advertising and marketing personnel were not permitted to set foot inside newsrooms. Now, marketers and editors hold planning meetings to coordinate advertising and coverage around certain events, and news organizations sponsor some of the same events they cover. For example, Canwest, the *Globe and Mail*, and *La Presse* were "official media suppliers" to the 2010 Winter Olympics (VANOC n.d.). There was a time when no advertisements were permitted on the front page of newspapers. Now it is common practice, even for the so-called quality dailies. What were once advertising-free spaces are now up for sale.

Concentrated Capital

If the history of journalism tells us that change is constant, the pace of change over the past two decades has been breathtaking, and it has resulted in some fundamental shifts in the media landscape. The news industry, first of all, has become further concentrated in the hands of large corporations, and perhaps more important, concentrated in the hands of corporations that are confined neither to one medium nor to the news industry itself (see sidebar "Corporate Concentration"). The news business is only one of many businesses in which these corporations are involved. What is now Canwest Global Communications Corp., the largest media company in Canada, began in 1975 as a single conventional television station in Winnipeg. Canwest gradually expanded into network television and specialty channels, radio, daily and community newspapers, magazines, and digital media in Canada and internationally (Canwest n.d.). (Note: Control of the company has recently been in flux. By early 2010, suffering serious financial woes, it faced restructuring and the possible sale of some of its divisions.) CTVglobemedia Inc. owns properties in conventional and specialty television, newspapers, and radio (CTVglobemedia n.d.). Quebecor Inc., which started as the publisher of a single community newspaper in 1950, now has subsidiaries in newspaper, magazine, and book publishing, television broadcasting, cable television distribution, digital media, and book and music retailing (Quebecor n.d.). Even CBC/Radio-Canada, the public broadcaster, is a concentrated company, engaged in entertainment as much as it is in news and current affairs, across radio, television, and online platforms (CBC n.d.).

These are converged companies with holdings in various media platforms that seek to benefit from cross-promotion, multipurposing, economies of scale, and scope (see sidebar "Media Convergence"). Journalism is only a part, in some cases a small part, of what these companies do, only one of the products they sell. As part of larger corporations, news divisions are subjected to the same economic demands as other properties—ratings, readership, revenues—and their journalism becomes a component of the corporation's brand identity. Corporate ownership can be a good thing when the corporation's identity is closely associated with quality journalism, as in the case of the CBC or the *Globe and Mail*, and resources are invested to ensure that the brand remains prestigious and attractive to audiences and advertisers. But it can also be detrimental to journalism if the news division is denied adequate resources and becomes little more than a vehicle for advertising and the cross-promotion of the corporation's other businesses.

Canwest and Quebecor are publicly traded companies with interests beyond media; their business is no longer journalism per se, or even communications media, but making money in whatever field holds the greatest opportunity. Canwest started as a television broadcaster and has become Canada's single-largest owner of daily newspapers. Quebecor started as a newspaper company, but has expanded far beyond newspaper publishing; its most lucrative sector is Videotron, its cable company (Quebecor 2009).

SIDEBAR

Corporate Concentration

Corporate concentration is a measure of the competitiveness of any given industry sector. The fewer the competing companies, the more concentrated the industry is considered to be.

Corporate concentration is of particular concern in the news industry because journalism is a core democratic institution. A healthy democracy requires its citizens to have access to a diverse and reliable supply of news, information, and opinion. When the sources of information about current events are relatively few, citizens may not be getting a sufficiently broad perspective on complex news events. Worse, they are susceptible to manipulation by ideologically driven news providers.

The daily newspaper industry in Canada is considered to be highly concentrated. Many cities—Quebec City, Ottawa, Winnipeg, Calgary, and Edmonton—are served by just two major dailies, and Vancouver's two dailies are owned and operated by the same company. Victoria, British Columbia's capital, publishes only one daily newspaper. Newspapers belonging to two companies account for more than half of the country's daily newspaper circulation: Canwest's 13 daily newspapers account for 30 percent of total daily newspaper circulation, and Quebecor's 37 dailies add up to another 24 percent of daily newspaper sales. Of Canada's 98 general-interest dailies, only four are independently owned (Canadian Newspaper Association 2009). Canwest also owns 23 community newspapers, while Quebecor, through its Sun Media subsidiary, owns more than 100 (Canadian Community Newspapers Association n.d.). What we are seeing is the intensification of a problem first identified 40 years ago by the 1970 Special Senate Committee on Mass Media (the Davey committee) and the 1981 Royal Commission on Newspapers (the Kent commission).

Some would argue that the range of news offered by online sources alleviates concerns about corporate concentration in the news industry. But do online news sites simply provide us with more of the same kind of reporting, or do they in fact produce a more diverse array of news reports and analysis? We have seen a proliferation of news aggregators online, as well as sites specializing in opinion, but they tend to simply repeat, or comment on, news provided by the traditional media. According to a recent study by the Pew Research Center in the United States, which looked at 53 different news outlets in Baltimore, 83 percent of the stories tracked were "essentially repetitive, containing no new information." Of the 17 percent of stories that contained new information, almost all came from the traditional media (Project for Excellence in Journalism 2010).

SIDEBAR

Media Convergence

The term *media convergence* refers to the merging of previously distinct media platforms and companies. It is an economic strategy that companies use to derive maximum benefits from owning several media properties. This usually works by bringing together on a corporate website content and links to the corporation's different media properties. The CBC website (www.cbc.ca), for example, alerts visitors to all of the public broadcaster's radio and television programming, allowing people to listen to its radio programming or watch its TV shows online, as well as read supporting textual material, including blogs and audience comments. The site also promotes other CBC productions and services.

Media convergence is an exercise in economic efficiency with several dimensions. First, it allows the various media platforms to share resources. For example, a newspaper story can also be posted on the website; the same reporter is, in effect, producing the same story for two media platforms. Second, it allows for cross-promotion. The company can publicize its other businesses or other media programming across its platforms. For example, you often see promotional material for Global TV programming in Canwest's newspapers. Third, it allows media companies to offer package deals to advertisers who might be interested in advertising in more than one medium. Finally, media convergence is a branding exercise. By providing audiences with a range of media content across a variety of platforms, audiences are encouraged to show loyalty to the company brand, whether they are after news or entertainment, or whether they want to watch television or read a newspaper.

Publicly traded companies are those whose shares trade publicly on the large stock exchanges and are subject to the whims of both private and institutional investors. These investors have no loyalty to any particular industry sector but instead have an interest in maximizing the returns on their investments. That is the logic of capitalism. If any news property or industry—for example, daily newspapers or conventional television—loses the confidence of investors, it becomes vulnerable to downsizing, sale, or closure. Today, the news industry increasingly finds itself competing for revenues and capital investment with all other businesses; corporations no longer confine themselves to the news business but to the business of making money, in whatever industries offer the greatest opportunity.

Consider the example of Thomson Corp. (now known as Thomson Reuters). Thomson Corp. started as a small newspaper company in Timmins, Ontario, in the 1930s, became one of Canada's two largest newspaper owners by the 1980s, and boasted significant newspaper holdings in the United States and the United Kingdom by the 1990s. The company that was primarily a newspaper publisher for half a century had completely abandoned the newspaper industry by 2003 to become a "leading source of intelligent information" in what its directors perceived as greener pastures in other industries: sales and trading, enterprise, investment and advisory, legal, tax and accounting, and health care and science. Thomson only returned to journalism—but not newspaper publishing—when it merged with Reuters in 2008; Reuters remains one of the world's largest news services (Thomson Reuters n.d.).

A New News Medium

Another significant change, of course, has been the emergence of the Internet as the new central media arena, encompassing every kind of communications activity imaginable, including journalism. Although the news industry was thoroughly computerized by the early 1990s, and computer-assisted reporting had already become accepted practice in many newsrooms, the hypertext system we know as the World Wide Web only became public and easily navigable in late 1991. Online journalism (the widespread production and dissemination of news on the Internet) and media convergence (the merging of previously distinct media platforms and companies) were still in their infancy in the mid-1990s. But the Internet, particularly as its tentacles penetrated more and more Canadian homes—73 percent of Canadians aged 16 and over had Internet access from home in 2007 (Statistics Canada 2008)—provided the platform for the easy convergence of mainstream radio, TV, newspapers, and magazines, and fertile ground for new, stand-alone news organizations (for example, *The Tyee*, the Real News Network). Once the Internet platform became unplugged, wireless mobile technologies added a new intriguing dimension to the facility, convenience, and immediacy with which news content could be produced, circulated, consumed, and responded to.

Figure 5.2 Editorial staff at *The Tyee*'s offices in a lighter moment. The Vancouver-based "stand-alone" news organization is a product of the Internet age; with none of the logistical concerns of traditional newspaper distribution, it can maintain its focus on providing web-only news and commentary for its audience across British Columbia, and beyond. (PHOTO: Justin Langille.)

We are still coming to terms with the extent to which the Internet has changed the business of journalism. For one thing, the Internet has created a global newsstand, expanding the mediascape exponentially; once news organizations established a presence on the Web, they became available to everyone in the world with an Internet connection. Suddenly, world-renowned news organizations such as the BBC and the *New York Times* were side by side with the CBC and your local daily newspaper. This competition was further intensified by media convergence; once all content was digitized, it became just as easy to upload audio and video as it was to upload text. The more ambitious newspapers and magazines began featuring audio and video segments on their websites, and broadcasters started producing text. Newspapers no longer compete simply with other newspapers, they compete online with all other news media, breaking down the distinctions between media forms—print, radio, television—and the ways they practise journalism and conduct their news business.

New media technologies have also lowered considerably the barriers to entry to the business of news production and circulation, opening journalism to many more participants—and therefore competitors—whether they are devoted mostly to bringing together on one site news items collected from various mainstream news organizations (news aggregators) or committed to original news gathering, commentary (blogs), or advocacy. While the barriers to entry have not been removed entirely—having your own website does not mean you have either the information-gathering resources, the journalistic skills, or the marketing power to have much of an impact—there are nonetheless new opportunities, particularly in local news coverage and niche topic areas.

Combined with the fact that much of this content has become available for free, the Internet has created a new kind of competition for audiences in what economists refer to as an "attention" economy. As noted above, audiences have traditionally paid for media content in two ways: by paying money (for example, for newspaper subscriptions) and/or by paying attention (for example, to conventional radio and television). With so many news and information choices available online, the challenge of the Internet is getting peoples' attention and parlaying that attention into revenues. The top brands of the so-called legacy media—the BBC, the *New York Times*, CNN, and, in Canada, the CBC and the *Globe and Mail*—enjoyed the initial advantages of notoriety, credibility, and substantial financial and journalistic resources in the online world. And the established brands remain among the most popular online news sites, alongside Yahoo! and Google (see Alexa n.d.).

For the most part, though, the established news organizations have been timid and have only reluctantly committed resources to their online presence, yielding their initial advantages of notoriety and resources to corporate start-ups and smaller independents, who quickly built their reputations as innovators and leaders in a new era of journalism (for example, *The Tyee* in Canada, and the Huffington Post and *ProPublica* in the United States).

The New Media Ecology

In addition, the geography of journalism has changed, from the local, regional, and national to the global. James Carey (1998) asserts that the Internet forges a "new media ecology" as the global organization of media displaces the national, the "first instance of a global communication system." Carey argues that "the Internet is at the center of the integration of a new media ecology which transforms the structural relations among older media such [as] print and broadcast and integrates them to a new center around the defining technologies of computer and satellite" (28–34). Manuel Castells (2001) echoes these remarks: "The Internet is a communication medium that allows, for the first time, the communication of many to many, in chosen time, on a global scale" (2).

For journalism, this geographical change has meant that no longer is any one news organization's coverage area—its market—determined by the physical distribution of newspapers and magazines or the reach of atmospheric radio and television signals. Initially, satellite printing plants allowed the *Globe and Mail* to become a national newspaper and enabled the *New York Times* and the *Wall Street Journal* to hit the streets of major Canadian cities. Expanding cable networks and satellite television gave us CBC Newsworld (now CBC News Network), APTN, as well as the BBC, CNN, and Fox. However, the reach and the speed of the Internet have pushed the idea of news delivery to a whole new level.

The Internet also allows surfers to flit from site to site with a simple mouse click, meaning news organizations are losing their exclusive hold on audience members' attention. Reading the news online now means reading stories from several news sites, not simply that of your local newspaper, as well as viewing slideshows and video clips. What you watch and what you read are no longer dictated by your local news providers, but by your own judgment about who will best provide the news you want.

For this reason, news organizations are having to rethink their coverage areas and redraw their news maps as they sort out what kind of journalism they can do better than all of these new competitors. How far should we cast our news net? Should we continue to maintain expensive news bureaus in provincial, national, and foreign capitals? Or should we focus on local coverage, where we have more expertise and fewer competitors? (See Gasher and Klein 2008.) But it also has to do with topic. Should we continue with the department-store approach of providing a range of topics to suit everyone? Or should we specialize in the most lucrative topic areas, such as business and sports? These are not easy questions to resolve because they alter the news organization's relationship with its target audience. What community will we serve when "community" no longer means the people who live within a 30-minute drive of our newsroom?

The result of all these changes is a profound shift in what competition means. Competition in journalism used to mean "scooping" your rival; that is, reporters working in the same medium trying to get the story before their cross-town competitor. Quite suddenly, daily newspapers find themselves competing for audiences with all-news radio and television services and emerging online news sites in addition to news organizations from other places (for example, national newspapers, foreign newspapers, the BBC, and CNN on cable and satellite television, and everyone with a website).

Some of this competition is deliberately self-inflicted. That is, news organizations with newspapers, radio stations, television stations, and websites serving the same market hope to capture audiences and advertisers with whichever platform they choose at any given time. It's akin to betting on several horses in the same race. And it provides opportunities to cross-promote news platforms and cross-purpose news content. The clearest example of this is Vancouver, where Canwest owns both daily newspapers (the tabloid *Province* and the broadsheet *Sun*), the TV news ratings leader (Global BC), and a number of community newspapers.

The Contracting Labour Force

For journalists, the front-line workers who make their living producing news, the landscape has changed as well. Newsrooms are shrinking as companies try to cut costs. Senior journalists—that is, the most experienced but also the most expensive—are offered early-retirement buyouts. What new hiring there is consists of either temporary contract work for recent journalism-school graduates, one-off freelance contracts (at rates that have not risen in 20 years), or off-loading copy editing and page layout to independent contractors. The *Toronto Star*, for example, announced in November 2009 that it would cut 78 editing positions and contract the work out to Pagemasters North America, a division of Canadian Press (*Ottawa Citizen* 2009).

New collective agreements demand that journalists produce more stories, work longer hours, and share their work on the company's various media platforms. In the case of newspaper reporters, these agreements have dramatically changed their job descriptions and working conditions. Rather than filing, typically, one story per day—allowing time for research, interviews, and writing—they are now asked to file throughout the day to keep the website current, which means constantly rewriting and updating their story. It can also mean providing photos, video or audio files, and possibly a live, on-camera interview for the company's suppertime TV newscast. Instead of doing one job, reporters are in effect doing two or three, for the same salary, and no doubt feeling less pride in the quality of their work.

These changes to journalists' working conditions are the grounds for contemporary labour-management disputes, and Quebec appears to be the place where these battles will be fought first. Quebecor, the company most committed to the strategy of media convergence, locked out *Le Journal de Québec* journalists for 16 months in 2007 and 2008, and it locked out employees of *Le Journal de Montréal*, Montreal's largest-circulation daily as of January 2009. In both cases, workers responded to the lockout by producing their own newspapers: In Quebec City, a daily tabloid called *Média Matin Québec*, and in Montreal, a website called RueFrontenac.com. Journalists at Canwest's Montreal daily, the *Gazette*, have been without a contract since June 2008.

The Journalist as Entrepreneur

Paradoxically, the journalism field has grown substantially over the past 20 years. Besides the online news sites that have sprouted on the World Wide Web—belonging to both mainstream news organizations and independent start-ups—we have seen the emergence of free daily newspapers in Canada's major cities and a veritable explosion of so-called ethnic community media across Canada. (see Fishwrap n.d.; National Ethnic Press and Media Council of Canada n.d.). And Al Jazeera English, the international service of the Qatar-based TV news broadcaster, won distribution approval from the Canadian Radio-television and Telecommunications Commission in November 2009. It plans to open at least one Canadian bureau (Krashinsky 2009).

The question is whether the opportunities to make a decent living as a journalist have kept pace. The medium that most agree will be the principal news platform of the future, the Internet, lacks a viable business model. The mainstream media have tried various strategies to generate revenue online: the broadcast model of free content paid for by advertising, the magazine model of paying for content with subscriptions and advertising, the mixed model of providing some content for free and charging for premium content services. None has worked—so far. People are reluctant to pay for content they are accustomed to getting for free, and can usually get for free elsewhere. And while the amounts advertisers spend online increase every year, the $1.6 billion spent by Canadian online advertisers in 2008 accounted for just 11 percent of total media advertising, only slightly more than was spent on radio advertising, and still far behind the amounts spent for newspaper and television advertising (Interactive Advertising Bureau of Canada 2009).

These converged media companies, though, have a number of advantages that may be able to tide them over. They have recognizable brands to separate them from the online crowd, they can draw on existing reporting staff and repurpose their content, and at least a few have the financial resources to see them through these still-early stages in the development of online news.

The independent online start-ups face the same economic struggle, but with fewer resources. Some, certainly, are satisfied to rely on citizen journalists and advocacy journalists who are not trying to make a living from the provision of news, information, and commentary, and may be able to operate that way. But those sites seeking a more viable business model, that want to pay their staff—including their journalists—a living wage, may have to be creative, not only in their journalism, but in their search for the revenues to sustain it (see Basen 2009).

This may be the most important story of the coming years: whether journalism can free itself from the tight-fisted control of profit-obsessed corporations and find a new, more independent voice. New media technologies have lowered, not removed, the barriers to entry to the news industry. The entrepreneurs to watch in the coming years will be those navigating the spaces beyond corporate journalism, seeking new ways to tell important stories, and new ways to make a living doing it.

DISCUSSION QUESTIONS

1. Some analysts have described the new media initiatives we see online as a "revolution," a term that suggests a complete and fundamental change in the way the media are organized and operate. Do you agree that we are witnessing a true revolution? Or are we simply witnessing the migration of the commercial news industry to a new sphere of activity?
2. There is a great deal of talk about the need for a new business model for the news media, given the extent to which people are migrating online where they can access the information they need free of charge. Do we need to find a new way of paying for the production and distribution of news and commentary, or will subscriptions and advertising eventually work online as well?
3. Could the public broadcasting model, whereby media organizations rely on funding from governments (for example, the CBC), be a better economic structure for news organizations?

SUGGESTED RESOURCES

-30- [Lise Lareau's blog]. http://www.newsshift.blogspot.com.

Fagstein [Steve Faguy's blog]. http://blog.fagstein.com.

J-Source.ca, The Canadian Journalism Project. http://www.j-source.ca.

Outing, Steve [blog]. http://steveouting.com.

REFERENCES

Alexa. n.d. Top sites in Canada. http://www.alexa.com/topsites/countries/CA.

Baillargeon, Stéphane. 2009. Charitée bien coordonnée … *Le Devoir*, December 11.

Basen, Ira. 2009. Citizen rising. *Maisonneuve*, Fall.

Canadian Community Newspapers Association. n.d. CCNA member ownership chart. http://www.communitynews.ca/ownership/.

Canadian Newspaper Association. 2009. 2008 daily newspaper paid circulation data. http://www.cna-acj.ca/en/aboutnewspapers/circulation.

Canwest. n.d. About us. http://www.canwestglobal.com/about/default.asp.

Carey, James W. 1998. The Internet and the end of the national communication system: Uncertain predictions of an uncertain future. *Journalism and Mass Communication Quarterly* 75: 28–34.

Castells, Manuel. 2001. *The Internet galaxy: Reflections on the Internet, business, and society.* Oxford: Oxford University Press.

CBC. n.d. About CBC. http://www.cbc.radio-canada.ca/about/.

CBC. 2009. *CBC/Radio-Canada annual report 2008–2009.* http://www.cbc.radio-canada.ca/annualreports/2008-2009/index.shtml.

CTVglobemedia. n.d. Properties. http://www.ctvglobemedia.com.

Fishwrap. n.d. Every daily newspaper in Canada. http://fishwrap.ca.

Gasher, Mike, and Reisa Klein. 2008. Mapping the geography of on-line news. *Canadian Journal of Communication* 33: 193–211.

Influence Communication. 2009. *Canadian news review: 2009 report.* http://www.influencecommunication.ca/index.html.

Interactive Advertising Bureau of Canada. 2009. 2008 Canadian online advertising revenue grows to $1.6 billion and surpasses radio. http://www.iabcanada.com/newsletters/072709.shtml.

Krashinsky, Susan. 2009. CRTC gives green light to Al Jazeera English. *Globe and Mail,* November 27.

National Ethnic Press and Media Council of Canada. n.d. About us. http://www.nationalethnicpress.com/content/view/26/41/.

Ottawa Citizen. 2009. Toronto Star targets editors. November 25.

Picard, Robert G. 1989. *Media economics: Concepts and issues.* Newbury Park, CA: Sage Publications.

Project for Excellence in Journalism. 2010. How news happens—Still. http://pewresearch.org/pubs/1458/news-changing-media-baltimore.

Quebecor. n.d. Quebecor at a glance. http://www.quebecor.com/Quebecor/QuebecorAtAGlance.aspx.

Quebecor. 2009. *2008 annual report.* http://www.quebecor.com/InvestorCenter/QIAnnualReports.aspx?Culture=en.

Smythe, Dallas. 1977. Communications: Blindspot of Western Marxism. *Canadian Journal of Political and Social Theory* 1: 1–27.

Statistics Canada. 2008. Canadian Internet use survey. *The Daily,* June 12. http://www.statcan.gc.ca/daily-quotidien/080612/dq080612b-eng.htm.

Thomson Reuters. n.d. About us. http://thomsonreuters.com/about/.

Vancouver Organizing Committee for the 2010 Olympic and Paralympic Winter Games [VANOC]. n.d. About VANOC. http://www.vancouver2010.com/about-VANOC/.

CHAPTER 6

Sustainable News Models for a Digital Age

Donna Logan and Darryl Korell

Full fathom five thy father lies;
Of his bones are coral made;
Those are pearls that were his eyes:
Nothing of him that doth fade
But doth suffer a sea-change
Into something rich and strange.

William Shakespeare, *The Tempest*

Introduction

The traditional media model that worked well for most of the 20th century is basically quite simple. As Figure 6.1 shows, mass media traditionally were the intermediary that connected content, consumers, and advertisers. The number of media players was limited, in print by the huge cost of establishing a newspaper, and in broadcasting by government regulations (overseen by the FCC in the US and the CRTC in Canada). Broadcasting was also limited by "spectrum scarcity," that is, the finite number of channels that were available for television and radio (a restriction that in the digital age no longer applies). Since it was at one time possible to maintain borders and protect copyrighted material, the media business evolved as a business based on "protectable" scarcity (Canadian Media Research Consortium 2009). In this environment, many operators did very well. It was not uncommon for newspapers to turn a profit—before interest, taxes, and depreciation—in the 30 percent range.

CHAPTER OUTLINE

When Internet access increased immensely in the latter half of the 1990s, the proliferation of new technologies began threatening the mass media's role as intermediary, challenging

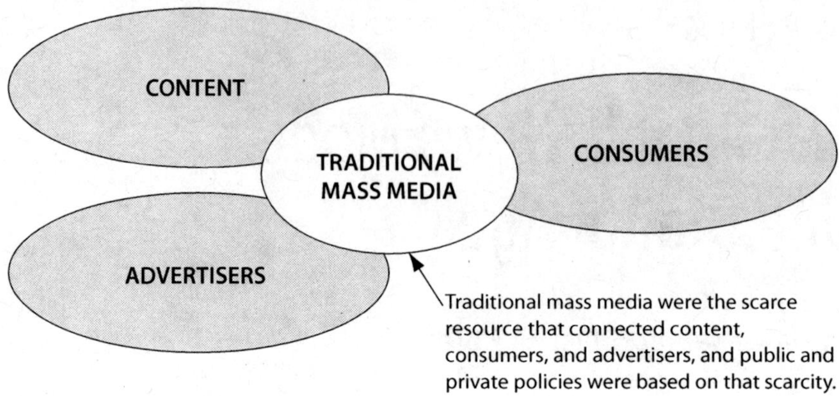

Figure 6.1 The traditional media model

SOURCE: © Communications Management Inc.

both regional borders and scarcity. Suddenly there were many new media players and content producers, including advertisers and consumers who were capable of sending media content directly to audiences. Advertisers, in particular, began to experiment with sending content directly to consumers. Today, most vendors have websites and not only communicate but also sell directly to consumers online.

The model that has emerged as depicted in Figure 6.2 is many times more complicated than the original. Instead of mass media being the sole intermediary, it is one

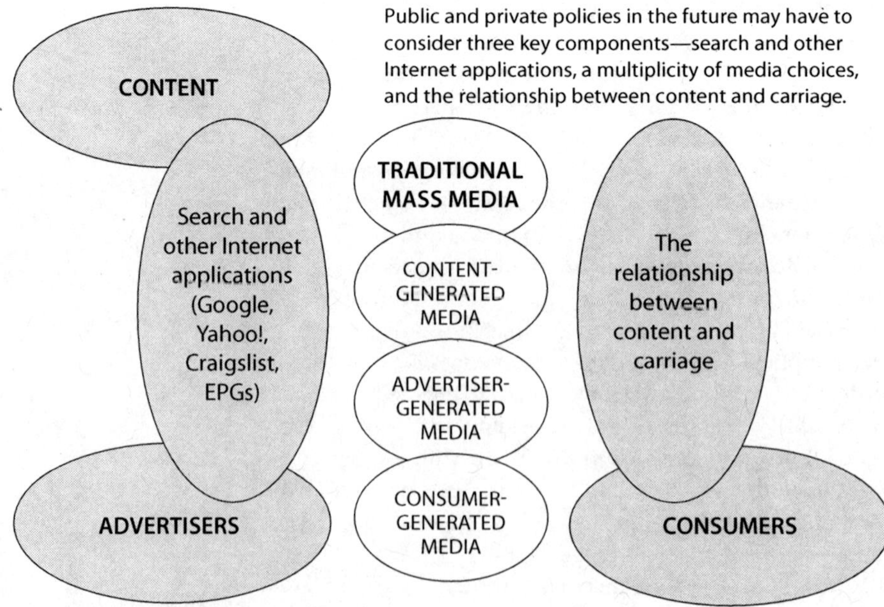

Figure 6.2 The emerging media model

SOURCE: © Communications Management Inc.

of many: content-generated media, advertising-generated media, and consumer-generated media.

The impact of this new model on revenues has been enormous. Most obviously, it provides more outlets for advertisers and increased options for consumers. Media companies now have many more competitors for every dollar spent by advertisers.

Advertising has long been the main revenue source for newspapers and broadcasters. It accounts for roughly 75 percent of the total. Circulation and online advertising account for the rest. As advertisers began to use the new means available to them to attract customers, advertising revenues in traditional media began to fall. Figures 6.3 and 6.4 show the fall of media revenues in Canada over the last ten years. The most acute losses have occurred in newspapers.

Although circulation is a minor part of overall newspaper revenues compared with advertising, it also fell as readers migrated online. Online advertising actually grew, but it has not made up for the losses in print. Even today, online advertising only amounts to 5 percent of overall revenues, with an online ad worth one-tenth the price of a print ad. The result is that many newspapers that once made 30 percent profits have seen their profits fall to 15 percent or lower. The situation might not have been all that bad if two other things had not happened. One is the concentration of media ownership in the last 20 years and the other is the 2008–9 recession that hit advertising revenues particularly hard. Media owners found themselves spending vast amounts of their reduced profits servicing debts they had accumulated during the concentration binge. When they should have been innovating to meet the challenges of new technology,

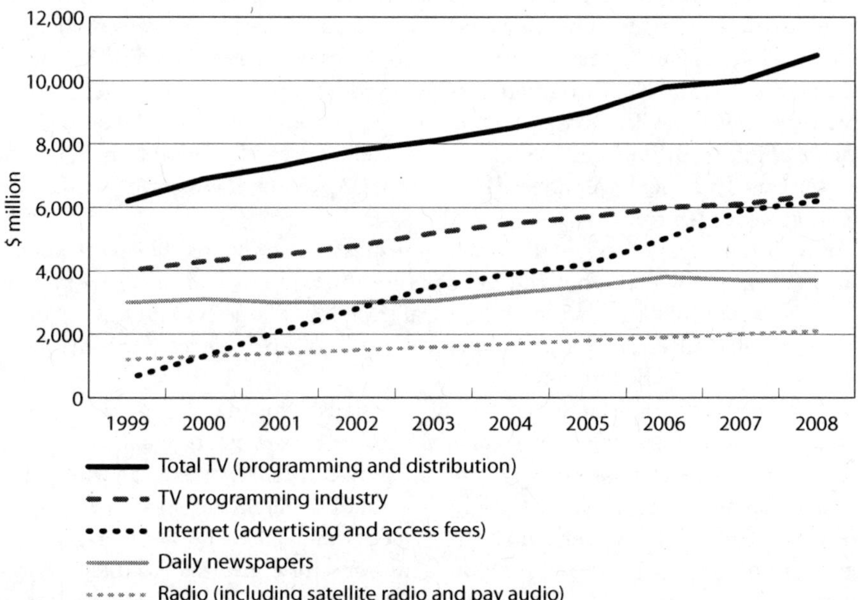

Figure 6.3 Trends in total revenues (from all sources) for selected media, Canada, 1999–2008

SOURCES: Statistics Canada; CRTC; CNA; © Communications Management Inc.

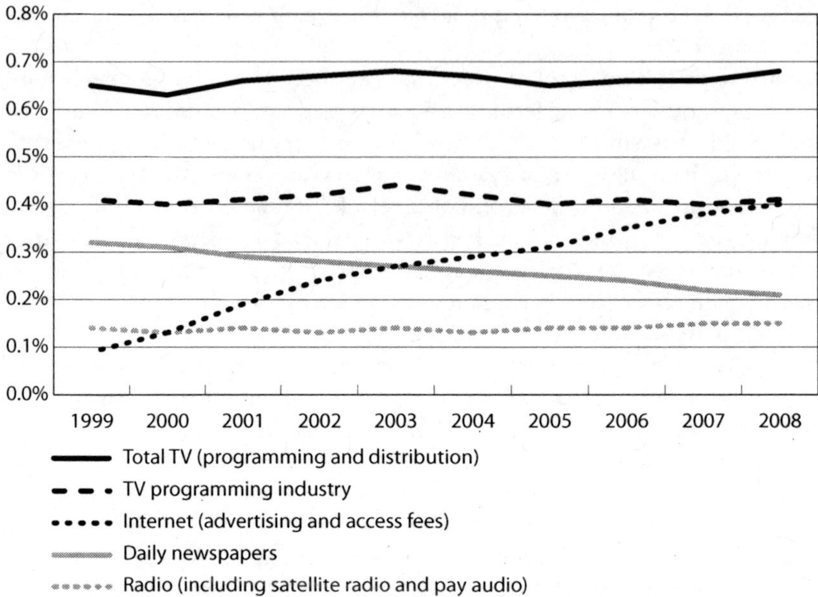

Figure 6.4 Trends in total revenues (from all sources) for selected media as a percentage of GDP, Canada, 1999–2008

SOURCES: Statistics Canada; CRTC; CNA; © Communications Management Inc.

they retrenched and starting slashing costs and outsourcing many of their operations. Many hundreds of media jobs were, and continue to be, lost across the country.

Meanwhile, as had happened in the United States, enterprising online innovators such as craigslist and Kijiji swooped in and started siphoning off newspaper classified advertising revenues. The share of these revenues across Canada has fallen by 2 percentage points from 1999 to 2008 (Canadian Media Research Consortium 2009), but some larger city dailies have suffered losses up to 13 percent. It is hard to see this trend stopping any time soon.

Why did newspapers not start similar websites? The only possible explanation is that they were in denial. They did not see the situation for what it was: a systemic change that required innovation and radical thinking. Many thought that when the recession ended advertising would return. Few recognized that even if that happened, it was never going to be the same.

The other thing traditional owners and journalists, for that matter, were slow to pick up on was the growing importance of consumer participation and interaction. The Internet allows the public to become amateur journalists, to engage with professional journalists, and to publish their own media content on social networks or blogs. Now a lot of newspapers and broadcast operations incorporate user-generated content into their products and provide many ways for consumers to interact. Journalists too have become bloggers, but many news organizations still make it difficult for readers to connect with them. Many traditional news organizations are still trying to catch up.

Media Market Changes Slower in Canada Than in the United States

In the United States, traditional newspapers and TV stations are closing or moving online, others are seeking bankruptcy protection, and a myriad of start-ups are exploring new ways of doing things. These events have led to numerous conferences and reports to promote a public dialogue on what this means for the state of journalism and democracy, including a US Senate subcommittee hearing on the future of journalism in May 2009, which looked at how the United States can sustain quality journalism in these troubled times.

The reason why little or nothing comparable is happening in Canada has much to do with the fact that the situation here is different. There is little doubt that the same trends that are causing so much turmoil in the United States are also affecting Canada, but at a slower rate. There are a number of reasons for this. The percentage comparisons in Figures 6.5 and 6.6 show that Canadian dailies have been less dependent on classified advertising than their US counterparts, and have done relatively better in terms of national advertising. We can also infer from these figures and from comScore data that the most serious online competitors for classified advertising, craigslist and Kijiji, have lower usage rates in Canada than in the United States (Canadian Media Research Consortium 2009).

The other point to note about these figures is that national advertising in Canada accounts for over 16 percent of total media revenue and has declined very little. National advertising in Canada brings a lot more revenue than retail advertising and has always accounted for a larger percentage of total profit than in the United States.

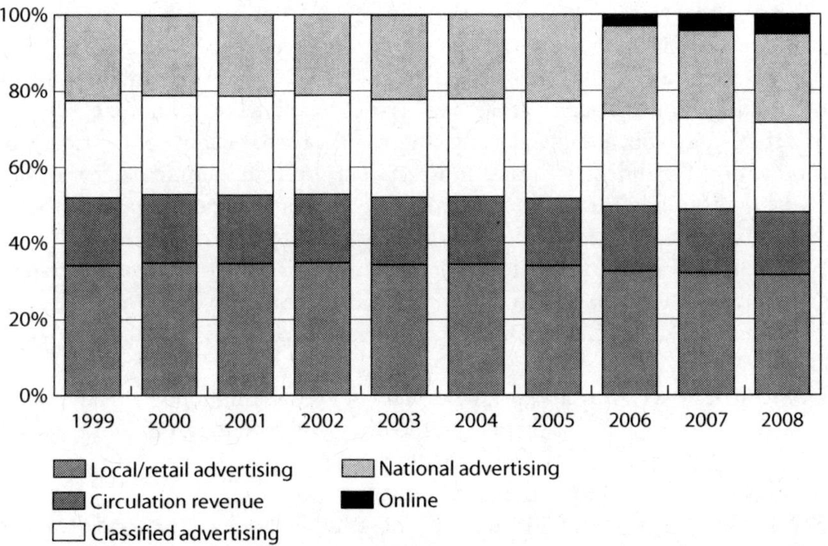

Figure 6.5 Advertising and circulation revenue trends, paid circulation daily newspapers, Canada, indicating percentage of total revenue, 1999–2008

SOURCES: CNA; TVB; © Communications Management Inc.

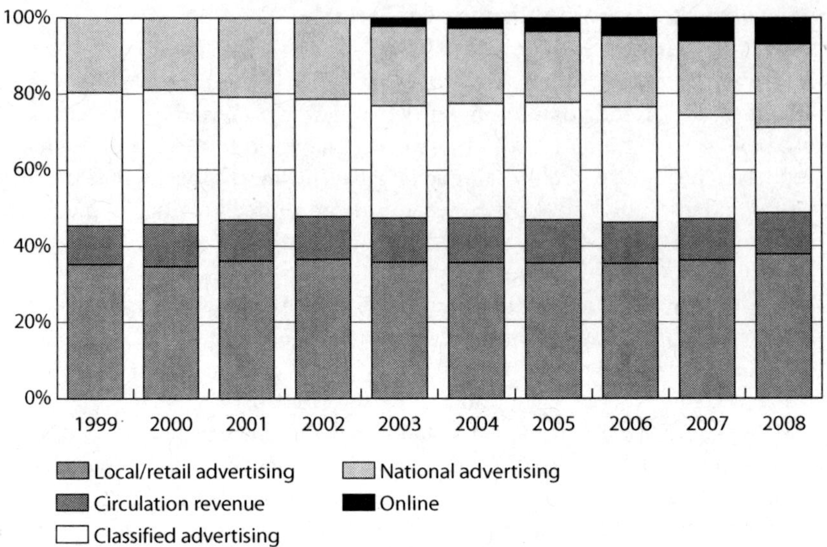

Figure 6.6 Advertising and circulation revenue trends, paid circulation daily newspapers, US, indicating percentage of total revenue, 1999–2008

SOURCES: NAA; © Communications Management Inc.

While all of this is good news in the short term, it should not be an excuse for complacency; it may mean that Canadian daily newspapers and broadcasters have at least a little more time to react to market changes.

Any efforts will be for naught unless traditional operators come to grips with the reality that they have to find ways to be paid directly for some content by consumers, start thinking more radically about cost structures, and revolutionize advertising approaches. This is not about tinkering. There will have to be more outsourcing, more sharing within the industry, and as much reduction in the duplication of resources and services as possible. Moreover, media have to do a far better job of collaborating with audiences and making content of greater value to the consumer. As the noted media scholar Robert Picard writes: "[I]t is essential for news organizations to rethink their activities and approaches to journalism today in order to improve value creation for five central stakeholders: consumers, advertisers, investors, journalists, and society" (2006, 3).

Unfortunately, as innovative as owners and operators might become, the new revenue streams do not look, at this point, like they will be enough to make up for the losses from traditional sources, principally advertising. The new cost structures for print and broadcasting must change drastically.

Fortunately, Canadian media are beginning to head down that road. Traditional owners are searching for new sources of revenue, and innovators are seeking to devise new models. Many more experiments are under way in the United States, hence the discussion of new models that follows looks at activities on both sides of the border. Regrettably, the number of new models in Canada is still minuscule by comparison.

What News Models Could Be Effective in Making Up for the Perceived Decline in Local News and Investigative Reporting?

Online Subscriptions or Micropayments

Many believe that the most obvious option would be to charge consumers for online news. Various newspapers are considering ways to charge for at least some online content by way of digital subscriptions or micropayments for individual news stories, as Apple does for music with iTunes. While access to free online news content has become a norm, some in the news industry now say offering free, unfiltered news is unfair to print subscribers (Kirchhoff 2009, 16–17) and creates the impression that content has no value, training new generations to expect quality journalism to come free of charge (Brill 2009). Online payment has been one of the most debated issues since the media crisis came to the forefront in 2008.

There are examples where newspapers have successfully charged for some content online. For example, the *Wall Street Journal* has succeeded by setting up paywalls. More than 1 million customers pay for online access, with annual rates varying from $103 for an online subscription to $140 for access to both print and online platforms (Liedtke 2009). Paying subscriptions for Britain's *Financial Times* online premium model have reached 121,000 at £99 per year (Andrews 2009a). But the success of business newspapers may be a special case because their customers have an interest in accessing valuable, up-to-date data that a competitor might not have, and many subscribers can claim costs as a business expense. Nonetheless, while not a business newspaper, Quebec's *Le Devoir*, an influential, high-quality daily, has managed to profit despite hiding much of its online content behind a paywall (Descôteaux 2009).

However, by erecting paywalls, some experts believe most newspapers would still reach a net loss even if they were to offer low fees (Langeveld 2009b). The gains made from online news payments would not be sufficient to make up for a loss in advertising revenue from reduced web traffic.

When considering daily newspapers that are intended for mass audiences, it is hard to believe that the necessary number of customers would be willing to pay for online content when other quality news organizations report on the same communities at no charge. For example, in areas where the CBC has a comprehensive local news website, it would be difficult for local newspapers to draw enough readers to their websites if they were to charge for online access. In fact, a poll released in September 2009 by Harris Interactive in the United Kingdom claims that three-quarters of respondents would switch to an alternative free news source if their preferred news site were to begin charging for content (Andrews 2009b). As mentioned above, the emergence of online platforms means traditional media organizations can no longer count on "protectable" scarcity (Canadian Media Research Consortium 2009).

Regardless, many newspaper publishers worldwide are planning to charge for at least some content. Most notably, the *New York Times* announced in January 2010 that it plans to introduce a metered online payment system by 2011. It will allow readers to access a certain number of articles each month at no cost before charging a flat fee for unlimited access. This comes as the New York Times Company reportedly made a loss of US$35.6 million between July and September 2009 (BBC 2010).

Drawing from 118 interviews with newspaper executives from the United States and Canada for the American Press Institute, 58 percent said they were considering online fees (Kaplan 2009). Over 1,000 newspapers and magazines have signed letters of intent to become affiliates with Journalism Online, a company that enables news publishers to charge for select website access and digital content (Liedtke 2009). Likewise, many newspapers are collaborating with e-reader producers and resellers to create online news platforms where readers can pay for news content that is wirelessly downloaded to their device. Electronics market research company iSuppli predicts that consumers will purchase 15 million e-readers in 2011 (Standage 2009, 121). Moreover, the much-heralded Apple iPad release in 2010 will undoubtedly help drive the market for e-reader-specific applications and content in the near future.

What is more, speaking on behalf of newspaper publishers to the US Senate Commerce subcommittee in May 2009, *Dallas Morning News* publisher and CEO James Moroney argued for an exemption to US antitrust law, so publishers could jointly impose payments for online content (Kirchhoff 2009, 16). So far in Canada, there is reportedly no such talk among newspaper publishers to cooperate, and compel readers to pay for some online content.

Non-Profit and Hybrid News Models

In response to a perceived decline in investigative, local, and regional in-depth reporting, a number of non-profit and hybrid start-ups have come into existence in the past several years. The non-profit VoiceofSandiego.org, for example, has generated much attention for its approach to news reporting since launching in 2005. It focuses on investigative news and is very selective about what it reports, strictly covering local stories. While it still has a relatively small audience, with fewer than 100,000 unique visitors a month, some of its articles about hidden pay raises in municipal government, unaffordable public housing, and misleading crime statistics have led to "prosecutions, reforms, and the kind of national journalism awards—from Sigma Delta Chi and Investigative Reporters and Editors—typically given to newspapers" (Downie and Schudson 2009). By emulating US public broadcasting models, it relies on contributions from foundations and trusts, audience donations, and advertising. Employing only 11 people, it pays its younger reporters what they would make at larger newspapers. Its operating budget increases yearly: from US$800,000 in 2008 (Pérez-Peña 2008) to US$1 million in 2009 (Downie and Schudson 2009), and its journalists also provide reports for free to local public and private radio and television stations.

The newly launched *Chicago News Cooperative* (ChicagoNewsCoop.org) brings an interesting approach to non-profit news. Funded through donations from several foundations and trusts, and led by former executives and reporters from the *Chicago Tribune*, it publishes local stories about Chicago's communities, politics, public policy, culture, and arts on its website, while collaborating with public media and selling its content to private media. It publishes a two-page section twice a week in the Chicago edition of the *New York Times*—its first paying customer—and has its own hyper-local section on the *Times*'s website. The co-operative's journalists also provide reports for Chicago's local public television station; it is in talks to collaborate with the city's local public radio station as well (Pérez-Peña 2009).

Canada has also witnessed the rise of alternative news models with local and regional focuses. For example, British Columbia's TheTyee.ca, a daily online magazine, has quickly earned a solid reputation for its investigative journalism, opinionated feature articles, and hybrid business model. In 2009, it won a Canadian Journalism Foundation Excellence in Journalism Award for small, medium, or local markets; a National Edward R. Murrow Award for excellence in electronic journalism in the United States and Canada; and three Canadian Online Publishing Awards.

The Tyee draws revenue from a number of sources and incorporates charitable, tax-deductible donations to fund its investigative reporting. Approximately 65 percent of its annual funding comes from two primary investors; 15 percent comes from advertising; and 15 percent comes from foundations or private donations for specific research or reporting projects. Five percent comes from reader contributions toward *Tyee* fellowship funds, where contributors make tax-deductible donations to support investigative pieces that look into issues of public interest (*The Tyee* 2009). Also, it achieves savings and subsidies by hiring and training interns, and publishing writers and photographers who have secured grants to cover their fees, contingent on exposure through *The Tyee*. Its annual operating budget varies between $500,000 and $600,000.

So far, *The Tyee* has attracted a relatively large audience. In March 2009, it drew 160,000 unique visitors, 292,000 visits, and 610,000 page views, an increase of about 30 percent over the previous year. Editor David Beers says a large majority of its audience is from British Columbia. Much of that audience comes from the provincial government, British Columbian universities, the federal government, and other media.

While it doesn't focus solely on local or regional news, another notable Canadian example is the non-profit *rabble*, which has existed since 2001. Supported by individuals, organizations, trade unions, and research institutes, www.rabble.ca publishes its own news stories, in-depth feature articles, blogs, commentary, podcasts, and video, along with reprints of articles from other "progressive sources" (*rabble* 2009, 2).

The news website relies on a strong and dedicated online community to engage its readers. Through babble, its multifaceted discussion forum, *rabble* provides a comprehensive platform for web users to share ideas, comment, post their own news stories, and become socially involved. In 2008, *rabble* reported averaging 140,000 unique visitors per month (*rabble* 2009, 40), with an annual operating budget of $154,000. Fifty-two percent of its revenue came from sustaining partners; 16 percent came from memberships; 6 percent came from advertising; and 26 percent came from grants, donations, and special events (39). Its content and support come from a small part-time staff, interns, and volunteers.

Government-Supported Models

Thus far, the above-mentioned models looked at how we can protect our local and investigative news by way of private, entrepreneurial initiatives. Yet, many believe government can also play a role in ensuring that citizens have the news and reporting they need.

There is significant talk in the United States of reorganizing existing newspapers as non-profit organizations. This designation would shield them from taxation on certain income, and make both subscriptions and donations tax deductible (Kirchhoff 2009, 18). There are also discussions of creating low-profit hybrids that combine non-profit and for-profit characteristics, including limits to profits.

In France, the government went so far as to give everyone in the 18-to-24 age group a one-year subscription to a newspaper of their choice, which is part of a €600 million aid package for French newspapers (de Pommerau 2009).

There is reason to believe that the public subsidization of news organizations could be supported in Canada. In October 2009, a Harris-Decima survey reported 51 percent of Canadians would support public aid for newspapers (Canadian Press 2009b). Although this question was directed toward existing newspapers, it shows there could be some type of support for any news organizations that would make up for a lack of local and investigative reporting in various communities across Canada.

A way to ensure more local news coverage would be to borrow from the US public broadcasting model. In this case, Congress funds much of the Corporation for Public Broadcasting, which in turn funds local, independent, public radio and television stations and program producers. The public radio stations, which are run by some paid employees, local community volunteers, non-profits, and universities receive income from a variety of sources. They contribute program fees and membership dues to National Public Radio (NPR; www.npr.org), which produces national and international news and current affairs content for its member stations. Each station is responsible for its own program schedule—a mixture of locally produced information and cultural shows, along with content from NPR and other sources including the BBC and the CBC. What is more, NPR recently created a new digital distribution platform on which its member stations can share local radio and web reporting with other affiliates across the country (Downie and Schudson 2009).

Thanks to its comprehensive and ambitious website, NPR has shown how the Web can be an effective medium for publishing original high-quality news by using a combination of media: text, audio, photos, and videos. Canada could take advantage of its already strong public broadcaster, the CBC, to implement a similar system. In areas not already serviced by the public broadcaster, a network of web-based, independent local news organizations could supplement local news coverage with national and international coverage from the CBC. The public broadcaster, in turn, could use any content produced by the independent local stations for its programming as well. Such an arrangement would require a sea change in current thinking in both the private and public sectors in Canada. But if that were possible, it could happen.

Premium/News Digest Models

In the for-profit sector, another readily available model is to charge consumers for a premium/news digest service. Much like some of the successful online pay models established by the *Wall Street Journal* and the *Financial Times*, it would allow news organizations to continue to report on hard, breaking news but charge a premium for added services. The *Christian Science Monitor* (CSM; CSMonitor.com), for example, has done very well since ceasing its daily print publication in March 2009. The news organization publishes its hard news stories online at no charge, and sells a newly created weekly news magazine. Ninety-three percent of its 43,000 former daily print subscribers agreed to switch to the weekly publication; moreover, by October 2009, the total number of fully paid subscribers had increased to 67,000. Online page views increased by 20 percent from April to October 2009, reaching 8.5 million per month. A monthly subscription to its weekly print edition costs 41 percent less than a monthly subscription to its daily print version had cost. Total revenues remain practically unchanged since saving on printing, paper, distribution, and staff costs (Edmonds 2009). The news organization still delivers investigative journalism and funds eight foreign bureaus for both print and online products.

Receiving a bundled news package in print every day has become for many less convenient than simply searching for news online at no charge; although, a premium/news digest service that lends insight to the news in a concise, finely edited manner is still convenient enough for readers to buy. Media expert Martin Langeveld (2009b) writes: "Daily print is not a long-term sustainable model, and forward-looking newspapers, rather than exploring an online paywall, should explore transitioning to a once- or twice-weekly frequency, focusing their print efforts on a weekend edition distributed Friday."

As there will always be websites that offer high-quality hard, breaking news at no cost—such as the BBC, NPR, or the CBC—it is hard to imagine how any news organization could profit by charging for its hard news content, at least at national or international levels. However, the CSM's experiment reveals that there is a desire for a well-curated selection of news and analysis. This probably explains why circulation for the *Economist*, a weekly news digest, has doubled in the past seven years (Pressman 2009). As AFP-MediaWatch concludes in its 2009 report on the future of the news industry, in order to survive, traditional media must commit to context, editorialization, intelligence, journalistic contribution, new technological platforms, and added value (Scherer 2009).

Hyper-Local News Ecosystems

In areas where local media coverage is inadequate, Canadian communities should consider hyper-local news ecosystems.

Hyper-local news provides more focused content, which reflects the interests of a specific, often tiny, geographic area. Hyper-local journalism is a very broad concept. It can refer to a local blog covering amateur hockey or one of the above-mentioned non-profit investigative news models.

Since news models are moving toward niche-oriented or specialty news and away from the less-convenient bundled news packages, there is an opportunity to develop a framework, or ecosystem, that would be made of "scores of companies operating under different means, motives, and models, each dependent on the others to optimize their success … creating critical mass they can sell to advertisers" (Jarvis 2009a). A hyper-local site could affordably hire editorial staff and advertising help from the network, while still maintaining its niche community focus.

Outside.in is a hyper-local network that incorporates over 4,000 hyper-local bloggers and news organizations, and covers 35,312 neighbourhoods in the United States (Reisinger 2009). It allows hyper-local publishers to use its tools to customize neighbourhood news pages for every community in its market. In December 2009, CNN announced it was investing in the hyper-local network, and would carry feeds from *Outside.in* on the network's website.

Providing an ecosystem, or support system, for hyper-local news sites could be a more effective way for larger news organizations to cover communities they either cannot afford to cover themselves or are unable to access. In May 2009, to expand its local digital coverage, the *Globe and Mail* reached a content-sharing agreement with Torontoist (www.torontoist.com), a comprehensive, hyper-local blog. This agreement provides the *Globe* with "intensely local" (Grant 2009) news features and event listings for its special online-only Toronto section. The *New York Times* has ventured into hyper-local networking as well, with the previously mentioned *Chicago News Cooperative* partnership; moreover, it launched two hyper-local sites of its own that cover several communities in Brooklyn and New Jersey.

Which Models Will Survive?

As Jan Schaffer (2009), executive director of J-Lab: The Institute for Interactive Journalism, writes, "So, what epiphanies are to be drawn from what is working?" The newspaper has long been viewed as the news medium that does the most to inform society. It has done the most to hold institutions accountable; many say the culture of good journalism depends on its survival. But the newspaper can no longer be viewed "as a general-purpose vehicle for publishing a variety of news and opinion … [that] only need[s] a digital facelift" (Shirky 2009; see Shirky's blog entry in Chapter 4).

If we are indeed in the midst of a media revolution, the old system must collapse before new systems are set in place, according to Shirky. What will happen? It is easier to see what is broken than what will replace it. As Shirky (2009) writes, "Even the revolutionaries can't predict what will happen."

The importance of the Web does not solely have to do with how we communicate and receive news; the online revolution affects most aspects of our lives. In fact, many recognize Internet access as a human right. Finland became the first country in the world to declare broadband Internet access a legal right in October 2009. In June 2009, UK Prime Minister Gordon Brown (2009) said the Internet is "as vital as water and gas"; every home should have access to broadband.

As Shirky (2009) notes, "Society doesn't need newspapers. What we need is journalism." So what will the future of journalism be? The answer is simple: No one knows. The models discussed in this chapter—online subscriptions or micropayments; nonprofit news models; government-supported models; premium/news digest models; hyper-local news ecosystems; database/real-time journalism; location-based, targeted technologies; ambient journalism; political observatory organizations or special interest advocacy; investigative funds and collaborative media—will most likely be part of what Shirky refers to as "overlapping special cases" for a few decades until society finally makes sense of how best to use them.

Who will come up with the sustainable news models of the future? Media expert Jeff Jarvis (2009b) does not know, but he believes that they will be developed by industries that embrace an entrepreneurial spirit: "The structure—the ecosystem—of news will not be dominated by a few corporations but likely will be made up of networks of many start-ups performing specialized functions based on the opportunities they see in the market."

Jarvis's assertion does not imply that news giants will cease to exist. Instead, he says they could help establish frameworks for news enterprises to exist.

Journalists are going to have to change as well. They will have to become entrepreneurs themselves. They will have to work in constant flux and within complex news ecosystems, generating revenue from a variety of sources (Jarvis 2009b).

GlobalPost.com is an example of a news organization embracing an entrepreneurial spirit. Hoping to fill the increasing void of foreign news content, it is an independent, for-profit agency of foreign correspondents committed to international reporting. It receives funding from online advertising, distribution of syndicated content to other news organizations, and Passport, a paid subscription model for premium content.

GlobalPost grants each correspondent 10,000 shares in the organization, "meaning that they have a vested interest in the enterprise's success" (Langeveld 2009a). While it pays its journalists just US$1,000 a month, *GlobalPost* allows them to freelance for other organizations as well. As of July 2009, it had 65 correspondents in nearly 50 countries. It drew 391,000 monthly unique users on its website in just five months (Balboni 2009).

How Else Could We Get Our News in the Future?

Database/Real-Time Journalism

Computer algorithms are being used in an abundance of ways to help give people a better understanding of the world around them. Terms such as *database journalism* and *computer journalism* are emerging to explain systems that use artificial intelligence to make sense of the plethora of information available online for use by citizens and journalists.

For example, when a user enters an address in EveryBlock.com, an American hyper-local database journalism website, a page appears with publicly available civic information—building permits, restaurant inspections, construction notices, and police reports—news and blog articles, consumer reviews of local businesses, photos, and anything else immediately related to the neighbourhood. Its creation was originally backed by a US$1.1 million grant from the Knight Foundation, and in August 2009, MSNBC acquired it (Stone 2009). Founded in 2007, *EveryBlock* had editions in 15 US cities as of December 2009.

AOL is also heartily adopting the concept of using algorithms for news editing and production. Combining the information drawn from algorithms with marketing partnerships and freelance writers, AOL aims to harness the Internet's capacity to alert its journalists to what the crowd is discussing, in real time. It examines search data and traffic patterns, finds the latest popular search topics, and automatically commissions related stories from freelancers. The goal is to reduce inefficiencies and editorial costs, and produce stories that are attractive to advertisers (Singel 2009). This strategy is part of an ambitious plan by AOL to produce an abundance of content via its large number of popular niche websites. As of December 2009, AOL employed approximately 2,000 full- and part-time journalists (Cauchon 2009), taking a very entrepreneurial approach to how it selects and pays journalists for original content.

An algorithm-based news system such as AOL's would not produce all the necessary information to replace today's news organizations, and it also poses some serious ethical questions about the selection of news stories for profit. All the same, it shows how crowd-powered research systems can rapidly exploit breaking news and trends that are happening in real time, and quickly alert journalists to them.

Location-Based, Targeted Technologies

Many entrepreneurs have looked into how news organizations could track their audience's news habits to connect them with high-cost, personally targeted advertising. Although not intended solely for news consumption, Google launched a new feature for its AdSense advertising network in March 2009 that allows advertisers to reach users that have shown interest in similar or related items. The web-search giant plans to track its users' online habits and build a collection of "interests" based on which websites they visit (Gilbertson 2009). It also plans to display ads to users that are based on their past online interactions and behaviours.

In addition, program developers are taking advantage of the massive increase in online mobile devices to create location-based marketing. Marketers can reach consumers by combining their "location, inferred intent and personal affinities to aggregate and deliver relevant information about the real world surrounding them at any given moment" (Klaassen 2009). For example, Geodelic's Sherpa application (www.geodelic.com/sherpa/) allows customers to find out instantly about their immediate surroundings—business locations, restaurant reviews, and real estate information. As they continuously use the application, Sherpa tailors its results to their personal interests.

News organizations will undoubtedly have to adapt these technologies for news purposes or risk being swept aside again by their online competition. Besides providing a valuable means for connecting news advertisers with their audience, location-based, targeted technologies would be very effective in distributing personalized news stories, reflecting a reader's interests and hyper-local community.

Ambient Journalism

The capabilities of database journalism and real-time networked digital technologies have led to the concept of ambient journalism. According to UBC Journalism professor Alfred Hermida, ambient journalism is achieved via "para-journalism" forms such as microblogging. These "broad, asynchronous, lightweight and always-on systems are enabling citizens to maintain a mental model of news and events around them, giving rise to awareness systems [Hermida] describes as ambient journalism" (Hermida, 2009).

Following the June 2009 disputed election crisis in Iran, scores of people undermined the state-controlled media by using various microblogging applications, most notably Twitter—a social network and microblogging tool that allows its users to post messages of up to 140 characters—by sending reports and photos of protests, street fights, government crackdowns, and casualties. For example, publicizing support for defeated candidate Mir Hossein Mousavi, one message read, "We have no national press coverage in Iran, everyone should help spread Moussavi's message. One Person = One Broadcaster. #IranElection" (Cohen and Stone 2009).

Not only was Twitter an effective tool for citizens to communicate and organize antigovernment protests, it was also an essential tool for reporting what was happening to other Iranians and the world. The BBC, CNN, the *New York Times*, and the CBC all used some Twitter postings in their reporting.

While individual "tweets" (as Twitter messages are called) may not have any effect and have some errors, value in an awareness system comes from the combined effect of communication (Hermida 2009). The collective messages reflect the reality and emotions of a moment, and help drive opinion (Cohen 2009).

Some organizations are already trying to exploit the capabilities of real-time search tools to support other customary search and news content. In December 2009, Google launched its real-time web search, which integrates tweets and Facebook updates into its normal search and news sections. What is more, it posts results chronologically, emphasizing the newest content from news articles, blog postings, and Wikipedia updates (Canadian Press 2009a).

Future models of ambient journalism may develop systems "that help the public negotiate and regulate this flow of awareness information, facilitating the collection and transmission of news," identifying the "collective sum of knowledge" from the plethora of individual messages, bringing meaning to the data (Hermida 2009). The key is to develop these applications in a way that supports the traditional notions of good journalism.

Although we believe in the importance of media in a democratic society, it does not mean that some of the media's most important duties—news, public forums, and checks on institutions—are exclusive to today's news industry. An absence of other options made the news media the purveyor of these responsibilities over the past two centuries; however, "changes in communication technologies and abilities have made other forums possible" (Picard 2006, 151).

Political Observatory Organizations or Special Interest Advocacy

Recent advances in digital compilation and distribution of public information have not only revolutionized how journalists do their reporting but also presented an opportunity for news organizations and non-governmental organizations (NGOs) to exploit these sources and create digital platforms to better inform the public.

In what could make some traditional elements of journalistic work redundant, citizens are gathering and disseminating public information themselves to keep track of government officials. OpenCongress.org is an example of how a non-profit-led initiative can become a comprehensive US federal government database, where use of official government data—every available piece of legislation, votes, committee reports, campaign contributions—and news and blog postings about Congress members are brought together to create a representation of all happenings in the federal government. OpenCongress uses open-source programming code and licenses its content under Creative Commons, inviting others to use its material and come up with new ways to filter the most attention-worthy issues in US Congress.

FactCheck.org and PolitiFact.com are two more interesting examples of how journalists, academics, and NGOs are using the increasing amount of available government data to hold the US government accountable. Set up by the Annenberg Public Policy

Center of the University of Pennsylvania, FactCheck.org monitors US political television advertisements, debates, speeches, interviews, and news releases. It follows local, state, and federal levels of government. The *St. Petersburg Times*'s PolitiFact.com rates the accuracy of statements made by members of US Congress, the president, Cabinet secretaries, and lobbyists as well as testimonies before Congress via its "Truth-O-Meter," "Flip-O-Meter," and "Obameter"; the last meter assesses over 500 promises that Barack Obama made during his presidency campaign. PolitiFact.com won the 2009 Pulitzer Prize for National Reporting for its fact-checking during the 2008 US presidential election.

As new systems of algorithms, alert systems, and information presentation platforms appear, there will be opportunities—most likely for technology companies—to create new forms of visual journalism that can help hold institutions accountable. For example, Sunlight Labs, a non-profit organization of web developers and designers dedicated to opening government, holds Apps for America, an annual competition that encourages web developers to create new applications that will make government more accountable, interactive, and transparent.

What We Know for Sure

Investigative Funds and Collaborative Media

Whatever happens, the future of journalism is collaborative. As *Guardian* editor Alan Rusbridger says, "I have seen the future, and it's mutual" (Downie and Schudson 2009).

Sponsored in most part by philanthropic contributions, non-profit ProPublica.org embraces the spirit of professionals and amateurs working together. A newsroom of over three dozen journalists and editors (Downie and Schudson 2009) prepares and distributes investigative news pieces to other news organizations for publication or broadcast at no cost. Up to now, its stories have appeared on *60 Minutes* and NPR, and in the *New York Times*, the *Los Angeles Times*, and many smaller newspapers. One of its pieces was shortlisted for the 2009 Goldsmith Prize for Investigative Reporting. Whereas most newspapers contribute 10 percent of budgets toward journalism, almost all of its resources purportedly go toward journalism (Pilkington 2008).

ProPublica launched its pro-am wing of reporting in May 2009. In six weeks, it had recruited over 1,000 volunteer citizens to monitor progress on a sample of 510 of the 6,000 projects that were approved for US federal stimulus money following the 2008 global financial crash. It hopes to someday use its network to collaborate on investigative reports with other news organizations; to reveal data and documents that are hidden from public view; and to create resources for people to assess what is happening in their communities (Myers 2009).

During the 2009 provincial election in British Columbia, *The Tyee* had its readers participate in its investigative journalism, by asking them to fund reporting on the issues that mattered most to them. The four top funding choices were "Tyee's Choice," privatization, environment, and clean government. The funding produced over 60 feature articles and over 200 blog postings in the lead-up to the election. Reader-funded reporters broke stories on growing payments to privatizers, losses in the BC Rail trust fund, and a flawed new government welfare-to-work program (Beers 2009).

When examining collaborative news models, there are many more excellent cases worth mentioning. Spot.us, for example, is an American non-profit, crowd-funded news organization where reporters appeal to readers for donations to help pay for reporting about often under-reported and overlooked topics. Contributions are tax deductible, and donations will be reimbursed if another news organization buys the exclusive rights to a story's content.

TalkingPointsMemo.com (TPM) has garnered a great deal of success since launching as a blog in 2000. Today, it is a profitable, US national news website, with an openly ideological slant, that reports on government and politics via breaking news coverage, investigative reporting, and guest blogging (Downie and Schudson 2009).

With two bureaus in New York and Washington, TPM has truly embraced the Web as a news medium, building itself around fast-paced online breaking news, and narrating and aggregating daily news, while still embracing the traditional news values of good news reporting and investigative journalism. Most particular to a new media organization, it has benefited from a strong online community of readers. As founder and editor Josh Marshall says, TPM depends on the involvement of an audience with "high interest and expertise": "We have a consistent, iterative relationship with our audience—people telling us where to look" (Downie and Schudson 2009). In 2007, TPM won a George Polk Award for Legal Reporting for its investigation of the Bush administration's handling of federal prosecutors, sparking the interest of traditional media, and eventually leading to the resignation of Attorney General Alberto Gonzales.

Canada has had its share of successful citizen journalism websites: *Orato.com*, *DigitalJournal.com*, and *NowPublic.com* publish user-generated news from around the world. And in what appears to be a movement toward more localized, niche-oriented user-generated news, the US *Examiner.com* (www.examiner.com) bought *NowPublic* in September 2009 (Stelter 2009) and has moved into the Canadian market, with editions covering Vancouver, Calgary, Toronto, Ottawa, and Montreal. The *Examiner.com* does not aim to compete with mainstream media, but to act as a forum where users can speak to others in their community, communicating something about which they are passionate (Oliveira 2009). Many articles may be of interest to very few, and may not be covered by mainstream media, but digital publishing's practically infinite storage capacity makes it easy for citizens to learn more about what they care most about, whether it be at a hyper-local or international level, so long as there is someone willing to write about it. As of December 2009, there was a total of 245 local *Examiner.com* editions in Canada and the United States.

Emerging Trends for Traditional Media and Journalists

Just as it is too early to know which of the new models explored in this chapter will survive, it is impossible to say with any certainty what will happen to traditional media outlets. Clearly, they are on a slippery slope at the moment, but predictions of their demise are premature. In the present context, it seems impossible to imagine a world without newspaper organizations and television. Newspapers, in particular, have always been the engine that drives the news, producing far more original journalistic content than any of the other media. Despite the plethora of new media, this is still the case, according to a 2009 study by the US Project for Excellence in Journalism. An examination of all the local news produced in Baltimore for one week found that 95 percent of the stories that contained new information came from traditional media—most from newspapers (Project for Excellence in Journalism 2010).

However, the same survey also showed that the overall amount of local news is declining as traditional media outlets shed reporters in an effort to remain profitable in the face of declining revenues. At this point, new media organizations have not yet come close to making up the difference.

Although the situation looks bleak for traditional media organizations, it may not be terminal. When they move to digital as their principal means of delivery, it will eliminate all kinds of expensive delivery costs: newsprint, trucks, transmission fees, et cetera.

As we have seen in this chapter, some newspapers have already eliminated their print version and moved online exclusively. When online delivery becomes more common, it is likely that online advertising will command a higher price, but given the alternatives available to advertisers, it will never generate the revenues that print advertising did, so new means of revenue will have to be found. These could include fees for specialized information, highly targeted and localized advertising, various forms of direct marketing, and radically different cost structures. The fragmentation of audiences also points toward smaller, more niche-oriented publications, using a variety of forms of distribution. For these reasons, we are unlikely to see the return of the huge newsrooms of the past. Not only will there be fewer staff reporters and correspondents, there will be more content acquired from freelancers, citizen journalists, independent production groups, and wire services. As well, there will be a greater number of partnerships across media and NGOs to fund investigations. In short, traditional media outlets are responding in many ways to the new directions available to aggregate audiences and augment revenues. It would be a mistake to write off traditional news organizations. They have been slow to adjust, but if they pick up the pace, they may be able to survive.

DISCUSSION QUESTIONS

1. What needs to happen in Canada before more innovative news organizations are created?
2. What kinds of news will Canadians be willing to pay for online?
3. Now that digital technologies such as algorithms, alert systems, and online databases are available to monitor civic institutions, how will journalistic practices be affected?

SUGGESTED RESOURCES

BuzzMachine [Jeff Jarvis's blog]. http://www.buzzmachine.com.

Canadian Media Research Consortium. Future of news survey. http://www.mediaresearch.ca/en/projects/FutureofNewsSurvey.htm

Downie, Leonard, Jr., and Michael Schudson. 2009. The reconstruction of American journalism. *Columbia Journalism Review*, October 19. http://www.cjr.org/reconstruction/the_reconstruction_of_american.php?page=all.

Project for Excellence in Journalism. 2010. How news happens: A study of the news ecosystem of one American city. January 11. http://www.journalism.org/analysis_report/how_news_happens.

Reportr.net [Alfred Hermida's blog]. http://reportr.net.

Shirky, Clay [blog]. http://www.shirky.com/weblog.

REFERENCES

Andrews, Robert. 2009a. "Because we're worth it": FT.com going even more premium. *paidContent.org*, December 16. http://paidcontent.org/article/419-because-were-worth-it-ft.com-going-even-more-premium/.

Andrews, Robert. 2009b. PCUK/Harris Poll: Only five percent of readers would pay for online news. *paidContent.org*, September 20. http://paidcontent.co.uk/article/419-pcukharris-poll-only-five-percent-of-readers-would-pay-for-online-news/.

Balboni, Philip. 2009. Message from president and co-founder Philip Balboni. *GlobalPost*, July 4. http://www.globalpost.com/mission-statement.

BBC. 2010. New York Times website to charge. *BBC News*, January 20. http://news.bbc.co.uk/2/hi/business/8470894.stm.

Beers, David. 2009. Guide to Tyee election reporting. *The Tyee*, May 9. http://thetyee.ca/Tyeenews/2009/05/09/ElectionReports/.

Brill, Steve. 2009. Brill's secret plan to save the New York Times and journalism itself. *PoynterOnline*, February 9. http://www.poynter.org/column.asp?id=45&aid=158210.

Brown, Gordon. 2009. The Internet is a vital as water and gas. *Times Online*, June 16. http://www.timesonline.co.uk/tol/comment/columnists/guest_contributors/article6506136.ece.

Canadian Media Research Consortium. 2009. *The state of the media in Canada: A work in progress*. http://www.mediaresearch.ca/documents/SOM_Canada_0702.pdf.

Canadian Press. 2009a. Google to display tweets, Facebook updates. *CBC.ca*, December 8. http://www.cbc.ca/technology/story/2009/12/08/consumer-google-facebook-real-time-search.html.

Canadian Press. 2009b. Majority would back newspaper bailout: Poll. *CBC.ca*, October 8. http://www.cbc.ca/arts/media/story/2009/10/08/newspaper-bailout.html.

Cauchon, Paul. 2009. Médias—Plus que du contenu, il faut du contexte. *Le Devoir*, November 30. http://www.ledevoir.com/societe/medias/278231/medias-plus-que-du-contenu-il-faut-du-contexte.

Cohen, Noam. 2009. Twitter on the barricades: Six lessons learned. *New York Times*, June 20. http://www.nytimes.com/2009/06/21/weekinreview/21cohenweb.html?ref=middleeast.

Cohen, Noam, and Brad Stone. 2009. Social networks spread defiance online. *New York Times*, June 15. http://www.nytimes.com/2009/06/16/world/middleeast/16media.html?scp=2&sq=iran%20election%20twitter&st=cse.

de Pommerau, Isabelle. 2009. France: Bailout for newspapers? Sarkozy gives free youth subscriptions. *Christian Science Monitor*, December 15. http://www.csmonitor.com/World/Global-News/2009/1215/France-Bailout-for-newspapers-Sarkozy-gives-free-youth-subscriptions.

Descôteaux, Bernard. 2009. Rapport annuel 2008—Préparer Le Devoir de demain. *Le Devoir*, May 21. http://www.ledevoir.com/non-classe/251324/rapport-annuel-2008-preparer-le-devoir-de-demain.

Downie, Leonard, Jr., and Michael Schudson. 2009. The reconstruction of American journalism. *Columbia Journalism Review*, October 19. http://www.cjr.org/reconstruction/the_reconstruction_of_american.php?page=all.

Edmonds, Rick. 2009. Online focus is working for *Christian Science Monitor*. *PoynterOnline*, October 23. http://www.poynter.org/column.asp?id=123&aid=172295.

Gilbertson, Scott. 2009. Google's new ad network knows where you've been, what you do. *Wired*, March 11. http://www.wired.com/epicenter/2009/03/googles-new-ad/.

Grant, Kelly. 2009. Introducing the new Toronto hub. *Globe and Mail*, May 30, 2009. http://www.theglobeandmail.com.

Hermida, Alfred. 2009. FoJ09 talk: Twitter as a system of ambient journalism. Reportr.net, September 15. http://reportr.net/2009/09/15/foj09-talk-twitter-as-a-system-of-ambient-journalism/.

Jarvis, Jeff. 2009a. The future of business is in ecosystems. BuzzMachine, November 11. http://www.buzzmachine.com/2009/11/11/the-future-of-business-is-in-ecosystems/.

Jarvis, Jeff. 2009b. The future of news is entrepreneurial. BuzzMachine, November 1. http://www.buzzmachine.com/2009/11/01/the-future-of-journalism-is-entrepreneurial/.

Kaplan, David. 2009. Glass half full? 51 percent of newspaper publishers believe charging for online content can succeed. *paidContent.org*, September 14. http://paidcontent.org/article/419-glass-half-full-51-percent-of-publishers-believe-they-can-charge-for-on/.

Kirchhoff, Suzanne M. 2009. The U.S. newspaper industry in transition. *Congressional Research Service*, July 8. http://www.fas.org/sgp/crs/misc/R40700.pdf.

Klaassen, Abbey. 2009. Places, please: How location changes digital marketing. *Advertising Age*, September 14. http://adage.com.

Langeveld, Martin. 2009a. Interview: Charles Sennott, executive editor of GlobalPost. Nieman Journalism Lab, March 31. http://www.niemanlab.org/2009/03/interview-charles-sennott-executive-editor-of-globalpost/.

Langeveld, Martin. 2009b. Paying for online news: Sorry, but the math just doesn't work. Nieman Journalism Lab, April 3. http://www.niemanlab.org/2009/04/paying-for-online-news-sorry-but-the-math-just-doesnt-work/.

Liedtke, Michael. 2009. Want to read all about it? Prepare to pay. *Globe and Mail*, September 21. http://www.theglobeandmail.com.

Myers, Steve. 2009. ProPublica reporting network adds 1,000 members; Starts with stimulus. *PoynterOnline*, July 6. http://www.poynter.org/column.asp?id=101&aid=165980.

Oliveira, Michael. 2009. Citizen journalism gaining steam, filling in blanks left by mainstream media. *Winnipeg Free Press*, December 9. http://www.winnipegfreepress.com.

Pérez-Peña, Richard. 2008. Web sites that dig for news rise as watchdogs. *New York Times*, November 17. http://www.nytimes.com/2008/11/18/business/media/18voice.html.

Pérez-Peña, Richard. 2009. Chicago news venture to sell content to New York Times. *New York Times*, October 22. http://www.nytimes.com/2009/10/23/business/media/23chicago.html.

Picard, Robert. 2006. Journalism, value creation and the future of news organizations. Working Papers Series, Spring, Joan Shorenstein Center on the Press, Politics and Public Policy, Harvard University. http://www.robertpicard.net/PDFFiles/ValueCreationandNewsOrgs.pdf.

Pilkington, Ed. 2008. The human search engines. *Guardian*, June 30. http://www.guardian.co.uk/media/2008/jun/30/propublica.

Pressman, Matt. 2009. Why *Time* and *Newsweek* will never be the *Economist*. *Vanity Fair*, April 20. http://www.vanityfair.com/online/politics/2009/04/when-will-magazines-stop-trying-to-copy-the-economist.html.

Project for Excellence in Journalism. 2010. How news happens: A study of the news ecosystem of one American city, January 11. http://www.journalism.org/analysis_report/how_news_happens.

rabble. 2009. 2008 annual report: News for the rest of us. *rabble.ca*. http://rabble.ca/sites/rabble/files/Annual%20Report%2008%20v5.pdf.

Reisinger, Don. 2009. It's time to go hyperlocal with these resources. *CNET*, August 18. http://news.cnet.com/8301-17939_109-10312295-2.html.

Schaffer, Jan. 2009. First read: Follow the breadcrumbs. *Columbia Journalism Review*, October 19. http://www.cjr.org/reconstruction/follow_the_breadcrumbs.php.

Scherer, Eric. 2009. Context is king. *AFP-MediaWatch*. http://www.mediawatch.afp.com/public/AFP-MediaWatch_Automne-Hiver-2009-2010.pdf.

Shirky, Clay. 2009. Newspapers and thinking the unthinkable. Clay Shirky, March 13. http://www.shirky.com/weblog/2009/03/.

Singel, Ryan. 2009. AOL becoming automated, on-demand content factory. *Wired*, November 30. http://www.wired.com/epicenter/2009/11/aol-automatic-content/.

Standage, Tom. 2009. The plot thickens: E-books will move further towards the mainstream. *Economist: The World in 2010*, November 13, 121.

Stelter, Brian. 2009. Examiner.com buys NowPublic, a citizen-media web site. *New York Times*, September 1. http://www.nytimes.com/2009/09/02/business/media/02public.html?_r=1&scp=1&sq=nowpublic.com&st=Search.

Stone, Brad. 2009. MSNBC.com acquires EveryBlock, a hyperlocal news start-up. *New York Times*, August 17. http://bits.blogs.nytimes.com/2009/08/17/msnbccom-acquires-hyperlocal-startup-everyblock/.

The Tyee. 2009. Tyee Fellowship Funds. http://thetyee.ca/About/Fellowshipfunds/.

CHAPTER 7

What's a Good Story? Recognizing Quality in Journalists' Work

Ivor Shapiro

CHAPTER OUTLINE

Introduction

Ottawa, 2009: At the Supreme Court of Canada, a lawyer for the Canadian Civil Liberties Association is arguing that journalists should enjoy the right to refuse to provide information about a confidential source. The justices mostly listen respectfully, but then one of them leans forward and asks the elephant-in-the-room question. In this day and age, he points out, any citizen can obtain and publish, on a blog, information in the public interest. So, he asks: "Who is a journalist?" (*National Post, et al. v. Her Majesty the Queen* 2009).

New York City, 2009: Three bloggers successfully sue the police for denying them press credentials. "The Police Department should not be in the business of determining who's a journalist," one says (Media Bistro 2009). In some places, government officials have stopped issuing media credentials to freelancers, or even issuing them at all—throwing up their hands at the business of deciding who's entitled and who's not. As one official is quoted as saying: "There are so many bloggers and others who aren't really professional writers … it is getting hard to tell who is a 'real' writer and who isn't" (Chan 2009).

Also in New York, way, way back in 2005: Jay Rosen, professor at New York University's journalism school and long one of the world's most passionate promoters of "civic journalism," announces: "Bloggers vs. journalists is over" (Rosen 2005).

Who is a journalist? In this day and age, anyone who wants to be. And not just this day and age. Journalists never required professional certification to do their work. When George Orwell took to the streets of England and France to find out what homelessness was like, he didn't carry his press card. When, a long time later, I submitted my first story to a daily newspaper at age 16, it was accepted on merit and I wasn't ID'd.

Defining Journalism

Who, then, is a journalist? The best answer is, Who cares? But tweak the question just a titch, and it becomes a bit more important: *What* is journalism? Or, more exactly: What is *good* journalism? Hmm. Whom shall we ask?

What Wins Awards

If you're trying to find out how journalists distinguish good work from mediocre, and excellent from good, a sensible first set of calls might be to judges in journalism awards programs. But be prepared for some pretty subjective answers. Members of judging panels tend to be reluctant to name specific standards. Instead, they will refer to their professional experience or personal tastes. "I can't really describe it," said one when a colleague posed the question. "Do [the pieces] compel me? Do they draw me in?" Said another: "If it gets my attention, keeps me reading, and I forget that I'm judging, then it's worthwhile. It comes down to how the writer speaks to me" (Shapiro, Albanese, and Doyle 2006).

One awards judge emphasized comprehensive reporting: "It took the reader into the story and I was able to visualize the problems. It was fair and balanced. The reporter interviewed all the important people in the story. The piece addressed a specific problem in the community that normally wouldn't get addressed because people in the story were powerless. And the reporter found the story himself." For another judge, excellence was all about the writing: "Great writing, passionate engagement with subject matter. The writer had a burning, sweating, heaving need to convey his thoughts on the matter" (Shapiro, Albanese, and Doyle 2006).

Personal preference aside, though, judges in some leading awards programs are expected to follow guidelines for identifying excellence. One of these programs, the National Newspaper Awards (NNA) of Canada, provides specific pointers for each category of submission. The Investigation category, for example, expects "enterprise and depth" and comprises a list of 13 questions to consider, including:

- Was this work a worthwhile allocation of this newspaper's resources—does the subject involve a matter of reasonable importance to the public?
- Is this a significant exposé? Is the public interest or the rights of individuals at stake?
- Does this work emanate primarily from the initiative of the reporter/newspaper?
- Does this work expose secrets and/or wrongdoing?
- Does fact-gathering go beyond routine, drawing on computer databases, analysis, public records and authoritative (perhaps reluctant?) sources for its information? (Canadian Newspaper Association 2010)

In all categories, NNA judges are also provided with a set of notes listing the following elements for evaluation:

- **Idea:** significance (was it worth reporter and reader spending time on?); newsworthiness; timeliness; originality and creativity; humorous; initiative
- **Reporting:** depth and breadth; context and background; accuracy; fairness and balance; comprehensive, relevant sources (officials and real people); detail that engages the reader; answers reader's questions; enterprise and effort

- **Writing:** language (precision of usage, elegance); style, tone, mood (appropriate to content); credibility/authority; compelling lead/opening; clarity; strong focus/theme—what is this story about?; structure and organization; effective anecdotes, quotes and examples; narrative and description; accuracy and fairness; creativity/risk-taking; reader interest
- **Overall impression:** excellent; good; indifferent (Canadian Newspaper Association 2010)

Figure 7.1 This photo won an inaugural National Newspaper Award in 1949 (Jack DeLorme, *Calgary Herald*). Determining what constitutes journalism is becoming increasingly difficult, but good journalism will always be engaging, fair, accurate, focused, and ultimately, worth the readers' and the reporter's time.

Although the lists of judges' values and guidelines are long, and vary from program to program, a few aspects clearly rise to the fore: judges tend to look for quality in a story's purpose and content, in the research (reporting) that it requires, and in the writing style.

What Editors Want

Let's turn now from adjudicators to a group of people who are in the business of assigning, selecting, and supervising works of journalism day by day—the editors. Over the years, surveys of editors have produced even longer and more varied lists of values than have surveys of awards judges. But a careful look at the various studies suggests that editors' values have much in common. Reviewing studies of US newspaper editors over the past few decades, one steadfast researcher, Leo Bogart, identified 13 words and phrases that surfaced repeatedly when editors described what quality journalism consists of:

- integrity
- fairness
- balance
- accuracy
- comprehensiveness
- diligence of discovery
- authority
- breadth of coverage
- variety of content
- reflection of the entire home community
- vivid writing
- attractive makeup, packaging or appearance
- easy navigability (2004, 40)

To this list, Bogart proposed one addition: "clear differentiation of reporting and opinion" (2004, 40). Bogart may have simply forgotten to refer to originality or freshness of content, or anything related to a story's content or benefit to society. But it is clear that journalists do place value in those areas—for example, a 2007 study of online news editors in Canada and the United States showed that they valued most such "traditional" criteria of quality as

- credibility
- utility
- content relevancy
- separation of fact and opinion
- good writing

The same study showed that "traditional" criteria trumped more web-specific values, such as

- immediacy
- ease of use
- "hyperlocalism"
- interactivity with communities (Gladney, Shapiro, and Castaldo 2007)

As one of the authors of that study, I strongly suspect that it's already badly out of date, reflecting something predating a true Web 2.0 sensibility. In any case, the various lists of ranked criteria produced by all these surveys of editors have not yet helped to produce a clear, widely accepted definition of what "good" means in "good story" or "good journalism." Bogart has said that the assessment of quality in journalism remains "as murky as critical judgment of poetry, chamber music or architecture" because the field's accomplishments are "as intangible as those of any art" (2004, 40, 44).

Journalism's "Values" and "Elements"

I know all these lists of indicators are a bit dizzying—relax, no one expects you to memorize them. But I hope you'll bear with me for just two more before we move on to try to draw their wisdom together.

The first comes from Mark Deuze (n.d.), a self-described "academic, author, blogger, tweeter, metalhead, brabo" who teaches communications at Indiana University Bloomington. (Nope, I don't know what a brabo is, either.) Deuze suggests that working journalists share a common "occupational ideology"—a "collection of values, strategies and formal codes characterizing professional journalism and shared most widely by its members"—whose essential elements can be recognized worldwide. This ideology can be described, according to Deuze, under the headings of "five ideal-typical traits or values," which are as follows:

- **Public service:** Journalists provide a public service (as watchdogs or "newshounds," active collectors and disseminators of information).
- **Objectivity:** Journalists are impartial, neutral, objective, fair and (thus) credible.
- **Autonomy:** Journalists must be autonomous, free and independent in their work.
- **Immediacy:** Journalists have a sense of immediacy, actuality and speed (inherent in the concept of "news").
- **Ethics:** Journalists have a sense of ethics, validity and legitimacy. (2005, 445–447)

But few have done more to help spell out the "elements" of good journalism than journalist-researcher team Bill Kovach and Tom Rosenstiel (2007), who drew together a series of discussions over a two-year period in the name of the Committee of Concerned Journalists to offer comprehensive and illustrated descriptions of how journalists themselves define their common purpose and principles. They began by stating the social purpose of journalism: to "provide people with the information they need to be free and self-governing." Then, they set out what is needed to achieve this goal in nine "elements," adding a tenth to the book's second edition. These are as follows:

1. Journalism's first obligation is to the truth.
2. Its first loyalty is to citizens.
3. Its essence is a discipline of verification.
4. Its practitioners must maintain an independence from those they cover.
5. It must serve as an independent monitor of power.
6. It must provide a forum for public criticism and compromise.
7. It must strive to make the significant interesting and relevant.
8. It must keep the news comprehensive and proportional.
9. Its practitioners must be allowed to exercise their personal conscience.
10. Citizens, too, have rights and responsibilities when it comes to the news. (5–6)

Okay, that's it for the available lists—or at least some of the main ones. If you glance back over them now, I expect you'll notice some themes that crop up again and again even if the words vary. In the rest of this chapter, I'm going to draw these themes together in a way that suggests a fair consensus on the key aspects of quality journalism.

In Search of Consensus

Can we produce from the survey results and proposed "values" and "elements" a template for quality-control standards in newsrooms? Hardly.

For one thing, journalists treasure their autonomy, and don't like the sense of being managed. They generally see themselves more as craftspeople than as professionals, and therefore see no impetus for spelling out quality criteria. Their shared values are more apt to be tacit assumptions based on handed-down common experience. As Ida Schultz (2007), a Danish researcher, puts it:

> What constitutes a good news story is often very evident for journalists, while a new intern or a visiting ethnographer will need some time and experience before the good news story becomes evident or even recognisable. (194)

Another reason the lists of quality indicators are not used in newsrooms is that news organizations are so varied. Although two daily papers serving mid-size cities may have similar practices and cover similar stories, there are big differences between their routines and those of large national papers, community and alternative weeklies, local and national TV, and the growing number of entrepreneurial web-based operations. As journalism becomes more diffuse in form and process, clarity about quality criteria is bound to become more, not less, elusive.

All the same, I don't think we need to give up on the idea of clearly and concisely describing what "good" journalism is—any more than we should stop expecting engineers and electricians, midwives and mechanics, police officers and public servants to understand and emulate the best practices of their domains. And although there are many ways to capture that understanding, I believe the studies of journalists' values point to core ideas that can be expressed under just five reasonably simple headings. Each of these headings describes an aspect of the actual practice of our discipline:

- **Discovery:** seeking information
- **Examination:** subjecting that information to scrutiny
- **Interpretation:** figuring out the story being told by the information
- **Style:** using the language of text, sound, and/or images to craft the story
- **Presentation:** engaging communities in the crafted story

These five proposed headings are not especially original. They are adapted from the study of rhetoric (loosely, the techniques of communication) as described by generations of thinkers going back to the times of Aristotle in Greece and Quintilian in Rome (Shapiro 2010). And I think they may apply to any work of journalism, whether it's conveyed in text, sound, or video, whether printed or broadcast or webcast. What I am suggesting is that if a work of journalism is to be any good, then the journalist or journalists responsible for it must have performed disciplined work in *all* of these five respects. Let's look into them, one by one.

Discovery

This first aspect of journalists' work comprises a few utterly foundational activities. First, a reporter, editor, photographer, or producer—or a team of several people—fix on a reporting idea or focus. A more academic crowd would call this a research question:

- Why have the potholes on Rutter Street not been fixed?
- What keeps Taliban militants fighting in Afghanistan?
- What's it like to race sled dogs from Whitehorse to Fairbanks?
- Who can get the Maple Leafs into the playoffs?
- Is Mark's Work Wearhouse really in merger talks with American Apparel, and if so, who came up with that idea?

Having determined a question, the journalist or team formulates a research strategy:

- Who am I going to call?
- What do I need to know first?
- What pictures do I need to get?

... and sets out on the hunt for answers.

What makes journalism good when it's seen as Discovery? Good journalism is the product of a vigorous curiosity; its choice of subject matter is focused, original, and relevant to its audience; the story or picture or interactive feature will interest and benefit citizens, shed light on what life's like, and even make a difference.

How can we know when the work of Discovery is done well? That involves looking not just at the published result but at the reporter's methods. Did she start out knowing (or thinking she knew) what the "truth" was, or did she actively seek out answers with an open mind? How widely did she cast the net for new sources, to represent not just predictable perspectives but knowledge and experience from various sectors of the community? Were just official sources relied on or did the reporter seek independent knowledge? What promises were made to sources? How imaginative and open-ended were the questions that the reporter asked? Who was in, and who was left out of, the picture? To what extent did the journalist's own experiences in life and work affect, enrich, or diminish her ability to probe to the roots of the issues?

At the root of much of this is the journalist's *stance*—the position adopted toward the subject matter, and toward the task of choosing and investigating issues and events. Many journalists believe in and advocate for specific positions, and journalists, being human beings, will inevitably carry their interests and biases into their work. All the same, most journalists aspire to some degree of impartiality in the conduct of that work. In other words, an underlying standard of Discovery is that *journalists are independent observers of events*. This is not to say they have achieved or can achieve the mental state of "objectivity." But their methods should reflect a self-conscious striving to be uninfluenced by personal connections; if not, such vested interests should be declared and managed.

Examination

If Discovery is a hunt for information, Examination is a test of what that information is worth. As discoverers, journalists read, view, or probe the findings, views, feelings, and experiences of other people, but as examiners, we ask ourselves whether we believe them! As the old saying goes, journalists are not stenographers. Kovach and Rosenstiel wrote that "the essence of journalism is a discipline of verification" (2007, 79). When we do quality work, we apply tests that allow us to form a conclusion about the truth of what we have been told and about whether what we have learned from different sources is consistent.

Examination can, and often does, lead to further Discovery. Let's say I talked to works city manager Sal Di Vito (*Discovery*), and he told me that Rutter Street's potholes are caused by excess traffic. So I check a traffic database (*Examination*). This confirms that Rutter is one of the busiest streets in town, but it also tells me that nearby Easy Street, paved at the same time, is even busier than Rutter. So I go out and take a look at Easy (*Discovery*) and take some pictures: the asphalt is as smooth as a football field. I call Di Vito and ask how come Easy's not rutted (*Examination*); he says, "Sometimes, a pothole is just a pothole," and hangs up. So I start wondering who repaired each street, what materials they used, and what they were paid … and I go on discovering and examining my discoveries until I believe I have uncovered the truth of why Easy's clean and Rutter's rotten.

Sometimes, we're involved in Discovery and Examination all at once: Talking to Di Vito, I might ask, "Who repaired Easy Street?" (*Discovery*) and then, "How do you know that?" (*Examination*). But seeking out purported facts, on the one hand, and testing their veracity and coherence, on the other, are still separate ways of thinking and acting. But how can I ever know that a piece of information is true, with sufficient certainty to merit publication? This is one of the toughest questions surrounding quality in journalism. We don't have the kind of clear evidentiary standards that scientists have—in different situations, we will accept different answers to questions such as the following:

- Which facts require verification?
- What constitutes adequate verification?
- Is verification required before publication of the news story (rather than afterward, in follow-up stories or in readers' responses)?

Some magazines, but not all, employ "fact-checkers" to verify facts following an established routine and standards; a few newspapers, at least in the United States, contact sources for partial prepublication reviews of sensitive or major stories, sometimes including "read-backs" of quotes and story segments (Smith 2008, 71; Stoltzfus 2006). Studies in North America and Europe have cast serious doubt on journalists' rigour in verification (O'Neill and O'Connor 2008; Lewis et al. 2008; Machill and Beiler 2009; Jones 2009; Owen 2003; Project for Excellence in Journalism 2005). It's even been suggested that verification isn't a feasible goal for routine news reporting, but the greater the importance or sensitivity of the story, the clearer it is that strict verification is required prior to publication (Rosner 2009).

One of the most novel, and difficult, questions raised by the way the Web transforms journalism today concerns whether prepublication verification is still important. After all, some say, if we get something wrong it will soon be corrected by user comments and social-media buzz. Some have gone further, arguing that the work of journalism is improved when the research and reporting itself is done under the glare of the social Web, benefiting from the ongoing responses of what used to be called the "audience": "by exposing our work transparently we invite audience participation and engagement early in the story's development. We encourage would-be readers of the final piece to help us shape the story, make it better, make it stronger, make it deeper and more true. We deliberately blur the line between author and audience. We want our audience to help us tell their story. We want to open source our journalism" (MacPhail 2009).

The lack of consensus on—and growing confusion over—what constitutes "best practices" for corroboration is one of the most conspicuous gaps in the quality standards of modern journalism. But for now, the culture of the best newsrooms is still one of skepticism: "If your mother says she loves you," a veteran will say, "check it out" (Chepesiuk, Howell, and Lee 1997, 68). So, what is "good" journalism under the heading of Examination? It is a journalism of verification. *Journalists take rigorous and clearly evident efforts to ensure accuracy.* If you tell me you own 100 oil wells in Venezuela, and I speak to your spouse and he says so too, is that adequate confirmation? Nope. Will I put it in my story? Not until you, or I, prove it.

Quality journalism doesn't rest only on interviews and email exchanges; it includes viewing documentary evidence and conducting bibliographic research; it may involve data-mining techniques and statistical analysis. It certainly involves distinguishing between reliable web sources (Statistics Canada, the Encyclopedia Britannica) and those that are unverified (Ask.com, Facebook). Good journalists are skeptical; they are interested in balance and fairness; they keep careful research records. Journalists avoid credulousness and seek independent confirmation both of individual facts and those facts' interrelationships. (See also Chapter 9, "Journalistic Research as Critical Thinking.")

Interpretation

A reporter's notebook may contain hundreds of facts, each of them examined and duly verified, but transcribing those facts into a computer file will not make them a story. The facts must be interpreted—the storyteller asks, What do these facts add up to?—and then arranged into a coherent narrative. The great Roman speechmaker Quintilian wrote that "arrangement is to oratory what generalship is to war" (1920, s. 7.10.13). For the journalist, interpretation means reflecting the facts' "meaning"—adding value to the "bare facts" by helping people figure out what to make of them.

If Examination involves something approaching a scientific detachment in testing for accuracy and coherence, Interpretation is a more passionate and intuitive affair, in which a journalist looks at the findings with both heart and mind engaged. To tell a story is (as historiographer Hayden White wrote) to find that events possess "a structure, an order of meaning, that they do not possess as mere sequence" (1987, 5, 44). The storyteller finds the connections between facts, the ways in which events affect other events, the ways in which people make history happen (Abbott 2002, 36–48).

If we view journalism as Interpretation (sense-making), what makes the work "good"? For one thing, we must look for *depth of analysis*—the intellectual scrutiny that's applied in order to illuminate the underlying meaning of the facts. We also seek *emotional engagement*—understanding the struggles and joys, hopes and tragedies, achievements and mistakes of fellow human beings. Plus, we want to see as much *breadth of context* as the circumstances allow: Is manager Di Vito solely responsible for those potholes, or are the city budget, its tax base, provincial and federal subsidies, the tender process, or even corruption part of the picture?

IN PRACTICE

A Paradigm Shift

The interpretive contribution of journalism has never been more vital than today, when so much information is directly available from primary and other sources, and when verification may arguably take place in the public space of the Web. Jane Singer (1997), a journalism professor at Colorado State University in Fort Collins, conducted a study of metro reporters and editors and described their attitude to stories this way:

> These journalists see themselves as professionals whose job is not just to gather information and shape it into a story but also to make sense of it for their readers. That emphasis on the interpretive role—and on the need to be a credible and fair source of interpretation in a world in which credibility is becoming harder to judge and fairness harder to come by—is especially strong. … [A] paradigm shift is occurring, in which the journalist's core function is changing from mere transportation of information to its processing. (15)

Here, some basic human values come into play, and should. The honest journalist will ask him or herself questions such as, Is this interpretation fair to all concerned? Am I getting things out of proportion? Am I giving too much emphasis to one side of the story? These questions raise even more tricky issues about the degree to which storytelling technique—and the constraints and opportunities of text, graphics, sound, and visuals—can shape and even distort the way a story is told. Good storytellers blend "showing" (scenes, details, point of view, quotations, and dialogue) and "telling" (summary, explanation, and transitions) in careful proportions; they select and omit details strategically but honestly; they see the narrative power of controversy, conflict, and contrast, but they neither invent nor exaggerate it.

Transparency is one of the pervasive issues underlying the questions just listed. *Good journalism is open to appraisal.* For instance, creative narration has the potential to obscure key facts about what lies behind the picture presented. And the necessity of selectivity should not be a licence to hide material that could change the meaning of events. Instead, journalists are expected to be transparent about their methods and to attribute both facts and opinions to their sources.

Style

Journalism encompasses both reporting and writing, both chase-production and scripting, both filming and editing. Good journalists are as concerned about content as about form; they can barely decide which matters more. Without attention to matters of Style—clarity, engagement, appeal—it's just not journalism.

You will read much more about matters of Style in the course of this book; for now, it is enough to say that quality in journalism will always be, in part, about the creative use of language, images, sound, and the full potential of whatever medium is being used. Quality in journalistic style places clarity at the top of the tree; a plain, conversational, unostentatious Style is our highest goal. We want reading to be easy, viewing to be instantly engaging, navigation to be intuitive. We want to engage and interact with those we used to call "audiences," to select words and images carefully for high impact. We want to choose voice, tone, pacing, and point of view that are appropriate to the topic and purpose, to use quotations and dialogue effectively.

With Style in mind, a defensible quality standard is that *journalism is edited*. In proposing this standard, I know I am entering a thicket of controversy. In a traditional newsroom, editing means that every story is vetted by at least one other journalist and usually more; the more important or controversial a story, the more likely it is to be read carefully by senior editors. But this is not necessarily the case for information posted online. Journalistic bloggers would argue vociferously and defensibly that work posted without editing qualifies as peer-reviewed through its submission to the judgment of the millions who may read and comment on it. But others would say that prepublication editorial review distinguishes a work of journalism from memoir or "sounding off," and helps to attach a degree of authority to its results.

Presentation

The line between Style and Presentation is, like most the others drawn above, somewhat shaded, and its location will in part depend on the medium being used. On a web page, Style refers to the care given to the individual elements (text, pictures, and audio, for instance), while Presentation refers to the way all these elements are gathered into one package. Within an individual feature story, Style may refer to word choice, tone, pacing, and syntax, while Presentation is about structure—the lead, the establishment of theme, the fundamental logic or "narrative arc," the ending. But, generally speaking, there's another difference, too: While Style is often the work of an individual person completing an individual item under an editor's supervision, the fruits of Presentation are seen in a bigger context—the newscast; the series; and the amalgam of effort that turns out a page of copy, pictures, video, comments, tweets, feeds, newsletters, and social-media interactions.

Presentation is, then, usually a corporate effort, involving the participation of reporters, producers, editors, photographers, videographers, illustrators, art directors, sound editors, programmers, and a growing list of others with specific skill sets. The final "product" reflects not only their collected efforts but also the nature of their interrelationships. "Good" Presentation involves attention to other kinds of relationships, too—the relationships between form and content, fact and opinion, subjects and genres. Quality in Presentation is about nuances of placement, design, and layout, about the difference between grabbiness and sensationalism.

As presenters of a final product (to the extent that any such product is ever "final"), journalists are concerned not only with luring and engaging audiences but also with ensuring that some important values are maintained. They seek to avoid unnecessary harm to people, to ensure that the whole truth is told despite legal and practical constraints, and to steer clear of conflicts of interest, including the conflict between a publication's business and editorial goals. For good journalism to be presented, the editorial team must be able to function as independently as possible of influence from shareholders and government. Their work must be presented without regard to personal loyalties, and without concern over whether an advertiser might be offended. The primary allegiance of journalists must be to the community they serve; their choices offer prominence to examinations of issues and events without undue regard to their popularity or public acceptability, and expose citizens to a wide variety of points of view. In short, *journalism must be uncensored.*

The Next Level: Excellence

Under each of the above five headings, I have suggested what I have called a "quality" parameter. What I mean to suggest is that journalism is not good journalism unless all five of the following statements is true: it is independent, it is accurate, it is open to appraisal, it is edited, and it is uncensored. These are *minimum* standards for quality journalism.

But beyond minimum standards, there is a world of greater possibility. If we work hard enough at the details and the vision of journalism, we hope that sometimes, perhaps often, perhaps even usually, we might attain excellence. Quality is about doing work that's good enough, but excellence is about doing the best journalism possible.

What might excellence look like? Here, again, I suggest, we may find guidance in the five core activities that comprise true journalism.

- **Discovery:** Excellence in reporting must have something to do with the social importance of its subject matter. While any topic can attract curiosity, and such curiosity should be left unfettered, journalism at its best aspires to leave society better for the work having been done. In other words, journalists, at their best, are *ambitious* in their goals and methods. In their best work, journalists observe, interview, and investigate as rigorously as possible, and they focus these efforts on helping citizens to understand their world better and to set the public agenda.
- **Examination:** The quintessentially journalistic act of verification can mean different things in different situations: anything from looking up a word in a dictionary to interviewing half a dozen participants in a closed-doors meeting before reporting what transpired. But the best journalism involves *undaunted* investigation. The best reporters do not choose easy paths to information; they do not rely on "usual suspect" sources, or stop their reporting at the first sign of a coherent and credible narrative. Rather, they shed light on complex topics and subject powerful people and institutions to special scrutiny. And the greater the potential impact of a story, the more demanding will be the expectation of rigour in reporting.
- **Interpretation:** To find the story hidden in the facts demands more than mere transparency. At their best, journalists seek to present facts and opinions "*in context*"—that is, in a way that is fully proportional and scrupulously fair, and that sheds light on how events transpire.
- **Style:** Journalists' best work does more than inform—it touches, stimulates, and involves communities in the story being told. So we might say that excellent journalism is *engaging* in both approach and technique.
- **Presentation:** The team effort involved in bringing the final fruits of journalism before the community, including the writing of headlines and the "packaging" of coverage, places prime value on avoidance of the yawn factor. No good purpose

is served by a bored audience changing channels. Freshness goes well beyond matters of Presentation, of course, but journalists at their best strive to be *original* in form, in substance, and in the way the two coexist.

Who is a journalist? You are, probably, if you're reading this. But what kind? To the extent that you bring your soul and your brain to this job, you're in for thrills, laughter, pain, and the satisfaction of doing a job that the world badly needs. To get good at it, better at it, *excellent* at it takes time, and practice, and severe self-criticism. And in those moments when, through determination, ethics and a refusal to settle for less, you arrive at a place that's better than "good," you'll know where you are, and you'll want to return again and again.

Meanwhile, enjoy the ride.

DISCUSSION QUESTIONS

1. Think back to a time in your life when you worked hard at something and, in the end, felt you had achieved an outcome to be proud of. What was it about the work you did that made it possible to feel that way? Do you think the work was "excellent" or merely "good," and what makes you say that?
2. In a newspaper, broadcast, or online source of journalism, identify a piece of work that you think is "good" journalism. What makes it so? Refer to the five core activities (Discovery, Examination, Interpretation, Style, and Presentation) in testing and expressing your answer.
3. Now, identify a piece of work that's substandard. What makes it so?

SUGGESTED RESOURCES

J-Source.ca, The Canadian Journalism Project. http://www.j-source.ca.

This website is filled with continually updated information and commentary about journalists' efforts to achieve quality and excellence in their work.

Kovach, Bill, and Tom Rosenstiel. 2007. *The elements of journalism: What newspeople should know and the public should expect*. Rev. ed. New York: Three Rivers Press.

REFERENCES

Abbott, H. Porter. 2002. *The Cambridge introduction to narrative*. Cambridge: Cambridge University Press.

Bogart, Leo. 2004. Reflections on content quality in newspapers. *Newspaper Research Journal* 25 (1): 40–53.

Canadian Newspaper Association. 2010. Judging guidelines [National Newspaper Awards]. http://www.nna-ccj.ca/wordpress_dev/wordpress/?page_id=104&lang=en.

Chan, Sewell. 2009. After police relent, bloggers get press credentials. *New York Times* City Room Blog, January 9. http://cityroom.blogs.nytimes.com/2009/01/09/bloggers-get-press-credentials-after-police-relent/.

Chepesiuk, Ron, Haney Howell, and Edward Lee. 1997. *Raising hell: Straight talk with investigative journalists*. Jefferson, NC: McFarland.

Deuze, Mark. n.d. User profile. http://www.blogger.com/profile/00646727527986293107.

Deuze, Mark. 2005. What is journalism?: Professional identity and ideology of journalists reconsidered. *Journalism* 6 (4): 442–464.

Gladney, George A., Ivor Shapiro, and Joe Castaldo. 2007. Online editors rate web news quality criteria. *Newspaper Research Journal* 28 (1): 55–69.

Jones, Deborah. 2009. Busted! *J-Source.ca*, May 7. http://www.j-source.ca/english_new/detail.php?id=3820.

Kovach, Bill, and Tom Rosenstiel. 2007. *The elements of journalism: What newspeople should know and the public should expect*. Rev. ed. New York: Three Rivers Press.

Lewis, Justin, Andrew Williams, Bob Franklin, Thomas James, and Nick Mosdell. 2008. *The quality and independence of British journalism: Tracking the changes over 20 years*. Cardiff, Wales: Cardiff University Press. http://www.cardiff.ac.uk/jomec/resources/QualityIndependenceofBritishJournalism.pdf.

Machill, Marcel, and Markus Beiler. 2009. The importance of the Internet for journalistic research: A multi-method study of the research performed by journalists working for daily newspapers, radio, television and online. *Journalism Studies* 10 (2): 178–203.

MacPhail, Wayne. 2009. Show students how to sculpt in a new medium. *J-Source.ca*. http://www.j-source.ca/english_new/detail.php?id=4348.

Media Bistro. 2009. Topic: Press pass/credentials. http://www.mediabistro.com/bbs/cache/t43504_1.asp.

National Post, et al. v. Her Majesty the Queen. 2009. SCC, court file no. 32601. Webcast, http://www.scc-csc.gc.ca/case-dossier/cms-sgd/webcast-webdiffusion-eng.aspx?cas=32601.

O'Neill, Deirdre, and Catherine O'Connor. 2008. The passive journalist—how sources dominate local news. *Journalism Practice* 2 (3): 487–500.

Owen, John. 2003. Now you see it now you don't. *British Journalism Review* 14 (3): 3–8.

Project for Excellence in Journalism. 2005. *The state of the news media 2005*. http://www.stateofthemedia.org/2005/.

Quintilian, Marcus Tullius. 1920. *Institutio oratoria*. Cambridge, Massachusetts: Loeb Classical Library.

Rosen, Jay. 2005. Bloggers vs. journalists is over. PressThink, January 21. http://journalism.nyu.edu/pubzone/weblogs/pressthink/2005/01/21/berk_essy.html.

Rosner, C. 2009. The higher the stakes, the more verification is required. *J-Source*. http://www.j-source.ca/english_new/detail.php?id=4020.

Schultz, Ida. 2007. The journalistic gut feeling. *Journalism Practice* 1 (2): 190–207.

Shapiro, Ivor. 2010. Evaluating journalism: Towards an assessment framework for the practice of journalism. *Journalism Practice* 4 (2).

Shapiro, Ivor, Patrizia Albanese, and Leigh Doyle. 2006. What makes journalism "excellent"? Criteria identified by judges in two leading awards programs. *Canadian Journal of Communication* 31 (2): 425–445.

Singer, Jane B. 1997. Changes and consistencies. *Newspaper Research Journal* 18 (1–2): 2–18.

Smith, Ron F. 2008. *Ethics in journalism*. 6th ed. Malden, MA: Blackwell.

Stoltzfus, Duane. 2006. Partial pre-publication review gaining favor at newspapers. *Newspaper Research Journal* 27 (4): 23–38.

White, Hayden. 1987. *The content of the form: Narrative discourse and historical representation*. Baltimore, MD: Johns Hopkins University Press.

PART TWO
Roles and Skills in the Digital Age

CHAPTER 8

Roles and Skills for Cross-Platform Reporting

Tim Currie

CHAPTER OUTLINE

Introduction

When Rob Curley invited applications for internships at the groundbreaking *Las Vegas Sun* in March 2009, he wasn't looking for people with advanced skills in web page design or a slick video resumé (Curley 2009).

As editor of the *Sun*'s new media division, Curley is head of one of the top online newsrooms in North America. He could have had—and did have—scores of applicants who were top of their class. In fact, he wanted interns with core journalism skills and, most important, a new media mindset. He wanted people who could think creatively across platforms. People who could apply traditional storytelling skills to emerging technologies. People who would know when a live chat would be appropriate or when a story could benefit from a 360-degree interactive photo. Some knowledge of HTML or video editing would be an asset. But having skills wasn't the point. Grasping the possibilities of multimedia platforms—and the willingness to learn new skills—was. "You need to be open-minded about learning to do things you've never done before," Curley (2007) stated on his blog. Reporters need to be "committed to the journalism, not the medium."

The next decade will be an exciting time to work in journalism. But it's going to be an uncomfortable ride for people who are set in their ways and unwilling to see new possibilities. Few newsroom managers want high technical proficiency from their journalists—but they do want interest in new skills and adaptability. For example, it requires little stretch of the imagination to see that mobile devices are set to profoundly change the way we deliver journalism—and the way we interact with audiences. Once GPS technology in these devices "sees" the locations mentioned in news stories, audiences will be able to easily discover the news that is all around them.

Traditional Skills Meet New Tools

Does this mean you have to be a tech nerd to survive in the coming decade? Not at all. But it does mean you should try new tools and see how they work. So when Metro Canada announced, as it did in January 2010, a partnership with foursquare.com, forward-thinking journalists took a look at foursquare for themselves. Foursquare is a social media network that allows mobile users to "check in" to a location—a restaurant, for example—so friends can see where they are. Metro promised in its announcement to begin offering alerts to point hungry wanderers to restaurant reviews on Metro's site. How do you author a restaurant review for someone who isn't just thinking about going to a restaurant but is actually there? How many geo-coding skills does a journalist need? Where will efforts such as this one lead?

Fortunately, the skills you need don't include using a crystal ball. The skills you need are traditional journalistic ones such as research and storytelling ... with a digital update. They start with basic writing and newsgathering, and grow to encompass superior audio and video production. They include strong involvement with your audience and a healthy dose of business sense. They are rounded out with solid news judgment extended to online platforms.

Jayson Taylor, multimedia editor at the *Globe and Mail*, says the people he hires to create interactive narratives possess a basic skill: "They have to be able to tell a good story—they have to be a really good journalist."[1]

Mary Sheppard, executive producer of CBC.ca, says the people she looks for are always accomplished writers who make journalistic decisions that reflect a solid understanding of their audience. "We do this story for this reason, we don't do this story for this reason. This story goes high in the lineup because it's important across the country; this story goes lower because it's not as important, or whatever—they know those things."[2]

She adds, however, that technical skills are high on her list of like-to-haves. Speaking of a recent hire, she says he has a unique skill in the news unit because he can collaborate effectively with other staff. "He's the writer—but he can talk to the web developer and he can tell him what he wants. They understand the same language."

The new skills for cross-platform reporting are all about understanding the language of each medium. Let's take a look at how those skills fit into five new roles:

- multimedia storyteller
- investigator/sense maker
- content manager
- community builder
- entrepreneur

The Roles of the New Journalist

Multimedia Storyteller

The days of "I'm a radio reporter" or "I'm a newspaper editor" are gone. Reporters in major newsrooms file stories for multiple platforms—and do it quickly and frequently. A reporter might file a radio report for 12:00 p.m. and a web update for 12:10 p.m. An editor will not only manage content for the print publication but also keep a blog and maintain a presence on Facebook.

IN PRACTICE

Stephen Northfield on Building Cross-Platform Coverage

Stephen Northfield is foreign editor of the Globe and Mail and managing editor of the multimedia series Talking to the Taliban (http://v1.theglobeandmail.com/talkingtothetaliban/) and Behind the Veil (http://www.theglobeandmail.com/news/world/behind-the-veil/). The author spoke with him about his experience in cross-platform coverage.[3]

The *Globe and Mail* has made major changes to the way it delivers online content in recent years. But according to Foreign Editor Stephen Northfield, one of the biggest is how it builds cross-platform coverage.

He says the *Globe* has evolved from using a cookie-cutter approach to interactive elements to a more nuanced consideration of each tool's strengths and weaknesses. "It used to be like there was a box we ticked off: We'll have an online chat tomorrow or we'll do a blog about it or something," he says. "Now that we've had some experience with it, we can talk about what actually works. Because sometimes online chats don't work and blogs don't work."

Now, he says, editorial staff discuss which particular online technique will do the best job of furthering the story. "The thing that has really changed for me is the recognition that every news story can be enhanced by having an online component and in some ways the online component actually overruns the news story itself," he says.

Northfield was managing editor for two major investigative series. The *Globe* published Talking to the Taliban in March 2008. The print and online series, which involved a number of interviews with Taliban fighters in Afghanistan, won a 2009 Emmy Award in the New Approaches to News and Documentary category. It also won a 2008 Online Journalism Award in the category of Investigative Journalism (Large Site). The Flash-based site included videos, timelines, and graphics to tell the story of Taliban fighters and their motivations to fight.

The second project was the Behind the Veil series, published in September 2009. This investigative feature looked at the lives of women in the Kandahar region of Afghanistan. The online component included content such as features on Pashtunwali, Afghan tribal law—"stuff that you really don't have room for in a newspaper."

"What a package like this says to the reader is you can spend five minutes, but you can also spend five hours," Northfield says. "And if you want to go deeper, we can take you in all sorts of different directions."

Creating newspaper content is a redactive exercise in which editors are constantly compressing a story to its essence, whereas web editors focus on expanding content, he says. The print audience is looking for a strong linear narrative, while the online audience is looking for a "cafeteria-style of presentation that lets readers get everything they want."

Integrating content across platforms is an increasingly important skill, Northfield says, and understanding how people consume content is an important first step. This includes understanding which kinds of stories work in which medium.

"Disasters are terrible print stories," he says, explaining that the flood of information ignores production deadlines. "The final evolution of this will be—and we're really not there yet—when we start saying 'That's a completely online story' and 'That's not even a print story at all.'"

It also means understanding that each medium has its own set of values.

"I'm pushing hard with our correspondents—whose impulses are to make all their online stuff perfect—to say: What works really well is just 90 seconds of you standing up and having someone point a camera at you," he says. "It will look like the film you took of your family at Disney World, but you know what? It's fine. Because people's expectations are different."

Journalists need to know how storytelling and interactive tools work, he says, but they don't need to master them. In big organizations such as the *Globe and Mail*, he says, the ability to work in teams and to coordinate the work of designers, editors, and programmers is key. "They need to understand the strengths and weaknesses of different ways of telling stories online and in print—and to be forceful in arguing where to put limited time and resources."

In fact, Northfield says, the jack-of-all-trades model doesn't work well in large organizations. "The danger here is that we know a little bit about how to do everything. But we don't know a lot about the things we really do the best. There's a real role within a news organization for people who are specialists. For web people who are really good with the web stuff, building websites, posting stories, understanding what works well. And then people who are oriented towards print. And working together."

"I don't think we should demand that everybody know what's happening inside the box," he adds. "They need to understand how these things work in terms of how they can tell an effective story."

The Taliban and Veil series were "institutionally exhausting," Northfield says. The future is finding ways to produce smaller, more focused cross-platform coverage.

"We need the big epic," he says. "But we need to figure out how to do the sitcom version as opposed to the three-hour, full-length movie version."

Committing yourself to journalism on any platform doesn't necessarily mean delivering it on all platforms. A key skill for the new journalist is understanding the strengths of each medium. At its most basic, it's understanding that some stories work better when told in a particular form. For example, a story filled with emotion works best in broadcast. The viewer can see the worry etched in the face of a person awaiting a kidney transplant. The listener can hear the exuberance in the winning team's dressing room. However, a story rich in numbers will work better in print or online.

At a higher level, it means understanding that the delivery platform is a consideration. Television viewers appreciate high production values and an engaging narrative. However, web viewers of video gravitate to short clips. Further, they will typically forgive—even welcome—amateur production values, finding a level of realism in imperfect lighting and awkward framing.

An even more nuanced understanding involves an appreciation of the audiences that different services attract. So, on the Internet, your Facebook audience might be younger and more interested in lifestyle issues. Your Twitter audience, on the other hard, might be older and more focused on news and business.

Audiences are fragmenting and the key is to reach them in the medium they prefer.

The ideal that a single reporter can do it all still exists. The image of the backpack journalist has been around since the early days of the Web: the mobile correspondent reaching into a kit bag to pull out the right tool for the right story, moving effortlessly from platform to platform, telling stories in the medium best suited to it. In reality, few journalists are expert storytellers in more than one medium. Nevertheless, the dream seems closer than ever.

For starters, a journalist's kit bag is a lot smaller than it was ten years ago. Today, an HD video camera with a good microphone provides excellent-quality video, stills, and audio for almost any form of storytelling. Radio reporters, however, will want a dedicated audio recorder for top quality. But the need for a separate still camera is waning, as many newsrooms now want HD video from which they can also pull stills.

"As far as photojournalism goes, we'll probably never hire a photographer-only again," says the *Globe*'s Taylor.

The new reporting environment means reporters need, at minimum, proficiency in audio, video, and image editing. Extended to the Internet, these skills involve tighter editing and closer visual cropping. The new reporting environment means reporters must think visually at all times, but remember that good quality audio is crucial: Viewers will brave poor video quality but will bail on poor audio. It means reporters must understand that an audio slideshow is sometimes more effective than a video.

It means outstanding writing skills are an absolute must. The highway to irrelevance is littered with typos, misspelled names, and sentences that have four verbs. Even a reporter who produces work mainly for radio will need to take competent photos for use on the Web and write captions. In days past, some reporters in broadcasting could get by with a shaky grasp of spelling and grammar—enough to write a phonetic intro for a radio story or a name and job title on screen. Not anymore.

Ultimately, the new reporting environment means we need to accelerate everything we do. A reporter's job is increasingly tied to the Internet and continuous updates.

As the news cycle tightens, the deadline on breaking stories becomes minutes, not hours away.

How has the new reporting environment affected a reporter working for a major broadcaster? He or she might cover a train derailment like this:

- Arrive on scene with a camera operator.
- Tweet the situation for followers.
- Conduct newsgathering.
- Provide a live-to-air radio report.
- Confirm facts with the newsdesk for website update.
- Return to the newsroom.
- Edit a video report for the evening TV newscast.
- Check for reaction online and engage with those who have commented.
- Take a deep breath.

Investigator/Sense Maker

When was the last time your web search returned fewer than 10,000 results? Information scarcity is not the issue it once was. We're awash in information. We can subscribe to email announcements of Supreme Court of Canada decisions, tweets from members of Parliament, and blog updates from local activists. We can find the name of the person who bought the building across the street, the quarterly earnings of the grocery chain we shop at, and how much our Cabinet representative spent on lunch last year—all from our home computer.

Canadians *can* do all these things—but most don't. They either don't know they can, don't have the time, or, more likely, don't have the ability to make sense of it all. Few Canadians can decipher a corporate earnings report or assess the relevance of a court decision. Journalists have always had a key role in investigating and explaining complex issues to their audience. But that role is more important than ever today. Canadians choose their own sources of information—citizen media, professional blogs, expert podcasts, business mailing lists—and they are better for it. But they are also bombarded by slick corporate ad campaigns, rumours, and half-truths spread virally in social media.

The journalist's job is to provide an anchor in the whirl of comment, hype, and talking points. To sort through what's important, what's relevant, and what's false. To expose the stories of real people amid rules, procedures, and laws. So-called citizen journalists can lay the foundation for great stories by bearing witness to important events with what we call user-generated content. They might contribute a cellphone video of a bus accident or a photo of high-rise window washers failing to use safety harnesses. But few will tie that accident to a history of failed mechanical inspections or those practices to lax adherence to workplace safety rules.

The role of the new journalist is to integrate the efforts of eager citizens—to take raw content from mere observation and supply verifiable meaning. In essence, journalists are the information experts for their communities. This role requires knowing what information you have a right to, how to access it, how to interpret it, and how to identify its relevance.

Think you're pretty good at using Google? That's a start. Much of the best information is available in databases online, but not in commercial search engines. Part of your job is knowing when to Google someone's name and comb through the results, and when to search for that name in a provincial land registry or a directory.

Being an information expert means being a computer enthusiast. It doesn't necessarily mean being a technical expert, but being eager to explore digital information. That means learning how to form advanced search queries and sort data in a spreadsheet.

Finally, a crucial skill for the new journalist is being able to discern what's *not* available online, for example, what's in the library or in the memory of a retired worker. As good as computers are for finding information, a journalist's best tool is still a cellphone.

Content Manager

In fall 2009, CBC Ottawa produced a series involving cross-platform coverage of health officials struggling to prepare the National Capital Region for the H1N1 virus. The radio coverage of Swine Flu: Ready or Not included interviews with health administrators. The TV coverage looked at preparations at homeless shelters. The online coverage included a timeline of key dates in the development of the H1N1 vaccine (Peloquin 2009).

The swine flu series took weeks to prepare. But the challenges of managing coverage across platforms are equally complex with smaller breaking news stories.

In January 2010, the *Toronto Star* covered the impact of Toyota Canada's halting sales of its most popular vehicles because of a problem involving sticky gas pedals (Associated Press 2010). The coverage began with an Associated Press wire story posted on TheStar.com in the late afternoon. The *Star*'s staff followed the story immediately with postings on Twitter and on Facebook, and shortly thereafter with a news alert via email. Staff updated the story over the next couple of hours with files from the Canadian Press. They built the coverage further with local stories on the Web and in the newspaper the next day.

The variations of cross-platform coverage are endless. A Saturday feature in a daily newspaper might consist of photos and text—but it will also point readers to the website for slideshows and video. The evening TV news will send viewers online to post comments.

Multiplatform journalism is the product of many people working together to turn chaos into streamlined coverage. The *Globe*'s Taylor says the news organization looks for people who understand a cross-platform workflow involving photographers, graphic designers, multimedia producers, and page designers. "An absolutely key component is being able to navigate the newsroom and find out who does what. If you're going to be a multimedia journalist you need to know who all the players are and how to get all the players moving at the same speed," he says. It requires solid news judgment and also an intimate understanding of one's audience.

Editors advance stories as the day progresses by adding layers of detail. Depending on the story and size of the news organization, they might do the following:

- issue basic facts first via news alerts and on social networks
- establish the story with radio reports and stories on the Web
- build the coverage visually with video for the Web or the next TV newscast
- prepare in-depth coverage for the next day's newspaper
- advance the story with reaction and context on the next day's radio and TV current affairs shows through reports, interviews, and radio phone-ins

On the Web, there are more ways to advance stories that require deft editing skills:

- **Live-stream video:** It can be used to cover events such as testimony at a public inquiry or the announcement of a winning bid for a major sporting event.
- **Interactives:** They deepen the audience's understanding of a story with timelines, maps, and polls.
- **Backgrounders:** They establish context for issues by explaining the history of an issue and providing links to source documents.
- **Web resources:** They point your readers to valuable content online.

Community Builder

"My readers know more than I do." That was Dan Gillmor's astute observation in his influential 2004 book *We the Media*, and it's a phrase every journalist can benefit from repeating. Gillmor's point is that journalists who adopt a lone-wolf attitude today are likely to find themselves beat by competitors who harness the knowledge of their audience. Call it the wisdom of crowds, strength in numbers, or an open-source workflow. It's about using your audience to improve your reporting; it's about your audience using you to make sense of their lives. News organizations that have built highly engaged communities have a natural support network for their journalism. They are positioned to get better stories, find more informed sources, achieve greater accuracy in their reporting, and have a more loyal audience base.

In radio, engagement is more than having record numbers of listeners, it's about getting people to phone in with comments and suggest ideas for stories. On the Web, it involves more than just acquiring Facebook fans or accumulating page views on a website. Media managers have come to consider online audience measures such as page views, or even unique visitors, as ineffective to useless. Publishers—and advertisers—see little value in the people who spend five seconds scanning a story and then disappear into the virtual crowd. They now focus on engagement—how long people spend on a website and what they do. Do they share the content? Click on interactives? Comment?

It sounds easy, but building engagement takes a lot of time and work. The *Globe and Mail*, the *New York Times*, and the BBC have communities editors dedicated to the task. At smaller organizations, however, you're it.

Building engagement is more difficult than simply installing a website commenting system or pumping headlines into Twitter. Communities rarely form themselves. The communities that do often consist of cranks and bigots who have long since annoyed or scared off reasoned thinkers and political moderates. Communities need nurturing and focus, which means being present and visible wherever your community is debating important issues online. The rewards for forming communities successfully are considerable—communities attract advertisers and advertisers bring money.

Tools that you can use to help build communities online include the following:

- **Social media:** Establish a Facebook fan page or build a following on Twitter. Build engagement by responding to comments, and re-posting or re-tweeting the best of them.
- **Blog:** Showcase your thoughts using a popular service such as Blogger or WordPress.
- **Live blog:** Offer moment-by-moment updates on a breaking story and engage the audience using a collaborative online tool such as CoveritLive.
- **Editors' blog:** Explain editors' decisions on topics such as story selection, editorial policy, or use of graphic images. In January 2010, for example, the BBC Editors Blog explained why editors don't report the number of Taliban casualties in Afghanistan (Wyatt 2010).
- **Hosted chat:** Involve audiences with reporters and newsmakers who answer questions on an important topic of the day. TheGlobeandMail.com frequently hosts these types of chats.
- **Website comments:** Moderate the reaction to stories online. Guide the discussion but act as a gatekeeper when subjects such as religion, sexuality, or death attract hateful or libelous comments.
- **Citizen media:** Integrate user-generated content into news coverage. News organizations such as the BBC and CNN encourage people to be part of the newsgathering process by using everything from storm photos to cellphone video (for example, see CNN iReport at www.ireport.com).

Strategies for building communities can include offering perks to the most active members, such as a free subscription to the newspaper or insider access to the editorial board. Building communities requires a complex but important skillset that involves the ability to frame a discussion, guide its evolution, feed it when it lags, and cool it when it boils over. It also requires the following:

- **Sharing:** Modify your workflow to make it more open and interactive.
- **Curating:** Be a filter and a guide for your audience, directing them to important content around the Web by linking and commenting on it.
- **Aggregating:** Become a centre for knowledge about your community.
- **Strategizing:** Set goals for your community—not just in the number of users, but in the volume and quality of their chatter.

Entrepreneur

Journalists have long left business matters to the suits working downstairs. The difficulty of getting a broadcast licence or buying a printing press insulated news outlets from new competitors. Not anymore. Content and the money that supports it are intimately linked.

If anything is clear in the rapidly changing media landscape, it is that the market is fragmenting. There will always be large institutional media outlets, but there will

Figure 8.1 Amber MacArthur began her journalism career as a media and technology specialist, but with her keen entrepreneurial skills has created a very successful career as a public speaker, strategist, author, and new media host and producer. (PHOTO: Sam Javanrouh/TopLeftPixel.com.)

also be nimble, niche news organizations such as British Columbia's *TheTyee.ca*, and business and political news outlet *AllNovaScotia.com*. And, of course, bloggers—professional and amateur.

As news organizations fold and others start up, journalists are adopting a credo familiar to entrepreneurs: "Fail early and often." The need to try new things and figure out how to make money is crucial—particularly when online stories can be ranked according to the number of people who view them and the ad money they bring in.

As a result, few journalists can expect to work at a single news organization for their entire career. Many will change cities and jobs multiple times. They will switch focus between broadcast, online, and print. They will jump from contract worker to full-time staffer and back again. Whether they work alone or with others, they will need to bring a spirit of entrepreneurship to their work that will spur the development of new editorial products (Glaser 2008). They will need the ability not only to create content but also to drive audiences to it.

You might not need a business degree, but if you have an idea for a new journalism venture, you'll need basic skills in the following areas to bring it about:

- **Market research:** Identify your audience—Is it young or old? How big is it? Is it growing?
- **Strategizing:** Create a business plan, get funding, and measure progress.
- **Marketing:** Understand how advertising works—particularly online—and be able to build a social media strategy.
- **Accounting:** Understand basic billing and payroll.

And don't forget about your own image. It's risky to tie your reputation to a single media outlet. The upheaval in the news business means you need to continually broadcast your assets. It's standard practice for employers to research their hires in social media networks before they offer any contracts. But you can't build your reputation in social media or position yourself highly in search results overnight. In short, you need to treat yourself as a brand. It means you need a personal website and at least a cursory understanding of how to promote your content in search engines (search engine optimization). It means you need to be active in social media and aggressive in maintaining your reputation online.

NOTES

1. Jayson Taylor (multimedia editor, the *Globe and Mail*), in a telephone interview with Tim Currie, December 2, 2009.
2. Mary Sheppard (executive producer, CBC.ca), in a telephone interview with Tim Currie, October 7, 2009.
3. Stephen Northfield (journalist, the *Globe and Mail*), in a telephone interview with Tim Currie, October 9, 2009.

DISCUSSION QUESTIONS

1. A commercial airliner has disappeared from radar east of Winnipeg. How would you build cross-platform multimedia coverage of this story over the next 12 hours?
2. Google yourself. What image do you portray online? How would you improve it?
3. Your city is hosting a big hockey tournament 30 days from now and your news organization is planning extensive coverage. What could you do to drive traffic and engagement on your website both before and during the event?

SUGGESTED RESOURCES

Mashable. http://mashable.com.
This blog offers social media news and tips.

PBS MediaShift. http://www.pbs.org/mediashift/.
This news and commentary site tracks emerging media forms.

Teaching Online Journalism. http://mindymcadams.com/tojou/.
This multimedia reporting blog is hosted by University of Florida professor Mindy McAdams.

REFERENCES

Associated Press. 2010. Toyota suspends sales of recalled vehicle. *Toronto Star*, January 26. http://www.thestar.com/business/article/756220--toyota-suspends-sales-of-recalled-vehicles.

Curley, Rob. 2007. What sort of things should an aspiring journalist be thinking about? RobCurley.com, January 14. http://robcurley.com/2007/01/14/what-sort-of-things-should-an-aspiring-journalist-be-thinking-about/.

Curley, Rob. 2009. Want an internship that might actually help you get a journalism job, even in this rotten economy? RobCurley.com, March 23. http://robcurley.com/2009/03/23/want-an-internship/.

Gillmor, Dan. 2004. *We the media: Grassroots journalism by the people, for the people.* Sebastopol, CA: O'Reilly.

Glaser, Mark. 2008. In digital age, journalism students need business, entrepreneurial skills. PBS MediaShift, January 30. http://www.pbs.org/mediashift/2008/01/in-digital-age-journalism-students-need-business-entrepreneurial-skills030.html.

Metro Canada. 2010. Metro and Foursquare announce groundbreaking partnership. *MetroNews.ca*, January 26. http://www.metronews.ca/toronto/canada/article/430567--metro-and-foursquare-announce-groundbreaking-partnership.
Peloquin, Christine. 2009. Key dates in the development of H1N1 vaccine. *CBC.ca*, November 9. http://www.cbc.ca/health/story/2009/11/06/f-swine-flu-vaccine-rollout-timeline.html.
Wyatt, Caroline. 2010. Reporting Afghanistan casualties. BBC—The Editors. http://www.bbc.co.uk/blogs/theeditors/2010/01/reporting_afghanistan_casualti.html.

CHAPTER 9

The Journalist as Critical Thinker

Paul Benedetti and Kim Kierans

Introduction

The problem: You are in the newsroom when three assignments hit your desk:

- A local health food store is bringing in a naturopath to lecture on detoxification diets to rid the body of built-up toxins.
- The business department received a press release about a paranormal "ghost-busting" service starting up in town.
- A former Playboy bunny and actress is in town to promote her book on how diet and vaccines caused her son's autism—and how she cured it.

CHAPTER OUTLINE

These are not invented stories. They are real "stories" that we have dealt with as reporters or teachers. They can and will come up for you. You may even recognize the last one; it's about Jenny McCarthy, who received enormous amounts of coverage for her unproven and unfounded claims about curing her young son's autism. Every day reporters and editors deal with these kinds of stories, and often they appear in print, online, or on radio and TV, uncritically presented to an audience all too willing to accept them.

As a journalist, what do you do? *How* do you decide whether to cover an event, *how* to cover it, and finally *what* to write? Difficult questions. We'll examine each of them, but first let's look at how not to respond:

- I don't make news. I just cover it. I cover anything.
- I write down what people say. I don't know whether it's all true or not.
- I just present the information and let readers decide.
- I'm neutral. That's my job.
- I just reflect the interests of our readers. They love it.
- Everyone has his or her own reality. There are many ways of "knowing." I don't judge.

You may have heard these responses—they're pretty common among some journalists and even some journalism instructors. But they don't wash. In their book, *The Elements of Journalism*, Bill Kovach and Tom Rosenstiel (2001) write: "Journalism's first obligation is to the truth." Not some big-T, philosophical Truth, but the more mundane, down-to-earth truth they call "practical truth." As journalists, we must come as close to the truth based on the assembly of verifiable facts as we can. To do less would be to fall short of the demands of the craft. We owe it to readers not to promote nonsense or purvey rumour and feed hoaxes. We owe it to readers not to sensationalize and exaggerate, not to promote quackery and its useless products and services, and not to misinform and mislead. But how do we do it?

SIDEBAR

What Makes a Good Critical Thinker?

Raymond S. Nickerson (1987), an authority on critical thinking, characterizes a good critical thinker in terms of knowledge, abilities, attitudes, and habitual ways of behaving. Here are some of the characteristics of such a thinker:

- uses evidence skillfully and impartially
- organizes thoughts and articulates them concisely and coherently
- distinguishes between logically valid and invalid inferences
- suspends judgment in the absence of sufficient evidence to support a decision
- understands the difference between reasoning and rationalizing
- attempts to anticipate the probable consequences of alternative actions
- understands the idea of degrees of belief
- sees similarities and analogies that are not superficially apparent
- can learn independently and has an abiding interest in doing so
- applies problem-solving techniques in domains other than those in which learned
- can structure informally represented problems in such a way that formal techniques, such as mathematics, can be used to solve them
- can strip a verbal argument of irrelevancies and phrase it in its essential terms
- habitually questions one's own views and attempts to understand both the assumptions that are critical to those views and the implications of the views
- is sensitive to the difference between the validity of a belief and the intensity with which it is held
- is aware of the fact that one's understanding is always limited, often much more so than would be apparent to one with a non-inquiring attitude
- recognizes the fallibility of one's own opinions, the probability of bias in those opinions, and the danger of weighting evidence according to personal preferences

Critical Thinking

The answer is critical thinking. This concept is not to be confused with "criticism," as in the judgments made by book or movie critics. Although *critical thinking* has been described in many ways, Lewis Vaughn provides a simple definition in his book *The Power of Critical Thinking*: "The systematic evaluation or formulation of beliefs or statements by rational standards" (2004, 4).

By that Vaughn means that each person—and every journalist—must ask him- or herself not *what* do I believe, but rather *why* do I believe it and whether it is worth believing. In other words, critical thinking leads us to ask, How do I think about things? and How do I decide what to believe? Vaughn (2004) writes, "Critical thinking offers us a set of standards embodied in techniques, attitudes and principles that we can use to assess beliefs and determine if they are supported by good reasons" (4). This is a key idea for journalists.

Journalist and writer Ernest Hemingway once famously wrote that any good reporter has to "develop a built-in bullshit detector." Good advice, but how do you build such a detector? Once again, the answer is critical thinking, which gives us the tools to do the following:

1. Logically assess a statement, claim, or information
2. Ask questions to help us understand, evaluate, and resolve the claim or information
3. Decide rationally, through a logical process what or what not to believe, or what is the truth

Why Do You Believe the Things You Believe?

The problem for most new reporters—and for many people—is that they aren't really sure what they think is B.S. or, more important, why they think that. Most people have not critically examined what they believe and frankly, don't even know *how* to do it. It's not their fault. Despite the fact that critical thinking is extremely important and often mentioned by employers as a key skill for new hires, it is not taught in the regular school system and most students complete college or university degrees with little or no contact with formal critical thinking instruction. As Richard Paul and Linda Elder (1996) of CriticalThinking.org point out, most people believe things for the following unchallenged reasons:

- It's true because I believe it (I assume that it is true, but I have never questioned the basis for my belief).
- It's true because we believe it (I assume the dominant beliefs of my group—family, work, political party, et cetera—even though I have never questioned the basis for those beliefs).
- It's true because I want to believe it (I believe what "feels good," what supports my other beliefs, what does not require me to change my thinking in any significant way, and what does not require me to admit I have been wrong).
- It's true because I have always believed it (I feel a strong attraction to beliefs that I have long held even though I have not seriously considered the evidence for the critique of these traditional beliefs).

- It's true because it is in my vested interest to believe it (I gravitate to beliefs that would justify my getting more power, money, or personal advantage, not noticing the evidence or reasoning against those beliefs).

Unfortunately, journalists are just as prone to these self-serving and self-deceiving ideas. It's pretty tough to decide what to accept and what to reject, what makes sense and what does not, what is truth, and what is fabrication, delusion, or worse (if you haven't given a moment's thought to *what* you believe and *why* you believe it). See Box 9.1 and test your beliefs.

BOX 9.1 Critical Thinking Exercise

What do you think about these things? Why?

- haunted houses
- alien space ships
- astrology
- psychic readings
- magnetic healing bracelets
- alien abduction
- Bigfoot
- herbal remedies
- Loch Ness monster
- psychokinesis

How to Think About Weird Things ... and Everything Else

People make all kinds of claims all the time. So reporters have to be careful—it's not our job to accept these kinds of statements on faith. You just can't take a person's word as fact or truth. Yet journalists do so all the time, and that is why our profession is so poorly regarded by the public. Oddly, we tend to be highly skeptical of politicians and salespeople, but we often naively and uncritically accept many other claims.

Critical thinking gives us a toolkit we can use to examine claims, events, issues, or controversies. Mostly, it involves asking good questions—something reporters are supposed to be good at! See Box 9.2 for a handy checklist of critical thinking skills.

BOX 9.2 Checklist of Critical Thinking Skills

- Ask questions.
- Define the problem.
- Examine the evidence.
- Analyze assumptions and biases.
- Avoid emotional reasoning.
- Don't oversimplify.
- Consider other interpretations, or alternatives.
- Tolerate uncertainty. Accept tentative answers.

(Lipps 1999)

Critical Thinking Basics

Three questions can help guide the critical thinking process:

1. What is being claimed?
2. What is the evidence?
3. Is the person making the claim an authority?

What Is Being Claimed?

People claim a lot of things, and sometimes it's hard to know exactly what they are claiming. I once had a city councillor say to me: "People are upset by this proposition. I've received a lot of calls." That looks like a simple statement, but you need to ask several questions to ascertain the veracity of what she is saying. What people? How many people? How many calls? What, precisely, are they upset about? Can I talk to some (or all) of these people?

I've interviewed people who have said, "I was very ill and I used alternative medicine to cure myself." This claim is loaded with questions. What was the illness? Was it formally diagnosed? What tests did you undergo? What mainstream treatment did you receive? What kind of alternative medicine, exactly? How do you know you are cured? Have you been tested?

Finally, reporters are often faced with claims that are fuzzy or incomplete: "Crime is way up in the downtown core. It's the druggies." What are the statistics? What kind of crime? What does "way up" mean? When did it go up (IF it did)? What do you mean by "downtown core"? Who are "the druggies," and what do you mean by that term?

Claims must be clear, accurate, precise, logical, and falsifiable. Let's unpack each of those terms:

- **Clear:** If the claim isn't clear, you cannot proceed. If you don't understand the claim, ask for an example or an illustration. Ask if the source can state it another way.
- **Accurate:** The claim must be factual. If the claim is that the city is doing nothing to control wild dogs, do you know for sure that there are wild dogs in the city? Check the facts.
- **Precise:** The claim must have specific details. If someone says that a neighbourhood is dangerous, what does that person mean? If a scientist says most people are overweight, what do "most people" and "overweight" mean?
- **Logical:** The claim must make basic sense. Does it meet the standard of "common sense"? If it's obviously fanciful or plainly loony, there's not much point in pursuing it.
- **Falsifiable:** This one is a bit tricky. Can you conceive of evidence that could prove the claim to be false? If no, then it's not really a claim. For example, if a person claims that the bracelet they sell to cure arthritis gives off energy that is currently undefined and completely undetectable by all modern scientific means, then the claim is impossible to disprove and therefore meaningless. (Conspiracy theories are based on nonfalsifiable claims: Once you prove that a claim is groundless, the conspiracy theorist merely says that your proof is just another part of the conspiracy.)

Once you have clearly figured out the claim, then you can move to the next step—how to decide whether the story is true and worth running.

What Is the Evidence?

Clearly journalists cannot do stories based on unsubstantiated claims. No good journalist would accept a claim from a businessman, a politician, an activist, or a citizen without some supporting facts. Those supporting facts are called *evidence*. Evidence plays a key role in the daily working of society. You wouldn't buy a house without making sure it existed. You wouldn't buy a car without looking it over and taking it for a ride. You want evidence for these important decisions. Similarly, no jury would convict a person without solid evidence; no responsible government would license a drug without evidence that it was safe and effective; no manufacturer should be able to make a claim about its product without evidence. But all too often, journalists accept stories with either no evidence or the weakest, flimsiest kind of evidence. Why?

Because most people and many journalists do not understand what evidence is and how it is used. They don't understand the scientific method or scientific thinking. The National Science Board's (NSB) 1996 survey of Americans showed that only 2 percent understood how scientific theories are developed and tested, and only 23 percent were minimally able to explain the nature of scientific study, laments professor Jere Lipps in an article on science in the media. "In general, those responsible in the media are as uninformed about science and its processes as the general public," writes Lipps (1999).

You may argue that journalists are not scientists and that the world is not a test tube and you would be right. But without the framework of critical thinking to guide journalists, far too often they fall back on irrational ways of thinking. As Steven D. Schafersman (1991) writes in his essay "An Introduction to Critical Thinking":

> Most people are followers of authority: most do not question, are not curious, and do not challenge authority figures who claim special knowledge or insight. Most people, therefore, do not think for themselves, but rely on others to think for them. Most people indulge in wishful, hopeful, and emotional thinking, believing that what they believe is true because they wish it, hope it, or feel it to be true. Most people, therefore, do not think critically.

This kind of thinking, or lack of it, leads journalists to produce poorly researched, unsubstantiated, erroneous, and just plain bad stories. The public, many of whom are experts in their respective fields, read these stories and are appalled. It's no wonder that polls repeatedly show that journalists are held in low esteem by the public and that fewer and fewer people have confidence in the stories we produce (Project for Excellence in Journalism 2009). This reaction is particularly justified when it comes to stories about science, alternative medicine, pharmaceuticals, epidemics and other health risks, environmental issues, climate change, and a host of other complex subjects.

The following guidelines will help you produce stories based on reason and evidence. Although they are derived from the scientific method, they can be adapted for everyday use.

1. **The proponent of any claim must provide the evidence.** Or, more simply put, the person making the claim has a duty to provide the evidence. This is a key point because it shifts the "burden of proof" to the person making the claim. Anyone who proposes an engine that runs on water, a cure for cancer, or a perpetual motion machine *must* provide evidence for that claim. And reporters must demand the evidence before writing the story.
2. **"Extraordinary claims require extraordinary evidence."** This phrase is said to have originated with science writer and astronomer Carl Sagan, and it is one of the most important ideas in critical thinking. Reporters don't demand proof for everything. That would be ridiculous. People tell us their age, where they live, where they grew up, what their job is like, how they bake a cake, and we

don't usually require proof. Of course, we check our facts, we seek out second sources, and we do background research, but if we demanded proof of everything everyone told us, we would never get our stories out to the public in a timely fashion. But, the greater the claim, the higher the burden of evidence. And when people make amazing claims, then we must demand a very high level of evidence.

3. **Anecdotes and testimonials are a low form of evidence.** Although journalists live on the stories that people tell us, we have to understand that in many cases, anecdotal evidence and personal testimonials are not considered high-quality evidence. People are easily fooled. People make mistakes. People see patterns and connections where none exist. People underestimate randomness and coincidence. And people often see cause and effect where there isn't any.

   Consider people's belief in dubious therapies. For example, a person has a cold; she drinks a glass of boysenberry juice and chews ten vitamin C tablets. After four days, the cold disappears. The conclusion: Vitamin C and boysenberry juice cures the common cold. Many, many people have made the same mistake, and many reporters have written stories about cures for the common cold (and many other things) based on evidence just as flimsy. Cutting out wheat and dairy cures hyperactivity. A change in diet cures autism. Eating raw foods cures cancer. Bee stings cure multiple sclerosis. The list goes on and on. University of British Columbia professor Barry Beyerstein (2003) often lamented these kinds of stories: "Essentially, these people say: 'I tried it, and I got better, so it must be effective.' The electronic and print media typically portray testimonials as valid evidence. But without proper testing, it is difficult or impossible to determine whether this is so." Why? Because it's simply not that simple. Beyerstein also points out that there are many reasons why people may think a particular therapy, although unproven, works:

   a. **The disease may have run its natural course.** Most illnesses are self-limiting, which means that they go away on their own.
   b. **Symptoms come and go.** Many illnesses (especially chronic ones such as multiple sclerosis and arthritis) are cyclical. The symptoms get worse and get better—all on their own.
   c. **The placebo effect may be responsible.** About 30 percent of people feel better just by taking a sugar pill, or placebo. Any intervention can have a temporary positive effect and make people "feel" better.
   d. **The diagnosis may have been wrong.** People may believe that they have a disease, take a treatment, and then claim they are cured when they never had the disease in the first place.
   e. **People who have a strong psychological investment in a cure can trick themselves into thinking they are better.** As Beyerstein explains, "They may be selective in what they recall, overestimating their apparent successes while ignoring, downplaying, or explaining away their failures."

   For these reasons and others, scientists came up with the idea of experiments and controlled trials to test theories and remedies. Because people—

patients and researchers—can easily trick each other and themselves to believe what is not the case, the gold standard for testing was developed: the double-blind, placebo-controlled trial.

Evidence Based on the Double-Blind, Placebo-Controlled Trial: The Gold Standard

In this kind of test, two matched groups of people are given a treatment. One group gets the real treatment, the other group gets a placebo. The researchers and the two groups are "blinded," meaning that none of them knows which group is receiving the real drug and which is receiving the placebo. After the trial is over, this information is revealed, and the researchers see which group benefited from the drug. In this way, no one can influence the outcome of the test. This kind of careful, controlled trial is the only way to test the true efficacy of treatments and remedies. Without controlled trials, doctors and patients have convinced themselves that many strange things—from drilling holes into people's skulls to release "the demon spirits" to performing frontal lobotomies with an ice pick—actually cured people! Today, treatments and pharmaceuticals are put through this rigorous process before being offered to the public as safe and effective. The study results are peer reviewed and published in scientific journals for everyone to read and critique. Then the trials may be repeated to ensure that the outcomes were correct. That is how science works today. Even with such testing there are problems, but it's the best system we have and anything less, particularly in the field of medicine, should be considered suspect.

Obviously, this kind of advanced science—whether in medicine or engineering or physics—is difficult for the generalist journalist to navigate. So, we must rely on experts. Which leads us to the next step in the wonderful world of critical thinking: a review of the experts.

Is the Person Making the Claim an Authority?

Journalists, it's often said, know a little about a lot—at our best, we're well-informed, quick-study generalists. But that also means that we have to rely on experts for many of the stories we write. Vaughn (2004) explains that experts provide us with reasons to believe a claim because in their area of expertise they are more likely to be right than we are. Obviously experts have greater access to the right information, and they are much better equipped to judge that information. In short, they are authorities on the subject.

But how can we judge who is an expert and which experts are trustworthy? Here are some questions to consider:

- Does the person have a proper education and training in his or her field of expertise (usually from reputable, accredited institutions)? Check the person's degrees and credentials.
- What is the person's reputation among his or her peers? Lots of people have advanced degrees, but checking to see how your expert is viewed in his or her field is crucial.

- Has the person published studies in peer-reviewed journals, and has he or she published books on his or her field of expertise? What accomplishments, awards, or other professional credits has the person received?

If all of these factors check out, you can probably trust the claims and evidence provided by the expert. However, even if you can establish the authenticity of an expert, you have to be on the look out for bias that may be part of professional rivalry, political views, ideology, and conflict of interest. Some of these influences are hard to figure out, especially if time is short, but it's always a good idea to directly ask the experts if they have any connection or associations that might be pertinent to the issue at hand, and who is funding their research.

It's always good to gather more than one expert's views and to read some of the material published on the subject. If experts disagree, make sure that you have a good sense of the overall expert view in the field. Don't just line up opposing views and give up. Get a sense of the general scientific consensus and relay that to readers. Science is a process, and the best you can do is provide your audience with current thinking on any subject.

Non-Authorities, *or* Will a Real Expert Please Stand Up?

Perhaps the biggest mistake that journalists routinely make is giving expert status to people who are not experts. In critical thinking this is called *appeal to authority*, but in simple terms it is giving authority to people who don't deserve it. The following people are non-authorities:

- **Celebrities:** Just because someone is handsome or famous or talented, it does not make her or him an expert. Pamela Anderson may be a spokesperson for PETA (People for the Ethical Treatment of Animals) but she is not an expert in animal welfare or animal experimentation. Children's entertainer Raffi may have an opinion about environmental toxins, but he's no expert. And, Jenny McCarthy may have a book out about autism, but she's neither a doctor nor an autism researcher.
- **Experts in the wrong area:** Nobel laureate Linus Pauling was certainly a renowned expert in chemistry. But he became widely famous for his unorthodox views on the curative powers of vitamin C for cancer. Unfortunately, Pauling was not an expert in nutrition, vitamins, or cancer. Be careful: an expert in one field, even one with a PhD, may not have expertise in another. Despite an expert's degrees and position, his or her opinion in a field outside the area of study is worth about as much as any other non-expert. In other words, not much.
- **Victims:** A person with cancer is an expert in what it is like to have cancer, not a cancer expert. A person who has been mugged may have some valuable insight into the experience of being assaulted but is not an expert in crime or violence. Victims' stories are important and their views and opinions can be used to great effect in our stories, but don't confuse them with experts.

As well, don't make the mistake of "false balance" in your story. This term describes the habit of some journalists of pitting a dubious or non-expert or an expert with radical, fringe views against another expert who expresses the general consensus of the scientific community, suggesting to readers that this is a fifty-fifty kind of debate. It's not and it's misleading. There are, for example, history professors who are Holocaust deniers, but it would be a gross misrepresentation to do a "He said/She said" story on that basis. Doing that and then copping out by "letting the reader decide" is bad journalism.

Finally, remember that even experts should be held accountable. We should feel comfortable that they are well informed, have assessed the currently available information, and come to well-supported conclusions. In the end, the weight we give them in our stories should be based on reasoned consideration of those factors.

What Information Can You Trust on the Internet?

There is no doubt that the Web has become a gold mine of information for journalists. Before Google, reporters researching a story had to comb through the "morgue" (the paper files housed by most newsrooms), check reference books and encyclopedias, and locate and read pertinent articles and books at the library. Today, a virtually endless supply of information is a keystroke away, but the question is, How credible and reliable is that information? Information researchers have documented "the growing belief that high-quality information will be impossible to find amidst the vast amount of lower quality, unfiltered information" (Wathen and Burkell 2002).

TOOLS & TIPS

Questioning Online Content

Journalists should apply basic critical thinking skills to information they find on the Internet. Here is a helpful checklist for assessing online content, adapted from the work of Lewis Vaughn (2004) and Kathy Schrok (n.d.):

- ☐ **Who?** Who wrote the web pages? Are they experts? Are their credentials and professional associations listed? Check the credentials to make sure they are bona fide.
- ☐ **What?** What is the purpose of the website? Is it news, advertising, opinion, scholarship, commercial, satirical, activism … ? What is the information, and is it consistent with other sites on the same topic? Is it well sourced, and are there references and citations for the material? Are the sources credible, well known, and authoritative?
- ☐ **When?** When was the website created? When was it last updated? Is the information current and up-to-date?
- ☐ **Where?** Where is the website located? Is it sponsored by a school, government, or some other well-known authority or source? Check the URL extension. Is it .gov, .edu, .com, or .org, and what does that tell you?
- ☐ **Why?** What is the purpose of this website? Why did the author put it up? Is it fair and balanced? Is it biased? Why? Is it useful to you? Why should you use it?

Many websites are highly partisan propaganda vehicles using dishonest and misleading tactics including "claims of conspiracy theories, the selective use of facts, the denial of known facts, the fabrication of facts, the use of hard to understand jargon, irrelevant conclusions, and the use of ad hominem attacks against those who dispute the revisionist's version of history" (Mathson and Lorenzen 2008).

If all of this sounds like a lot of work, it is. It's easier and faster not to be a critical thinker, not to ask the tough questions, and not to check your sources and your facts. But the price of being a gullible, superficial journalist is high. At best your stories will be one-sided, incomplete, and weak; at worst they will be misleading, misinformed, and potentially damaging.

Conclusion

Carl Sagan feared for our future because of what he saw as a wave of irrational thinking spreading around the world. In his 1997 book *The Demon-Haunted World*, he wrote:

> I worry that, especially as the Millennium edges nearer, pseudoscience and superstition will seem year by year more tempting, the siren song of unreason more sonorous and attractive. Where have we heard it before? Whenever our ethnic or national prejudices are aroused, in times of scarcity, during challenges to national self-esteem or nerve, when we agonize about our diminished cosmic place and purpose, or when fanaticism is bubbling up around us—then, habits of thought familiar from ages past reach for the controls.
>
> The candle flame gutters. Its little pool of light trembles. Darkness gathers. The demons begin to stir. (24)

In the end there are two kinds of reporters: those who are critical thinkers and those who are not (see Box 9.3). Which kind do you want to be?

BOX 9.3 Critical and Non-Critical Thinkers

Critical thinkers

- are hard-working
- are clear
- are accurate
- are precise
- are relevant
- are deep
- are contextual
- are logical
- are fair to all sides
- are open-minded
- have breadth

Non-critical thinkers

- are lazy
- are prejudiced
- stereotype
- distort
- rationalize
- are prone to self-deception
- are simplistic
- jump to conclusions (impulsive)
- are unfair
- are closed-minded
- are inflexible
- react emotionally

DISCUSSION QUESTIONS

1. Choose a controversial health story such as "autism and vaccines," "wheat grass juice," or "fluoride" and type it into Google. Take the top five or ten sites and evaluate them. Are they credible? Biased? Unsupported? Balanced? What have you learned about online information?
2. Read a mainstream media story on a difficult subject such as legalizing drugs, privatizing health care, or the seal hunt. List the "experts" used in the story and research each person. Are they really experts? Are they celebrities? Activists? What are their credentials? Does the reporter "balance" her use of experts in the story?
3. Test yourself! Take a belief you have held, but have never critically examined. Perhaps you take echinacea for colds or believe gun owners commit more crimes than non-gun owners or believe that climate change is a myth. Now, seek out information and sources that *challenge* that belief. Compile and evaluate the evidence as impartially as you can. Is your belief supported?

SUGGESTED RESOURCES

Critical Thinking and Skepticism

The Committee for Skeptical Inquiry. http://www.csicop.org.

Geisler, Jill. 2005. Critical thinking: What do you mean by that? PoynterOnline, April 27. http://www.poynter.org/column.asp?id=34&aid=81581.
This article offers a terrific list of 35 individual skills for critical thinkers.

James Randi Educational Foundation. http://www.randi.org.

Quackwatch. http://www.quackwatch.org.

Skeptic [Skeptics Society]. http://www.skeptic.com.

University Libraries, University at Albany. 2009. Evaluating web content. http://library.albany.edu/usered/eval/evalweb/.

University of Wisconsin, Eau Claire. n.d. Ten C's for evaluating Internet sources: Guide. http://www.montgomerycollege.edu/Departments/writegt/htmlhandouts/Ten%20C%20internet%20sources.htm.

Woloshin, Steven, Lisa M. Schwartz, and Barnett S. Kramer. 2009. Promoting healthy skepticism in the news: Helping journalists get it right. *Journal of the National Cancer Institute* 101 (23): 1596–1599. http://jnci.oxfordjournals.org/cgi/content/full/101/23/1596.

REFERENCES

Beyerstein, Barry L. 2003. Why bogus therapies often seem to work. Quackwatch, July 24. http://quackwatch.com/01QuackeryRelatedTopics/altbelief.html.

Kovach, Bill, and Tom Rosenstiel. 2001. *The elements of journalism: What newspeople should know and the public should expect*. New York: Random House.

Lipps, Jere. M. 1999. Beyond reason: Science in the mass media. In *Evolution! facts and fallacies*, ed. J.W. Schopf, 71–90. San Diego, CA: Academic Press. http://www.ucmp.berkeley.edu/people/jlipps/Beyond.html.

Mathson, Stephanie M., and Michael G. Lorenzen. 2008. We won't be fooled again: Teaching critical thinking via evaluation of hoax and historical revisionist websites in a library credit course. *College & Undergraduate Libraries* 15 (1–2): 211–230.

National Science Board. 1996. *Science and engineering indicators—1996*. NSB 96-21. Washington, DC: U.S. Government Printing Office.

Nickerson, Raymond. 1987. *Reflective reasoning*. Hinsdale, NJ: Lawrence Erlbaum. Quoted in Schafersman 1991.

Paul, Richard R., and Linda Elder. 1996. The critical mind is a questioning mind. Foundation for critical thinking. http://www.criticalthinking.org/articles/critical-mind.cfm.

Project for Excellence in Journalism. 2009. Public attitudes. *The state of the news media: An annual report on American journalism*. http://www.stateofthemedia.org/2009/narrative_overview_publicattitudes.php?media=1#2ethics.

Sagan, Carl. 1997. *The demon-haunted world: Science as a candle in the dark*. Toronto: Ballantine Books.

Schafersman, Steven D. 1991. An introduction to critical thinking. http://www.freeinquiry.com/critical-thinking.html.

Schrock, Kathy. n.d. The five W's of web evaluation. http://kathyschrock.net/abceval/5ws.pdf.

Vaughn, Lewis. 2004. *The power of critical thinking*. New York: Oxford University Press.

Wathen, Nadine C., and Jaquelyn Burkell. 2002. Believe it or not: Factors influencing credibility on the Web. *Journal of the American Society for Information Science and Technology* 53 (2): 134–144.

CHAPTER 10

Practical Research and Web Navigation Skills

Kelly Toughill and Fred Vallance-Jones

CHAPTER OUTLINE

Introduction

Honest, critical research is the foundation of all great journalism. This is true in every medium and across every subject area. Both Bernhard Drax, a journalist who works exclusively in the virtual world of Second Life, and Stephanie Nolen, the celebrated foreign correspondent for the *Globe and Mail*, built their reputations by painstakingly piecing together facts and opinions to create stories of meaning for their audience. Whether you are covering sports, entertainment, politics, or war, the quality of your work and the lustre of your own reputation will rest on your ability to ferret out crucial information, test the integrity of that information, discern the important from the irrelevant, and then identify and interpret the patterns and relationships that transform raw data into knowledge.

Some journalists draft a formal research plan before they begin; others scribble a few points on a piece of paper as a rough guide. Regardless of your personal style, most of your research will begin with two basic questions: What do you need to know? How will you get that information?

The first is the most important. Good research is driven by a key question. When Peter Cheney researched his seminal series on the taxi cab industry in Toronto, the question he asked himself was, "Why are Toronto cabs so filthy and broken?" The answer revealed a regulatory system that allowed wealthy professionals to exploit new immigrants—at the expense of taxi customers. When Daniel Leblanc began investigating the story that turned into the sponsorship scandal, he simply wanted to know why the RCMP had commissioned an elaborate hot-air balloon. The answers to that question toppled the Liberal government of Prime Minister Jean Chrétien and sent several people to prison. The best research is guided by a question that is simple, open, and free of assumptions and bias. The central question will dictate what you need to know. Finding the answer is the fun part.

Sources for Journalism Research

There are three types of sources for journalism research: people, records, and numbers. You can get stories from people, stories from records, and stories from numbers. Most great stories require all three.

People

Interviewing is a key research skill that is covered in depth in Chapter 14, "Interviewing in the Digital Age." But before you interview anyone, you must figure out who has the information you want, and how you will find them.

Many journalists waste their own precious time—and that of their sources—by interviewing the wrong person. Before you pick up the phone or send off an email, think about who is affected by your topic, who is the decision-maker at the centre of the issue, and who understands the issue but is not directly involved. Most sources fall into one of three categories: affected subject, accountable subject, and third-party or involved expert. There is also a fourth crucial category of sources you will use, and may or may not quote: helpers.

Inexperienced journalists often think that victims or affected subjects are the most difficult people to find. In fact, they are generally the easiest. Affected subjects are usually found through simple location or through helping organizations. Go to the location of the story. If it is a story about education, go to a school. If it is a crime story, go to the scene. If it is a story about a development controversy, go to the neighbourhood and knock on doors or go to the crucial city council meeting and talk to people in the crowd. The easiest way to get great interviews from affected subjects is to get out of the office and show up where they are. But it is not the only way.

Non-profit and professional organizations can also help you find affected subjects. For example, if you are writing about a change in prostitution laws, you may not be able to find a prostitute to interview by trolling the street, but you might get a good interview by enlisting the help of one of the many organizations that deal with sex-trade workers. Most of those groups will rightly refuse to give you the name and contact information of their clients, but they might agree to pass your business card around or allow you to post a note on a bulletin board. Finding the organizations is not hard. A simple Internet search using appropriate keywords and your location will usually turn up helping agencies, as will a search through www.sources.ca, a guide to Canadian associations. Most cities and towns have a guide available in the public library that lists all community groups and helping agencies in the area. This technique is useful for finding any kind of affected subject, whether it be tardy taxpayers, delinquent teenagers, or championship tennis players.

Finally, enlist the power of the Internet in your search. Crawl Facebook, LinkedIn, and email lists (LISTSERVs) to get the message out about the story you are doing and the people you are seeking. There are email lists for every demographic, psychographic, and interest group imaginable.

The strategy for finding accountable subjects is a little different. The first task is to figure out who is your accountable subject. That isn't always easy. Who is responsible for creating or resolving the conflict at the centre of your story? Who has the power to make decisions that will change the outcome? Accountable subjects are often

TOOLS & TIPS

Political Resources

The horse race of elections is barely the beginning of covering politics. Think about how power is used, and what that means for your readers, listeners, and viewers.

The following underused resources will give you an edge over your competitors. They will generate exclusive stories and add depth to the big stories of the day.

- **Committee testimony:** The Canadian House of Commons and the US Congress hold hearings in which all sorts of reluctant people are forced to testify about things that they would never discuss with a reporter. The hearings make it to CNN and CBC News Network (formerly Newsworld) only when they focus on a huge story that everyone already knows about, such as the subprime mortgage fiasco. If you have a beat or an area of interest, look up the verbatim transcript of past committee hearings on the topic, and find out who is scheduled to testify in the future. Good stories are guaranteed.
- **Committee reports:** Canada's Senate and House of Commons, and the US Congress, produce all sorts of bipartisan reports that languish in obscurity. Most of them are excellent pieces of research on interesting issues. Mine them.
- **Government and regulatory agency reports:** Sure, reports from Canada's Auditor General or the US Congressional Budget Office get play, but reports from Fisheries and Oceans Canada or the US Federal Communications Commission can have far more impact on real people's lives. Look at the publications of every government agency and regulatory body in your area of interest. Chances are that no one else has.

shielded by gatekeepers: executive assistants, secretaries, public relations firms, official spokespersons, and even bodyguards. Often the gatekeeper's job is simply to protect a busy boss from strangers who would waste his or her time. So your first job is to convince the gatekeeper not only that you have a good reason to speak to his or her boss but also that *it is in the boss's best interest to speak with you.*

You must always understand both why you need to speak with someone and why they need to speak with you. Whether you are trying to interview an affected subject, an accountable subject, or an expert, you must know and be able to articulate what's in it for them. The answer to that is usually simple, for most people have a clear interest in ensuring the truth is widely known. If you can't articulate why someone should speak with you, you will have a very difficult time landing the interview.

If you can't get through the gatekeeper, try reaching the accountable subject directly, either through phone, email, a helper, or in person. Try calling the accountable subject after the gatekeeper has left. In many offices, an assistant's number will bounce to the boss after the assistant has gone home. Many phone systems are also set up so that the number of the boss is one digit higher or lower than his or her assistant. So, if the secretary's number is 555-3892, try dialing 555-3891 or 555-3893. Or, try reaching the person at home. Find the home number either through a simple search of the phone book or by using a digital reverse directory, if you know the address. Some powerful people keep their phone number listed in the name of a child or a spouse.

A key resource for finding accountable subjects is the directory. There are directories for organizations, schools, alumni groups, and governments. Most private schools have a parents' directory that includes home phone numbers and addresses, and many of the key decision-makers in society send their children to private school. The Canadian government has a very good online directory that often coughs up the direct phone number for key government bureaucrats. It is called the Government Electronic Directory Services (GEDS). It can be searched by name, title, department, or role and is easily found by searching "GEDS" in your favourite browser.

Directories are also useful for finding experts. Almost every story needs an expert to help explain key facts or the central conflict. Some people are experts because they have a great deal of education, while others are experts by virtue of experience. A beat cop might be an expert on crime in a particular neighbourhood. A criminologist might be a better expert on national crime trends. Every major university has an online directory that lists faculty members by their area of expertise.

So where do public relations people fit in this system? The best ones are helpers. Spokespersons are rarely experts on anything, and they almost never have decision-making power, so they are not accountable subjects. But they can—and should—help you find experts and decision-makers. A good government spokesperson can help you connect with the bureaucrat who can explain the design of a new program, or the minister who can explain why the government has vowed to adopt it.

Public relations people are not the only helpers. Some of the gatekeepers mentioned earlier can also be helpers. Executive assistants, secretaries, and even chauffeurs can help you track people down on deadline. Perhaps the most important type of helper is the one who connects you to an unknown community. Getting a quick read on a new community is one of the key skills of any good journalist. The community may be geographic—a town, a country, a neighbourhood. Or it may be defined by interests or professions. It doesn't matter if you are trying to understand forensic accountants, sex club patrons, Rwandan immigrants, or women with breast cancer—you are better off with a guide.

The best guides to a new community are people who know everyone within it. It is a cliché of journalism that reporters rely on cab drivers, bartenders, and barbers for quick quotes. There is a reason that reporters gravitate to those professions. All three talk with a broad cross-section of their community. Look for people who have reason to speak with both the powerful and the powerless. For example, if you could talk to only one person to get a quick understanding of a university, you may be better off talking to a popular cafeteria worker than the president of the institution.

Records

Some of the best research is done in libraries and databases. Don't underestimate the power of records to tell a story. And don't underestimate how many of the world's events are recorded on paper or in cyberspace. The key to records research is to learn to think sideways. Most of the documents, pictures, and video you review will have been created for another purpose. Few people write things down because they suspect a journalist will want to look them up someday. They write them down because they need clear proof of changes in power, money, or thinking. Your job is to think creatively about where to find the records that reveal your story.

IN PRACTICE

Covering the Beat

Beat reporters rely on records to find new stories and advance stories they have already told. The core of a beat reporter's job is to figure out which records are key to their beat and then to check those records every month, week, or day. Gillian Cormier is a reporter for *AllNovaScotia.com*, an online news outlet that focuses on business in Nova Scotia. She covers telecommunications for the site. This is the list of records that she checks every day to cover her beat:

- Campaign finance (Elections Nova Scotia)
- SEDAR
- Labour Standards Tribunal
- Federal environmental assessments
- Provincial environmental assessments
- Personal bankruptcy filings
- Industry Canada (business bankruptcy)
- Orders in council
- Tenders
- CanLII (Canadian law database)
- Nova Scotia Utility and Review Board
- Courts
- Registry of Joint Stock Companies
- Canadian Radio-television and Telecommunications Commission
- Wire services (back files)
- Disciplinary wing of professional organizations
- Statistics Canada
- Nova Scotia Securities Commission
- Property Online

Most of the records used by reporters are instantly available to the public. Others must be accessed through a freedom of information request. Almost all levels of government in Canada and the United States have some form of freedom of information law. The laws work differently in different jurisdictions. The principle behind all of the laws is that every record held or created by government should be available to the public. This principle is important. You don't have to prove you have the right to the record; it is up to government to prove why you shouldn't have access to the record under a specific exemption.

Most bureaucrats are not familiar with freedom of information laws. You may be told by someone at a front counter that you can't see the university president's employment contract, the engineering report on a failed sewage plant, or a city council member's expense report. The person barring access may honestly believe they are doing the right thing. In fact, all of those records are public under freedom of information laws in most jurisdictions in Canada and the United States.

All agencies and government departments have an information officer responsible for handling access requests. Contact the information officer before you file the request, to ensure the material isn't already available elsewhere.

There are two types of access requests: fishing expeditions and surgical requests. Both can generate very good stories. Many reporters file "fishing expedition" requests on a slow news day in the hope they might turn up something interesting. That's what Daniel Leblanc, of the *Globe and Mail*, did when he asked for all contracts from a federal sponsorship program. Later, when a secret source began to guide his query, Leblanc used the surgical technique to request specific reports and documents key to

TOOLS & TIPS

The Courts and Court Records

Never underestimate the power of the courthouse to cough up a good story on a slow news day. And never underestimate the power of court records to enrich other stories.

The courts are set up and named differently in different parts of the world, but every courthouse has a clerk's office with an index of cases arranged by date and by name. Browse the index and pull the file. A civil case will have a narrative of allegations and a statement of defence. A criminal case will have the allegation, details of the accused, probation and pre-sentencing reports, and sometimes witness depositions.

You can even get good court stories without going to court. CanLII is a database of court judgments and tribunal rulings across Canada. Find it at www.canlii.org. The United States has an even more comprehensive database called PACER. It includes every scrap of paper filed in every federal court in the United States. All the racy details of the Michael Jackson and the Conrad Black allegations were posted to PACER before the courthouse even opened for the day. Find PACER at pacer.uspci.uscourts.gov.

the story. His work broke the sponsorship scandal that is widely credited for the electoral defeat of Liberal Prime Minister Paul Martin.

When drafting an access request, be careful of your wording. It is better to ask for all records regarding a topic than just a report or an email. It is often better to limit your request to a specific time frame, to speed reply and reduce search fees.

Most jurisdictions charge a nominal fee for filing an access request. After reviewing your request, the information officer will give you an estimate of how much it will cost to search your request, and how much it will cost to copy the documents. There is often room for negotiation at this stage. Most agencies must respond to your request within 30 days. There are differing rules on how long an agency or department has to actually fill the request. If your request is denied, most jurisdictions have an appeal process. In some jurisdictions and some departments, freedom of information requests are returned within days or weeks. In others, the process can last years. Former Reform Party researcher Laurie Throness filed a request in 1999 for Prime Minister Jean Chrétien's agendas. It took 11 years for that case to make it to the Supreme Court of Canada.

Numbers

Many journalists are uncomfortable with math. We tend to be word people or visual thinkers who dismiss quantitative analysis. Because we don't have the confidence to analyze numbers, we miss good stories and let people get away with all sorts of spin. There are three reasons that the profession in general should pay more attention to numbers.

The first is that we don't scrutinize numbers the way we should, and that is a disservice to our readers, listeners, and viewers. We miss stories and are led astray by professionals more adept at numerical analysis. The truth is that numbers are very often opinions disguised as facts. For example, major corporations often choose to "restate" their financial statements from past years. General Motors once claimed that it simply missed $5 billion in losses when drafting up its annual report. Financial statements, like many spreadsheets, are carefully crafted to create a specific portrait of reality. General Motors needed to change the portrait.

The second reason to focus on numbers separately is that our credibility as journalists is often tested by our capacity—or incapacity—to deal accurately with numbers. We mess it up all the time. For an amusing and terrifying read, check out Craig Silverman's blog, RegrettheError.com, particularly the section "Fuzzy Numbers etc." The range of numerical errors on any given day is astonishing. The smallest numerical error casts doubt on every other part of your story.

The last reason is the most important. Facility with numbers is vital to connecting with readers who are linear thinkers. Some people can understand a truth expressed numerically that they simply cannot accept when presented with words or pictures. That realization is sparking a trend in number stories and packages. The key is to find the narrative link. As you will see, numbers really can be used as a language of narrative. If you can recognize the narrative potential of numbers, and manipulate them honestly and accurately, you will enhance your own stories and have a rare and marketable skill.

Some number stories are obvious. From global warming to unemployment, many of the staple stories of the news cycle are based on numbers. Science stories, health

TOOLS & TIPS

Money

Follow the money was the advice given Bob Woodward and Carl Bernstein by their secret source when they were pursuing the Watergate scandal. It is still good advice today. Money records reveal a person's allies, their place in a community, and, sometimes, their secrets. These top five money sources should be familiar to every journalist working any beat.

- **Management information circular:** This source gives you the salary, bonuses, stock options, and golden parachutes of every top executive and every director of every publicly traded company in North America. For Canadian companies, go to www.sedar.com. For US companies, go to www.sec.gov/edgar.shtml.
- **Public accounts:** Budgets tell you how the government planned to spend its money. *Public accounts* tells you how it actually did. Use this resource to track payments to consultants, hospitals, and even politicians.
- **Lien check:** Almost every state and province has a system that allows you to look at who owes money to whom.
- **Business registrations:** Look up business partners and the web of business connections using federal, state, and provincial business registries. Even when a company is privately owned, it still has to file registration or incorporation papers.
- **Property records:** Usually found in a local land registry office, these records reveal who owns a property, how much they paid for it, whom they purchased it from, the names of the lawyers involved, and details of the mortgage.

stories, stories about tax rates and the economy, and many sport stories have numbers at their core. Other number stories are less obvious. Consider, for example, the story Robert Sheppard wrote on Tim Hortons' Roll Up The Rim To Win contest in 2006 for CBC.ca (Sheppard 2006). Sheppard analyzed the contest and discovered that residents of Quebec and the ten US states in which the contest is held had a much greater chance of winning the donut chain's grand prize than residents of Ontario and other provinces. The story has been repeated by CBC and many other outlets every year since.

So, how do you find good stories in a sheet of numbers? In general, look for one of three things: a sharp change in a number; a gradual and consistent change in a number, or a number that is surprising. In the case of Tim Hortons, Sheppard based his story on a number that was surprising.

A sharp change in a number usually signals a big event. For an extreme example, think of a very bad earthquake. It is registered as a sudden change in seismometer readings and measured by the Richter scale. It can also be measured by a sudden spike in the death rate. A less dramatic example is a plunge in the stock market.

A gradual and consistent change in a number signals a trend. The steady change in meteorological data first showed the trend of global warming. When an economy constricts for several months straight, the trend is labelled a recession.

The important trick is figuring out which numbers are significant. Some are obvious: budgets and batting averages, unemployment statistics and cancer rates. Some are not. One task of any journalist covering a specific subject area is to figure out the signal numbers of that beat. Which numbers begin to signal a trend or event before it is otherwise obvious? Signal numbers on the economy beat include housing starts, unemployment rates, labour participation rates, and interest rates. Changes in any of those numbers can help predict what will happen next in the economy. But every subject area has its own signal numbers that help perceptive journalists accurately predict the future. Where do you find those numbers? Many places, but a key source for any Canadian journalist covering any subject area is the Statistics Canada website at www.statcan.gc.ca. This federal agency collects data on everything from the production of pork bellies to urban homicide rates and the number of Canadians employed in the fine arts. Its tables can reveal whether Canadians are more likely to die from a lightning strike or a dog bite, which Canadian province has the highest rate of throat cancer, and what communities have the highest rate of volunteering.

Statistics Canada publishes a newsletter, *The Daily*, that is a wealth of eclectic story ideas. Its website also has a feature called "Community Profiles" that allows you to look up and compare the vital statistics of any community in Canada. You can build your own tables from its vast store of information by accessing its CANSIM database.

To find out how your math skills compare, try the online test hosted by Investigative Reporters and Editors (IRE) at www.ire.org/education/math_test.html.

• • •

Great journalists use all three types of sources—people, records, and numbers—to weave stories of power and meaning. Regardless of the type of source, great research will keep you asking, "What happened?" "What does this mean to my readers?" "How can I verify what I have learned?" In the end, great research is the only way to find the truth.

Navigating the Web

There is a paradox of plenty about the World Wide Web. While it has made it possible to access more material online than any person could use in a dozen lifetimes, it is also a chaotic place.

While physical libraries maintain collections that are carefully built, catalogued, and culled by professionals, the Web is just an interconnection of billions of computers around the world. There is no acquisition policy, no central catalogue, and no records-disposal policy to ensure that materials that have outlived their usefulness are removed. There is only an illusion of order created by search engines such as Google and Bing, and you have no idea of the qualifications of the person who has posted information.

So while it seems easier to find information than it used to be, it is harder to build a comprehensive picture of anything. There is just so much out there that is either not organized particularly well or is presented in a way that obscures any real understanding. Plenty more seems invisible because it is part of the so-called hidden web of databases and other resources beyond the reach of search engine robots.

Smart researchers need to find their way around this electronic jungle. In this section, we'll explore how your research can take advantage of the Web's strengths and weaknesses.

Following Someone's Trail on the Net

There was a time when it was easy to live a largely private life. For most people, the only traces that one might leave might be a yellowing birth announcement, a few school yearbook entries, a wedding announcement, and a death notice. Unless someone clipped the notices from the paper or went to a library to scroll through microfilms, the information effectively vanished. Aside from one's phone book listing, the city directory, and paper records at land titles and assessment offices, one could live and die without leaving much of a public record.

But today people leave traces everywhere, and the more public the person, the more likely that you can find out a great deal about the person just by following his or her trail online. Even people who deliberately keep a low profile leave clues that can pry open the door to finding other information.

It is the very vastness of the Web that makes this possible, and the fact that a lot of material, once posted, just stays there, often half forgotten by the people who put it there but quietly indexed by search engine robots. Smart researchers can go looking for all those fragments of information and gather enough details to start asking good questions of human sources.

Key to this technique is how one looks at information. Your interest in a piece of information may have little relationship to the reason it was posted in the first place. So a press release mentioning your quarry may serve to tell you where the person worked at that time. A mention on a club website may give clues to a person's wider network of associates. A biography may tell you where someone has lived or worked before, giving you valuable leads on people who may know the person. Perhaps most important, material found on the Web this way will point you to a wealth of human sources who will know and may have worked or lived with the subject.

Let's look at how easy it is to build a profile of Fred Vallance-Jones, one of the authors of this chapter. Using Google's unmatched ability to search out content on the visible Web, one can quickly find out the following:

- His official bio says he lives in Halifax, Nova Scotia, with his wife and four children, teaches at the University of King's College, and worked previously at CBC and the *Hamilton Spectator* (www.ukings.ca/fred-vallance-jones). This kind of official biography is usually carefully written to provide only certain details, usually those that will be most flattering, but it provides the researcher with endless avenues to pursue. In this case it points the way to colleagues at the university, and former colleagues at the CBC and the *Spectator*. It suggests other online searches, for example, research papers the author might have written. And while it doesn't say where he lives in Halifax, knowing this nugget should be enough to use Canada411.ca or land title records to track down where he does live. That, of course, opens the door to talking to neighbours or tracking down the subject for an interview if he proves elusive.

- He graduated from Carleton University with a Bachelor of Journalism (lists.caj.ca/pipermail/caj-list/2002-September/013290.html) as indicated by this post to an email LISTSERV that lives on years after it was created. The message refers to faculty who taught Vallance-Jones, offering hints at the time period and pointing the way to faculty from the time and fellow students, some of whom may still be in touch with the subject.
- The author has specialized expertise in advanced research techniques and writes a column for J-Source.ca on computer-assisted reporting (www.j-source.ca/english_new/category.php?catid=210), has co-authored two textbooks on investigative and computer-assisted reporting (www.oupcanada.com/catalog/9780195424577.html), and does research on freedom of information in Canada (www.cna-acj.ca/en/news/public-affairs/cna-releases-4th-annual-freedom-information-audit). All of this information provides an important window on the author's professional activities and points the way to reading some of the author's writings to get a sense of his interests. Doing this kind of careful background research is crucial when preparing for an interview because people are flattered when you take the time to find out something about them.
- According to this online picture—www.flickr.com/photos/27004867@N05/2530989951/—captured and posted without his even knowing, the author is mostly bald and, at least in 2008, wore his remaining hair quite short. More important, you now know what the author looks like in case you ever have to identify him without meeting him directly.
- He keeps a Facebook account (www.facebook.com/fred.vallancejones). The security settings on this account are fairly tight, but some people allow anyone to look at their personal information. Also, if you have your own Facebook account—and you should—it is a pretty reliable way of reaching someone.
- He led a lobbying effort in 1997 against changes to Manitoba's *Freedom of Information Act* (list.flora.org/pipermail/action-forum/1997-June/000140.html and www.gov.mb.ca/hansard/hansard/3rd-36th/ed_004/ed-004.html). If nothing else, this information shows that the subject's interest in freedom of information is long-standing. If you read the Hansard entry, it also tells you that he lived in Winnipeg at that time, another detail as you build a profile of your subject that leads you to still other records and sources.

Of course, the author has been a very public person, so there is probably more available online about him than about many people. But the point is that people leave a trail behind on the Net, and you can follow it.

Using Google to search someone's name is just one of many strategies you can follow. For example, if you put in someone's name and just the expected area code, you can find phone numbers that may not be listed in the public directory. Searching the person's name along with that of known associates will often turn up times they have collaborated, helping build the picture further. And of course you can use Google Advanced Search to look for references to your subject on specific websites or in files with particular formats, such as PDF reports.

Giving Web-Based Information a Workout with a Spreadsheet

It is pretty common these days for governments and corporations to post lists of information, budgets, or financial results online. But as discussed earlier in the section on numbers, the information is often presented in a way that will lead you to a desired conclusion or one that prevents you from developing a deeper understanding of the information.

A simple tool that most of us already have on our computers, or which we can download at no cost, can take us over these hurdles to new understanding. That tool is a spreadsheet.

Many reporters have avoided using this ubiquitous application, perhaps because it seems to create extra complication or because of a deep-seated aversion to math. But the nice thing about this tool for digging into web-based information is that it's really easy to use, and either no math is involved at all or if there is math, the program does it for you. It's like math without math: What more could a journalist want?

For our demonstration, we'll use a free downloadable spreadsheet program called OpenOffice. You can get it at www.openoffice.org. The figures presented below are from the version that was current as of publication; over time, some features may change. If you use a Mac, NeoOffice (www.neooffice.org) is a similar open-source program.

For the data, we'll use financial reports from the Proactive Disclosure website of Industry Canada. Since 2004, federal government departments and agencies have been required to publish online all contracts valued at $10,000 or more, travel and hospitality expenses for senior staff, grants and contributions to businesses and organizations, and position reclassifications. The website is becoming a vast storehouse of information on how the government spends money. But it isn't organized in a journalist-friendly fashion. The information is divided by department and agency, and within each, by quarter. So looking at all of the information for one department or agency involves opening up four files for every year. You can see why so few journalists make use of these data.

But a spreadsheet program such as OpenOffice makes the job quite a bit easier by allowing one to combine and look at several files at the same time. You can now see how figures change over time and who the ongoing beneficiaries of government business are.

We'll begin by going to the Proactive Disclosure website. You can find it at www.tbs-sct.gc.ca/pd-dp/gr-rg/index-eng.asp, a central site maintained by the Treasury Board Secretariat, a central agency of the federal government. Under **Industry Canada**, pick **Contracts** and then **Disclosure Reports**. Click on the most recent fiscal quarter listed. Figure 10.1 presents an example of one of the quarter listings as it appears at the site.

As you will note, the contracts are listed by date, which may be logical from the point of view of the department but probably the least useful configuration for a journalist who would like to see which contracts are the largest or who got the greatest

Date	Vendor Name	Description	Contract Value
2009-07-01	LEXIS-NEXIS	859 Other business services not elsewhere specified	$10,273.00
2009-07-01	BITQUEST CORPORATION	670 Computer equipment - hardware and software	$11,944.00
2009-07-01	WORKDYNAMICS TECHNOLOGIES INC.	670 Computer equipment - hardware and software	$16,490.00
2009-07-01	HEWLETT-PACKARD (CANADA) LTD.	670 Computer equipment - hardware and software	$79,899.00
2009-07-01	CISION CANADA INC.	341 Communications Research Services	$50,001.00
2009-07-01	GENOMEQUEST INC.	859 Other business services not elsewhere specified	$241,102.00
2009-	INTEGRA NETWORKS CORP	1229 Computer equipment parts	$44,792.00

Figure 10.1

SOURCE: Industry Canada. 2009. *Disclosure of contracts: July 1 to September 30, 2009.* http://www.ic.gc.ca/app/ic/cr/lstCntrcts.do?lang=eng&qrtr=221.

number of contracts for what. The spreadsheet will allow us to reorganize the information any way we like.

To begin, copy the URL for the page from the address bar at the top of the browser (see Figure 10.2). We used Firefox, but you can use any browser you like.

Figure 10.2

Now, start up OpenOffice Calc. From the **INSERT** menu, choose **Link to External Data**. In the URL of external data source box, paste in the URL you copied from your browser and press Enter. OpenOffice will work for a few moments before providing you with a list of tables on the web page (note that this process only works if your computer has an active Internet connection). Select HTML_tables so as to import the data (but not the rest of the page) in the table. You should end up with the dialog box presented in Figure 10.3.

Click OK and OpenOffice will import the data into the spreadsheet (see Figure 10.4).

As with all spreadsheet programs, your working area is a grid of rows and columns that intersect to form cells. The cells contain the individual pieces of information, or

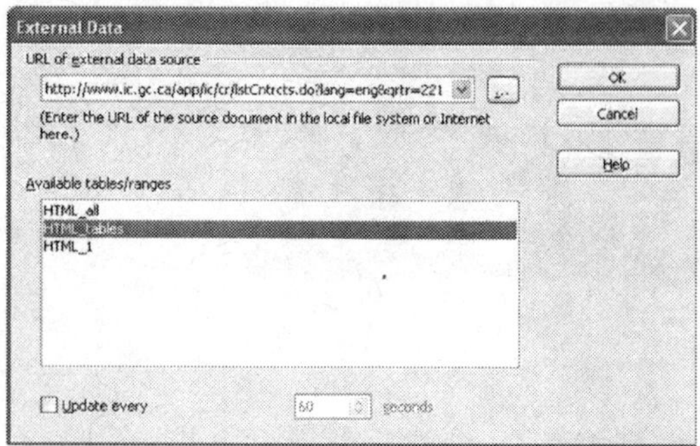

Figure 10.3

data. Each column contains all of the information about one aspect of what is being recorded, in this case the date, the vendor name, the description of the contract, and the value of the contract.

To get rid of the hyperlinks in the Vendor Name column, click on the column header (the "B" at the top of the column) and from the **FORMAT** menu, choose **Default Formatting**.

Your spreadsheet is now ready to use to make more sense of the data.

If you want to see who got the largest contracts, sort the spreadsheet. Click on the top number in the Contract Value column, and then click on the **Sort Descending** (Z→A) icon on the Standard toolbar.

To view all of the contracts in alphabetical order by vendor, click on the top number in the Vendor Name column, and then click on the **Sort Ascending** (A→Z) icon on the Standard toolbar.

To see all of the contracts from one vendor, from the **DATA** menu, choose **Filter > AutoFilter**. Click on the down-arrow button beside Vendor Name at the top of the column, and choose the name of the vendor you would like to view. The sheet will be reduced to just those contracts.

To add up all of the contracts in the quarter, click on a cell below the last Contract Value entry and click on the Sum icon (it looks like "Σ" and is located in the formula toolbar just above the spreadsheet). OpenOffice will suggest a sum formula. Make sure it includes the top cell and the bottom cell in the column you are adding up. Cells are identified by the letter and number of the intersecting column and row, as in A2,

Untitled 2 - OpenOffice.org Calc

	A	B	C	D
1	Date	Vendor Name	Description	Contract Value
2	07/01/09	LEXIS-NEXIS	259 Other business services not elsewhere specified	$10,273.00
3	07/01/09	BITQUEST CORPORATION	670 Computer equipment - hardware and software	$11,944.00
4	07/01/09	WORKDYNAMICS TECHNOLOGIES INC	670 Computer equipment - hardware and software	$16,490.00
5	07/01/09	HEWLETT-PACKARD (CANADA) LTD	670 Computer equipment - hardware and software	$79,899.00
6	07/01/09	CISION CANADA INC	341 Communications Research Services	$30,001.00
7	07/01/09	GENOMEQUEST INC	859 Other business services not elsewhere specified	$241,102.00
8	07/02/09	INTEGRA NETWORKS CORP	1229 Computer equipment parts	$44,792.00
9	07/02/09	GRAND & TOY LTD	1172 Office and stationers supplies	$12,205.00
10	07/02/09	TERAMACH TECHNOLOGIES INC	1226 Computer equipment - large/medium - mainframe, mini	$78,982.00
11	07/02/09	HARRINGTON STAFFING SERVICES LTD	813 Temporary help services	$14,015.00
12	07/02/09	MAXSYS PROFESSIONALS AND	213 Temporary help services	$12,260.00
13	07/02/09	EXCEL HUMAN RESOURCES	472 Information technology consultants	$65,625.00
14	07/02/09	AME DESIGN ASSOCIATES	421 Architectural services	$11,970.00
15	07/03/09	MARKETRESEARCH.COM, INC	859 Other business services not elsewhere specified	$10,775.00
16	07/03/09	EKOS RESEARCH ASSOCIATES INC	491 Management consulting	$21,000.00
17	07/06/09	SYSTEMSCOPE	472 Information technology consultants	$76,388.00
18	07/06/09	HILL & KNOWLTON CANADA	492 Research contracts	$15,708.00
19	07/06/09	INFOTECH ALBERTA	491 Management consulting	$15,000.00
20	07/06/09	ÉCOLE DE LANGUES, LA CITE INC	447 Tuition fees and costs of attending courses including seminars not elsewhere specified	$17,934.00
21	07/06/09	FIRST CLASS LANGUAGE TRAINING	447 Tuition fees and costs of attending courses including seminars not elsewhere specified	$23,400.00
22	07/06/09	PHIRELIGHT E-BUSINESS SOLUTIONS	491 Management consulting	$125,832.00
23	07/06/09	COMMISSIONAIRES (THE)	460 Protection services	$45,205.00
24	07/06/09	BARBARA PERSONNEL INC	813 Temporary help services	$12,301.00

Figure 10.4

G23, et cetera. To accept the suggestion, press Enter, and the total of contracts will appear. If the formula suggested doesn't include the whole range you need, edit it before pressing Enter. You can edit it later by double-clicking on the cell with the formula in it to open it for editing.

These same methods will work on any table that you import from a web page.

With the Proactive Disclosure data, you can use the Link to External Data feature to add as many quarters as you like. Just make sure that you put your cursor in the first cell in column A *below* your existing quarters before adding another. You will also need to manually paste in each new URL each time you import another table of data. Hint: Convert the new entries in the Vendor Name column to default formatting each time you add a new quarter. Doing so will make saving the file faster by getting rid of file overhead.

Really Getting to the Heart of the Numbers

OpenOffice can also create quick summaries of data using its DataPilot feature.

Before we begin, we'll add to our sheet all of the quarters of data for the past three years. Next, click on the label of the column header at the top of the second column (the "B" at the top of the column) and, from the **INSERT** menu, choose **Columns**. This action will create a blank column B and move the remaining data to the right.

Click on the column header for the new column and, from the **FORMAT** menu, choose **Cells**. Now, within the **Numbers** tab, choose All in the Category box. Doing so will ensure that when we are finished the next step, we will see ordinary numbers in the column.

Label the new column "Year" (in what should be cell B1). In cell B2, manually write in the formula =Year(A2). This will put a number corresponding to the year from the date in cell A2 into cell B2. Move the cursor to the bottom right corner of cell B2 until it changes to a small plus sign. Double-click to fill in the formula to the bottom of the sheet. If double-clicking doesn't work, move the cursor until the small plus sign appears, then hold and drag down to fill in the remaining year entries. Figure 10.5 presents what your screen should look like.

	A	B	C	D	E
1	Date	Year	Vendor Name	Description	Contract Value
2	07/28/03	2003	ATRIA NETWORKS LP	223 Digital channel communications services for the combined transn	$2,423,440.00
3	03/01/04	2004	ATRIA NETWORKS LP	223 Digital channel communications services for the combined transn	$1,089,662.00
4	12/21/05	2005	VOX POPULI COMMUNICATIONS	819 Non-professional personal service contracts not elsewhere specif	$21,420.00
5	01/01/06	2006	POI BUSINESS INTERIORS	859 Other business services not elsewhere specified	$23,216.00
6	04/01/06	2006	OGILVY RENAULT	859 Other business services not elsewhere specified	$24,982.00
7	05/10/06	2006	MAGELLAN ENGINEERING	819 Non-professional personal service contracts not elsewhere specif	$29,574.00
8	09/25/06	2006	TESTCOR INC.	1243 Measuring, controlling, laboratory, medical and optical equipme	$18,240.00
9	10/05/06	2006	PHOENIX STRATEGIC PERSPECTIVES INC.	1143 Printed matter, including books, newspapers, pictures, manuscri	$26,500.00
10	10/11/06	2006	GENERAL MOTORS OF CANADA LIMITED	1261 Road motor vehicles	$38,501.00
11	10/25/06	2006	DAIMLER CHRYSLER CANADA INC.	1261 Road motor vehicles	$22,397.00
12	10/31/06	2006	PHOENIX STRATEGIC PERSPECTIVES INC.	351 Communications professional services not elsewhere specified	$94,808.00
13	11/01/06	2006	IPSOS-REID CORPORATION	341 Communications Research Services	$100,855.00
14	11/01/06	2006	SOFTWARE SPECTRUM	670 Computer equipment - hardware and software	$35,552.00
15	11/02/06	2006	DANIELS ELECTRONICS LTD.	1243 Measuring, controlling, laboratory, medical and optical equipme	$14,640.00
16	11/06/06	2006	ROHDE & SCHWARZ	1243 Measuring, controlling, laboratory, medical and optical equipme	$44,984.00
17	11/06/06	2006	SIGNAL TECHNOLOGY ASSOCIATES INC.	1211 Special industry machinery	$57,012.00
18	11/06/06	2006	ROHDE & SCHWARZ	1243 Measuring, controlling, laboratory, medical and optical equipme	$44,984.00
19	11/08/06	2006	BOLD TECHNOLOGIES, LTD	1228 Computer software .	$11,069.00
20	11/09/06	2006	DECIMA RESEARCH	491 Management consulting	$43,162.00
21	11/14/06	2006	UNIFY CORPORATION	670 Computer equipment - hardware and software	$16,521.00
22	11/14/06	2006	PHOENIX STRATEGIC PERSPECTIVES INC.	492 Research contracts	$51,405.00
23	11/21/06	2006	GENERAL MOTORS OF CANADA LIMITED	1261 Road motor vehicles	$21,135.00
24	12/05/06	2006	RATEL MOBILE COMMUNICATIONS LTD	1223 Image/video equipment	$12,688.00

Figure 10.5

Note: There are some contracts for earlier periods that Industry Canada included in the online data.

Now, we can have some fun.

To begin creating the summary table, select the entire sheet of data by placing your cursor in the upper left cell, then using the keystroke combination SHIFT + CTRL + END (successively press each key until you are pressing all three). Now, from the **DATA** menu, choose **DataPilot > Start**. Choose the Current Selection button and click OK, and the dialog box in Figure 10.6 appears.

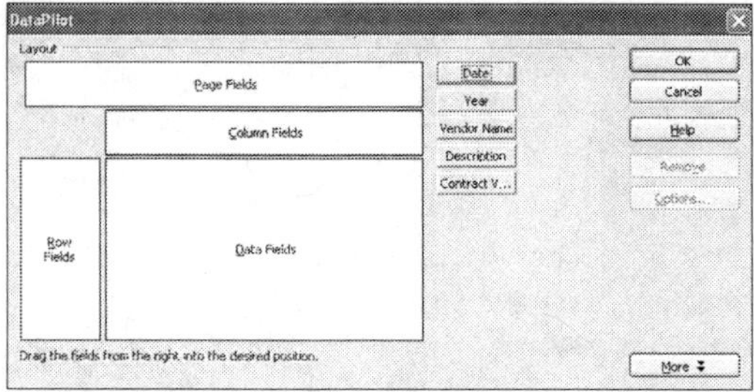

Figure 10.6

From here, creating a powerful summary is as simple as dragging and dropping.

In the DataPilot dialog box, drag the Year button into the white area labelled "Column Fields." Drag the Vendor Name button into the area labelled "Row Fields." Drag the Contract Value button into the white area labelled "Data Fields."

Click on More in the right bottom corner of the dialog box, and change the Results to box to "- new sheet -." Click OK to see the result, which will total up each vendor's contracts for each year.

To the far right, you will find a Total Result column (whether this column is added can be changed under More in the DataPilot dialog box you just worked with). You can click in the top entry of this column and sort it to see who got both the largest value of contacts and how much they got each year (noting that in the last year, there are only three of four quarters included here). Figure 10.7 presents the sorted result.

In the image above, you will note that the column headers jump from A to G. Columns B to F are hidden as they contain totals for contracts from previous years. In reporting these figures it would be important to check with the department to find out why this was the case. For information on how to hide and "unhide" columns, see the online help guide for your spreadsheet program.

	A	F	G	H	I
1	Filter				
2					
3	Vendor Name	2007	2008	2009	Total Result
4	**Total Result**	$78,180,858.00	$80,463,128.00	$59,827,786.00	$222,918,595.00
5	COMMISSIONAIRES (THE)	$3,088,165.00	$3,503,904.00	$3,460,628.00	$10,052,697.00
6	AJILON CANADA INC	$3,007,463.00	$1,606,867.00	$2,110,982.00	$6,725,312.00
7	BRAINHUNTER OTTAWA INC	$1,699,114.00	$3,385,886.00	$1,115,502.00	$6,200,502.00
8	EXCEL HUMAN RESOURCES	$1,472,411.00	$1,805,459.00	$2,320,116.00	$5,597,986.00
9	DELOITTE & TOUCHE LLP	$562,054.00	$3,114,944.00	$802,540.00	$4,479,538.00
10	VERITAAQ TECHNOLOGY HOUSE INC.	$373,121.00	$1,480,379.00	$1,790,350.00	$3,643,850.00
11	ROHDE & SCHWARZ CANADA INC	$1,087,096.00	$1,518,433.00	$940,313.00	$3,635,009.00
12	ATRIA NETWORKS LP				$3,513,102.00
13	TRM TECHNOLOGIES INC	$2,604,971.00	$50,086.00	$132,484.00	$2,787,541.00
14	KPMG	$10,600.00	$2,572,773.00	$147,000.00	$2,730,373.00
15	PRICEWATERHOUSECOOPERS LLP	$1,947,746.00	$539,210.00	$161,790.00	$2,648,746.00
16	PUBLIC WORKS AND GOVERNMENT	$759,141.00	$949,069.00	$885,105.00	$2,593,315.00
17	EUROPEAN PATENT OFFICE		$2,583,253.00		$2,583,253.00
18	IBM CANADA LTD.	$655,881.00	$125,550.00	$1,650,613.00	$2,432,044.00
19	ORACLE CORPORATION CANADA INC.	$872,448.00	$616,253.00	$664,893.00	$2,153,594.00
20	SOFTCHOICE CORPORATION	$1,115,906.00	$436,197.00	$507,837.00	$2,071,236.00
21	INTEGRA NETWORKS CORP.	$964,550.00	$489,289.00	$506,286.00	$1,960,125.00
22	BELL CANADA	$830,321.00	$115,328.00	$995,100.00	$1,940,749.00
23	ERNST AND YOUNG		$1,897,467.00		$1,897,467.00
24	NISHA TECHNOLOGIES INC.	$1,298,281.00	$526,837.00	$41,202.00	$1,866,320.00

Figure 10.7

As you can see, a spreadsheet is a remarkably powerful tool that you can use to bring real understanding to data commonly presented online.

The procedures shown here are similar for other spreadsheets, including Microsoft Excel. In Excel, the DataPilot feature is called PivotTable. Complete instructions on how to do the same analysis in Excel as well as how to do math such as working out percentage changes from year to year can be found in *Computer-Assisted Reporting: A Comprehensive Primer* (see Suggested Resources, below). The book covers a wide range of techniques from Internet research strategies to analyzing vast social networks, as we have just scratched the surface of what is possible.

Searchable Databases—Everywhere

Partly as a result of the efforts of journalists to make data public, governments have started to make more and more of their databases available for public searches. This accessibility is important because it allows you to tap directly into raw data on a wide range of government programs, particularly those that involve public health and safety. You can bypass the press releases and spinners and see directly which drugs have caused people to get sick, which airlines are having a lot of mid-air mechanical problems, who is giving money to political parties, who the directors are of corporations, which restaurants have violations of food safety laws, where wildfires have happened, and so on.

In almost all cases, the databases provide users with the ability to search on names, dates, and other relevant criteria, and results are returned either as a spreadsheet table or as a text report.

Two databases that became public directly as a result of journalists pushing for access were Health Canada's database of adverse drug reactions—people who get sick or die because of the drugs they take—and Transport Canada's database of aviation incidents. You can find links to these databases and a long list of other searchable databases at www.emp.ca/newjournalist.

Data from searchable databases can be combined with other research or with results from other database searches. So, an enterprising reporter might search the boards of directors of companies getting the most businesses from the government using the federal incorporations searchable database, then search for those director names on the database of contributors to federal political parties.

And this is just the beginning of what is possible. Some journalists like to go further, and obtain data in bulk form from government departments. If there is a searchable database, there are bulk data as well. And there are hundreds of valuable databases that are unavailable online.

Sorting the Wheat from the Chaff

One of the challenges of modern online research is that there is no obvious difference between information that has been carefully sourced and verified and something created by a hobbyist in his basement, between that intended to inform and that intended to persuade, or between accurate facts and inventions. To use the library comparison again, there is no librarian carefully sifting through the material and ensuring that only the most credible material is stacked on the reference shelves. So most of the responsibility for understanding the nature of information is shifted to the researcher, that being you. Discernment and verification become important skills in deciding whether one can just use the information, or if it needs to be verified further.

It's key is to understand the reason why any particular piece of information might be provided. You need to make a judgment of the likelihood that information is self-serving or prone to error. One caution: Sometimes hackers or hobbyists create fake or spoof websites that look identical to the legitimate ones. One way to check is to Google the genuine website, and compare the URL that actually appears in the address bar of your browser. The fake one likely looks different, perhaps having another top-level domain or a particularly lengthy URL full of slashes and subdomains. *Beware* is the operative word, because the Web is a jungle.

Obviously, information that appears to be second hand, one person saying something about another or some other organization, is no more reliable than hearsay or second-hand information anywhere else, and should always be checked.

Here are some reference points that can help you evaluate the information you find.

Information produced by government statistical agencies and other bodies whose purpose is to gather information objectively and disseminate it is at the top of the reliability heap. So you can put a high degree of faith in the hundreds of reports prepared by Statistics Canada and in accident reports prepared by the Transportation Safety Board of Canada. The research is thorough, and people working for such agencies know their own credibility is on the line if details are mistaken or presented without full integrity.

The descriptions of activities of governments, labour unions, and business organizations provided by those organizations on their own websites are also reliable as far as they go. Although the information is likely to be largely truthful, it may not be thorough, and the details may be selected (indeed, likely are selected) to produce a positive picture. This information accurately reflects what an organization says about itself, but you probably want to seek alternative viewpoints in your research.

In the case of disclosures by publicly traded companies on securities websites such as SEDAR or EDGAR, there are penalties for improper reporting, but these do not provide bulletproof assurances of accuracy. Consider, for example, how Nortel "restated" several years of financial results filed with regulators.

The information made available by advocacy organizations, charities, lobby groups, think tanks such as The Fraser Institute, and the like is further down the reliability food chain, but is still useful. The factual information itself is probably reasonably reliable, but there is a greater chance that the information is being presented to persuade you of a particular point of view, or at least to reflect a broad point of view that the organization maintains.

The websites of tens of thousands of small volunteer organizations, clubs, social groups, and the like require more caution in their use. These websites may not always take great care in providing accurate information, but they do provide useful information about organizational activities as well as contact information for members and board members.

Finally, blogs, online forums, Twitter, other social network sites such as Facebook and, yes, Wikipedia vary wildly in reliability. When you obtain information from any of these sources, it is impossible to know without researching further if the information you have obtained is reliable. It may be, but it may not be. It is not good enough to simply attribute such sources. Information from any of them needs to be verified with other human or online sources. This is not to say that you shouldn't use such sources at all. In fact, Facebook has become a hugely important reporting resource, especially for finding sources and story tips. Just be careful, and verify what you find with other sources known to be reliable. Wikipedia may appear first on many searches, and it provides many leads on information, but you need to verify anything you find there.

DISCUSSION QUESTIONS

1. How should journalists use numbers as a research tool or as a storytelling device?
2. Review stories and media packages that have recently won a national or regional journalism prize. Do you think the research or the storytelling techniques were more important to their success? Why?
3. What are the three types of interview subjects you need most often, and how do search techniques differ for each? How would you find a chief executive officer for an interview? A victim of a fire? An expert on breast cancer?
4. Consider how you can make the best use of the tremendous resources of the World Wide Web. How can you take advantage of its vastness while not being undermined by its wild nature? Give reasons for your answers.

SUGGESTED RESOURCES

Research

Investigative Reporters and Editors Resource Center. http://www.ire.org/resourcecenter.
This site is a research portal for journalists, dedicated to investigative journalism.

J-Source.ca, The Canadian Journalism Project. http://www.j-source.ca.
This site is a project of the Canadian Journalism Foundation and leading journalism schools and organizations across Canada. It has an excellent resource page with tips on researching beats, interviewing, and web research. At the homepage, click on the Resource Centre link, or use the following direct link to the Resource Centre page: www.j-source.ca/english_new/category.php?catid=11&PHPSESSID=9bac2f1d703a4bb28dd3ca4108795dfe.

Poynter's News University (NewsU). http://www.newsu.org.
This online training program is run by the Poynter Institute. It has several good classes about research techniques. In particular, look at the section on math skills for journalists and how to read polls.

Web Navigation

CAR*in*Canada. http://www.carincanada.ca.
This site is a Canadian resource for computer-assisted reporting. It is maintained by the University of King's College.

National Institute for Computer-Assisted Reporting. http://data.nicar.org.
This site is an excellent resource for those interesting in digging more deeply into using computers to mine information from the Web and other data sources.

Statistics Canada. http://www.statcan.gc.ca.
As highlighted elsewhere in this chapter, this site is a gold mine of data just waiting for a reporter with a spreadsheet.

Vallance-Jones, Fred, and David McKie. 2009. *Computer-assisted reporting: A comprehensive primer*. Toronto: Oxford University Press.

REFERENCE

Sheppard, Robert. 2006. Reality check: Rrrolling up the rim on the real odds of winning. *CBC.ca*, March 14, 2006. http://www.cbc.ca/news/background/realitycheck/sheppard/20060314.html.

CHAPTER 11

Developing Story Ideas

Shane Holladay

Introduction

The aim of this chapter is to demystify the process of generating story ideas and converting them into actual pieces of journalism. Seasoned journalists were not born with innate qualities that somehow made them better able to generate story ideas. They learned how to recognize what is and what is not a story, and they invariably did this by immersing themselves in stories. Practically speaking, that simply means that they consumed a great deal of content in the medium in which they planned to work. This approach continues to work because stories have patterns.

CHAPTER OUTLINE

Every story has a recognizable main idea, and, over time, someone who is attentive to surrounding events begins to recognize story ideas as they crop up. Newsworthy stories offer something new or unconventional, a twist on the expression of a typical main idea. After journalists know what's typical, they can spot what's unusual. So the first part of learning to recognize patterns in information and events is to start collecting that information in a useful way. And thanks to the Internet, journalists now have at their disposal an unprecedented number of tools that make it easier to find out what's going on locally and beyond.

Armed with that body of knowledge, journalists can spot new and interesting details in the stream of otherwise everyday and ordinary stories they're exposed to. The raw beginnings of story ideas start to emerge from the background of facts and information. The real business of developing a story idea begins—the journalist takes a nugget of an idea and tests it in the real world.

How does an idea become a story idea? The key to developing any idea into a story idea is to explore it with the right people. Stories always come from people. Even when you find a story idea in data or documents—reports, analysis, court rulings, or securities filings—the true origin of those facts or events is what other people were doing.

The First Task: Find Out What's Going On

Back in the day, journalism professors made sure that prospective reporters subscribed to have the local paper (and a national one) delivered every day. This was a good idea. They wanted to get students to learn about the world around them and, more precisely, learn about their community. The only thing dated about this practice is that there's no longer any need to handle the hard copy.

Anyone with an Internet connection can access just about any newspaper—or any other source of news, sports, or entertainment—quickly and easily. If anything, too much information is available.

Trying to stay informed by visiting websites and blogs is challenging: systematically clicking through a site's navigation is time-consuming, and it's easy to miss a great deal of the content. Very few websites manage to simultaneously balance the look and feel of their site with making most new content visible. This is where newsreaders, alerts, and, perhaps surprisingly, social media networks become invaluable tools. Given the speed at which Internet technologies evolve, it's more practical to talk about how these tools can help new journalists find out what's going on around them than it is to discuss how specific tools work. A few examples of useful online tools are presented below.

Newsreaders

Instead of forcing a user to navigate to various topical sections of a website, good newsreaders use RSS feeds to present every published story, photo gallery, video (or what have you) from a given website. In a feed list, the most recent items appear at the top of the screen. Typically, the list displays headlines, short summaries or samples of the content, and links to the content's web page.

As one example, Google Reader offers feed bundles based on the most popular feeds for news, sports, entertainment, and recommended items. You can subscribe to these feed bundles or click on the "Add a subscription" button and plug in keywords (such as "hockey" or "fashion") to find feeds that reflect your own niche interests.

Getting Started with RSS Feeds

Here are some tips on getting started with RSS feeds:

- Subscribe to one of Google Reader's feed bundles, just to see what it offers and whether it's of interest to you.
- Look for local and national publications that relate to your interests. Subscribing to their feeds is an easy way to stay in touch with what's happening in your community.
- Undertake keyword searches in areas of interest to try to find feeds from independent blogs and websites.
- Try to narrow your choice of feeds from a publication. You probably don't need to see the whole *New York Times* news feed; the paper's technology news feed may be enough.

The RSS links on most websites don't always automatically feed into your reader of choice. Clicking on them will often lead to a page that's just a block of XML code. In such instances, copy the link address and paste it to the reader manually.

TOOLS & TIPS

What Is RSS?

RSS typically stands for "Really Simple Syndication," and it's a very common way for websites and blogs to push content out to an audience. An RSS feed is a stream of data that's updated on a regular basis. It can include text, images, links, and metadata (information about the information) in a summarized format. From the user's side, that stream of data—called a feed—is interpreted and displayed by so-called RSS readers (or *feed readers* or *aggregators*).

There are two big advantages to using a good RSS reader to view feeds from sources. The first is exposure to new information. Novice journalists typically follow the most salient sources—the most prominent TV stations in their area, the most reputable newspapers and the biggest magazines—and their websites. RSS readers are good research tools because they are neutral—they don't really know your location or your political or cultural affiliations—so they will serve up a set of feeds you probably would never have thought of. Many of those feeds will be independent blogs and alternative or unconventional news sources, all of which are important because the last thing you want is content from one point of view. It's very important to get started with feeds from a broad selection of websites, not just feeds from typical sources.

The second big advantage, especially when using software with a social dimension like Google Reader, is that you are exposed to content that other people find interesting. An RSS reader that allows you to view popular feeds, follow other users, view items shared by those followed, view what those followed like, and potentially view the feeds that others follow is tremendously useful because it exposes you to information you wouldn't otherwise have discovered on your own.

The Goals of Using RSS Readers

- to find out about the world
- to establish a base of knowledge that will help you recognize stories and spot new story ideas
- to create a system that will tell you about new things that are happening, in ways you might not always anticipate

The Advantages of Using RSS Readers

- They make it much easier to find out what's being published.
- You can customize your feeds and the information you receive.
- If they include social bookmarking tools, you can quickly find out what other people find interesting.
- Your base of knowledge will be vastly more diverse than it otherwise might be.

Message Boards, or Internet Forums

Message boards, also known as *Internet forums*, are probably the most venerable form of social communication on the Internet. Usenet newsgroups and Yahoo! Groups are two examples of aggregate groups (or, groups of groups), and practically any community (researchers, political activists, neo-Nazis, gamers, law societies) can quickly and easily set up public or private message boards to talk about issues.

Message boards are a great resource for understanding smaller communities with niche interests. Essentially, message boards are a group of people talking about what they really care about. Every message board has its own set of social rules and conversational tone, some of which can be off-putting. Different from news feeds that simply present stories, message boards are typically used by people to share facts and opinions (and often flame wars) about topics at a pre-story level or to discuss mainstream stories. As a result, they are a good source for emerging stories and a good way to develop some expertise about a topic. If you're willing to get involved in the conversation, other participants are almost always willing to educate you (whether you like it or not). Be careful, though: Message boards are rarely objective and balanced in their opinions or facts.

Getting involved in the conversation opens some interesting doors for journalists to collaborate with others online to develop story ideas.

Depending on the software hosting the message board, you can arrange for email alerts when new topics are posted, send personal messages with specific questions to other forum members, or search for keywords in existing posts.

The Goals of Using Message Boards

- to gain exposure to the ideas of niche communities
- to access conversations unfiltered by other media

The Advantages of Using Message Boards

- They're collaborative—they're conversations in which you can get thoughts and opinions from the other participants. They're a good way to find sources when developing story ideas as well.

- They're often built around communities with specific interests. Thus, they're specialized and offer more insight into the topics that communities care about than you can get from general reports or articles aimed at mass audiences.

Mailing Lists

Mailing lists, which date back to the earliest days of the Internet, are another method of sharing information. They're almost always focused on a narrow topic or community—for example, education technology, bisexual rights and advocacy in the United Kingdom, or sports betting systems. Some lists are closed and require permission from an administrator before you can subscribe.

Essentially, participants email one central administrative address, and that email is redistributed to everyone else on the mailing list. Depending on the number of people involved, an inbox can become quickly flooded (you get a copy of everyone's email), although some lists allow you to subscribe to weekly or daily summaries of list conversations.

Mailing lists are very much like message boards, with conversations happening entirely through email threads. Like message boards, they offer a window into communities dedicated to in-depth debates or conversations about their particular passion.

The Goal of Using Mailing Lists

- to gain access to opinionated experts—they can provide story ideas and serve as potential sources for your stories

The Advantages of Using Mailing Lists

- They're focused on the topic or community that participants care about, so they can offer deep and potentially uncommon knowledge.
- They're a good source for stories that no one else is aware of.

Alerts

Alerts are simple but powerful tools that can be used to find out what's happening in the world and what's being written about it. Alerts essentially come in two flavours: curated and custom.

Curated alerts are managed by people. An editor decides that a major newsworthy event just took place and alerts subscribers about it by email or text message. These kinds of alerts need some sort of subscription.

Custom alerts are automated and based on user-defined parameters. Some of the more technologically sophisticated news agencies, such as the *Toronto Star* and the *New York Times*, allow subscribers to add keywords to their profiles. In turn, alerts are emailed automatically when stories are published featuring those keywords. Custom alerts are excellent tools for researching specific topics.

Google offers an alert service that leverages its massive Internet search index. Google Alerts allows you to define keywords that generate news updates, with the added benefit of a vastly broader reach than a single media site. A list of related material from mainstream publications and websites arrives in your inbox, along with links to blogs or forum posts that match the keywords. Again, the advantage here is in getting information from sources that you wouldn't have realized are out there.

The alerts you subscribe to require some degree of management. As your needs change, you should update your list of alerts so that they remain relevant.

The Goals of Using Alerts

- to receive active updates on topics you care about
- to discover new information sources

The Advantages of Using Alerts

- Curated alerts help you recognize what are considered important stories. They're based on the judgment of experienced editors, although they also represent the biases of those editors.
- Custom alerts take advantage of automated systems to sift through massive amounts of content and data on your behalf.

Social Media Networks

The tools presented above (alerts excepted) are essentially online social networks; they just exist with a more narrow scope than social media networks such as Facebook, LinkedIn, and Twitter. Some newsreaders offer social connections—they show you what other people are reading or what they say they like. Social media networks, unlike the collection of message boards, RSS feeds, and mailing lists, are concerned with the connections among people. Depending on their privacy settings, you can usually see who someone has friended.

Social media networks will help you recognize stories. Pay attention to the stories that matter to people, the ones that they re-post, and the ones that they share.

Given the deluge of information you can set yourself up to receive online, social media networks become powerful tools for finding out what information is important. Have you ever followed a link sent by a friend? Doing so is essentially using a social filter. Considering the vast number of things people could potentially pay attention to, they often rely on friends and family—or people in their social network—to help them decide what's important to check out.

Social media networks are also powerful tools in developing stories. They're especially handy when you need to find people, either to help you develop a story idea or a full-fledged story.

A 2010 Pew Research Centre report called "Understanding the Participatory News Consumer" suggests that the American public regularly turns to their social networks to get news. According to the study, some 72 percent of American news consumers follow news because they want to know what's going on in the world and be able to talk about it with their friends. The authors note that "social networks act as alert systems for the most engaged news consumers." Equally significant are the reported rates of participation:

> Some 37% of internet users have contributed to the creation of news, commentary about it, or dissemination of news via social media. They have done at least one

> of the following: commenting on a news story (25%); posting a link on a social networking site (17%); tagging content (11%), creating their own original news material or opinion piece (9%), or Tweeting about news (3%). (Purcell et al. 2010)

Examples of social media sites and how they can be useful follows.

Facebook

Facebook groups spring up on just about any conceivable topic, and they are communication hubs for activists of all stripes (political, environmental, legal, vegetarian, you name it). You'll find people you can contact who are passionate about, and likely knowledgeable in, the topic in question. Tribute groups (devoted to people who have passed away or died tragically) also appear on Facebook, and can help you locate people who cared about the deceased.

LinkedIn

This site is probably the best single repository of potential experts. LinkedIn is a site designed expressly for business people looking to network. People list their qualifications and experience at the site and try to build connections with other professionals. For a journalist, this site operates as a directory of potential sources. You won't always be able to contact people directly through LinkedIn, but it should be a simple matter to track down their professional contact information with a Google search.

Like any other social media network, LinkedIn offers the most value after you build a profile and make full use of its features. It's also a good idea to build a LinkedIn profile in the interests of your own employment prospects.

Twitter

Sometimes referred to as a microblogging site, Twitter is more than just a quick way to tell people about your personal habits in 140 characters (and through the judicial use of URL shorteners). It's an excellent way to keep abreast of real-time events and solicit help in developing stories and story ideas.

However, Twitter is only as useful as the people you follow. It works this way: When a person sends out a tweet (a short message), everyone following that person gets a copy. That message can then be re-tweeted by others to their network of followers. Twitter is one of the best examples of how friend filters work—or how you can count on the people you think are trustworthy to alert you to stories.

Similar to curated alerts, curated Twitter feeds are available from major media publications and popular blogs. You don't need to follow every single one. Network effects will guarantee that as long as you build a broad and fairly diverse group of people to follow, you'll find out about interesting things as they happen. Make sure to re-tweet messages that you find interesting too—doing so will help you build a network of people who follow your tweets and become a new reciprocal source of information.

Don't hesitate to use Twitter to contact potential sources for interviews; it works. And finally, don't hesitate to ask your followers for advice or suggestions for sources or stories.

The Goals of Using Social Media Networks

- to find out about emerging stories—watch for trends in what the people you follow are talking about, and be aware of what your friends and colleagues are sharing
- to gain help from your social network in filtering the deluge of news and information that's out there
- to build contacts that will help alert you to stories, help you develop stories, help you understand events, and help you find potential sources

The Advantage of Using Social Media Networks

- Your social media network becomes part of your story development toolkit. People in your network can help you answer questions, suggest sources, and point out angles that you wouldn't necessarily think of on your own.

Crowdsourcing and Collaborating

One thing that should be obvious is that the above online tools have some sort of social dimension. Although you could approach each tool as a solo research effort (by ignoring the comments and feedback you get from your social network, focusing instead on the content they're sharing), you would be bypassing the potential advantage of having even more people enrich your knowledge and contribute to your work.

Historically, journalists have had little or no interaction (apart from the occasional letter or email) with their audience, but that all changed when websites began offering the public the option to comment on stories. Depending on the site (and how its comments are moderated) most of the feedback can be drivel. On occasion, though, the general public can offer some genuinely good feedback.

SIDEBAR

Social Networking Sites and News Distribution

The Pew Internet research report "Understanding the Participatory News Consumer" points to the emerging role of journalists as nodes in social networks (Purcell et al. 2010).

Just over half of online Americans (57 percent) use social networking sites like Facebook, MySpace, and LinkedIn, and 97 percent of those users are online news consumers. Overall, a third of all Internet users gets their news from friends as well as specific journalists and news organizations they've decided to follow on social networking sites.

Just what degree of public participation is appropriate when researching and writing stories is now an open debate. Journalists that do engage with their audience usually benefit when they collaborate with the people who read their work. This type of journalism has been dubbed *crowdsourcing* or *collaborative journalism*, and its potential contribution to story development has been alluded to during most of this chapter's discussion of social media.

The benefits are clear: extra ideas, sources, and tips or facts when developing a story. But don't forget that collaborating with your audience or the people in your social network still demands that the same standards of journalism be applied to their contributions: Double-check their facts and ensure the story is accurate and balanced.

Cooking Up Your Own Story Ideas

After you've set up some systems to find out what's going on—you've subscribed to some feeds, you're reading the paper every day, you're getting alerts about community sports, you're involved in a municipal affairs newsgroup—potential story ideas will start to hit you. This is a property of being well informed.

Developing great and original story ideas is a byproduct of skill and planning, not instinct, luck, or some innate potential to recognize news. It is partly learning to know what is a nascent story idea and what isn't, but mostly it's a matter of positioning yourself to be well informed and knowledgeable about the world around you. Remember that a story idea must always be something actionable, which means it's not so vague or broad that there's no clear way to start figuring out who you need to talk to.

Another way to look at developing great story ideas is to learn to know what *isn't* a story idea. Although a story idea can start with a topic, a topic is definitely not a story idea. Topics are general areas of interest, a category of events, or the subject of a discussion. Here are some examples of topics:

- the economy
- tattoos
- athletes and creatine
- poverty in the city
- media bias
- net neutrality

These are almost proto-ideas. They're what a journalist might have a step or two before he or she gets to a practical story idea. The common thread in of the above examples is a lack of specificity. In every case, the topic is broad and somewhat vague. Prefacing a topic with your intent to investigate doesn't help in any way. In other words, the following doesn't work either:

- I'll look at the economy.
- I'm interested in doing something about tattoos.
- I want to do a story on athletes and creatine.
- And so on …

Even so, a topic isn't a dead end. It needs to be associated with specific ideas. For example, simply strip away the intent to investigate ("I would like to compare and contrast …") and set some boundaries to the idea so it's possible to frame questions about it and figure out who you need to talk to in order to find answers.

Let's go back to the list of topics presented above, pick one, and show how it could evolve into a story idea.

Select a proto-idea.

- Poverty in the city

Add some boundaries.

- People in some of the most desperate situations are homeless, which is an example of the most extreme form of poverty.
- Wealth isn't evenly distributed—there are rich areas and poor areas.
- Some people are active in assisting the homeless.

Frame some questions.

- Who can tell me how many homeless are in the city?
- What are the poorest neighbourhoods?
- Who is helping out? How are people helping?
- How effective is that assistance?

Formulate the story idea.

- Establish the homeless population and where it's concentrated.
- Find out who is active in helping the most disadvantaged in the city.
- Find out what they're doing and what they're not doing.
- What are the results of their efforts? Has there been any change? Are those changes anecdotal or measurable.

It's clear that a bona fide story idea has some defining traits. When you generate your own story ideas, you'll know you're on track when

- you can make true or false statements about the idea
- you can figure out who to interview to find out if those statements are true or false

In other words, there must be a clear path of action on the idea. Always identify your assumptions going into a story and double-check them. A healthy bit of skepticism—even about things you assume to be true—will not only ensure you get the story right but also help keep your eyes open for a more interesting angle on a story.

Some common story ideas come out of actionable ideas.

A story idea can be about a person.

EXAMPLES:

- A poverty activist has an important role in securing funding for a shelter. How long has he been working in the community? What do the people who that person works with have to say? Are there any critics?
- A local professor gets a multimillion dollar research grant. What other work has she done? What got the professor into this line of research? Why does she think this research is important? Can anyone else in the professor's field offer some insight?

  Digging deeper: Who is this person? Where does this person come from and how did he or she get to where they are now? What do others have to say about this individual?

A story idea can be about a place.

EXAMPLES:

- A derelict hotel notorious for violent crime and drug trafficking is being closed and demolished. When did the hotel first open? Was it always notorious? Where can you find former patrons or guests? Are any of them famous? Are there any archived reports or stories about the place? What does it look like now?
- A café in the city is a hotspot for young artists. What makes it attractive to the young artists who go there? How do the young artists benefit? What kind of atmosphere do you find there?

  Digging deeper: What happened at the place that's interesting? What's the history of the place? Who can tell you why that's important? Who was actually there? How can you describe the place?

A story idea can be about information.

EXAMPLES:

- Health Canada issues a product recall. How did the ministry conclude that the product was dangerous? What facts were used in this decision? Has the product been recalled in other countries? Who was affected by this product? Can you find and speak with them?
- A poll is released suggesting that Canadians are heavy beer drinkers. Who conducted the research? Who paid for the research to be done? How was this study conducted? Who can you find to explain what the results mean?

  Digging deeper: Who can explain what the information means? Whom does it affect? What tools do you have to relate that story?

A story idea can be a statement with a question.

EXAMPLES:

- A new hockey arena will be built in the city. Does the municipality really need one? Who was behind the push to get a new arena? How could the same money otherwise be spent? Who benefits from this new arena? Are there any critics?
- The RCMP announces that violent crimes are down in rural areas in Alberta. How did they measure this change? What do they consider "violent crime"? How does this change compare with other jurisdictions? How significant is this change? Who can put this change in perspective?

  Digging deeper: Consider every idea to be a theory that can be either confirmed or discarded. Turn the idea into a statement. What do you need to know if this is true? Take the idea you have and re-frame it as a statement and a series of questions that will test the truth of that statement.

Note that every one of the preceding examples features at least one question that involves talking to people. There's always going to be someone out there who knows much, much more about the story idea you have in mind than you do. In just about every case, they'll suggest a way of looking at your story that you've never thought of. Learn to run with that.

Handling Assignments

Many stories are assignments. A reporter can be sent to cover a trial, a protest, or a city council meeting or gather random opinions through streeters. The objective of each of these stories is usually pretty clear:

- Report the outcome of the trial.
- Cover the protest. Establish what it's about and who cares about the issues and why.
- Report the outcome of the city council meeting and spot the important issues.
- Get reactions from the public and look for interesting points of view.

Going Further with Assigned Stories

Working in a newsroom guarantees that a significant part of your workload will be assigned stories. Those stories could be based on ideas generated by your editor or, quite simply, newsworthy events or people that need to be covered.

Treat these assignments like nascent story ideas, but always be alert for unexpected elements that could lead to completely original angles on the story or a new story altogether.

For example:

- You're sent to the scene of a house fire where firefighters rescued a child from a smoke-filled room. You're talking to a member of the public outside the home, and that person mentions that there have been two similar fires in the neighbourhood in the last month. Is there a bigger story here?
- You've been sent to city hall to cover a vote likely to approve a small increase in taxes on local businesses. You also check the agenda and discover an item added at the last minute to discuss a possible transit fare hike for seniors.

Press Releases

Even the most innocuous press releases have an agenda. In many cases the announcement is worthy in and of itself, but the information in any press release should never be taken at face value. Even if the facts have not been spun, an opportunity always exists to create an original story that's better than the obvious one presented in the press release.

For example:

- Hasbro announces the launch of a fan-driven version of Monopoly, with the public's choice of Canadian cities on the board. You talk to the company. But then you decide to ask a professor of new media studies about tabulating public votes to create a product, and you discover a better story about other crowdsourcing initiatives.
- Virgin Mobile announces a new mobile technology on its network and promises new phones and features. You realize you need to get some perspective on this story and track down an industry analyst. That person tells you Canada lags behind European and Asian cellphone markets, and the announcement is more froth than substance; in the analyst's opinion, consumers will get more of the same.

Tips from Sources and Suggestions from Friends

Tips will come into a newsroom or from sources who trust you. Sometimes friends or family will hear about something that is potentially newsworthy. Such tips should always be treated with caution. The first thing a journalist must do is seek independent confirmation of a tip.

Let's say a defence attorney tells you that she's worried about the safety of her client in remand. Her client told her that inmates have figured out how to open some secure doors. The province denies that this is true, but you get in touch with the union representing guards and they reveal they've discovered the same thing. They were told that there's no budget to upgrade locks at the prison.

Tips should always be approached with caution and, ideally, are stories only when there's independent confirmation from someone willing to go on the record.

Conclusion

Developing story ideas is possible after you've established a rich understanding of the world around you. Once again, this is not a mysterious process; every expert was once a novice. There is a learning curve that takes place before a seasoned journalist can bring to bear tacit knowledge about a topic or invent innovative angles on a story that's been told a thousand times.

Most novice journalists are stymied by two challenges when they set out to develop their own stories. The first lies in recognizing what a story is (and conversely, realizing when an idea they have is not a story). This is largely a byproduct of the second challenge they face, namely, that they have not yet developed a deep and broad base of knowledge about the field in which they want to report.

Thus the first task outlined in this chapter—to find out what's going on. Be curious. Exploring the tools outlined above, and any others you discover along the way, is essential to developing an understanding of the events around you and how they affect your community. You will become well informed. Once you've immersed yourself in the stories that are being told around you, you'll start to recognize stories that have not yet been told.

The next step is to anchor your stories in the real world. Start talking to people. The planning portion of this process (gathering knowledge) is complete. Now, another set of skills a journalist must bring to bear will come into play. This is where sources are identified, tracked down, and interviewed. This is where story ideas are tested against reality and either enriched by your sources, modified to fit reality, or discarded as irrelevant, inaccurate, or fictional.

Taken together, those two steps help novice journalists develop good judgement and critical thinking. They lead to a conceptual understanding of storytelling and the ability to recognize the big picture, to address important aspects of a story, and to ignore irrelevant information.

This state of story development proficiency is the goal of every successful journalist, where you are able reflect on how you find stories, how you shape your knowledge base, and how you can continually improve the process by which you generate great stories.

DISCUSSION QUESTIONS

1. How do you know you are making good choices about your sources of information? What are the benefits and disadvantages of the sources you are turning to for information, and the tools you are planning to use?
2. When you are developing story ideas in a social medium, what is the right level of collaboration? How do you identify reliable and trustworthy contributors to a collaborative effort to develop a story idea?
3. Why are interviews with real people essential to developing good story ideas?

SUGGESTED RESOURCES

Journerdism. News and commentary website by Will Sullivan, the Interactive Director at the *St. Louis Post-Dispatch*, in St. Louis, Missouri. He covers "online journalism, multimedia, social media, mobile, tech news & ideas." http://www.journerdism.com.

McLachlan, Gregg. 50 places to shop for story ideas. http://www.notrain-nogain.org/Train/Res/Report/50places.asp.

Nieman Journalism Lab. Collaborative project at Harvard University funded by the Nieman Foundation. Its goal is to "attempt to figure out how quality journalism can survive and thrive in the Internet age." http://www.niemanlab.org.

10,000 Words. "Where journalism and technology meet." http://www.10000words.net.

REFERENCE

Purcell, Kristen, Lee Rainie, Amy Mitchell, Tom Rosenstiel, and Kenny Olmstead. 2010. Understanding the participatory news consumer. Pew Internet & American Life Project, March 1. http://pewinternet.org/Reports/2010/Online-News.aspx.

CHAPTER 12

Reporting Basics: Accuracy, Precision, and Balance

Rick MacLean

Introduction

Andrew Gilligan had a scoop he wanted to share. Right away.

So at 6:07 a.m. on May 29, 2003, he sat in front of a radio microphone and did just that. The British government's claim that Iraq could launch weapons of mass destruction in 45 minutes was nonsense, the BBC defence correspondent said. The government had fudged the facts to trick the public into supporting the war. His source had helped write the report that made the claim.

"Downing Street … ordered it to be sexed up, to be made more exciting," Gilligan said, paraphrasing what he'd been told.

In his rush to be first, however, Gilligan was wrong. Twice. His secret source was Dr. David Kelly, a biological weapons expert. But Kelly didn't help write the report, and he had never used the words "sexed up." The government suspected that Kelly was the source and leaked his name, apparently in a bid to discredit the story. Caught in a media storm, a few weeks later the scientist told his wife he was going for a walk. He headed to a wooded area near his home, swallowed 29 painkillers, and slit his left wrist. His body was found the next morning.

Gilligan's story was inaccurate. But in an Internet environment, increasingly defined by the ability to get the story first, the incident was probably inevitable. It's a warning for any journalist operating in an era that includes Twitter, Facebook, YouTube, the blogosphere, and 24/7 news. In this chapter we'll look at what you can do to ensure your stories are accurate, precise, and balanced, despite the rush to be first.

CHAPTER OUTLINE

Accuracy

My teenage son was never much of a newspaper reader, except for the sports pages the day after he'd played in a high school basketball game. He would flip to that section, scan for the story, and start reading.

"Yep," he would sigh. "They did it again."

"It" was the spelling of his last name. There are at least four ways to spell it—MacLean, Maclean, McLean, and Mclean. Our spelling is the first one, a fact I gently pointed out to the paper one day when I noted that I had once been the paper's editor—for about 15 years—and my photo and name still appeared weekly on my column.

Research suggests that my complaint—and my son's—is not unique. Studies indicate that about half of sources feel there are errors in stories involving them. Many of those complaints are judgmental, not factual, and a case of emphasis. Some complain about distorted headlines or misquotes. But about one-third of errors involve typos or factual errors. Most involve incorrect names, times, dates, numbers, addresses, locations, and titles (Fedler et al. 2001, 123).

If a working definition of *accuracy* is "getting things right," then accuracy comes in two basic flavours: facts and emphasis. Getting the basic facts right is relatively easy. Check. Then check again. Never assume. John Smith may spell his name Jon Smyth. Don't ask sources how to spell their name; print it in block letters in your notebook and show it to them. Same thing with titles and addresses. I use a red marker to write "Fired" across a story if a student fouls up a name.

And check the source's age. Is his or her birthday soon? Someone might be 18 today, but 19 in a month. You'll need that information for follow-ups. Also, ensure numbers add up. If you have 10 people on the committee, you shouldn't have 11 names. Finally, read your copy out loud. Reading it silently won't work. You skim. And in skimming the the story, you can miss typos like that one. Did you see it? Your brain processes the words differently when it hears them. You'll spot errors and clunks—sentences that are just plain ugly.

This is an online age. If you get something wrong, or worse, make it up, you'll get caught.

IN PRACTICE

Inconvenient Truths

Sportswriter Mitch Albom once filed a lovely colour piece for the *Detroit Free Press* about a pair of NBA players who returned to their roots to watch the national college basketball championships. All popcorn and pompoms. Problem was, the players changed their minds at the last minute and didn't go. The story had been filed in advance. Albom had to apologize. Similarly, a freelancer in Canada filed a story to the *Boston Globe* talking about blood on the ice at the start of the annual seal hunt. One problem: The hunt was delayed. That story was also filed in advance.

Stick to what you know to ensure accuracy. I once covered a meeting where a committee member appeared to be drunk, but there was no way to be sure. I did the only thing I could, I described exactly what I saw, a man who slurred his words and seemed to struggle to understand the discussion going on around him. He and his family were angry at the story, but they didn't argue that it was inaccurate.

Knowing What to Emphasize

The real difficulty with accuracy isn't ensuring that the names and numbers are correct. The problem is getting all the relevant facts and knowing what to emphasize. Simply getting the necessary information can be difficult. And people eager to spin you might provide their side of the story, omitting anything that hurts their case, in an effort to influence what you consider important.

Journalists must pick and choose from the facts they collect, deciding what's useful and how prominently it will play. Often, they depend on experts to help them. But every reporter has had an experience like the one described by professor (and Chapter 10 co-author) Kelly Toughill of University of King's College in Halifax. In the fascinating CBC Radio series *Spin Cycles*, she described working at the *Toronto Star* and watching spin expert Paul Rhodes deliberately leak stories to chosen reporters in such a way that gave the government a clean hit, a story without the other side's point of view in it.

One of the more infamous recent examples of such manipulation involved then *New York Times* defence reporter Judith Miller. Eager to appear on the front page, she began writing stories about the suspected weapons of mass destruction program in Iraq. One story featured a defector laying out work done on storage sites for nuclear, chemical, and biological weapons. Another, using US government sources, said Iraq was importing aluminum tubes needed for nuclear weapons.

It was all hooey.

Looking back, Bob Woodward of Watergate fame said Miller's excuse (that her sources had lied to her) wasn't good enough; she needed to talk to more sources. The few reporters who went looking—reporters not caught up in the war hysteria following the September 11, 2001 attacks on the United States—found doubters willing to talk.

Figure 12.1 Journalist Edward R. Murrow's willingness to confront US Senator Joseph McCarthy over his misleading attacks on supposed Communist sympathizers—including Murrow himself—represented a crucial turning point in public sentiment toward McCarthy. (Photo: Prelinger Archives Collection.)

The need to challenge the accuracy of assertions is a lesson journalists sometimes forget. One such challenge occurred on April 13, 1954. TV journalist Edward R. Murrow of CBS responded on air to an attack on his character by powerful US Senator Joseph McCarthy, the head of a committee investigating communism in America:

> He claimed, but offered no proof, that I had been a member of the Industrial Workers of the World. That is false. I was never a member of the IWW, never applied for membership. Men that I worked with in

> the Pacific Northwest in western Washington in logging camps will attest that I never had any affiliation or affinity with that organization. The senator charged that Professor Harold Laski, a British scholar and politician, dedicated [a] book to me. That's true. He is dead. He was a socialist—I am not. He was one of those civilized individuals who did not insist upon agreement with his political principles as a pre-condition for conversation or friendship. (Murrow 1954)

Today, a number of groups try to unspin dubious claims. FactCheck.org, a project of the Annenberg Public Policy Center of the University of Pennsylvania, holds political feet to the fire, whatever side of the political fence they call home.

In Canada, DeSmogBlog.com tries to pull back the veil on who pays the bills in the climate debate. It's led by Jim Hoggan, founder of the public relations firm James Hoggan & Associates based in Vancouver. In the United States, Greenpeace's Exxon-Secrets (www.greenpeace.org/usa/campaigns/global-warming-and-energy/exxon-secrets) does the same thing.

Journalist Craig Silverman of Montreal keeps reporters on their toes with his blog RegretTheError.com and his book *Regret the Error*. The *Hamilton Spectator* earned a mention for this mistake: "A cutline in Saturday's *Spectator* incorrectly identified Jes-Lynn Chaplin's new baby as a boy. Baby Harlow, Hamilton's first baby of the new year, is a girl." The *Denver Post* earned a spot for this gem: "Because of a reporting error, a story on Page 3E on Sunday listed author John Updike as still living. He died in January."

Oops.

Silverman also includes a checklist on his website for those hoping to avoid future embarrassment (see Tools & Tips below). Among his suggestions: Ask sources to spell their name and title, and verify the math when using numbers.

Journalism, the old chestnut says, is history on the run. That means accuracy is what you can get *now*. The rest must wait for tomorrow, when it might not rate as big a headline. That is unfortunate, but the pressure to publish or broadcast is unrelenting. Still, in the push for speed, it's important to remember what you're being given, what you're being denied, and why. And it's vital to get it right.

Early in the 1996 movie *Up Close & Personal*, hard-bitten veteran Robert Redford snarls at budding young reporter Michele Pfeiffer when she screws up the location of a double drowning.

"In the blue waters off Miami today …" she begins.

"Miami Beach," he snaps.

Details matter. After all, if you can't get the basics right, what else did you screw up?

Precision

Being accurate is one thing. Being precise is another. Consider the beginning of this story:

> Bobby Brown of Cloudy Corner was convicted yesterday of theft of over $5,000 in a case involving a break-in at his church. His sentencing is set for Monday.

It's accurate, but it's not precise. Turns out, Brown is a pretty popular name in Cloudy Corner, a small community with a history dating back more than a hundred

TOOLS & TIPS

Accuracy Checklist

Story: ______________________________

Sources: ______________________________

____

____

While Reporting

- ☐ Ask sources to spell name and title
- ☐ Record or transcribe interviews
- ☐ Verify claims with reliable sources
- ☐ Save links and other research
- ☐ Ask sources what other reports got wrong

Final Checks Before Submission

- ☐ Numbers and math
- ☐ Names
- ☐ Titles (people, books, etc.)
- ☐ Locations
- ☐ Compare quotes to notes/recording
- ☐ Quote attribution
- ☐ Definitions
- ☐ URLs
- ☐ Spelling and grammar
- ☐ Spellchecker errors

Story-Specific Items

- ☐ ______________________________
- ☐ ______________________________
- ☐ ______________________________

SOURCE: RegretTheError.com. Reprinted by permission of Craig Silverman.

years. And there are Bobby Browns galore there. So many, in fact, that the locals add their wives' names to them to tell them apart. There's Judy's Bobby and Sally's Bobby and …

This is a true story. Well, the wives' names part, at least. And you can imagine the number of calls you'll get tomorrow if your story slaps every Bobby with the thief handle. Rightly so. The situation could be the same in places like Cape Breton Island,

Nova Scotia, where middle names help people understand if you're talking about singer John Allan Cameron or some other John Cameron down the road.

Precision, in this case, requires that the reporter name the one person convicted of theft from the church. Bobby Brown, 32, of 112 Church Lane in Cloudy Corner is precise, as well as accurate. Similarly, people charged with serious crimes are further identified with their middle names, in order to avoid misidentification (for example, Robert William Pickton, Mark David Chapman).

And accuracy is not enough when it comes to tech talk, the language used by experts in their fields of study. A police officer at a trial may say the victim had "petechial hemorrhages," but we'd rather say blood vessels in the eyes had burst, a sign the person suffocated (Philbin 1996, 170).

It's translation, and it's a specialty of journalists like Bob McDonald, the host of CBC Radio's science show, *Quirks and Quarks*. Consider this example from April 14, 2001. Scientist Robert Devlin describes his work trying to grow bigger fish:

> We isolated genes from the salmon which are responsible for regulating growth and engineered them in the lab such that more growth hormone could be produced. These genes were then introduced back into strains of various species of salmonids, including coho salmon, rainbow trout, Chinook and Atlantic salmon. And what we basically observed is that there is a very dramatic enhancement of growth relative to the growth rate seen in the wild strains. And this looked like there was a fair bit of potential for accelerating the growth of fish then, which brought along a lot of questions associated with the risk of this kind of technology to wild stocks. And that's our current research program.

I was lost at *salmonids*. Fortunately, McDonald jumped in: "So basically, you took a gene, you put a gene into the fish that produces growth hormone just to basically make it grow faster."

"That's right," Devlin agreed.

McDonald chopped 116 words to 24, and you could edit that to 16, easily, with not a salmonid in sight: "You put a gene that produces growth hormone into the fish to make it grow faster."

And McDonald ran the translation by the expert, who said the translation was accurate and precise. Remember, it's easier on the ego to tell someone you don't understand and ask for clarification than it is to see a correction appear with your name attached to it.

Then there's *said*. Some writers can't seem to leave well enough alone when it comes to the word. Get over it. It's both accurate and precise. *Said* means one thing, someone opened his or her mouth and sounds came out. That's it. And that's enough. Don't believe me? Listen to Elmore Leonard (2001), author of books such as *Get Shorty* and *Killshot*:

> Never use a verb other than *said* to carry dialogue. The line of dialogue belongs to the character; the verb is the writer sticking his nose in. But *said* is far less intrusive than grumbled, gasped, cautioned, lied. I once noticed Mary McCarthy

ending a line of dialogue with "she asseverated," and had to stop reading to get the dictionary.

It's a case of showing readers, not telling them. Let readers consider the facts and decide for themselves. That's also why Leonard (2001) is death on adverbs:

> Never use an adverb to modify the verb *said* … he admonished gravely. To use an adverb this way (or almost any way) is a mortal sin. The writer is now exposing himself in earnest, using a word that distracts and can interrupt the rhythm of the exchange. I have a character in one of my books tell how she used to write historical romances "full of rape and adverbs."

Replace *said* with *claimed* and you're suggesting the person is lying. "He didn't take the money, claimed the mayor." Best call your lawyer and your accountant, the defamation suit is on its way. *According to*, same thing. There's too much baggage, too much imprecision in such words.

There is such a thing as being too precise, especially in a lead. Saying the mayor is suing you for $996,987.63 for writing he "claimed he's innocent" is swell, but in the lead you could say "about $1 million" and save the gory details for later. Similarly, readers might better understand it if you say about one person in eight will get the flu this year, rather than 12.59 percent of the population.

A quotation is a quotation. I once had a high school principal scold me in a hallway during a career day because one of my reporters wrote a story in which a grade 12 boy said, "I didn't do nothing all weekend." It made the school look bad, the principal said. The paper should have cleaned it up. I politely informed him if my reporter had done that, I would have fired her. The double negative was awkward, but it was accurate and precisely what the kid said.

The Impact of Language

But the principal was right about one thing: Language is important on an emotional level. That's something experts know very well, so they try to shape the discussion in their favour using language. Reporters need to understand that. An obvious example is abortion. Reporters use *pro-life* and *pro-choice*, not *anti-abortion* and *pro-abortion*, to describe the two sides. Is one set of terms more precise than the other? That's an interesting question. Certainly many groups prefer to be known for what they support, not what they oppose.

When it comes to language, and its impact on the audience, Frank Luntz is considered an expert. When you say *climate change* instead of *global warming*, you're using language devised by the Oxford-educated American who wrote the book *Words That Work: It's Not What You Say, It's What People Hear*. So why *climate change*?

> "Climate change" is less frightening than "global warming." As one focus group participant noted, climate change "sounds like you're going from Pittsburgh to Fort Lauderdale." While global warming has catastrophic connotations attached to it, climate change suggests a more controllable and less emotional challenge. (Luntz 2002, 142)

Climate scientist Andrew Weaver of the University of Victoria in British Columbia considers *climate change* less accurate than *global warming* in the present context:

> The term *global warming* applies specifically to what is happening now, as a consequence of increasing greenhouse gases associated with human activity. Climate has always varied and it will continue to vary no matter what we do. This truism sounds innocent enough, but it's the rallying cry for the denial industry looking to delay emissions reduction policy. This is why the term *climate change* is less accurate. Climate has always changed and always will.
>
> I use the term *global warming* to let people know specifically what I am referring to. It is the climate change caused by humans. I don't want it to be buried in with all the other climate changes of the past and future. When I use it, I want to be very clear that we are talking about human-caused climate change as opposed to natural climate variability.[1]

Balance

The man who handed me the secret government report has his reasons. Among them was his desire to discredit a political rival. What the report said was damning. The rival—call him Joe—was accused of being a liar, a thief, a drug dealer, and a bootlegger.

There was one problem. The report contained accusations, not proof. Legally, I was in deep water. Ethically, I had the same problem. Fortunately, there was a solution to both problems. I had to go to Joe and get his side of the story. I left the door to my car slightly ajar when I got out at his house and walked up the front steps. A man the size of a door greeted me.

"Is he here?" I asked before I realized Joe was sitting in the shade at the far end of the porch.

"No," The Door said.

Then Joe laughed.

"Never mind him. Come on up." The Door moved aside, slowly.

I wasted no time. In minutes I'd asked Joe if he was a liar, a thief, a drug dealer, and a bootlegger. He denied the charges, talking in detail about the accusations. That done, I made my excuses and headed back to my car, squeezing past The Door on my way. The story ran the next page on page one. There were no complaints.

Getting both sides—perhaps all sides is more accurate—is crucial in a story. Avoid the temptation to run one side today and the other tomorrow. Legal problems aside, and they are considerable, it's wrong. And it's bad journalism. Readers, viewers, and listeners have a right to expect the full story, if you can get it. If you can't get the full story, put that in the story. I've put *declined to comment* in more than one story over the years after one side thought hiding would kill the story. But I've also pushed hard to get that other side.

One memorable case I called *Giving Oxygen to a Dead Man*. A health specialist was accused of billing a business for providing oxygen to a man who had died months earlier. I had the court decision against the specialist. I had the false paperwork he had filed. And I had the death certificate of the dead man. It was open and shut. But

I chased the specialist for days, finally catching him at home. He hedged. I promised the story was running either way. Finally, I agreed to fax him a copy of the story so he could read it. It worked. I got the comment. The story ran on page one. There were no complaints.

The Illusion of Balance

There is, however, a danger in the journalistic desire for balance. Perhaps we should be using the word *fair* instead. Sometimes, the desire for balance really masks a desire to find conflict, making the story more appealing. And that can get in the way of an accurate story.

The climate debate is an example. For a time, a retired geography professor from the University of Winnipeg, Tim Ball, was the go-to guy in Canada for reporters looking for the other side. Journalists doing stories about the changing climate would interview someone like Andrew Weaver at the School of Earth and Ocean Sciences at the University of Victoria, then call Ball. He could be counted on for a comment saying the science is wrong or the issue is still open to debate. The desire for balance satisfied, reporters would file their stories. The problem was, they didn't check to see if Ball was publishing significant amounts of peer-reviewed research on the subject in learned journals—the gold standard for evaluating a scientist's credibility. He wasn't. Weaver's list of publications, on the other hand, filled pages and went back years.

That's not balance. It just looks like it. Reporters using Ball should have noted his research record, and its relevance, in any story quoting him.

Exploiting a reporter's desire for balance is an old game. The tobacco industry was a master at it, even setting up something called the Tobacco Institute to give its claims credibility. David Michaels documented that work in his book *Doubt Is Their Product: How Industry's Assault on Science Threatens Your Health*. A 1938 Johns Hopkins study noted a strong link between smoking and life span. The tobacco industry spent the rest of the century fighting the science. Their tactics became public years later as result of legal action.

> Perhaps my favorite of the many, many self-incriminating documents uncovered in the forty million pages now in the public domain … is the 1969 memo in which a tobacco company executive gloated, "Doubt is our product since it is the best means of competing with the 'body of fact' that exists in the minds of the general public. It is also the means of establishing a controversy."
>
> Another personal favorite is a letter dated 1972, in which a staffer for the Tobacco Institute wrote to a colleague that the strategy of the past twenty years or so—"litigation, politics and public opinion"—had been "brilliantly conceived and executed" but was not "a vehicle for victory." It was only a holding action based on "creating doubt about the health charge without actually denying it …" (Michaels 2008, 11)

Setting up fake grassroots organizations is another tactic developed by tobacco lobby groups and now used by many lobby groups with enough money and motivation to make it work. Such groups pressure the media, demanding equal time for their point of view, all in the name of journalistic balance. The names of such "Astroturf" groups can be wonderfully perverse, such as "Citizens to Protect the Pacific Northwest and Northern California Economy." It was backed by more than $1 million from the forest industry, which wanted to do more clear-cutting (Pryne 1994).

SourceWatch.org in the United States tries to keep tabs on such groups. The Wikipedia-style website is run by the Center for Media and Democracy based in Madison, Wisconsin. The centre describes itself as an "independent, non-profit, non-partisan, public interest organization … countering propaganda by investigating and reporting on behind-the-scenes public relations campaigns by corporations, industries, governments and other powerful institutions" (Center for Media and Democracy n.d.).

The use of doubt and the abuse of the desire for balance were explored in the darkly satirical movie *Thank You for Smoking* in 2005. It featured exchanges like this one between industry spokesman Nick Naylor and a little girl in a classroom:

GIRL: My mommy says smoking kills.
NICK: Oh, is your mommy a doctor?
GIRL: No.
NICK: A scientific researcher of some kind?
GIRL: No.
NICK: Well then, she's hardly a credible expert, is she?

Conclusion

My 21-year-old daughter came running into the kitchen one day recently.

"Dad, the Opera House is on fire."

The bar had been owned by a good friend until he died. He'd spent years collecting movie memorabilia displayed in the century-old, three-storey, brick building. A prize possession was a dress once worn by movie star Marilyn Monroe. My daughter heard about the fire on her cellphone, by text. She ran to her laptop and opened up Facebook. There we watched four videos of the fire her friends, still at the scene, had filmed on their cellphones and posted. A day later I read about the fire on CBC.ca and clicked on the link to YouTube, where the same videos I'd watched the night before appeared.

Welcome to the 21st century.

Some of the stiffest competition news outlets face today comes from their own customers, who can scoop them with a cellphone. Technology and the rush to be first with the story put tremendous pressure on reporters. Meanwhile, accuracy, precision, and balance—crucial to meaningful reporting—take time. Finding a solution that lets news organizations prosper in this new world, while maintaining the kind of reporting needed to earn and keep credibility, is a significant challenge facing journalism in the new millennium.

NOTE

1. Andrew Weaver, email message to author, January 11, 2010.

DISCUSSION QUESTIONS

1. What issues surround "accuracy" in the age of digital journalism? Consider the following: Some journalists rely on crowdsourcing (which CBC Radio producer Ira Basen [2009] explores in "News 2.0: The Future of News in an Age of Social Media"). On October 3, 2008, Mathew Ingram checked Twitter on his way to work. A former editor at the *Globe and Mail* newspaper in Toronto, he read a report saying Apple CEO Steve Jobs had been rushed to hospital with a heart attack. The report on CNN-I hadn't been verified, but it was interesting and Ingram reposted it. He wasn't alone. Between 9:40 a.m. and 9:52 a.m., Apple shares tumbled by almost 11 percent, a $5 billion loss. By 10 a.m. Apple said the story was untrue and its shares began to recover.

   That's journalism at work, Ingram says.

   Jeff Jarvis agrees. He blogs about media and news at BuzzMachine.com and wrote *What Would Google Do?* Blog entries are part of a process, not the final word, he says. "In professional journalism, we look at mistakes and corrections as a mark of shame. In the blog world, we look at mistakes and corrections as a mark of honesty" (Basen 2009). Do you agree?
2. Why worry about balance when everyone can publish his or her views online? When American TV personality Glenn Beck of Fox News explored global warming in his 2007 show *The Climate of Fear*, he began by saying, "This is not a balanced look at global warming. It is the other side of the climate debate that you don't hear anywhere. Yes, Al Gore, there is another, credible, side."
3. Who cares what language is used—*global warming* or *climate change*, *pro-choice* or *pro-abortion*? It's all just a matter of opinion, isn't it?

SUGGESTED RESOURCES

To Keep You Honest

FactCheck.org. http://www.factcheck.org.

Regret the Error [Craig Silverman's blog]. http://www.regrettheerror.com.

Silverman, Craig. 2007. *Regret the error: How media mistakes pollute the press and imperil free speech*. Toronto: Penguin Group Canada.

On Spin

DeSmogBlog.com [on global warming]. http://www.desmogblog.com.

SourceWatch. http://www.sourcewatch.org/index.php?title=SourceWatch.

REFERENCES

Basen, Ira. 2009. News 2.0: The future of news in an age of social media. *Journalism Ethics for the Global Citizen*, August 17. http://www.journalismethics.ca/feature_articles/future_of_news.html.

Beck, Glenn. 2007. *The climate of fear*. Transcript of videotape. http://www.desmogblog.com/sites/beta.desmogblog.com/files/GlennBeck_ClimateOfFear.pdf.

Center for Media and Democracy. n.d. About CMD. http://www.prwatch.org/cmd/index.html.

Fedler, Fred, John R. Bender, Lucinda D. Davenport, and Michael W. Drager. 2001. *Reporting for the media*. 7th ed. Fort Worth, TX: Harcourt College Publishers.

Leonard, Elmore. 2001. Easy on the adverbs, exclamation points and especially hooptedoodle. *New York Times*, July 16. http://www.nytimes.com/2001/07/16/arts/writers-writing-easy-adverbs-exclamation-points-especially-hooptedoodle.html?pagewanted=1.

Luntz, Frank. 2002. "Straight talk" memo to the U.S. Republican party: The environment—A cleaner, safer, healthier America. http://www.sindark.com/NonBlog/Articles/LuntzResearch_environment.pdf.

Michaels, David. 2008. *Doubt is their product: How industry's assault on science threatens your health*. New York: Oxford University Press.

Murrow, Edward R. 1954. Response to Senator Joe McCarthy on CBS' *See It Now*. Audio file. http://www.americanrhetoric.com/speeches/edwardrmurrowtomccarthy.htm.

Philbin, Tom. 1996. *Cop speak: The lingo of law enforcement and crime*. New York: John Wiley and Sons.

Pryne, Eric. 1994. New timber coalition to join forest debate. *Voice of the Wild Olympics* 2 (1). [Excerpted from *Seattle Times*, November 18, 1993.] http://rdpayne.drizzlehosting.com/opa-news-v2n1.html.

CHAPTER 13

Structure and Story Online

Paul Benedetti

CHAPTER OUTLINE

Change and Continuity: The Surprising Survival of the Inverted Pyramid

You may have read that the Internet changed everything about journalism and storytelling. You may have even read that in this book. But like most sweeping statements, it's true and not so true. The Web with all its immediacy, its reach, its social networks, and new tools has changed the way we find stories, research stories, and structure and write stories. Some might argue that the Internet changes the very nature of story.

Oddly, perhaps even ironically, most observers first hypothesized that the endless space afforded by working online would make the classic hard news story a thing of the past.

Not true.

Why? Well, the Internet brought both good and bad news for journalists and their audience. First, the good news. It offered unlimited space, a boon for every reporter forced to cut a great story because the news hole was too small (and that's *every* reporter). It offered a huge audience who, the polls tell us, are getting more and more of their news online. According to a recent survey, about half of the people polled in the United States go online for their news, and Canadians are increasing their use of the Web for news (Reuters 2008; Canadian Media Research Consortium 2008).

Reading on the Web: Not Really Reading

The bad news is that surveys show that most people don't read online. That's right. They don't read online. At least, not much. They scan.

Web design and usability expert Jakob Nielsen (1997) writes: "People rarely read Web pages word by word; instead, they scan the page, picking out individual words and sentences. In research on how people read websites we found that 79 percent of our test users always scanned any new page they came across; only 16 percent read word-by-word."

Eye-scan research (where readers' eye movements are tracked) consistently shows that people are looking for headlines and chunks of information they can easily digest. Not surprisingly, this means that traditional journalism skills—the ability to write brisk, informative headlines and clear, compelling leads and comprehensive, tight stories—are now, more than ever, extremely valuable.

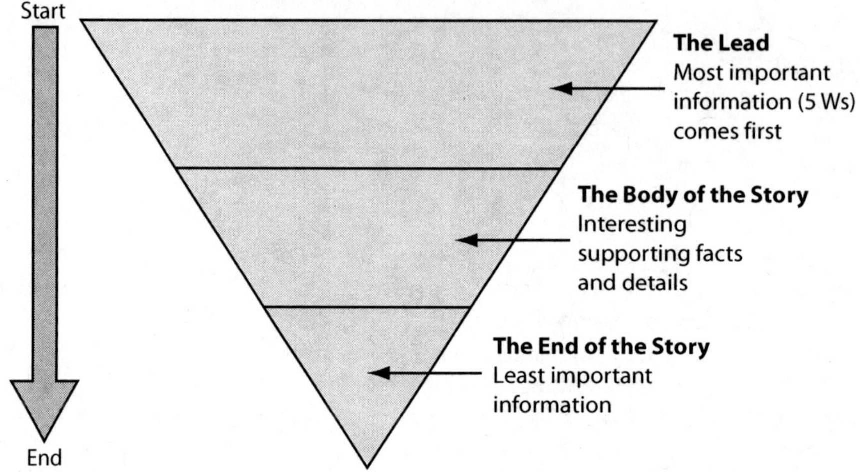

Figure 13.1 The inverted pyramid

Oddly, the writing structure that has for some time now been the object of scorn—the classic inverted pyramid—turns out to be the best "new" way to get online readers to read! (See Figure 13.1.) In fact, says Nielsen, the best online text is structured much like a good, tight, hard news story: He suggests that online writers stick to

- one idea per paragraph (users will skip over any additional ideas if they are not caught by the first few words in the paragraph)
- the inverted pyramid style, starting with the conclusion
- half the word count (or less) than conventional writing (Nielsen 1997)

So, even though space is unlimited online, the most effective text for most people is short. In other research, Nielsen (2008) suggests that, on average, users have time to read at most 28 percent of the words on screen, but much of the time they read only 20 percent.

Imagine, your audience is only taking in less than one-quarter of what you have written. Nielsen (2008) looked at the data and estimated that users spend, on average, about 60 seconds on a page containing 800 words (the average length of a typical columnist's piece). Even allowing for a generous 200-words-a-minute reading speed, the average reader is taking in less than a quarter of what you have written. Nielsen thinks it's even less: "More realistically, users will read about 20% of the text on the average page."

How to Engage an Online Audience

Don't despair. But ditch your illusions. Web pages jammed with text are very likely not being read. (There are exceptions: Some users will read certain stories almost no matter what the length. But the story has to be compelling, engaging, and rich with valuable and relevant content.) Nevertheless, there are solutions.

Keep in Mind That Less Is More

- **Rule number one: Write tightly, cleanly, and economically.** Forget about being paid by the word. Nobody will read flabby, bloated stories online.
- **Rule number two: Cut useless verbiage.** Or as online writing consultant Steve Krug (2000) puts it, "Happy talk must die" (46). This is the amateurish, chatty stuff that fills a lot of web pages. It usually begins, "Welcome ..." and then goes on for several hundred words telling you ... well, nothing. Reporters have a huge advantage here. We've been trained to cut the chat and get to the facts.
- **Rule number three: It's harder to write short than to write long.** As Mark Twain famously said: "I didn't have time to write you a short letter, so I wrote you a long one."
- **Rule number four: Cut. Cut. Cut.** In his book *Don't Make Me Think*, Krug (2000) advises writers to craft the piece. Then cut it. Mercilessly. His Third Law of Usability is, "Get rid of half the words on each page, then get rid of half of what's left" (45). One way to do this is to use what's been called the 20-20 rule. That is, readers tend to zone out if sentences go over 20 words and you can cut most of your sentences by 20 percent.

If you think this can't be done, remind yourself that it is done every day—by editors. Broadcasters and wire service editors, in particular, are experts at this kind of compression. Canadian Press editors routinely take 400-word stories, turn them into 200-word stories, and then boil them down to wire service alerts and then down to headlines.

Here is a 180-word piece from the Canadian Dairy Commission website:

> The Canadian Dairy Commission is a Crown corporation which was established in 1966 with the mandate of coordinating federal and provincial dairy policies and creating a control mechanism for milk production which would help stabilize revenues and avoid costly surpluses. The CDC plays a key role as facilitator and stakeholder in the various forums that influence dairy policy in Canada and offers a framework for the management of the industry as a whole, which is a **jurisdiction** shared by the federal government and the provinces.
>
> Since **supply management** was first applied to the dairy sector, the CDC has been in charge of two of the three pillars of the system: **support prices** and **market sharing quota**. Once a year, the CDC sets the support price of butter and skim milk powder following consultations with industry stakeholders. These prices are used as a reference by the **provincial milk marketing boards** to establish the price of industrial milk in each province. The CDC also monitors national production and demand and recommends the necessary adjustments to the national production target for industrial milk.

Now here's one way to revise the piece so that it's less than half as long (78 words):

> The Canadian Dairy Commission, established in 1966, is a Crown corporation that controls milk production and coordinates federal and provincial dairy policies.
>
> The CDC oversees dairy policy and manages the industry. It governs:
>
> - **support prices**
> - **market sharing quota**
>
> Each year, the CDC sets the price of butter and skim milk powder. These prices are used by the **provincial milk marketing boards** to establish the prices of industrial milk.
>
> The CDC also monitors:
>
> - national milk production
> - demand
> - production targets

Here's another version that's about half as long again (33 words):

> The Canadian Dairy Commission.
>
> Key Facts:
>
> - Crown corporation founded in 1966
> - Coordinates federal and provincial dairy production
> - Governs **support prices** and **market sharing quota**
> - Monitors national milk production and demand through **supply management**

Let Headlines and Blurbs Tell the Story

Because readers "scan" online rather than read, headlines and well-crafted leads become what's called "microcontent" online. Users are often on a mission—they want to be updated on the news, find the answer to a specific question, or find information on which they can act (for example, "Is the swine-flu vaccine safe? Where can I get it?"). So, they scan pages looking for keywords and for content that contains information. The microcontent must be "content rich"—that is, the words must convey clear information.

So, a piece on Indian fashion might have a print headline, along with a deck (the sentence summarizing the story or providing additional information, and typically appearing below the headline), such as this:

> **Whose sari now?**
> Indian style hits North American runways this spring

In a print publication, the headline would run above or below a picture of Indian models on a runway or a series of pictures of new fashions from Mumbai. The play on words would be immediately understandable and funny. But online?

Can you see the problem? The web scanner reading from left to right sees no content words in the headline (and the lengthier deck would likely not appear online at all). As well, the play on words is unlikely to work online, and the lack of clear keywords will distract and confuse. Today, lots of folks read news headlines via

1. Google searches
2. RSS (whether they actually know they're reading RSS feeds or not)
3. small screens (tablets, cellphones, smartphones, and other information appliances)
4. news aggregation tools
5. Twitter feeds with links
6. custom homepages like iGoogle

Imagine the same headline displayed on those platforms and interfaces. It would mean nothing. The online microcontent should instead read something like this:

Indian fashions hit North American clothing market
Bollywood style picked up by US designers

This headline drops the wordplay, has key content words on the left, and is information packed. Even on a small screen, users would know what the piece is about.

The other trick to online content is paying attention to the visual presentation of the story. Just as a good headline and strong photo can draw a newspaper or magazine reader into a story, so too the correct design of online content can spell the difference between a second-long scan followed by a quick click to another page and a user actually reading the piece.

Chunking

Chunking is essential to keep people reading. Because users scan, they can more easily digest "chunks" of information that the eye can quickly decipher. So, rather than present a block of grey text, break up your material using the following:

- headlines
- decks
- leads
- summaries
- subheads
- pull quotes
- lists
- tables
- links (Shewchuk and Mietkiewicz 2009, 68)

Using different fonts, and changing text size and even colour (sparingly and effectively), can all enhance the page and increase a user's uptake of the content. As well, we have to acknowledge that users are often "seekers" rather than readers. That is, they are looking for discrete pieces of information. Answers to questions. Stats or facts.

Instead of burying your facts in densely written paragraphs, consider delivering the information in lists—numbered, lettered, or bulleted. These formatting devices break the text up visually and allow for easy "digestion" of the key points.

Similarly, it's a good idea to parse your story into chunks. Doing so has two effects. First, it allows users to scan for subheads that interest them and dive directly into a section. And second, it provides users with much needed visual variability. A good rule of thumb that I've used in creating web stories is to ensure that every "screen" has some kind of visual break—a subhead, a boldfaced pull quote, a photo, or some other graphic element. Nothing puts off people like screen after screen of grey text. Scrolling down through a mile and half of uninterrupted print will exhaust even an interested user.

Once you've broken your story into chunks, you need to "flag" those chunks in some way, that is, provide users with a clear indication of the parts of your story. You can do this by putting hyperlinks at the top or side of the story that will guide users directly into the piece. CBC.ca did a good job of this in Influenza: Battling the Last Great Virus. The series topic's main web page provides users 24 entry points to dive into the story. See it here: archives.cbc.ca/health/disease/topics/1965/.

Editors chunk content and add headlines so that users can easily read any part of the story in any order. As a result, narrative control is relinquished to the user—which is a recent and challenging aspect of new journalism. Normally, reporters guide readers through material in some kind of chronological order ordained by the reporter and editors; read this, then read this, and then read this. But online, the control moves from the author to the user, and we must create stories that work that way. Links, clearly marked by informative headlines, allow users to move on to other material at any time. This last point leads us to the next great challenge of new journalism: structuring stories online.

The Non-Linear Story, or the New Narrative

The ability to "read" a story any old way you want is a new wrinkle engendered by the interface functionality of the Web. Sure, readers of a non-fiction book might dip into the introduction, then skip a few chapters, then read the end, but the author has a measure of control by laying out the book's contents in a certain order and by crafting a narrative arc that guides readers through the material—particularly if the book is based on "story"—from beginning to end.

The nature of the online environment, to some extent, dismantles that structure (see Figure 13.2). For one thing, we have hyperlinks.

Links, Links, and More Links

Hyperlinks give users lateral connectivity to a story—the ability to move "sideways" in the story and jump over to another story in the series, to an internal sidebar, or out altogether to a separate website or story. As a journalist, how you apply hyperlinks to your story is crucial. Hyperlinks can be very effective for providing explanations, definitions, and background without slowing down your story. Overused (see most pages on Wikipedia!), they can distract, lose, or drive users crazy. You want your hyperlinks to enhance your story, providing depth, texture, and additional information without interrupting the flow of the story too much.

Here is a piece with way too many links. The interruptions in the flow of ideas are distracting.

> ***Truthiness*** is a **term** first used in its recent **satirical** sense by **American** television comedian **Stephen Colbert** in 2005, to describe things that a person claims to know **intuitively** or "from the gut" without regard to **evidence**, **logic**, **intellectual** examination, or **facts**. **[1]** Colbert introduced this definition **[2]** of the word during the **pilot** episode of his political satire program ***The Colbert Report*** on October 17, 2005, as the subject of a segment called "**The Wørd**." *Truthiness* was named **Word of the Year** for 2005 by the **American Dialect Society** and for 2006 by **Merriam-Webster**. **[3] [4]**
>
> By using this "**stunt word**" as part of his routine, Colbert sought to satirize the use of **appeal to emotion** and the "gut feeling" as a **rhetorical** device in contemporary socio-political discourse. **[5]** He particularly applied it to **U.S. President George W. Bush**'s **nomination** of **Harriet Miers** to the **Supreme Court** and the **decision to invade Iraq** in 2003. **[6]** Colbert later ascribed truthiness to other institutions and organizations, including **Wikipedia**. **[7]** (Wikipedia n.d.)

As each user chooses different links, making a new path through the story, they are, in effect, creating a "new" story each and every time. No two users will have the same experience reading your story online.

This is even more true—and challenging—for the multipart story, series, or special report. Although the authors set out a structured set of text stories, audio, video, graphics, and interactives, it's important to remember a number of facts:

1. Not everyone takes in the piece in the order you have suggested.
2. Not everyone lands on the homepage. People coming to your story through search engines may land in the middle of the series or project.
3. You must plan for users entering, experiencing, and exiting the project in myriad ways. How do you maximize their experience?

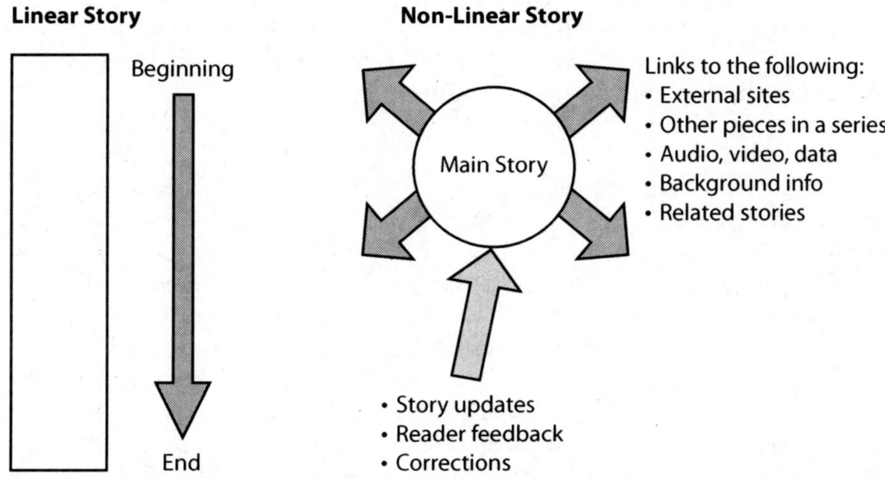

Figure 13.2 Linear and non-linear story structures

Let Them Drive but Provide a Good Map

You can enhance a user's experience by admitting one big fact: You are not in complete control of the story. Your user may watch all the video first; may read all the stories, but not in order; may check out the audio clips and then the photo gallery; or do any combination of the above.

The key for you is to structure the story in a way that allows users this flexibility without getting lost. How do you do that? By following web navigation conventions:

1. **Provide a clear map of the story.** Navigation should be designed to provide users with a clearly labelled list of links to all story parts. Remember to include this type of navigation on every page of your story to allow users to orient themselves in the story and to move seamlessly among its parts.
2. **Give users a sense of the size of your story.** Navigation should also provide users with a strong sense of the size and scope of your piece. Unlike a book that can be picked up and weighed, or a newspaper or magazine in which readers can easily see the story length, online stories can be deceptive. It's up to you to provide a clear overview of the story so users are clear about how many parts or sections or chapters your story has.
3. **Never "dead-end" users.** Don't let users get to the bottom of a story with no exit in sight. Forcing users to click on the "back" button to get around is an admission of structural defeat. Provide a navigation bar that contains links to the major parts of the story at the bottom or, at least, a series of links to "Related Stories" or "More Information." Again, you are "guiding" your readers by providing suggestions for the next story or other stories, but remember that they'll do whatever they please.

The CBC's Indepth: Forces of Nature series is a good example of a well-mapped story. The right-hand navigation bar is clear and simple with all the subsections of the series, including Earthquakes, Flooding, and Forest Fires. See it here: www.cbc.ca/news/background/forcesofnature/index.html.

Make Each Part a Whole

Because users will move through your story in a number of ways, it's important to make sure that the story's pieces are comprehensible no matter how users arrive at them.

Rather than provide in every story a "nut graph" or "context graph" (that is, the nutshell paragraph that lays out the news value, broader relevance, or central topic of a piece—and something that print journalists were forced to do in multipart newspaper stories), you need to give users clearly labelled links to background and contextual sections of your story. Also, you can hyperlink keywords to a definitions or glossary page. Linking to original documents, reports, white papers, and other supporting evidence also saves space and adds depth to your story. If people want to see the original sources for your story, they can do so simply by clicking the link.

Many reporters include a section or link called "About This Series," which provides an overview of the story parts and a brief backgrounder on the story and its authors.

The Key Structure Question: What Is the Best Way to Tell This Story?

Most of the discussion so far has been on how to make sure the story you are telling is clear, accessible, navigable, visually pleasing, and compelling. But before you take care of all those factors, you have to make an even more important structure decision about your story: *What is the best way to tell it?*

Of course, this used to be a non-question not long ago. Newspaper reporters used words and pictures, TV reporters used video and sound, and radio producers used words and sound to tell their stories. Even today, many legacy news organizations make the mistake of playing to their historical strengths—print, video, or audio—without considering the demands of the story. That's not good enough anymore.

The CBC tackled this issue head on: "Although CBCNews.ca could be mostly audio and video files, this wouldn't meet the demands of our web audience ... Publishable words are at the heart of online journalism and that has major implications for the CBC and other broadcasters on the web" (Shewchuk and Mietkiewicz 2009, 52).

In a bold move, the *Globe and Mail* decided to use audio interviews with members of the Taliban to anchor its award-winning series Talking to the Taliban. (See Figure 13.3 for a screenshot of the series main page.) Although Graeme Smith is primarily a print reporter and the *Globe*'s legacy platform is the newspaper, this compelling story was told in audio, with photo galleries and text to support it.

Figure 13.3 Talking to the Taliban

SOURCE: Smith, Graeme. 2008. Talking to the Taliban. *Globe and Mail*, March 22. http://v1.theglobeandmail.com/talkingtothetaliban/.

Similarly, the *Boston Globe* chose an audio slideshow format to tell Emily's Story: Finding a Way at Harvard. (See Figure 13.4 below.) The story is told mainly through an audio slideshow, but it is augmented by photo galleries, audio clips, songs, and some video.

Figure 13.4 Emily's Story: Finding a Way at Harvard
SOURCE: *Boston Globe*. 2005. Emily's story: Finding a way at Harvard. http://www.boston.com/news/specials/emily/multimedia/.

The key to success now is to rethink the whole story process, from inception to research to information gathering and, finally, to writing and production. It's no longer good enough to go about the story in the same old way and then worry about "adapting" it to the online world.

Jonathan Dube, who writes about online journalism in his blog, CyberJournalist .net, says that you have to "think different" about journalism on the Web. Dube (2000a) writes: "Collaborate with audio, video and interactive producers. Develop a plan and let that guide you throughout the news gathering and production process, rather than just reporting a story and then adding various elements later as an afterthought. Look for stories that lend themselves to the Web stories that you can tell or differently from or better than in any other medium."

Journalists may feel challenged by the seemingly unlimited number of media combinations they can now use to tell a story online. However, basic online storytelling forms are now fairly well established:

- Use text to explain.
- Use multimedia to show.
- Use interactives to demonstrate and engage. (Dube 2000b)

Of course, you can use any combination of these forms to tell your story. Dube (2000b) sets out the most common storytelling forms used by online news websites:

1. **Print plus:** This is essentially a print story or series of stories augmented by photos, charts, audio or video clips, interactives, et cetera. This form is widely used by newspaper websites; it plays off of their strength in print, but adds value with photos, maps, charts, and other helpful material.
2. **Audio:** Audio has become an extremely popular way to tell stories and inform. The podcast form (that is, downloadable recordings such as digital radio shows and audio documentaries) is often accompanied by supportive text transcripts, photos, and other material.
3. **Video:** Like the audio podcast, the video clip online can be an effective storytelling tool, although it's important to note that merely putting up five minutes of a talking head is not good. Online video stories are fast-paced, short, and often use a combination of text screen, narration, photos, and video footage to tell the story.
4. **Slideshow:** A slideshow is essentially a moving photo essay. Well suited to a story with strong visuals, the slideshow can showcase powerful images with crisp, tight writing in the captions.
5. **Narrated slideshow:** More like a slideshow on steroids, this form involves a series of powerful images augmented by narration, interviews, and sounds. As the photos move along, the audio plays with it and creates a documentary-style presentation.
6. **Multimedia interactives:** This is the name Dube gives to stories that use everything and the kitchen sink—text, photos, animations, clickable quizzes, polls, audio, video, slideshows, and pretty much anything else to create fully integrated "comprehensive interactive packages that tell stories in ways no other medium can" (Dube 2000b).

Obviously, the Web offers a vast array of tools and techniques with which to tell a story. Still, fundamentally, your story, whether in text, audio, video, animation, or a combination of media, must be well written. It must be structured to capture and hold the attention of users. It must be flexible and transparent enough to accommodate updates, changes, and corrections. It must engage with a human story, with solid facts, with compelling narrative, with high-impact information.

As well, it must respect the independence of users. They will access your story, read it, use it, enter it, exit it, and even add to it in ways you will have anticipated (you hope) and in some ways you may never have imagined. And that's okay.

Today, you must structure your stories, big or small, with users in mind. Journalism on the Web makes the writer–reader partnership complete; in many ways, the online story is now created and recreated each time it is read.

DISCUSSION QUESTIONS

1. Outline the main medium you would use to cover the following stories. What would you use as secondary elements? Why?
   - a school board meeting
   - the annual rural fall fair
   - a local indie-band show
2. Go online and compare the coverage of the same story at three different sites, such as CBC.ca, globeandmail.ca, and thecanadianpress.com. What works? What doesn't? What would you change, add, or delete?
3. Revisit a story you have done recently. Redo the story in a different medium—audio, video, text, slideshow, et cetera. Did you improve the story? Did you change it significantly? Can you marry the two versions?

SUGGESTED RESOURCES

BBC Wales. 2009. A guide to digital storytelling. http://www.bbc.co.uk/wales/audiovideo/sites/about/pages/howto.shtml.

CyberJournalist.net [Jonathan Dube's blog]. http://www.cyberjournalist.net.

Lasica, J.D. 2006. Digital storytelling: A tutorial in 10 easy steps. Techsoup.org, October 2. http://www.techsoup.org/learningcenter/techplan/page5897.cfm.

Project for Excellence in Journalism. 2005. *The state of the news media 2005.* http://www.stateofthemedia.org/2005/.

Shewchuk, Blair, and Mark Mietkiewicz. 2009. *Online news fundamentals: An introduction to journalism.* Toronto: CBC News.

REFERENCES

Canadian Dairy Commission. n.d. Homepage. http://www.cdc-ccl.gc.ca/cdc/index_en.asp.

Canadian Media Research Consortium. 2008. *The credibility gap: Canadians and their news media.* Vancouver: CMRC. http://www.mediaresearch.ca/en/projects/documents/THECREDIBILITYGAP.pdf.

Dube, Jonathan. 2000a. A dozen online writing tips. CyberJournalist.net, November 10. http://www.cyberjournalist.net/news/000118.php.

Dube, Jonathan. 2000b. Online storytelling forms. CyberJournalist.net, July 10. http://www.cyberjournalist.net/news/000117.php?Publisher.

Krug, Steve. 2000. *Don't make me think: A common sense approach to web usability.* Indianapolis, IN: New Riders Publishing.

Nielsen, Jakob. 1997. Alertbox: How users read on the Web. Useit.com, October 1. http://www.useit.com/alertbox/9710a.html.

Nielsen, Jakob. 2008. Alertbox: How little do users read? Useit.com, May 6. http://www.useit.com/alertbox/percent-text-read.html.

Reuters. 2008. More Americans turning to web for news. Reuters.com, February 29. http://www.reuters.com/article/idUSN2824760420080229.

Shewchuk, Blair, and Mark Mietkiewicz. 2009. *Online news fundamentals: An introduction to journalism.* Toronto: CBC News.

Wikipedia. n.d. Truthiness. http://en.wikipedia.org/wiki/Truthiness.

CHAPTER 14

Interviewing in the Digital Age

Jennifer Wilson-Speedy

CHAPTER OUTLINE

Introduction

Thanks to email, instant messaging, and cellphones, we're connected 24/7 with potential sources. The Internet is immensely useful for newsgathering, researching, and filing on the go. But it brings special considerations to a core part of the reporting process—interviewing.

Four experienced journalists tell us how the Internet can help and hinder everything from finding sources to getting quotes:

- David Akin, Canwest News Service's national affairs correspondent in Ottawa
- Steve Buttry, Complete Community Connection (C3) coach at Gazette Communications in Cedar Rapids, Iowa, at the time of interview (he's now director of community engagement at Allbritton Communications in Washington)
- Ken Kidd, *Toronto Star* feature writer
- Kirk LaPointe, managing editor at the *Vancouver Sun*

Interview Prep

Finding the Right People

Finding the right sources is essential for any interview. Interviewees will vary greatly from story to story, but may include experts, witnesses, politicians, and people affected by an event—as well as their friends and family.

There are many ways to find sources online, including media services such as

- HelpaReporter.com, an email service that shares journalists' requests for sources
- MediaLink.Andara.com and www.sources.com, databases of experts and information providers in Canada
- ProfNet.PRNewswire.com, a service that connects journalists and professionals

Social networking sites and public institutions can also yield valuable sources. Business networking site LinkedIn.com can be searched to find professionals in specific fields and regions. Many university websites feature searchable directories of professors and their areas of expertise.

To find sources in a particular neighbourhood, for example after a fire, try a site like Canada411.ca, which lets you conduct proximity searches by address, landmark, or postal code, giving you a list of phone numbers for people and businesses in the area.

Don't forget your personal connections. Friends and family can surprise you with excellent sources, so make phone calls, send emails, and poll your social networks for help. Be warned: Sharing your source request online can tip off the competition to your story idea.

Colleagues may be willing to share contacts from their own lists, filled after years of working on all sorts of stories.

Once you've found one source, that person can often recommend other people who can add to your story, so remember to ask.

You should also start a file listing everyone you speak to in your reporting—try a free online service such as Google Docs for easy access anywhere—so you can have your own database of sources to mine in the future.

Getting the Interview

Once you've got contact details for potential sources, it's time to find out whether they're willing to talk to you.

Many new journalists worry about having their interview requests turned down, but "people are amazingly accommodating," says *Vancouver Sun* managing editor Kirk LaPointe. "It's highly flattering to be interviewed. We often forget that as journalists. We kind of think we're an intrusion, and it's not true."

Of course, some sources will be reluctant. They may require convincing to speak or just refuse. But even if you think they won't want to speak on the record, you should always ask, says Steve Buttry, former C3 coach at Gazette Communications. Some people may be thankful for the opportunity to tell their side of the story or to have someone to talk to during a difficult time. Others may slam the door in your face, but at least you'll know you gave them a chance and tried your best for your readers.

Making Contact

How you approach sources will depend on the story, your deadline, and your proximity to the news. During an event or breaking news situation, knocking on doors or walking up to people is usually the only way to interview. But in most cases, you'll use the phone or Internet to make first contact.

A phone conversation creates a strong personal connection and is a good alternative to speaking in person. But you'll often get an answering machine. If you have to leave a message, always be clear about who you are, why you're calling—and your deadline.

While potential sources may not always have listed phone numbers, most have an email address or online presence. The Internet is a fast way to touch base with sources, and it allows them to respond on their own time. But email and instant messaging feel less personal than phone or in-person contact, which makes it easier for sources to deny interview requests. Also, requests can be ignored in the steady stream of newsletters, spam, and correspondence.

As a result, David Akin, Canwest News Service's national affairs correspondent, doubles up to ensure he makes contact: "I typically send an email request and make a telephone request for an interview simultaneously. So if spam filters catch my email, the phone message usually gets through."

Buttry also recommends combining an email request with a phone call to overcome spam filters and email overload. "Sometimes your message makes it to the inbox but doesn't get read. A clear, concise subject line helps. But making the first contact by phone is often a good idea. And you should follow up by phone if you don't get a prompt response," he says.

The email's subject line could provide details such as your publication and the reason you want to speak with the source. Some journalists also include their deadlines so sources know the timeline and can evaluate when—and whether—they'll be able to respond.

Setting the Tone

Always be clear with sources about who you are, who you're working for, and what you're working on, says Akin. That first contact is also the time to establish that you

Figure 14.1 Professional journalists agree that in-person interviews are always preferable to electronic exchanges, as they allow for non-verbal communication, spontaneity, and the gathering of additional valuable details that can be useful for a story.

want to speak with them on the record. Anonymous sources are normally a last resort, so check newsroom policies before agreeing to any conditions. Establishing what you need at the outset will give you time to hunt down another source if your first contact is unwilling to participate.

Your introduction could also include how you got their contact information, as a shared acquaintance can help establish a relationship and even encourage sources to speak with you.

Whether the meeting's real or virtual, find a mutually convenient time and be punctual. Following through on your plans shows that you're professional and respect your source's time. Aim for a place where the source will feel comfortable, such as the person's home or office. Or, if you're writing about an event, meet at the location to help jog his or her memory about details.

Getting to Know Your Source

The bulk of interview-related work isn't communicating with your sources but rather researching them. You may spend several days learning about interviewees only to speak with them for an hour or two.

Research helps frame your story and guides your questions. It helps build rapport. It confirms that you're speaking with the right people, and can lead to other sources.

"The more research you do, the more comfortable you'll be," says *Toronto Star* feature writer Ken Kidd. "Also, the more research you do, the more comfortable, or maybe uncomfortable, the person you're interviewing is." That knowledge shows sources either that you know what you're doing, boosting their confidence and encouraging them to open up, or that they've been checked out and can't lie to you.

"Preparation is a huge part of a successful interview. If you know what you're talking about, and know what to ask about, it makes a huge difference," says Buttry. "I don't think preparation has any bad results."

And preparing requires "more than a Google search on the topic," says LaPointe. "You can't wing it."

Not only do you want to know your source's name, job title, and area of expertise, you also want to learn about his or her personal life to help build a relationship and add depth to your story. Your research might include the following:

- **Basic web searches:** A great place to start. However, it can also bring up results for other people with the same name, so check carefully before accepting results as fact.
- **Online profile sites:** LinkedIn.com, Facebook.com, and MySpace.com are examples of social networking sites that will provide you with personal information and professional connections.
- **Blogs and microblogging services:** A source's blog entries and Twitter updates will provide a glimpse of what makes that person tick.
- **News archives:** Check whether your source has been in the news before, and if so, why.
- **Academic journals:** Previously published research on your topic will help teach you the basics so you can ask better questions.

- **Friends and colleagues:** These people can give you a broad sense of your source, so you can drill down further when it comes time to do the main interview.
- **Books:** Reading your source's previously published works will teach you more about him or her, and help you build rapport.
- **Secondary documents:** Not everything will be online. Look for supporting documents, such as printed journals, reports, or legal records.

As you research, note important findings, potential sources, questions that come to mind, and any discrepancies in facts so that you can raise them during the interview.

Despite all this research, it's also important to keep an open mind, says LaPointe: "Don't lead anybody to believe that you've already decided what the story is and that you simply need them to validate your thesis."

The Right Questions

What to Ask

Your questions will depend on the topic and may change as the interview progresses, but there are a few key areas to hit:

- **Your source's name, age, and job title.** Online spellings can be wrong and information can be outdated.
- **Facts, such as your source's experience and relationship to the story.** Ask how he or she knows the details being shared. Also, memories fade and stories can get skewed in multiple tellings, even with reliable sources, so it's always wise to back up your facts with supporting documents.
- **Any questions or discrepancies that came up in your research.**
- **Any other sources or supporting documents the interviewee can provide.**

Some journalists also have a broad "must ask" question, often for the end of the interview, that helps draw out great quotes, finds new leads, and safeguards against anything they could have missed. For example:

- What else should I know about this?
- Did I miss anything?
- Is there anything else you'd like to say?
- Who else should I speak to about this?

LaPointe says a great question, which came from his wife, is "What surprised you most?" He adds, "It stops people dead in their tracks … It forces anyone to just rack their brain, right away. You don't always get fantastic answers, but it puts somebody on notice that you're not prepared to just take the easy route out."

Preparing Your Questions

"You should always have a road map in an interview," says LaPointe, who suggests having questions written out, starting with fact-finding then open-ended questions.

Akin suggests shaping the structure of the story in advance, then looking to see where more background, colour, or anecdotes are required to shape your questions and interviews.

But don't let yourself become a slave to your plan. Journalists "have to be prepared for surprises," says LaPointe. "You should have good questions, and you should be able to reframe questions on the spur of the moment, but you shouldn't know the answers."

Framing Your Questions

The way you phrase your questions will affect the way your source responds.

- **Ask open-ended questions.** "Ask every question with a how, what, or why," says LaPointe. He adds that when we see these words at the beginning of a sentence, "we're hard-wired to open up, because they're questions of pure curiosity."
- **Ask any question that cannot be answered yes or no.** Akin suggests starting a question with "tell us," "describe," "how," or "why." He cautions, "Ask a politician a question to which [she] can answer yes or no and then [she'll] go and change the topic and give you the spin line or the message of the day."

Don't ask sources to cite the funniest, most amazing, or best thing, says LaPointe. "People don't rank things easily that way. They want to tell stories with a beginning, middle and end to them."

Looking for the Narrative

Like a story, an interview should follow the logical timeline of beginning, middle, and end, says LaPointe.

For example, if you're interviewing a firefighter who just pulled a baby out of a house, you shouldn't start by asking what was going through his mind after the rescue. "Get him to rewind his tape and to build the drama himself," LaPointe says. Ask about the sequence and senses. "Get the person to chronologically order the story. That's when natural drama comes out."

How to Conduct the Interview

"Every interview and every interviewing tool or circumstance has upsides that you need to use to your advantage and a downside that you need to watch out for and try to overcome, or at least be aware of," says Buttry. So, with journalists able to connect with sources in person, over the phone or via Voice over Internet Protocol (VoIP), by email, by instant messaging, and by video chat, how does one choose? Here's how each of these approaches stacks up:

In Person

All four journalists agree that in-person remains the best way to interview. "Electronically we've got more ability to connect, but truly, nothing is as good as the in-person interview," says Buttry.

IN PRACTICE

Face Value

David Akin says that face-to-face interactions are essential to becoming a good interviewer and, as a result, a good journalist. "To be able to spot trends, to offer nuance, description, analysis, context, those are the value-added jobs of journalists nowadays, and all that stuff happens the closer you get to your subject," he explains, offering an example from his first day at the Thunder Bay *Chronicle Journal*, when he was asked to report on striking grocery store workers. His editor expected him to make phone calls, but by driving to the store Akin says he got better details for his story, including that some workers had brought along their children, which likely wouldn't have come up in phone interviews. "You have to use good old gumshoe stuff," he says. "Using technology's great to find all these people, but then go to them once you've found them."

That's because 70 to 80 percent of communication is non-verbal, says LaPointe. He adds that a journalist really has an opportunity to understand more about someone's approach, attitudes, and insights by observing that person. "So in a setting where you're doing face-to-face interviews, you obviously have the opportunity to gain a lot more understanding and context for the quotes."

Kidd, as a feature writer, says those in-person details, such as mannerisms and even what's in a source's office, are essential to weaving a powerful narrative and would be difficult, if not impossible, to replicate virtually or even over the phone.

In addition to getting great details and a greater understanding of your sources, in-person interviews are also likely to give you better answers. You're essentially catching sources off guard with thoughtful questions, taking them away from their script. Also, you can instantly follow up and pursue new leads.

Of course, there are drawbacks to in-person interviews. The Internet provides an increasingly large pool of potential interviewees, but we're often not in the same time zone, much less the same city, as our sources. While in-person interviews provide more depth for our readers, not all newsrooms are going to be willing to spring for airfare to meet all your sources, even if you do have time to do so before your deadline.

Moreover, spontaneous answers are not always the best a source has to offer. "You ask me a question and I answer it off the top of my head, and if I think of something a half hour later that would have been a better answer, you don't get it, unless I take the initiative to get back to you," explains Buttry. Plus, sources put on the spot may not feel comfortable admitting that they need to check their facts, leaving you to cite guesses.

Phone or Voice over Internet Protocol

The phone or VoIP services, such as Skype, give you the immediacy of an in-person interview without the plane fare bill.

Akin says the phone is "still the most important piece of technology for reporters." You can pick up the tone of a source's voice, which gives you insight into that person's mannerisms and what questions hit a nerve. Plus, you can instantly follow any new avenues that come up.

In addition to convenience over distances, phone interviews also help with fact verification. Sources can check their notes without feeling embarrassed, and you can simultaneously confirm what they're saying. For example, when Akin was chatting with a source on "Republicans for Ignatieff," then a relatively unknown group, he was able to conduct web searches to verify what he was being told.

"That's exactly what [the Internet's] built for—to do some background checks, in this case in real time, and that sort of moved our interview in different directions," he says. "It's pretty useful to have that there just to answer questions that pop up in your head as you're just talking over something." This sort of verification would also work in email and instant-messaging interviews.

Really, Akin says, the only downside to a phone interview is having to transcribe.

However, LaPointe notes that the phone also presents "the ability for the interview subject to be doing other things, checking things, reading from script, that kind of thing, it's fairly common." Thoughtful questions can help steer your source away from a script, but a distracted source can give you bad facts or incoherent quotes, while a distracted journalist can miss the audio clues that could lead to a better story.

Email

Email can reach virtually anywhere in the world, at any time. Akin describes email interviews as a classic example of a "technology crutch" for journalists. But he acknowledges that email is useful for contacting sources who would otherwise be unreachable, for example in remote locations or embedded in war zones.

Thanks to email, Buttry was able to interview a retired professor with a hearing impairment who lived in another state. The professor had conducted research on lead poisoning from industrial pollution in the neighbourhood of an Omaha smelter. She was essential to his story, but was not comfortable conducting an interview with phone assistance. "We had a great interview by email," says Buttry. "I got bits of her personality and everything just like I would if I was sitting in her living room."

Email also means that sources can answer at their convenience with well-thought-out responses.

"If you ask me a question by email, I might type a draft and think, 'Let me leave that a while,' and I get back to you on my time frame so you get a more thoughtful and complete answer," explains Buttry, adding that sources will also have time to check their facts. The downside is that sources could run answers past their lawyer or PR person first, giving them a chance to speak on the record while sticking to an approved script.

Other potential downsides include the following:

- **There's no guarantee as to when, or if, you'll get an answer.** Email can be overlooked, accidentally deleted, or sent to the spam folder—leaving you without a source come deadline.

- **All that time to think can lead to stiff answers.** LaPointe says that email "saps spontaneity out of expression" and doesn't do a good job of conveying tone or intention. "The ability to fine-tune your quotes and review them repeatedly and stage-manage them and largely answer as you wish and not be provoked or held accountable is a real problem for journalists," he adds.
- **Your source can pick and choose which questions to answer.** A question in an email, especially if it's part of a list, can easily be ignored. In real time, you can call the source on an attempt to evade a topic, and even write it into your story, but virtually it's hard to say for sure whether the omission was intentional or oversight.
- **You can't follow up immediately.** If something's unclear or begs for more information, there's no telling when or if the source will respond, leaving you with incomplete research and a looming deadline.
- **You may not get to really know your source.** Much depends on how comfortable your source is online and how much he or she wants to share.
- **The response may not come from your source.** It could come from an imposter or the source's PR person or lawyer. "Even if I verify that this is a particular politician's email, I still don't know that he's the one sending me the answers," says Buttry.
- **You may get quotes rife with typos and syntax errors, which pose the question of whether or not to edit.** In these cases, it's often best to paraphrase to avoid having to alter the quote—but it also means that you could miss out on an otherwise powerful quote.

Emailing lists of questions should be avoided because it gives sources too much control, says LaPointe.

"That's not an interview. It's not an interview at all … because there's no back and forth," says LaPointe, who encourages journalists to "resist [email interviews] as strenuously as possible."

Instead, try emailing one question at a time, which allows you to respond and react to what your source is saying. Buttry and LaPointe both prefer this method, and Kidd also worked this way in his only, accidental, email interview. He emailed a source in England in the middle of the night, and the source happened to be awake and replied with a few thoughts. In some cases, you might ask if your subject can send photos to help provide you with more details about themselves or the topic.

It's also important to make your interviewing method clear to your readers, for example by writing in the story that the interview was conducted via email, says LaPointe. If your source would only answer via email, especially if he or she is someone publicly accountable, such as a politician, you should explain in your piece that you had to accept these conditions to get the information.

"Provide as much transparency to your own process as possible," LaPointe says. "Let the reader decide then if it's been compromised or if it's been doled out very carefully."

Instant Messaging

"Chat is not too bad, because it's somewhat close to real-time thinking aloud, although even with chat, of course, you can hesitate and frame, and veer this way and that way," says LaPointe.

Because it's in real time, you can pursue answers and react instantly to new leads. And especially if you're working with sources accustomed to communicating online, an instant-messaging session can provide insight into their personality, tone, and pacing. You can also check facts on the fly.

Like email, it's tough to confirm a source's identity in instant messaging, so you need to be clear with your readers that you have used this interviewing approach. You may also face the same problems with quote quality, such as stilted answers, responses copied and pasted from a script, or poor grammar.

And like the phone, distraction may be a problem. Sources could be chatting with other people, watching videos, or surfing the Net, leading to less thoughtful answers and slow responses.

Video Chat

LaPointe suggests that journalists use technology to maximize their reporting. "Try to do something that is going to give you a sense of who [sources are] and what they look like, how they respond, what their tone of voice is, how quick they are at things, whether there's any possibility they're reading a bit of a script in their answers. All those things are really useful."

Video chat may be the one technology that offers journalists all of those things: the ability to connect with and see sources in real time without actually having to go to their physical location. You get the colour and details, tone, personal rapport, and some identity confirmation with the convenience of the phone or instant messaging.

But, it too isn't perfect. In addition to the difficulties of arranging a convenient meeting time, your source needs a robust Internet connection to handle the chat, as well as a webcam and the technological savvy to get it up and running. While video chat services are becoming increasingly user-friendly and more widely accepted, the biggest obstacle to interviewing this way may just be finding sources—and newsrooms—equipped to use it.

The Interview

The best interview is like a conversation. You establish trust and rapport, listen intently, and respond. But an interview cannot go on indefinitely, and you will have points you need to cover, so a bit of structure helps ease the process along—so long as you're prepared to adapt or even throw your entire plan out the window to get the best for your readers. (For more on interviewing for broadcast, see Chapter 19.)

Building Trust and Rapport

You will always get better answers from comfortable sources, which requires establishing trust.

"I think the questions are really secondary to the rapport," says Buttry. "If you've got a good rapport, it doesn't matter the questions you ask, they'll just pour out their hearts."

Even if sources want to discuss a topic, they may still have a plan or script, and to get honest answers "you've got to make a connection where it turns into more of a conversation than a performance," says Buttry. "It's trust, it's empathy, it's listening well."

So seek common ground, like cheering for the same sports team or sharing a hometown, which takes you from a total stranger grilling them with questions to a real person with a job to do.

Instead of starting with questions, Kidd says you should "talk to them like they're neighbours on the street."

Asking Your Questions

Firing a dozen questions at your source can be intimidating, and it also doesn't give you a chance to listen, respond, or follow up. So, "Don't give 10 questions at once, give one," says LaPointe, even if it means it will take a few days to complete the interview via email.

He adds that this approach will also help you maintain control over the interview. "Put yourself in the driver's seat to the greatest degree possible," he says. "The other person is the star, but you're in control. And don't hesitate to assert your rights in these cases."

Some interview subjects will be eager to speak, only requiring an occasional "How do you know that?" or "Please tell me more" to plow through all your hoped-for topics and then some. More reluctant or nervous sources may need a bit of guidance, and a logical arc of questioning can help you get the answers you need.

- **Start easy.** If you start by asking something confrontational, your source can leave/hang up/block/ignore you, and not only will you not get an answer to that tough question, but you won't get anything else either. This is the time to confirm facts such as name, job title, and story basics. "I think people make a fundamental mistake with interview subjects. They think that they're ready to answer the most difficult question at the beginning. Human nature just doesn't work that way," says LaPointe. Instead, he says, you need to start by making it clear to sources that you understand their interest or point of view but that you haven't reached any conclusions.
- **Ask an open-ended question.** This is a good general rule, but it's also an excellent way to open discourse once you've got the basics covered. Examples include "Please tell me about that" and "What happened that day?"
- **Listen, respond, and follow up.**
- **Ask the tough stuff.** Now that you've established a foundation and rapport, it should be easier to ask, and get answers to, the harder questions. If it's a sensitive source, acknowledge that it may be difficult to discuss the topic, but explain that you need to ask. Kidd says the most important thing to do when asking tough questions is to keep the source communicating with you. If things become tense, step back and ask an easier question to try to continue the conversation.
- **Cool your source down with easy questions, such as fact confirmation, before ending the interview.** "You've got to let [people] give you the prime

> material, and then you've got to bring them back down to a level where you can leave with a certain amount of trust and where you can also have them help you," says LaPointe. "The sense of inquisitiveness almost stops with most interviewers when they've kind of got their money shot, and that's not a good thing."

Remember to take notes throughout the interview. While audio and video recordings are great for improving accuracy, if you rely on them alone, a dead battery or a lack of storage space can leave you with nothing. Emailed and instant-messaging conversations should be backed up in case of an accidental deletion.

Being Ready for Surprises

With all that research, it's easy to have a story half-written in your head before you talk to your source. Sometimes you'll get what you expected. Other times, your source will shock you, so you need to be listening carefully and be ready to scrap your expectations, questions, and that well-crafted lead to follow the new story wherever it may take you.

"You do prepare, but you can't be wedded to a script or you're going to lose good stories," says Buttry.

Understanding the Power of the Pause

It's human nature to feel awkward in silence. But it can be integral to a good interview, explains Kidd. "Don't be worried about gaps in the conversation," he says. "Pregnant pauses are important, because sometimes the subject leaps in to fill the void and says something he or she wishes she hadn't. This can also provide leads to other angles."

Buttry says journalists should speak only to build rapport or steer the interview. "If you ask a thoughtful question, a thoughtful answer takes some thought and some time," he says. "But if we have some patience to catch up on your notes or just pause and let it sit there awhile … that silence is working on the character that you're interviewing as well and you're getting those more thoughtful answers."

Looking for Added Value

Journalists working in any medium need to be on the lookout for things that can add value to their story's online presentation. An interview is a great chance to find out what your source has to share, for example, physical images and documents that can be scanned or links to digital images or research.

"Part of the purpose of an interview to me is to get to the stuff that's better than the interview," says Buttry, citing the example of a woman whose ex-husband had killed several people, including her daughter. This woman had a bag full of letters, journals, records, and other items from their life together. These items showed details far more intimate than she would have shared in an interview, no matter how good her rapport with the journalist.

Ask your source to share the following:

- **Photos.** Ask for digital and physical photos of the places, events, and time pertaining to your story. Snap your own photos too as the source speaks and shows you things.

- **Video.** Does your source have video from the time in question? Cellphone video or VHS can be ripped for online presentation. You can also shoot your own video of the interview or your source walking you around the site of an event.
- **Audio.** Your source may have a relevant audio clip on a computer, phone, or voice mail that adds depth to your piece. You may also choose to post all or a portion of your recorded interview.
- **Documents.** Letters, emails, papers, and receipts can all provide an extra layer of information.
- **Links.** Find out if your source has images posted to a Flickr account or a related blog post and link out from your story for detail-hungry readers.

Following Up

Once you've hung up the phone, left the meeting, or thanked someone for spending time on email or instant-messaging exchanges, you'll often think of four other things you should have asked. Or you'll be writing and hit on something that would really add to your piece or that needs confirmation.

Buttry encourages following up to check facts and confirm that nothing has changed since the interview, but also to check in to see whether a source has anything else to share. "It's amazing how often they do," he says. "I think follow-up is a huge part of a successful interview."

Your source will have given spontaneous answers during the interview. However, if you asked thoughtful questions, the source may continue to ponder the conversation and come up with more to say, says Buttry. "If you call them back for a follow-up interview, you kind of harvest the bounty of those seeds that you planted in the interview."

In addition to the potential for better answers, you may also ask better questions the second time around, based on what you learned from the first interview and any new research.

An email, instant message, or phone call is widely accepted for the follow-up, as it's convenient and is building off an established relationship with a source.

Learning to Be Better

Interviews get easier over time. And, while experience certainly helps with your confidence and comfort, you've also got to examine yourself and your methods. Look over your notes and tapes for areas of improvement as well as successes—did you interrupt the source? Should you have let that pause linger longer? Did you ask a really great question? These things will become apparent even when you're reviewing your notes for your story, and acknowledging them will help you continue to hone your skills.

Akin says the best interview practice is streeters—walking up to random people and asking them their thoughts. "If you've never, ever been an interviewer before, I think that is a great way to just dive in," he says. "You learn how to approach somebody with enthusiasm, not seem like a telemarketer, and get [that person] to open up about something. And … you have to think really quick on your feet." Not only will you get comfortable walking into a crowd, but it will also help teach you what kinds of questions work and which fall flat.

DISCUSSION QUESTIONS

1. What would be the appropriate interview format for a politician? A grieving family member? An author promoting a new book? Why?
2. Do you think having a "must-ask" question could be useful? Why? What would yours be?
3. You're interviewing a politician on a new agricultural policy. What research would you do to prepare?

SUGGESTED RESOURCES

Alvar, Marcia. 2002. The art of the interview. *PoynterOnline*, July 11. http://www.poynter.org/content/content_view.asp?id=9572.

Buttry, Steve. n.d. Shut up and listen: Getting the most from your interviews. No Train, No Gain. http://www.notrain-nogain.org/Train/Res/RepARC/interv.asp.

McLachlan, Gregg. n.d. Add some offbeat to your questions. No Train, No Gain. http://www.notrain-nogain.org/Train/Res/Report/offb.asp.

REFERENCES

Akin, David. 2009. Interview by Jennifer Wilson-Speedy. Telephone. September 1.

Akin, David. 2009. Interview by Jennifer Wilson-Speedy. Email. September 28.

Buttry, Steve. 2009. Interview by Jennifer Wilson-Speedy. Telephone. August 4.

Buttry, Steve. 2009. Interview by Jennifer Wilson-Speedy. Email. September 28.

Kidd, Ken. 2009. Interview by Jennifer Wilson-Speedy. Telephone. September 21.

Kidd, Ken. 2009. Interview by Jennifer Wilson-Speedy. Email. October 10.

LaPointe, Kirk. 2009. Interview by Jennifer Wilson-Speedy. Telephone. August 11.

LaPointe, Kirk. 2009. Interview by Jennifer Wilson-Speedy. Email. September 28.

CHAPTER 15

The Beat Reporter

Various Authors

Introduction

CHAPTER OUTLINE

For decades, the beat reporter has been in many respects the backbone of journalism, bringing intimate knowledge of a specific topic to his or her regular reportage. Whether it is stalking the corridors of city hall to cover the daily minutiae of local politics, reporting crime stories and breaking news on the police beat, or keying furiously late at night in a cold arena to report the outcome of a junior hockey game for a pressing deadline, it is the work of the beat journalist that has, to a great extent, provided the "bread and butter" content of most newspapers, radio and television newscasts, and online news sites. While this chapter cannot cover the many different types of journalistic beats in any detail, it does provide a sense of the role played by beat reporters in journalism today.

With the expertise, inside knowledge, and influential contacts built up over years of reporting on countless stories in a particular area, the seasoned beat journalist inevitably becomes a subject expert and a repository of important information. In fact, it is not uncommon for a beat journalist to become such an expert on a subject that he or she becomes eminently qualified to write an important book about it. For example, years of reporting on the business beat and Bay Street dealings allowed Theresa Tedesco, now with the *National Post*, to write the best-selling book *Offside: The Battle for Control of Maple Leaf Gardens*. Reporters Geoffrey York and Loreen Pindera parlayed their front-line experiences during the Oka Crisis into the critically acclaimed book *People of the Pines*. Similarly, sportswriter Stephen Brunt has penned many sports books, including *Facing Ali* and *Searching for Bobby Orr*.

But as with so many other aspects of contemporary journalism, the nature of beat reporting is also changing. Indeed, it has almost become a cliché to analyze the current crisis in journalism in terms that are very much about beat reporting: "As traditional media decline," observers ask, "who is going to trudge out on a winter night and cover the local city council meeting?"

Figure 15.1 Camera at council meeting. As economics and technology redefine how journalism is practised, some have expressed concern over how well traditional beats, such as local politics, will be covered. (PHOTO: Ursula Bennett/MississaugaWatch.ca.)

The answer to that question has much to do with the changing economics of journalism, but it leads to important questions about the roles, and skills, of the beat reporter. A leaner newsroom often means that a reporter who used to spend the vast majority of his or her time on a single beat may now be asked to be more of a generalist, and cover multiple beats. Any potentially negative effects on the quality of journalism produced by this altered role are partially offset by the benefits of reporting in the digital age. That is, even a reporter covering a beat part-time today can work much more efficiently, and, with the help of social media tools, be able to reach more sources and access much more information quicker than a beat reporter in years gone by could have ever imagined. As discussed elsewhere in this book, flexibility is one of the defining characteristics of the new journalist, whether it relates to the roles, tools, or media being used—or in some cases, the multiple beats being reported on for a news organization.

One of the ironies of the current revolution in journalism is that the very things that have undermined traditional journalism—the Internet and social media—have also become indispensable tools that allow a reporter to become better at his or her job. Another irony, or paradox, is that while journalists now must think more broadly about their roles and skills, a new premium on more focused information (or niche reporting) is simultaneously emerging within journalism.

It is perhaps telling that in 2007, the name of the Pulitzer Prize for Beat Reporting was changed to the Pulitzer Prize for Local Reporting (and, as of December 2009, online-only journalism now qualifies for Pulitzer Prize consideration). In an age in which readers can instantly access news sources, and when there is usually no scarcity of coverage of the big, national stories of the day, the work of a specialized or local reporter can become that much more important. Now that media are truly global in their reach, there can be tremendous value in niche reporting, or "narrowcasting." The need for good coverage of local beats—providing relevant information that serves a specific community—is attested to by the recent proliferation of community-oriented blogs and hyperlocal news and information sites such as Outside.in, which has a presence in almost 60,000 locales. It also explains why city-specific sites such as Torontoist (www.torontoist.com), "a website about Toronto and everything that happens in it," have emerged.

As well, newspapers such as the *Toronto Star* (TheStar.com) have in recent years worked to *expand* local coverage to enhance their appeal to readers (and local advertisers) in a very crowded online news environment.

What's more, the work of a local reporter on, for instance, city hall corruption, can now be easily accessed by anyone in the world with an interest in that topic, and the potential exists for a local story to "break out" of a local news environment, if it has resonance with people elsewhere. The disappearance of dozens of women from the streets of Vancouver was a local story for a long time, until it exploded into the story of a serial killer preying on prostitutes and drug addicts. The coverage of the trial of serial killer Robert Pickton went from being local to making headlines around the world. Similarly, NYU professor Clay Shirky often cites the legwork of *Boston Globe* reporters who broke a local story about child sexual abuse in the Catholic Church that subsequently had worldwide repercussions.

What's important to note is that in the age of global, digital journalism, there is—somewhat paradoxically—a new currency and value in specialized beat or local reporting. Young bloggers are advised to maintain a certain thematic focus and consistency to their posts, so that the audience that was attracted by the original topic of the site keeps coming back, and so that the blog can become established and gain readers within a community. (For more on blogging, see Chapter 17, "Blog to the Future: Telling Digital Stories in the Post-9/11 Decade.")

Serving a Community

To get a sense of what constitutes the best beat/local journalism, consider this list of some recent Pulitzer Prize winners for local/beat reporting, and the range of topics that they have covered:

- 2009: *Detroit Free Press* staff, notably Jim Schaefer and M.L. Elrick

  For their uncovering of a pattern of lies by Mayor Kwame Kilpatrick that included denial of a sexual relationship with his female chief of staff, prompting an investigation of perjury that eventually led to jail terms for the two officials.
- 2008: David Umhoefer of *Milwaukee Journal Sentinel*

  For his stories on the skirting of tax laws to pad pensions of county employees, prompting change and possible prosecution of key figures.

- 2007: Debbie Cenziper of the *Miami Herald*
  For reports on waste, favouritism, and lack of oversight at the Miami housing agency that resulted in dismissals, investigations, and prosecutions (The Pulitzer Prizes n.d., 2009).

In Canada, the National Newspaper Awards includes an entry category for Local Reporting, which applies specifically to newspapers "of 30,000 average daily circulation or less." Here are some recent winners:

- 2008: Monte Sonnenberg of the *Simcoe Reformer*
  For stories about the Ontario government's Home Owner Employee Relocation plan that led to changes. Runners-up were Gordon Hoekstra of the *Prince George Citizen* for stories about the state of the forest industry in British Columbia, and the *North Bay Nugget* team for coverage of an *E. coli* outbreak at a local hamburger fast-food outlet.
- 2007: Gordon Hoekstra of the *Prince George Citizen*
  For stories about air quality issues in the city. Runners-up were Elisabeth Johns of the *Cornwall Standard-Freeholder* for a series on domestic violence in the community, and Ann Lukits of the *Kingston Whig-Standard* for stories on declining care for seniors and a shortage of doctors in nursing homes.
- 2006: Paul Schliesmann of the *Kingston Whig-Standard*
  For stories about his wife Tracy's battle with cancer that ended with her death. Runners-up were Carole Morris of *Valley Today* in Windsor, Nova Scotia for her stories about the mysterious disappearance and search for a young man later found dead in a bog, and a team from the *Guelph Mercury* for stories about the 10th anniversary of Guelph's pioneering waste management system. (National Newspaper Awards n.d., 2007, 2008)

TOOLS & TIPS

Tips for the Beat Reporter

Wade Hemsworth

1. Don't expect a home run on the first day. Prime the pump with some straightforward stories to familiarize yourself with the material and people on your beat, which will also help spread the word that you are there to cover it.
2. Write profiles of key players on your beat. Use the interviews to establish the relationships that help you develop other story ideas. Writing these stories also establishes with the top figures on your beat that you are credible, accurate, and fair.
3. Go to events related to your beat. Receptions, announcements, and launches may not be the most newsworthy functions (you'll get this kind of news in advance once you are established on the beat), but the events themselves

are great opportunities for face time with newsmakers and learning through conversation what's really happening. Appearing at these events also establishes your commitment to the subject in the eyes of the people you write about, which goes a long way toward your sources seeing you as a go-to person.

4. Set up Google searches to bring you everyone else's coverage of your subject. This has a double effect: making sure you are covering your backside, and turning up a lot of story ideas that you might not have thought of. Use QuickWire the same way. Nothing going on? Try typing in some keywords from your area of responsibility and see what you can localize from what's happening in other places.
5. Read the sources your sources are reading. Do your homework by reading agendas, reports, and journals. These often produce the best stories and help you to keep up your knowledge of the topics you cover.
6. Find and monitor any websites and blogs that deal with your subject matter, whether official or unofficial, and be sure you mine the comment sections. Knowing what community members are talking about and what they think of current subjects is a good way of monitoring the pulse of your beat.
7. Set up Google Alerts using terms that bring up stories from your beat. You'll get an email every time one pops up on Google News. Seeing what other media are doing makes sure you're the first to know if you've been scooped, but more important, it gives you ideas for other stories.
8. Be honourable. Don't break embargoes without good reason. Keep off-the-record information off the record (after you have tried to get it on the record, of course).
9. Be economical with your questions when talking to busy people by preparing thoughtfully. If community leaders know they can get on and off the phone fairly quickly, they are far more likely to return your call when you really need them.
10. Keep a good list of your contacts, including cellphone numbers, home numbers, office numbers, email addresses, and assistants' names. Be disciplined about keeping this list up to date and be sure to mark it in your permanent list (for example, a database). If you have call display on your work phone, be sure to write down the number when someone calls you back. This is a simple but effective way to get cellphone numbers from sources who hesitate to give them out. That said, be careful not to use such "special" numbers unless you have to.
11. When requesting an interview, if you don't get the person right away, leave a phone message and send an email. Some people hardly ever play their messages, while others hardly ever look at their email, and trying to guess is

a loser's game. In your messages and notes, be sure to say that you are calling *and* writing and that the person should ignore the other message.

12. Within reasonable limits and budgetary restraints, try to dress like the people you cover. The less you stand out, the more your sources will relax, because they see you as being like them. Covering corporate board meetings in jeans, for example, sets you back before you've even asked the first question. So does covering an agricultural show in a suit. Always be neat and clean. No exceptions.

Wade Hemsworth has worked for the *Hamilton Spectator* since 1987, where he has been a reporter, a columnist, and an editor. His beats have included police, city hall, the courts, entertainment, the Hamilton Tiger-Cats, and post-secondary education.

New Roles for Beat Reporters

American journalist Dan Froomkin (2009) has written about the changing roles of beat reporters, and the value they can bring to journalism.

> Knowledgeable beat reporters aren't just stenographers, they are translators, educators, referees and analysts. If we've got people in our newsroom who really understand how a certain city or county works, or who are experts in certain policy areas, they should be sharing and showcasing their expertise in live discussions and blogs; should be answering reader questions and composing FAQs, should be on Facebook and Twitter, should be publishing and allowing readers to contribute to their beat notes, and should be writing and updating primers on key players and key issues .... They should essentially become the anchor for a community of people who share an interest in that beat. And by making it clear that our beat reporters are not faceless drones, but knowledgeable and accessible figures, we can reconnect with readers who may otherwise decide they may as well go somewhere else for their news.
>
> A renewed emphasis on beat reporting would be good for our newsgathering efforts overall, as well. It would remind us of the value of keeping experienced, knowledgeable, well-sourced journalists covering the same communities or topics over time; and it might encourage us to revisit our beat structures for the new era, as well as create mini-beats for urgent topics that we otherwise only cover reactively.

Froomkin described a new role for beat reporters in greater detail in the piece that follows, which is excerpted from the *Online Journalism Review*.

Dan Froomkin
"Why Beat Reporters Could Be News Sites' Greatest Secret Weapon" (excerpt)
www.ojr.org AUGUST 26, 2004

Ten years into this grand experiment of online journalism, I've come to realize that beat reporters could be the secret weapon of newspaper Web sites.

Their potential is unrealized as long as they're working only in the print world—and the online world needs their wisdom.

After all, covering a beat isn't just about producing an endless stream of incremental stories, punctuated by the occasional six-part series. It's about a deep, full-bodied understanding of the subject or area at hand. But at most newspapers, readers don't get nearly enough exposure to that expertise.

Meanwhile, on the Web, we've long realized the value of FAQs, primers and timelines. They work well in newspapers, but they perform even better on the Web, where they can be enhanced with images, be made multi-dimensional with links, can be expanded, collapsed and augmented by readers and—most importantly—where they don't get thrown in the recycling bin after one short day of life.

Primers, FAQs and timelines may not be the newest or fanciest tools in our toolbox, but readers love them. One big reason: Deprived by these formats of the ability to hide behind incremental news pegs, anecdotal leads or flowery prose, their authors have no choice but to explain themselves forthrightly and with authority. We just don't do them very often, because they're really hard to do. Or at least, they're really hard for online producers and editors to do.

Enter: The Beat Reporter

Only beat reporters can produce primers, FAQs and timelines with relative ease. There are, of course, plenty of reasons why this doesn't happen more frequently. Primers, FAQs and timelines are time-consuming, even for the most knowledgeable beat reporter. They can frustrate the flow of daily, incremental copy. Lacking a news peg, they are less likely to get a front-page byline. And there are still some newsroom managers—and some newsroom union leaders—who frown on doing anything that is considered primarily for online's benefit.

But there's something in this for newspaper reporters, editors, and readers, too.

Primers, FAQs and timelines offer beat reporters a great way to share the breadth of their knowledge with their readers—while at the same time demonstrating their authority to their sources. Say you're writing a primer about the town you cover—or about a topic on a beat like the environment. A good primer is sweeping in scope. It identifies and describes the big challenges in your chosen area. It offers you a chance to share your hard-won expertise in a more effective and expressive way than the daily, reactive, incremental story—or even the occasional trend story.

Primers also force reporters to state the obvious—which is often left strikingly unstated in the hurly-burly of daily journalism. For instance, how often does your newspaper describe the social, economic and racial stratification that is, inevitably, one of the most defining aspects of daily life in your communities?

Timelines, for their part, require us to know how we got to where we are. Beat reporters should know that—and if they aren't sure, or if there are large gaps in their knowledge, well, then, building a timeline is just what the doctor ordered.

FAQs require reporters to identify and ponder the important questions—and ideally ask readers what they are curious or worried about. FAQs can even force reporters to acknowledge that there are questions for which they don't have the answers. (In fact, I think we should not just be doing FAQs, but Frequently Unanswered Questions—or maybe even Frequently Unasked Questions. But the acronym is … problematic.)

My Personal Experience

In a strictly print universe, primers, FAQs and timelines rarely offer enough obvious bang for the buck. But if you add online into the mix, where such evergreen content can live for a long time—longer if it's updated once in a while—they become hugely valuable.

And while writing them is never easy, they're a lot harder when you're starting from scratch.

Forgive me if I use some of my own work as examples, but it's what I know best.

I've written dozens of primers over the past decade. The first ones I wrote were for Education Week on the Web, a site I helped launch in 1996. I had been an education reporter for many years before that, so I knew what I was writing about. I found writing authoritative, straightforward explanations—of such complicated, loaded and misunderstood topics as phonics vs. whole language and vouchers—to be hard, but deeply satisfying. Check out the Topics page on EdWeek.org to see what this has turned into over the years. It's wonderful work by talented beat reporters.

Once I came to WashingtonPost.com, I set myself to writing primers and FAQs about subjects with which I had only a passing acquaintance. Writing the idiot's guide to campaign finance or Whitewater, starting from essentially scratch, was devilishly hard.

It's amazing what you find when you're a generalist poring through the work of even the best beat reporters. While looking for some authoritative overview of the topic at hand, you find instead how incremental developments and anecdotes can really cover for the absence of simple, basic, explanatory journalism. You read everything you can find, and you still end up having to do a lot of your own reporting.

But again, I found the act of researching and writing them deeply satisfying. And the response from readers was deeply gratifying: Sure, none of my primers ever got in the top-ten daily page view list, but over time they wildly outperformed daily stories. And I was overwhelmed by the e-mails from readers—particularly students and teachers—who found them useful. Six years later, even, I still get e-mails a few times a month about a primer I wrote on affirmative action. Admittedly, most of them are from students trying to get help with their term papers—but, when you think about it, the ability to help students with their term papers is a pretty good litmus test for a news Web site … .

My career as a general-interest primer writer collapsed as I got sucked into covering L'Affaire Lewinsky. But on my new "beat" I constantly used primers, FAQs and timelines to tell that story online and help make WashingtonPost.com the pre-eminent destination on the Web for all things Monica. See http://www.washingtonpost.com/wp-srv/politics/special/clinton/faq.htm.

These experiences taught me that a beat reporter has a tremendous advantage over a generalist. In fact, plunk a beat reporter down to make a list of the half-dozen things that interest them the most about their beat—and voila!—you've already got the outline of a great primer. They've already covered the events that make up the timelines. They've already asked the questions that make up the FAQs. I'm not saying these are ever easy to do. It's never easy to boil things down, which is what these formats require. It takes a lot of time, a lot of energy—and, often, strong editing.

Next Steps for Newsrooms

… In many newsrooms, newspaper reporters are now filing on our clock, and that's a huge victory. But they're still not filing on our terms. A lot of the things I would like folks in print newsrooms to start doing for online—narrating photo essays, adding Web links, shooting video, creating blogs—don't necessarily provide a lot of obvious, immediate return to the newspaper itself. Maybe they are a bit too risky for some managers out there.

So it seems to me that primers, FAQs and timelines—written by beat reporters and edited by their regular editors—are the obvious next step for newsrooms to take, because they are perfectly adapted to the new medium while still serving the newspaper.

Genuine Connections

I have a theory about why newspaper circulation is down. It's not so much the Internet or demographics—at least not in and of themselves. I think it's at least in part because newspapers have failed to give readers evidence that reporters really know the community, least of all care about it. That used to be a given, decades ago.

Similarly, newspapers have failed to showcase how deeply knowledgeable and caring their reporters are about the issues they cover.

And in the absence of evidence of that sort of connection, readers feel free to drift away, either to ignorance or to commoditized news on the likes of Yahoo.

Primers, FAQs and timelines—particularly if they are produced in a way that encourages and responds to reader input—can reestablish the bond that once existed between newspapers and their readers. And it was that bond, I believe, that made newspapers essential, more even than the news.

So here's an idea that will make newspapers better, make Web sites stronger and maybe even be an antidote to declining circulation. What's wrong with that?

Stop hiding your secret weapons, people. Deploy them!

TOOLS & TIPS

Social Media for the Beat Reporter

Wayne MacPhail

1. Participate in social media, not just when you need sources, but, more importantly, when you don't. Contribute and engage. Nobody likes the guy at the cocktail party handing out business cards, and that's what you look like when you show up on Twitter, Facebook, or buzz.com and start asking for sources or answers. Reporters, especially tech reporters, who aren't engaged with social media and/or who haven't amassed a good deal of hard-earned social capital aren't doing their job.
2. Listen to podcasts and read blogs in your area of interest. Often bloggers have highly specialized knowledge about specific fields. Very often they know much more than mainstream journalists who need to be wide and shallow on subjects. Get over the idea that bloggers just write opinions. Read John Gruber on Apple products and user interface design and see if you still feel that way.
3. Use RSS feeds daily. If you're still browsing the Web instead of letting it come to you, you're wasting hours a week. Plus RSS feeds can be fed to your phone, tablet, netbook, or whatever mobile device you're using.
4. Use social media metric tools to track trends and firms. There are a variety of tools (search.twitter.com, socialmention.com, and other more complex ones like www.radian6.com) that allow you to see who's talking about what and how trends and memes are circulating on social networks. Use them.
5. Use geo-location to track trends and social media experts in your community. More and more social media tools allow users to share their locations via GPS or assisted-GPS radios. So, you can easily find local experts and local trends that might turn into stories.

Wayne MacPhail is a Hamilton-based journalist and new media consultant. Visit his blog at www.w8nc.com.

Beat Blogs

Jay Rosen, professor of journalism at NYU, has been a leader in exploring how traditional beats can be reimagined, and improved, for the world of digital journalism. Since 2007, he has been conducting experiments with beat reporters and other writers and journalists, in which social networking tools are actively incorporated. He explained the motivation behind this enterprise with the following proposition: "Maybe a beat reporter could do a way better job if there was a 'live' social network connected to the beat, made up of people who know the territory the beat covers, and want the reporting on that beat to be better" (Rosen 2007).

Rosen maintains a website devoted to networked beat journalism, BeatBlogging.org, which provides the following definition of a *beat blog*:

> **What's a Beat Blog?**
>
> A beat blog in the expansive sense is any blog that sticks to a well-defined beat or coverage area, whether it is the work of a single person or a team, whether it is authored by a pro or an amateur journalist. A beat blog can be part of a large site, or it could stand on its own. Normally, the beat is explicit and obvious from the home page of the blog, but it is possible for a beat blog to have an "implicit" or unusual beat that isn't immediately apparent to a casual user.
>
> Content-wise, a beat blog presents a regular flow of reporting and commentary in a focused area the beat covers; it provides links and online resources in that area, and it tracks the subject over time. Beats can be topical (like Dot Earth [dotearth.blogs.nytimes.com], which is about natural resources and the environment) or narrowly geographic (West Seattle blog [westseattleblog.com/blog] or both (Atlantic Yards Report [atlanticyardsreport.blogspot.com) or activity-related (Family Life [blog.syracuse.com/family], which is about "raising a family").
>
> When beat blogs are part of a pro reporters work, the best ones are not incidental to the reporter's work but an integral part of it; sometimes the blog is the main platform for the beat … .
>
> Our ultimate interest is to push forward the practice of using a beat blog in a more "networked" fashion, where the site becomes a two-way knowledge system that feeds the beat. Some have called this the "journalism of the inbox." It's editorial production, social media style. The ultimate promise of such a system—and we're not there yet—is to bring lots more people, with their beat-specific knowledge, connections, interests and talents, into the production of good reporting, quality features, great posts: better stories! (Rosen 2009)

TOOLS & TIPS

Developing a New Beat

Journalist, blogger, and trainer Steve Buttry devised the following plan as a guide to developing a new beat:

Beat:

- Reporter: ______________________________
- Editor: ______________________________

Getting started

- How do you define your beat? What does it encompass?
- Who will your readers be? Who will be watching for your stories?
- If you're starting from scratch, what will you do the first week on the beat?
- What other reporters/editors have worked this beat you can tap into now?
- How can your team be of assistance?
- What can news research do to help you discover and develop your beat? (reading materials, websites, experts)

Developing the beat

- Who are the official sources for your beat?
- Where will you go to find them?
- Who will you need to call? How often?
- Who are the unofficial sources for your beat?
- Where will you go to find them?
- Who will you need to call? How often?
- How does your beat overlap with other beats and writers?
- How will you structure time to stay connected and in sync?
- What can you do to develop your beat online?
- How can you push your beat (old or new), your reporting and writing to keep it fresh, more accessible and relevant?

Setting goals

- What percentage of your job will be:
  - Covering breaking news?
  - Breaking your own news?
  - Investigative reporting?
  - Storytelling?
  - Context, issues, trends?
  - Brites and quick hits?
- What are five stories you want to do in the first month?
- What does success look like in six months?
- What's one project you'd like to do in the next year?

(No Train, No Gain n.d.)

DISCUSSION QUESTIONS

1. Using the guide to developing a new beat above, plan a new beat on a topic that interests you. Which aspects of developing a new beat plan did you find the most difficult?
2. Choose a beat reporter working for a newspaper or website that you regularly read, preferably in your community. Review his or her archive of stories and look for common themes, threads, or topics. How many main topics does the journalist tend to cover? Did you see any old stories that developed "legs," and which the reporter subsequently wrote about as the story developed?
3. Find a local reporter who has a Twitter page and look through its various postings. What sorts of information do you see gathered there? What sorts of contacts and connections does the reporter appear to create or maintain via Twitter?

SUGGESTED RESOURCES

Beatblogging.org [Jay Rosen's blog]. http://beatblogging.org.

Froomkin, Dan [blog at The Huffington Post]. http://www.huffingtonpost.com/dan-froomkin.

McKercher, Catherine, Allan Thompson, and Carman Cumming. 2010. *The Canadian reporter: News writing and reporting*. 3rd ed. Toronto: Nelson Education.

REFERENCES

Froomkin, Dan. 2009. How to better use our biggest assets, beat reporters. Nieman Journalism Lab, May 28. http://www.niemanlab.org/2009/05/dan-froomkin-how-to-better-use-our-biggest-assets-beat-reporters/.

National Newspaper Awards. n.d. Winners and runners-up for 2008 NNAs. http://www.nna-ccj.ca/wordpress_dev/wordpress/?p=701&lang=en.

National Newspaper Awards. 2007. Finalists announced for 2006 National Newspaper Awards. News release, March 9. http://www.newswire.ca/en/releases/archive/March2007/09/c8988.html.

National Newspaper Awards. 2008. Winners announced for 2007 National Newspaper Awards. News release, May 9. http://www.newswire.ca/en/releases/archive/May2008/09/c7001.html.

No Train, No Gain. n.d. *Atlanta Journal-Constitution* beat development plan—new beat. http://www.notrain-nogain.org/Man/NRO/newb.asp.

The Pulitzer Prizes. n.d. Local reporting. http://www.pulitzer.org/bycat/Local-Reporting.

The Pulitzer Prizes. 2009. Current winners and finalists. http://www.pulitzer.org/awards/2009.

Rosen, Jay. 2007. Figuring out beat reporting with a social network. PBS MediaShift, November 1. http://www.pbs.org/idealab/2007/11/figuring-out-beat-reporting-with-a-social-network005.html.

Rosen, Jay. 2009. What we're talking about when we say "beatblog." Our definition. BeatBlogging.org, March 4. http://beatblogging.org/2009/03/04/what-were-talking-about-when-we-say-beatblog-our-definition/.

PART THREE
Social Media and Multimedia

CHAPTER 16

Social Media

Lisa Lynch

CHAPTER OUTLINE

What Are Social Media and How Are They Changing Journalism?

If you have a Facebook page—or, for that matter, an account on Flickr, YouTube, or Twitter—then you are one of the two-thirds of all global Internet users who have discovered the benefits of social media. In a few short years, social media applications have changed the way we use the Internet in profound ways. They facilitate "social networking," or socializing with people in online communities through the exchange of public and private messages and images. They empower ordinary people to become producers and publishers of online content—photos, videos, articles, blogs, even graphics—using free or low-cost Internet tools to create and distribute work. For these and other reasons, social media applications also change the traditional relationships between institutions and individuals, including the relationship between media outlets and their audiences.

As a journalist, you will likely engage with social media on a variety of levels. You may use social media to build communities around your content. You may use social media to enhance your own "brand" as a journalist or the brand of your media outlet. And, you may find yourself negotiating with social media audiences who want to integrate their user-generated content into your publication. It is even possible that some of you will find that your entire career revolves around social media; for example, as a crowd-funded public interest reporter, a social media manager for a news outlet, or a professional editor at a citizen media site. Or, you may discover that your true talent is as a "news curator," using social bookmarking as a tool to aggregate linked content for a news site.

It cannot be emphasized enough that the world of social media continues to be new territory for journalists and audiences—one filled with both promise and conflict. Still, when used correctly, social media tools have helped reporters write stories that are more extensively sourced, more accurate, and more widely read than before. The same tools have helped media outlets re-establish connections with readers and audiences, and engage new audiences as well.

This chapter will help you understand the various ways in which journalists have begun to use social media, whether they are freelancers, full-time reporters at news outlets, or editors or managers focusing more exclusively on social media. At the same time, you'll also learn how to get started with your own social media identity, or how to adjust your current use of social networking and microblogging services to find sources and information, and build contacts with an audience interested in your work.

Social Networking Sites

Going Where Your Readers Are

Social networking sites are platforms that allow users to build communities around shared interests or offline acquaintances. Although such platforms have been around for almost a decade, only in recent years have they become an important tool for journalists and editors. There are two reasons for this. The first is that social networking has emerged as a mass phenomenon outpacing many other forms of online activity, including online news consumption. The second is that the nature of social networking has changed, as many users have come to rely on their networks not only for online camaraderie but also for recommendations about which films to see, what products to buy—and what news items to read and discuss.

Depending on your age and interest, you may have been a member of any number of social networking sites, including Friendster, Tribe, MySpace, Skyrock, and Ning. The majority of social networking users in Canada have embraced Facebook, so for the purposes of this chapter we'll examine journalists' use of that network. And since—as any Facebook user knows—the design, functionality, and even demographics of the site are in flux, we'll focus on establishing a presence on the site and mining it for information rather than specific features and secondary applications.

It's a safe bet that most of you have a page on Facebook or know someone who does, so you're probably aware of the way the site is used by most of its members. After logging in to the Facebook platform, a user is directed to a homepage where he or she can read posted "status updates"; see photos, videos, and links that friends have posted; send and receive private emails; post public messages on a friend's "wall"; or keep abreast of the activities of groups, publications, or notable individuals whose "fan" pages send them updates.

It's easy to see why this mundane, highly personalized activity might seem anathema to journalists and editors. But as the site has matured, social network scholars and industry observers have noted that Facebook members are sharing content with one another on the platform far more than they are sharing content through any other means, including email. And as users spend more time on Facebook, sharing and commenting on news items has become an increasingly important function of the site. Relying on their "trust networks" to deliver the news and information they need, many Facebook users are spending less of their Internet time on news sites and news portals—an unfortunate reality that media industries must reckon with.

So while it's tempting not to take Facebook seriously—and until recently, many news outlets didn't—the site has become a valuable place both to cultivate audiences and to search for story ideas. Consequently, it's important for journalists to use Facebook, albeit with a continual eye on the way in which their identities as journalists might influence their use of the platform.

Building a Network

Whether you're a freelance journalist, a staff reporter for a radio program, or a social media manager responsible for your publication's overall online image, you need to carefully consider how you want to present yourself or your publication before establishing a presence on any social network. If you're setting up a Facebook page, you can choose either to carry out your networking entirely on a "friend" page or to concentrate your efforts on developing a "fan" page (there's an option to create a "group" as well, but generally group pages are for causes or events). While a friend page is open only to friends that have been accepted by the page owner, the fan page is open to anyone who chooses to join. Although it is a more passive interface, a fan page allows visitors to comment on what has been posted, write a note on the page "wall," and talk to other fans on the page.

Figure 16.1 There now exists a wide range of social media tools for both freelance and staff journalists and managers to choose from, and careful consideration should be given to what type of social media will best represent you or your publication.

It might seem like fan pages are the obvious choice for organizational efforts, while friend pages are the obvious choice for individuals. But while the former is certainly true (many CBC programs, such as Nora Young's *Spark*, now have Facebook fan pages, as Nora Young discusses at the end of this chapter), a fair number of well-known journalists, such as the BBC's Jeb Sharp, have both a friend page for their personal network and a fan page dedicated mainly to broadcasting activities and soliciting comments.

Once you've set up a page on Facebook, remember that you're essentially in a public space. Whether you're putting up comments on your own page or responding to the posts of others, steer away from crossing lines you might not otherwise cross in your professional life. Mostly, this means using common sense: If your place of employment discourages you from expressing political affiliation, for example, you should avoid joining groups that might indicate a preference for a party or candidate. If a source wants to "friend" you after they've appeared in one of your stories, think about how this might appear to readers. Overall, fan pages are more neutral sites of engagement, where those who follow you do so because they're interested in what you do professionally—not because they're hoping you might reveal something deeply personal about yourself that they wouldn't find out elsewhere.

Using Social Networks as a Reporter's Resource

Once you've set up your page on Facebook, you can begin to experiment with the many ways in which the platform can serve as a tool to circulate material and report on and source stories. Social networking services can be an excellent guide to the zeitgeist: Aside from the links and recommendations that your friends might provide, a number of interest groups and causes have pages that you can browse to find story ideas. But be aware as you're doing so that you're dealing with an interface that many users assume is more private than it actually is. For example, you may be able to identify the members of an organization by visiting its public Facebook page, but those members may still be surprised that that information is "public" to a journalist if you mention their names in an article or contact them through the platform.

Journalists have used Facebook to find sources by visiting the publicly available information of persons involved in a crime or tragedy, searching through that person's "friend list" for possible contacts. In the wake of the Virginia Tech shooting in April 2007, for example, journalists sought out and contacted friends of victims through Facebook. Although such searches can save a considerable amount of legwork, there are some important caveats. First, recent changes to the site have made the display of such friend lists optional, making it harder to conduct such searches. Second, although this information is ostensibly public, it often is not considered so by those on the network, so it's an ethical judgment call as to whether you'll want to use Facebook in this way. If you do decide to contact people you don't know on a social networking platform, make sure that you identify yourself as a journalist, since the default assumption on such platforms is that conversations are purely private and social in nature.

IN PRACTICE

Facebook Privacy

How private is your private Facebook page? The answer is, it depends. Facebook allows users to restrict what information is seen, but that information is still only as private as those who have been friended want it to be. For example, in the summer of 2009, Audra Shay, vice-chairperson of the Young Republicans in the United States, garnered national attention when someone in her friend circle revealed that she'd reacted approvingly to racist comments posted to her private Facebook page. Around the same time, an Associated Press reporter was formally reprimanded when a comment he made on Facebook was reported to management by one of his "friends."

Incidents such as these—whether or not they are directly related to a reporter's use of Facebook—have prompted many news organizations to establish guidelines for reporters who use social media. In October 2009, National Public Radio (NPR) issued a policy that, among other things, reminded its reporters that they were essentially representing NPR in a public forum whenever they chose to use social media:

> You should conduct yourself in social media forums with an eye to how your behavior or comments might appear if we were called upon to defend them as a news organization. In other words, don't behave any differently online than you would in any other public setting. (NPR 2009)

For those who are uncomfortable with negotiating the shaky line between public and private spaces on social networking platforms, there are other ways to use Facebook in your reporting practice. You can, for example, pose sourcing questions to friends or fans. And you can report on whatever material appears on public pages or fan pages. However, beware that the latter use can be ethically problematic. Some politicians, perhaps most notably Sarah Palin as an American vice-presidential candidate, use Facebook to release public statements and bypass questions from the media. As a result, reporters must understand that while social media in some ways have democratized communication, they have also created new platforms for information to circulate without being challenged or fact-checked.

Twitter and the "Microblogging Revolution"

Although not as ubiquitous as Facebook, Twitter's success in Canada has shown that microblogging—publishing ideas, opinions, and resources in 140-character bursts—also has potential to reinvigorate journalism. The capability of microblogging to produce real-time information that journalists can sift, curate, and aggregate has contributed to making Twitter an important new tool for newsgathering. Moreover, media outlets are realizing that Twitter users spend a large part of their time linking to information about news and current events. Twitter has thus become an important means for news stories to "go viral," or spread with astonishing speed as users recirculate information through the network.

A series of key events helped convince journalists of Twitter's value as a reporting tool. On April 12, 2007, an earthquake in Mexico City was reported on Twitter several minutes before the US Geological Survey took note. News of an earthquake in China the following May appeared first on Twitter as well. On November 28, 2008, during a terror attack in Mumbai, Twitter users at the site were able to provide on-the-ground accounts of events, while traditional media were prevented from reporting owing to a press embargo. The Mumbai events led many to speculate that Twitter would soon become the most-used platform for those wanting to obtain first-person accounts during crises, but the accuracy of these accounts quickly became an issue when, less than a month later, a conflict in Gaza resulted in an avalanche of conflicting accounts.

But even as its potential for accuracy came under fire, Twitter continued to prove its value to journalists as a source for eyewitness accounts. On January 15, 2009, news of the crash-landing of a US Airways plane into the Hudson River was once again scooped by Twitter users; in fact, a picture of the landing, posted on Twitter as the plane was still settling in the water, became one of the iconic images of the event. In May, Twitter itself became newsworthy when the judge presiding over the criminal trial of Ottawa Mayor Larry O'Brien allowed reporters to Twitter from the courtroom, despite blocking television cameras from the event (see Figure 16.2). And in June, international interest in the service surged after demonstrators protesting the results of the Iranian presidential election began to Twitter about what was happening in their country, communicating with raptly attentive Westerners despite a media shutdown that cut off access to "official" news of the events.

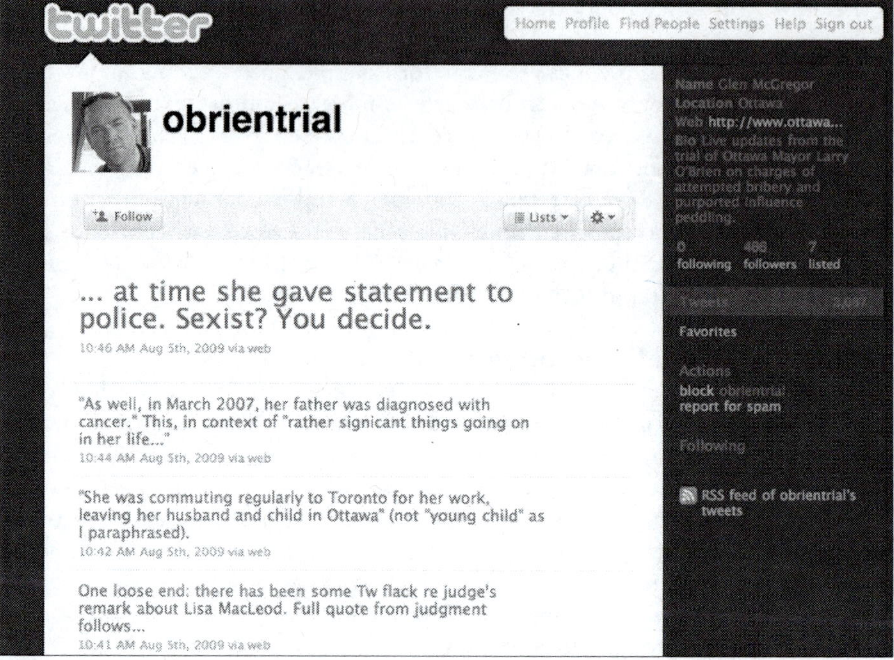

Figure 16.2 *Ottawa Citizen* reporter Glen McGregor was able to use Twitter to report on the 2009 court case of Ottawa Mayor Larry O'Brien after a judge ruled that television cameras were not allowed into the courtroom.

Getting Started with Microblogging

Listening In

Ask any regular Twitter user, and they will immediately tell you the most important part of the service is not what you have to say, but what you stand to learn from fellow users. So, before you start worrying about amassing followers, spend some time thinking about just who you might like to follow. The best thing about Twitter is that, with rare exceptions, you can sign up for almost anyone's updates: journalists, politicians, musicians, non-profit organizations, scholars, members of your community … the possibilities are mind-boggling, so it pays to be somewhat selective. Visit the homepages of those whom you are most interested in following and see who they might be following, including their lists of followers organized by topic. There are several third-party services that allow you to search for users in your area, or you can use Twitter's "Advanced Search" feature to find users near a particular postal code.

What if you work in a region where the service isn't used much? Is Twitter useless as a journalistic tool? Hardly. If you are a topical reporter, Twitter is a great way to listen in to conversations happening elsewhere on whatever you might cover. Following journalists around the country—or the world—provides a constant stream of story ideas that might be adapted to your community.

In addition to learning what readers to follow, it's also important to learn how to follow hashtags. *Hashtags*, which begin with the "#" symbol, are labels applied by users to their tweets to give those tweets added context and metadata (for example, #newmedia). Sometimes these tags are preordained, especially in the case of an event such as a technology conference (#GTEC), but they often arise spontaneously, and at times competing hashtags fracture what should be one continuous conversation into several threads. If you're searching for information about an event, try several obvious words or combinations as hashtags, and look for tweets that contain multiple tags as means of consolidating disparate lists.

Once a topic becomes popular—either spectacularly so, as in the case of the Iran elections, or simply popular enough to stand out at any given moment—it will appear on Twitter's site as a "trending" topic. For the most part, Twitter trends reflect the same conversations people are having both around the Internet and offline on a particular day: celebrity scandals, football games, television shows, et cetera. From time to time, however, Twitter trends can bring something to the public eye that might have escaped the attention of the conventional media. For example, a British court injunction preventing the *Guardian* newspaper from reporting on a parliamentary debate attracted international attention after it became a Twitter trend, eventually resulting in the lifting of the injunction by the court.

As the above examples suggest, Twitter can be a valuable source of breaking news. But those who cover breaking news on Twitter need to be vigilant about checking the accuracy of what they read. Journalism professor Steve Buttry (2008) advises that it's better to "consider everything bogus" until proven otherwise, while journalist Craig Kanalley (2009) suggests an eight-step process for verifying tweets that includes checking the time-stamp, attempting to contact the tweeter directly, looking up the person on Google, and searching for other tweets that seem credible and repeat the information. These "contextual tweets," as Kanalley calls them, can be found by searching through hashtags related to the event. Sometimes such hashtag searches can lead to contact with eyewitnesses.

Broadcasting Out

After you've gotten accustomed to using Twitter, it's time to figure out how and what to contribute to the site. It's your own contribution to Twitter that will help you establish a community of followers interested in what you have to say. For a reporter, the idea of having followers beyond his or her media outlet's readers can often be intoxicating and empowering; as *Chicago Tribune* general assignment reporter James Janega noted in an interview with J.D. Lasica, developing your followers as a reporter is like "a garden that you tend" (Lasica 2009).

Part of tending your garden on Twitter—as with any social media service—is establishing boundaries between your work identity and your social identity. You must decide whether you want to express any kind of political, religious, or other affiliation, and whether you want to mention family members or personal events. Some journalists blend both identities seamlessly, while others rarely, if ever, mention personal details; still others create two accounts, one personal and one professional.

Twitter cultivation is also highly dependent on your local climate: in this case, the "climate" of your workplace. If you're employed at a news organization, chances are that there are already guidelines for microblogging. Thus, depending on where you work, you may be either encouraged to use or discouraged from using microblogging services, or you may be restricted from using microblogging services in specific ways. For example, the *Washington Post* has a fairly defined Twitter policy that reflects the paper's aspiration to present itself as a bastion of neutrality in a politically charged environment. Reuters, on the other hand, has adopted a notably flexible policy for Twittering; Reuters editor Dave Schlesinger even "scooped" the wire service with his tweets when he reported on the 2009 World Economic Forum in Davos, Switzerland.

Once you've established how to present yourself, you need to think about how you might use your microblog. Many journalists, photographers, and videographers use Twitter to post links to their work, thus ensuring that readers see what they're doing. If you're a freelancer, this is especially useful: Your followers can see work by you that might be in a publication they don't read. But be aware that some followers don't like when Twitter is used purely for advertising purposes. If you put up links to your own work, also be sure to link to other kinds of content that you think your followers might find interesting.

Finally, although most of what you do on Twitter will involve listening to, and broadcasting to, a larger community, don't forget the platform's potential to facilitate conversation. After you establish a following, it's likely that people you've never met will begin to respond to your tweets. And once they do, you should make it a practice

TOOLS & TIPS

Real-Time Reporting with Twitter

One of the most innovative ways journalists use Twitter is to post bits of information on a story as it unfolds, giving audiences a sense of the process of reporting. Some news outlets ask reporters to steer away from this practice for fear of reporting inaccurate information, but others embrace it. If you are allowed to file such "process" reports, think as well about posting links to photos of events you are covering that may not make it to a blog post or to the news site later on—that way your audience can access material that would otherwise be unavailable.

Another approach to reporting on Twitter, perhaps less hair-raising than tweeting breaking news events, is to cover speeches, meetings, or sports events in real time. If you do this type of reporting, make sure you understand the regulations of doing so: The event you are at may be embargoed.

Yet another use of Twitter is the Twitter interview, a challenge owing to the restricted number of characters per tweet and the fact that the audience needs to follow both parties to see the entire conversation. One of the most notable Twitter interviews was between George Stephanopoulous and John McCain during the 2009 US presidential elections.

to respond to them. You may want to think about entering into a discussion with others on Twitter about professional matters or an ongoing news event. This sort of spontaneous contact is encouraged on Twitter; use common sense, however. Jumping into a heated debate between two politicians, or for that matter two impassioned newspaper editors you might be following, is not likely to provoke a response.

Here Comes Everybody: Journalism and Crowdsourcing

While individual journalists are harnessing the power of social media through social networking and microblogging, news media are doing the same primarily through crowdsourcing. Media outlets are increasingly using crowdsourcing to come up with interview questions and story ideas, collect photos and videos of events, and collectively analyze primary source documents.

Perhaps the most common use of crowdsourcing by media outlets is to solicit and collect reader/viewer photos and videos. For example, the *New York Times* collected readers' photos of Woodstock for a piece on the anniversary of that music festival, and the *Globe and Mail* collects readers' photos of snow and ice storms. At times, the line between crowdsourcing and citizen journalism can seem a bit confusing; there is admittedly a slippery slope between using media audiences as a resource and getting them to generate content for a newspaper in lieu of professional reporters and photographers. But when it's well done—as was the *Times*'s Woodstock coverage—crowdsourcing still and moving images allows a media outlet to document an event more completely and from a wider range of perspectives, while still retaining control over the eventual shape of the material.

If photos and videos can be used as primary source material to be interpreted and framed by journalists, data and documents, on the other hand, can be presented by media outlets as primary source material to be sifted through and analyzed by readers as part of a group investigative effort. One of the more ambitious attempts at this has been the *Guardian* newspaper's decision in Spring 2009 to create a database of financial records from British members of Parliament accused of mismanaging their funds. Reader response was immediate, and eventually about half of the 450,000-page database was analyzed by over 25,000 readers. Other newspapers have followed the *Guardian*'s example—including the *New York Times*, which has collaborated on a grant-funded software project called *DocumentCloud*, which will eventually enable even smaller news organizations to set up databases for crowdsourcing projects.

Social networking, microblogging, and crowdsourcing are but three examples of the journalistic uses of social media. As social media practices and technologies continue to evolve, journalists and news organizations will likely find more ways to harness audience dialogue and collaboration. The best way to be apprised of new developments in social media is to embrace what's out there right now, by establishing a social media identity and entering into conversations with journalists, editors, and audiences who are collectively exploring how social media are changing what it means to produce and consume the news.

• • •

Figure 16.3 Nora Young (PHOTO: William Stodalka)

Interview: Nora Young on Integrating Social Media

Canadian Broadcaster Nora Young is the host of the CBC technology show Spark, *one of the most innovative programs at the CBC in terms of social media use. Through the show's weblog, Facebook page, and Twitter feed, users can not only give feedback to* Spark's *team but also post ideas or possible interview sources for upcoming shows and suggest interview questions for guests.*

Aside from Spark, *Young—whose prior radio experience included an eight-year stint as the founding host of the CBC pop culture show* Definitely Not the Opera*—has her own distinct online presence, including a Twitter feed, a technology and culture blog (formerly called Crisper and now a part of NoraYoung.ca), and a weekly podcast series,* The Sniffer, *with co-host Cathi Bond. We asked Young how she manages to juggle these online identities, and how she negotiates the new frontiers of social media in her professional life as a journalist.*[1]

LISA LYNCH: I've been doing an inventory of your online presence. You have your own Twitter account, @nora3000, but you also tweet for @sparkcbc. You have a blog, you do a weekly podcast with Cathi Bond. *Spark* has a recently launched Facebook page. How did you establish all these online outlets, and how do you manage them?

NORA YOUNG: First, I should explain that I began to experiment with social media after I left *Definitely Not the Opera* and began to freelance. The blog started in 2005; the podcast started in 2006. In 2007, after doing a story on Twitter for my CBC Radio Tech column, I gradually began to use Twitter.

I'd describe my Twitter Feed and *The Sniffer* as both personal and professional. By that, I mean that if you're a journalist, especially a self-employed one, the line between what's "you" and what's professional is blurred. For me this is a good thing but it also means if you go to my Facebook page, you won't find anything deeply personal. I primarily view my social media presence as a "scratch pad" to test out ideas I'm thinking about, as well as a way to connect with like-minded people, and extend my journalism into more of a conversation with interested listeners and readers.

LISA LYNCH: Yet when *Spark* began, you kept up with your blog, podcast, and Twitter feed …

NORA YOUNG: Yes, that's why you see these parallel worlds—the Nora Young presence online and the *Spark* presence. @nora3000 features Nora Young's observations about the world—but again, I keep my professional hat on. The *Spark* feed, on the other hand, is updated by both me and my colleagues.

LISA LYNCH: Is everyone on the show as excited about social media as you are?

NORA YOUNG: We knew when we started *Spark* that it was a natural outgrowth to experiment with social media. For one thing, we felt we needed to workshop ways to do public broadcasting in a 21st century world. And that meant trying to make connections with our audience in a new way. For example, as far as the Twitter feed was concerned, we felt that in order to keep people interested, we would have to not just publish announcements about show; we also try to feature breaking news things related to things our followers might be interested in. We also wanted our social media presence to be a two-way conversation. We blog and tweet under our own names: There's often a back-and-forth with people who follow us, or who comment on the blog. Basically, we've come to understand that if you're going to create innovative media—print, online, or broadcast—you can't just focus on putting out your own message. Instead, you need to embrace the opportunity to learn from your audience.

LISA LYNCH: It might be a good idea to get your definition of "social media" on the table. Do you consider it a "social media" interaction when people go to your website and suggest stories ideas? Or only if they do so through Facebook or Twitter?

NORA YOUNG: For me, the most relevant aspect of social media for journalistic practice is the "many to many" characteristic of social media interaction: that is, the ability to comment (in the case of *Spark*, for example, via Twitter, the blog, or on Facebook) and to have that comment be seen not only by us, but by the entire *Spark* community. For me, one of the best developments at the *Spark* blog is that people are not just responding to the contents of the show: they are starting to respond to, and dialogue with, other commenters on the blog. That is part of what 21st century public media should be doing: acting as a platform that allows a community to develop.

LISA LYNCH: Are there other ways in which *Spark* monitors this kind of audience engagement?

NORA YOUNG: We have a *Spark* "superfeed" that lets us know any time someone mentions the show online. The point is not to be slavishly worried about everything people say, but we do want to be aware if there are conversations like, "Why isn't *Spark* covering X?" or "*Spark* is doing an especially good job covering Y."

In the early days, whenever a blogger would mention *Spark*, my colleague Dan Misener would comment on their blog, letting them know that we were out there, reading what they wrote. We don't do that every time now—that would take too much time—but we still try to instill the sense that there is a conversation between ourselves and our audience.

LISA LYNCH: Compared to Twitter, the show's Facebook presence is rather small, which I found kind of surprising.

NORA YOUNG: That's because it's new. I have to admit, I resisted putting the show on Facebook. I personally don't like using Facebook; Twitter is where I like to hang out. But we had a conversation that convinced us that for a lot of people, Facebook is their news feed. So we began sending our Twitter feed there.

LISA LYNCH: Yes, I noticed that it's mainly a site for your Twitter posts. But then conversations start on Facebook about those posts, conversations that aren't taking place on Twitter.

NORA YOUNG: Yes, and now we need to go check them as well! I have to say, part of our learning curve has been figuring out how can we use all the tools and find people where they are without spending so much time that we can't do the show. As much as we love engaging with the people in social media, the reality is that the people who listen on-air is still way higher. We need to make sure that the hundreds of thousands of people who listen to us and who might not be using social media are getting their share of our attention.

LISA LYNCH: We've been talking about what you contribute to the dialogue with the *Spark* audience via social media; let's turn to how you, as a *Spark* producer, benefit from using social media. There's promotion, of course, but it's also true that you find sources for *Spark* programs via your Twitter feed.

NORA YOUNG: We use it all the time for this, and it can be an incredibly effective tool. Of course, it can also be a lazy tool, and you need to realize you're dealing with a tiny subsection of the population. That said, it's a good tool for following a beat—and *Spark* is an example of that. Many of the people who follow us are the very people with the pool of expertise we might need to call on.

Maybe the best thing about how social media have influenced us at *Spark* is the way in which their use affects the aesthetic of the show itself. For instance, when we're organized enough, we blog or tweet about an interview and get suggestions for questions. Then we post the full, unedited interview at the blog, before it goes to air. This way, interested listeners can not only get access to extra content before it goes to air; they can also comment on the raw interview. So, when the episode is broadcast, it might actually contain questions from the *Spark* community and follow-up comments as part of the final edit! I think we're just beginning to see what the potential of social media might be in changing not only what content we use, but how that content is eventually shaped.

LISA LYNCH: You have mentioned the idea of "social media hygiene." So how would you define good social media hygiene?

NORA YOUNG: That's a hard one. We really haven't figured out all the protocols for engaging with social media. I mean, we all know by now how long we should take to respond to an email, but we don't have the same set of common assumptions about how to use Twitter, Facebook, et cetera. As journalists, we still need to figure out how much to reveal in our use of social media, how responsive we want to be to our audiences, how we protect our autonomy, or how we protect any research we might be doing. Personally, I know I tend to err on the side of keeping my professional hat on; I think that's partly because I started to get involved in these things when I was self-employed. Not all journalists feel the same as I do; I've seen among journalists that I respect a wide range of approaches, some more personal, some less.

LISA LYNCH: So what kind of advice would you give to a journalist just beginning to use social media, who is trying to sort through all of these various approaches?

NORA YOUNG: If I was to give someone who was starting out advice, I think the first thing is just to remember the persistence of what you write online, even while you're still training as a journalist. These days, most people who hire you are going to look at your Facebook page, for example, so think about what you put there.

Second, I'd say that you should think about what you're passionate about, think about what you'd like to be an expert in, and get out there and start using social media to get your ideas out. While I think expertise and thoughtfulness are as important in our profession as they ever were, there is a lot less credentialism now, and sometimes becoming an expert in something can open amazing doors for you.

Third, it's important to learn how to become part of a conversation. On Twitter, that means trying to engage with people who share your interests. Twitter's so open that it allows for a lot of connections between like-minded people to happen organically. Don't try to be overly strategic about it, though—for example, don't constantly try to engage with important people in an effort to be noticed. Just remember: Behaviour that's obnoxious in a real-world social situation is probably obnoxious on Twitter as well. After all, the goal is to develop a dialogue with people you find interesting and who are interested in you.

NOTE

1. Nora Young (broadcaster, CBC), in discussion by telephone with Lisa Lynch, September 23, 2009.

DISCUSSION QUESTIONS

1. What privacy issues are involved when journalists use social media? How can journalists use social media effectively while protecting their privacy and that of others?
2. What's the best way to strike a balance between speed and accuracy when using Twitter as a resource in reporting? What kind of information should journalists *not* send out over a Twitter feed?
3. How important is it for those who work primarily as print or broadcast journalists to develop an online persona? Should all journalists in a news organization be required to establish a professional presence online, or should some journalists be able to opt out? Should journalists who work for a news organization with a presence online be allowed to have an independent online persona?
4. Here are the Twitter accounts of three authors in this book who are active users. How do they use their accounts? What sorts of sites to they tend to link to? How do they manage their work and social identities?
   - Hermida, Alfred, on Twitter: http://twitter.com/Hermida.
   - Ingram, Mathew, on Twitter: http://twitter.com/mathewI.
   - Lynch, Lisa, on Twitter: http://twitter.com/lisallynch.

SUGGESTED RESOURCES

Akin, David, on Twitter: http://twitter.com/DavidAkin.

Canadian Association of Journalists on Twitter: http://twitter.com/CAJ.

Globe and Mail Facebook page: http://www.facebook.com/theglobeandmail.

J-Source on Twitter: http://twitter.com/jsource.

Spark Facebook page: http://www.facebook.com/cbcspark#!/sparkcbc?ref=ts.

Spark on Twitter: http://twitter.com/SparkCBC.

Tossell, Ivor, on Twitter: http://twitter.com/IvorTossell.

Young, Nora, on Twitter: http://twitter.com/Nora3000.

REFERENCES

Buttry, Steve. 2008. Ethics in social networks. Lecture at Upholding and Updating International Standards seminar, New Jersey Press Association. http://www.notrain-nogain.org/Train/Res/Multi/ethicnet.asp.

Kanalley, Craig. 2009. How to verify a tweet. Twitter Journalism, June 25. http://www.twitterjournalism.com/2009/06/25/how-to-verify-a-tweet/.

Lasica, J.D. 2009. Using Twitter at the Chicago Tribune. Socialmedia.biz, March 28. http://www.socialmedia.biz/2009/03/28/using-twitter-at-the-chicago-tribune/.

NPR. 2009. NPR news social media guidelines. http://www.npr.org/about/ethics/social_media_guidelines.html.

CHAPTER 17

Blog to the Future: Telling Digital Stories in the Post-9/11 Decade

Vinita Srivastava

CHAPTER OUTLINE

Social Media Grows Up

On November 14, 2005, a student walked into the crowded UCLA campus library with his knapsack, sat down, and began to read his course material alongside others studying for their mid-term exams. What he did not realize is that within three days his actions would spark a media frenzy and become one of the top searches online, launching him into the centre of heated discussions in the blogosphere. What happened to him that night and the way his story was covered grew into a perfect example of the new symbiosis of bloggers,[1] journalists, and netizens.

Just after 11 p.m., campus police asked the student to show his identification. Mostafa Tabatabainejad, a 23-year-old Iranian American, refused and turned to leave the library. Campus police, nervous of what they perceived to be his "suspicious appearance," decided to use a Taser to stun him. "Get off me!" the student cried out. "I said I would leave!" he yelled. A witness in the library took out a camera phone and began to video-record the scene. According to reports, security stunned the peaceful student up to five times as he screamed out in pain (Goodman 2006).

The cellphone recorder knew just what to do with his eyewitness account; the next day, he posted it on YouTube. The day after that, the campus paper, the *Daily Bruin*, ran the story with a link to the footage, and the popular blog Boing Boing circulated the story (see Figure 17.1).

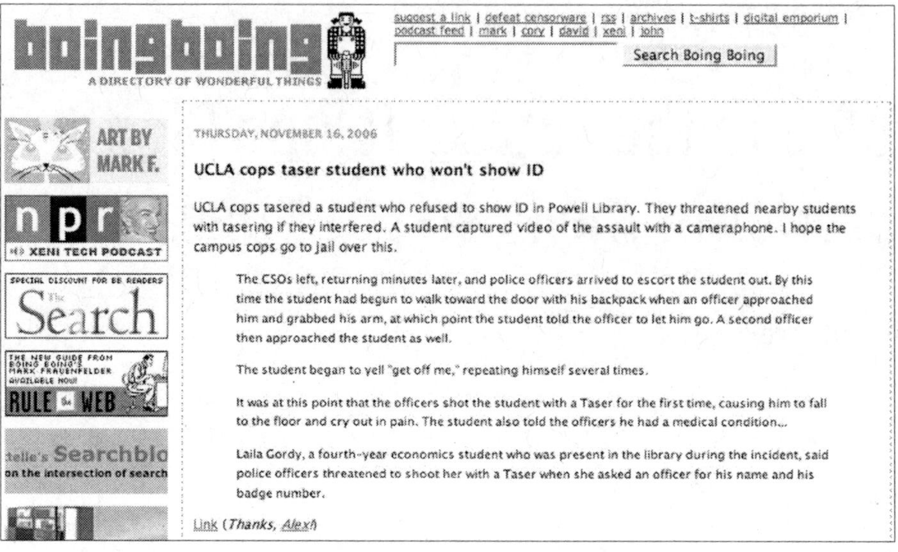

boingboing
A DIRECTORY OF WONDERFUL THINGS

suggest a link | defeat censorware | rss | archives | t-shirts | digital emporium | podcast feed | mark | cory | david | xeni | john

Search Boing Boing

ART BY MARK F.

npr XENI TECH PODCAST

SPECIAL DISCOUNT FOR BB READERS The Search

THE NEW GUIDE FROM BOING BOING'S MARK FRAUENFELDER AVAILABLE NOW! RULE the WEB

telle's Searchblo on the intersection of search

THURSDAY, NOVEMBER 16, 2006

UCLA cops taser student who won't show ID

UCLA cops tasered a student who refused to show ID in Powell Library. They threatened nearby students with tasering if they interfered. A student captured video of the assault with a cameraphone. I hope the campus cops go to jail over this.

> The CSOs left, returning minutes later, and police officers arrived to escort the student out. By this time the student had begun to walk toward the door with his backpack when an officer approached him and grabbed his arm, at which point the student told the officer to let him go. A second officer then approached the student as well.
>
> The student began to yell "get off me," repeating himself several times.
>
> It was at this point that the officers shot the student with a Taser for the first time, causing him to fall to the floor and cry out in pain. The student also told the officers he had a medical condition...
>
> Laila Gordy, a fourth-year economics student who was present in the library during the incident, said police officers threatened to shoot her with a Taser when she asked an officer for his name and his badge number.

Link (*Thanks, Alex!*)

Figure 17.1 Boing Boing's posting on the UCLA taser incident

A mere three days after the incident, Technorati, a blog-tracking site that monitors millions of blogs, reported that six out of the top 15 videos linked to by bloggers during the week showed the Taser incident (Padania 2006). By day five, the *Los Angeles Times*, MSNBC, and the *New York Times* had picked up the story. Tom Zeller Jr. (2006) of the Lede, a blog created by the *New York Times* to analyze the onslaught of multimedia information streaming online, wrote, "all of the facts aren't in, but even without context, it's hard not to get a chill from the latest bit of on-the-ground footage to wend its way from the street, to YouTube and into the heart of controversy." News and video of the incident, disseminated via blogs and YouTube, led to widespread protests by UCLA students who denounced the unnecessary violence. A look on YouTube today reveals that the Taser video has been viewed over 1.6 million times.

Of course people have used simple web tools to spread information and news online before the UCLA incident. Images of the bombings in London in July 2005 and the Paris riots in November of the same year were recorded and widely circulated by citizen eyewitnesses thanks to the ubiquity of cellphones and the accessibility of blogs. Eyewitness accounts from citizens are not an invention of either the Web or video tools such as camera phones. However, their proliferation on the Internet confirms that the news is now spread by what the Pew Research Center's Project for Excellence in Journalism (2010) calls the "three central elements of today's news ecosystem—the mainstream media, blogs and Twitter."

More recently, major events have been "broadcast" first by eyewitnesses using camera phone technology and Twitter, such as the November 2008 terrorist attack in Mumbai and the January 2009 emergency landing of US Airways Flight 1549 on New York's Hudson River (see Figures 17.2 and 17.3). The tweets on these events were not in any way seen as journalistic reports; instead they were seen as the quickest first-hand information available. People are not only posting eyewitness accounts but also

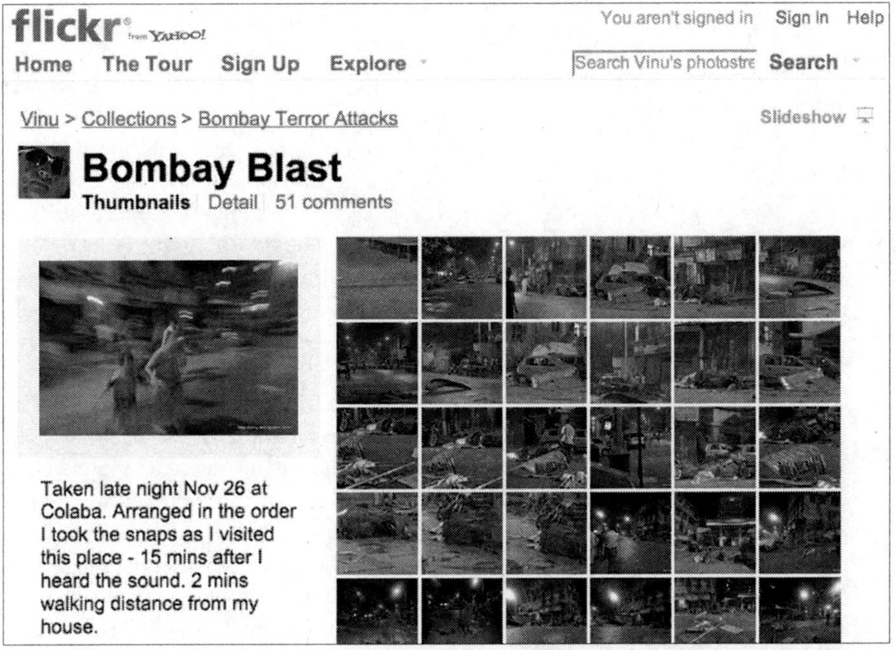

Figure 17.2 Photos of the Mumbai attack posted on Flickr

sharing sources and expertise using their cellphones, Twitter, and online tools like Flickr, created to work with social media.

Today, six out of ten people in the world own a cellphone. And the interconnection among cellphones, blogs, and microblogging site Twitter is growing stronger. Blogs are no longer just textual accounts organized by date posted: They are hyperlinked, include multimedia, are interactive, go viral, are networked, and have a global reach.

Blogs represent a shift in power within the media landscape. With simple but powerful tools like blogging software, social networking sites, and video and photo publishing sites, the average person can tell and circulate stories that would have previously taken weeks, if not months or years, to share.

Figure 17.3 presents the first photo of the emergency landing of US Airways Flight 1549 in New York City, posted by a bystander. Janis Krums, who uploaded his image on Twitter, tweeted, "There's a plane in the Hudson. I'm on the ferry going to pick up the people. Crazy." Vinu, a photographer who lived two minutes away from the blasts in Mumbai, used the photo-sharing site Flickr to post his photos of that event (see Figure 17.2). After he posted his photos on Flickr, he then used Twitter to share the link. The photos were picked up by the mainstream media within a matter of hours.

The New Media Ecosystem

In December 2006, *Time* magazine acknowledged the existence of the new media ecosystem by voting "You" as Person of the Year. According to *Time* writer Lev Grossman, self-publishing web tools have created new communities with unprecedented avenues of collaboration. He said, "It's about the many wresting power from the few

There's a plane in the Hudson. I'm on the ferry going to pick up the people. Crazy.

Figure 17.3 US Airways Flight 1549 in the Hudson River, Manhattan

SIDEBAR

A New Word Enters the Journalist's Lexicon

The word "blog" is a contraction of the term "weblog," which was coined by American blogger Jorn Barger in 1997, and which is itself a condensed version of the phrase "to log the web." The earliest blogs were for the most part personal online diaries, but within a few short years, blogs had become an essential part of journalism. Jonathan Dube of *The Charlotte Observer* is credited with pioneering the use of blogs for reporting, when he helped create a weblog to cover Hurricane Bonnie in 1998. For more, see the Blogging History Timeline later in this chapter.

and helping one another for nothing and how that will not only change the world, but also change the way the world changes" (Grossman 2006). The same *Time* article asserted optimistically that we were at a crucial point in the history of media, poised to create a more egalitarian world with digital media as its true champion. Although "[blogging's] truths are provisional, and its ethos collective and messy," wrote long-time blogger Andrew Sullivan (2008), "it heralds a golden era for journalism."

Sullivan was writing during the US presidential election campaign of 2008. Barack Obama was leading the race, and it looked like he might actually win. It helped that Obama had fully embraced the changing technological culture. In clear recognition of the power of the Web, Obama's campaign managers used social media to successfully solicit millions in donations and build a grassroots support network. Over 94 percent of donations for Obama 2008 came in small increments of $200 or less from over a million people (Green 2008).

It is widely accepted that the "golden era for journalism" Sullivan refers to began after 9/11. "Weblogs, once the preserve of a technologically savvy elite, have gained popularity since the terrorist attacks of September 11 2001," reported Neil McIntosh of the *Guardian* newspaper in 2003. On and after 9/11, broadcasters replayed the disaster, and newspapers such as the *New York Times* provided daily coverage of breaking news of the terrorists, accounts of those who had escaped and those who had been rescued, as well as unforgettable profiles of those who had not survived. Yet something else was occurring outside the mainstream media. The "former audience" (Gillmor 2004) had something to say, and they now had an accessible way to disseminate their ideas. North American media outlets like the *New York Times*, the CBC, and the *Globe and Mail* were not the only places people were turning to for the official story.

TOOLS & TIPS

Blogging Best Practices

If You Want to Blog ...

Have a point. Stick to the point.

- Blog about what you know or want to explore.
- Dig deep into one topic area.
- Follow standard journalism ethics.

Make your blog content-rich and attractive.

- Include multimedia in your posts: photos, videos, audio, and text.
- Use short, accurate, and alluring headlines to describe your posts.
- Read the Poynter Institute's EyeTrack07 study about how people read online.
- Include hyperlinks in your text.
- Write short paragraphs.
- Write in your own voice and style.
- Use bulleted lists to catch the reader's eye.
- Boldface subheadings.
- Write! She who hesitates is lost.

Participate in the blogosphere.

- Read other blogs.
- Take part in group blogs and conversations.
- Comment on other blogs.

In the United States, the press was not aggressive in fighting for access to information on the war in Afghanistan (O'Regan 2002), and many television stations, crunched for time, broadcast government-produced video news releases and passed them off as their own reporting (Barstow and Stein 2005). In the months and years that followed 9/11, bloggers provided critiques of traditional media coverage. A spike in online news searches was reported after 9/11 and "generated the most traffic to traditional news sites in the history of the Web" (Rainie, Fox, and Madden 2002). In Canada, *rabble.ca*, an online alternative news site, reported an increase in visitors in the months following 9/11 (Rebick 2001).

Multiple Points of View

The story of 9/11 and the US government's response to it was told from multiple angles and by multiple voices. A variety of websites and bloggers gave the public what it seemed to crave: a dialectic of questions and answers, historical context, and multiple points of view. Earlier media consolidation in North America (for example, the merger of AOL and TimeWarner, and the media acquisitions by Rupert Murdoch's News Corporation) had wiped out many reporters, publications, and foreign bureaus and shifted the industry toward a reliance on wire sources and "repurposed" content (CBC Digital Archives n.d.). As a consequence, in broadcast news, foreign news coverage had dropped by almost 40 percent and was rarely included unless it involved a crisis or a bomb (Arnett 1998). By 9/11, the public had grown healthily skeptical of the potential vulnerabilities of the mainstream media. Online publishing tools were accessible to many Internet users, and some began to challenge the importance and diligence of reporters working for large news outlets. Bloggers and web self-publishers exploded the idea that "reality was out there and journalists merely reflected it—objectively" (Stephens 2005).

In fact, the death of objectivity surfaced as a theme in journalism in 2004, coming not from the margins but the middle. Geneva Overholser, now director of the School of Journalism at the University of Southern California's Annenberg School for Communication and former ombudsman of the *Washington Post*, said, " 'objectivity' makes the media easily manipulable by an executive branch intent on and adept at controlling the message. It produces a rigid orthodoxy, excluding voices beyond the narrowly conventional" (Rosen 2005). Steve Lovelady, managing editor of CampaignDesk.org, and a former editor at the *Philadelphia Inquirer*, agrees that the mainstream press in 2004 "was hopelessly hobbled by some of its own outdated conventions and frameworks" (Rosen 2005). Perhaps not coincidentally, blog readership in the United States increased by 58 percent around that time (Rainie 2005).

On May 26, 2004, the editors of the *New York Times* printed an apology to readers, saying that they had "found a number of instances of coverage that was not as rigorous as it should have been." The editors did not name Judith Miller (or other reporters) at the *Times*, but they did mention misinformed articles written by Miller that painted terrifying pictures of weapons of mass destruction in Iraq. As well, they charged that the paper's editors should have pressed reporters "for more skepticism." The editors wrote, "It looks as if we, along with the administration, were taken in." *New York Times* columnist and theatre critic Frank Rich (2004) charged the Bush administration with creating a theatre of lies for the American public throughout its administration, and he accused the media, including his own paper, of tacitly supporting the administration's expert spin.

As a result, news blogs such as the Huffington Post, with its large network of volunteer contributors, photo streams, uploaded videos, opinion pieces, repurposed content and original reporting, are becoming increasingly important sources of information to audiences skeptical of their fourth estate.

Obama's administration recognized the legitimacy of bloggers when it invited a Huffington Post blogger/reporter to ask a question at the president's first official press conference (Luscome 2009). The president called on a Huffington Post reporter again in June 2009: "Nico, I know you, and all across the Internet we've been seeing a lot of reports coming out of Iran," Obama said. "I know there may actually be questions from people in Iran who are communicating through the Internet. Do you have a question?" (Cooper 2009).

International news sources and eyewitness reports have become crucial windows on reality. For example, Riverbend (a.k.a. Girl Blogger) blogged poignant and lucid reports from Baghdad that were seen as more "real" and "raw" than stories filed by foreign correspondents or stringers to North American papers. On December 26, 2003, she wrote, "Explosions and bombing almost all day yesterday and deep into the night … To see the news on CNN, Abu Dhabi, and Al-Arabia you'd think there was nothing going on in Baghdad beyond the usual thumps and thuds. Yesterday was *very* unusual … I hate the sirens. I can stand the explosions, the rattling windows, the slamming doors, the planes, the helicopters … but I feel like my heart is wailing when I hear the sirens" (see Figure 17.4).

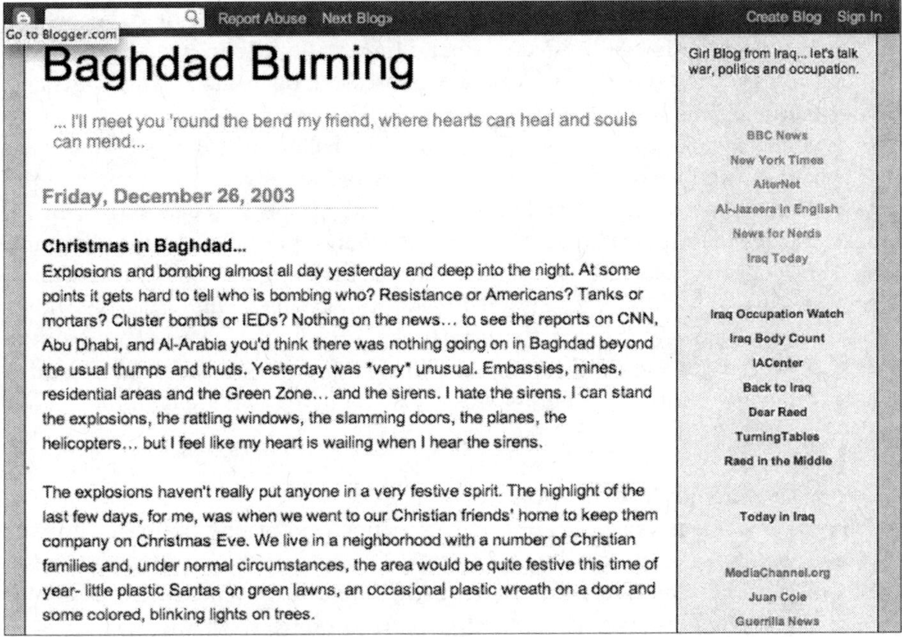
Report Abuse Next Blog» Create Blog Sign In
Go to Blogger.com

Baghdad Burning

... I'll meet you 'round the bend my friend, where hearts can heal and souls can mend...

Friday, December 26, 2003

Christmas in Baghdad...

Explosions and bombing almost all day yesterday and deep into the night. At some points it gets hard to tell who is bombing who? Resistance or Americans? Tanks or mortars? Cluster bombs or IEDs? Nothing on the news... to see the reports on CNN, Abu Dhabi, and Al-Arabia you'd think there was nothing going on in Baghdad beyond the usual thumps and thuds. Yesterday was *very* unusual. Embassies, mines, residential areas and the Green Zone... and the sirens. I hate the sirens. I can stand the explosions, the rattling windows, the slamming doors, the planes, the helicopters... but I feel like my heart is wailing when I hear the sirens.

The explosions haven't really put anyone in a very festive spirit. The highlight of the last few days, for me, was when we went to our Christian friends' home to keep them company on Christmas Eve. We live in a neighborhood with a number of Christian families and, under normal circumstances, the area would be quite festive this time of year- little plastic Santas on green lawns, an occasional plastic wreath on a door and some colored, blinking lights on trees.

Girl Blog from Iraq... let's talk war, politics and occupation.

BBC News
New York Times
AlterNet
Al-Jazeera in English
News for Nerds
Iraq Today

Iraq Occupation Watch
Iraq Body Count
IACenter
Back to Iraq
Dear Raed
TurningTables
Raed in the Middle

Today in Iraq

MediaChannel.org
Juan Cole
Guerrilla News

Figure 17.4 Girl Blogger's report from Baghdad

In 2005, Riverbend published a book consisting of blog entries, emphasizing the new weave of "old" and "new" media. In the introduction to Riverbend's book, veteran *Village Voice* journalist James Ridgeway wrote, "this anonymous 'girl blog' has made the war and occupation real in terms that no professional journalist could hope to achieve." Blogs like Riverbend's gave the public access to unfiltered reports in a time of intense government spin and PR—and reports from the "common" person at the scene were what the public wanted.

Still, the rise of news blogs such as Gawker (www.gawker.com) and Talking Points Memo (TalkingPointsMemo.com) does not herald the death of professional journalism. In fact, increasingly blogs and the mainstream media feed off one another in an ongoing dialogue.

Merely Endless Chatter?

In the race to blog, the increasing and seemingly endless stream of information that comes at journalists today is daunting. The idea that anyone can comment on a blog or create a blog without the benefit of an editorial filter is both exciting and frightening. Has the resulting increase in and diversity of opinion led to quality journalism? Are blog conversations the "new journalism"? Or, are they just a constant drone of voices with no organized rhythm?

Has the openness of the Web simply led audiences in different directions to pursue their own private interests—creating a lot of chatter, but nothing of quality? "What if all of the voices that are piling on end up drowning one another out?" asked online pioneer Jaron Lanier (2010). If everybody is following their own piece of the "Long

Tail," suddenly the discussion at the water cooler becomes complicated: Where are our commonalities? How do we decide what is important as a society? As readership of blogs increases and that of newspapers decreases, are we losing crucial leadership in journalism as "one voice" morphs into a million voices?

Everyone may not be as optimistic as Blood, who believes that bloggers and journalists can draw on each others' strengths. Some old media feel threatened by the proliferation of sites being generated by a young blogosphere. Over 50 percent of bloggers in North America are under 30 (Lenhart and Fox 2006). Mathew Ingram, long-time blogger and former community editor at the *Globe and Mail*, said teaching people how to use new technology is not difficult, but, "changing the way people think and the culture they work in is the hard part." Ingram left the *Globe and Mail* for the online network GigaOM in 2010, saying that while the *Globe and Mail*, Canada's "paper of record," has made progress using new technology, "there is still much left to do" (Ingram 2010).

Navigating a Sea of Information

Journalists describe the sheer volume of information they receive online as "drowning," an "onslaught," and even a "bombardment," and it's coming at them at a faster pace and in greater amounts than ever before (Project for Excellence in Journalism 2009b). As facts and information arrive from various sources, what is a journalist to do? Facts are not only harder to sell but also harder to distinguish. How should a journalist handle the overload of information with news sites, tweets, blogs, podcasts, YouTube videos, status updates, blog feeds, and news alerts? How can a journalist decide what is important news in a sea of information? Who should newsrooms trust? How should a journalist's message be packaged for people who have shorter attention spans and can jump to competitors' sites with the click of a mouse?

Consider the aftermath of the 2009 Iranian elections, in which Twitter played a major role in news dissemination. Jack Shafer (2009) of *Slate* wrote, "Unlike several other technology-friendly journalists I've found it more noise than signal in understanding the Iranian Upheaval ... my cognitive colander isn't big enough to strain out Iran information I can rely on."

Mainstream media blogs like the Lede are examples of news sites working within the new ecosystem to sift, judge, and probe the stream of reports, pictures, and videos coming from citizens and other professionals. On June 17, 2009, the Lede's Comments section was alive with dialogue, fact-checking, and information sharing. "Robert Mackey and his colleagues at the Lede have put out so much in such a timely fashion that I have relied on the blog as my primary source of information as the situation unfolds," wrote a reader from San Diego. "Many times over the past few days I have been moved by the courage and determination of the people in Iran, tears in my eyes and all my hair standing on end, imagining the events in Tehran brought to me through the compilation of resources and reporting on the Lede."

The lone blogger taking on media giants is a romantic image, similar to the heroic journalist who risks it all to get the story and expose the truth. But a Cornell University study concluded that in 2008, only 3.8 percent of blogs led the news cycle and effectively broke news (Leskovev, Backstrom, and Kleinberg 2009). In other words, most blogs followed the mainstream news. So, while bloggers occasionally offer flashes of original reporting, they are generally more valuable for the speed in which they respond to stories published in main media outlets.

Yet blog readership is up. Why? Blogs can achieve a kind of "meta reporting—reporting on the process by which news and opinion are formulated" (Stephens 2005, 7). For example, bloggers quickly pointed out that smoke in photos published by Reuters of the aftermath of an Israeli air strike in Beirut appeared to have been digitally altered and made darker (BBC 2006). Bloggers can make important contributions to national and international conversations and help hold the mainstream media accountable.

Occasionally, a blogger with time and money will break and give sustained attention to a story. For example, Josh Marshall, founding blogger of Talking Points Memo, won a George Polk Award for his dogged legal reporting on circumstances surrounding the firing of eight US Attorneys by the Bush administration. Marshall lassoed the collective intelligence of his readers and relentlessly pursued his story, providing context, collective information, and a report that led to the resignation of the US Attorney General. Marshall is a blogger who considers himself to be an investigative journalist. He first earned substantial funds for his blog from advertising when his readership grew in 2003. He believes that at the time, audiences were looking for alternative viewpoints regarding Iraq (McDermott 2007; Cohen 2008). For Talking Points Memo, blogging is not a style, but a medium used to deliver high-quality journalism.

The Potential for Distraction

While some blogs are shaped by the craft of journalism, many others are not and can distract us from urgent and important news and issues. The blogosphere's obsession with remarks made by US Chief Justice Sonia Sotomayor (Jurkowitz 2009) just a week before her appointment in 2009 points to a dangerous reliance on blogs to define the news. When reporters are swamped, amateur bloggers can end up leading a news cycle, as they did that week. Three bloggers from Orange County were praised for doing the "journalistic" footwork required to find an old Sotomayor university speech in which she called herself a "wise Latina woman." But was this news urgent and important? Where was the context? Was it relevant to the news cycle that week? The major media outlets followed the bloggers, leading to a news week with a story that had very little substance and little context. "Is Sotomayor a reverse racist?" cried the Orange County blogs. As the major media outlets searched for ways to make Sotomayor interesting, they grabbed the bloggers' chatter and the editorial filter got lost.

Now that power has shifted from one editor in a mainstream media outlet to many voices, how does one decide what is important news and what is simply the ravings of a few people? Consider that Sotomayor's "wise Latina" remarks took up more space than the North Korean nuclear tests, the spiralling economy, and the impending bankruptcy of General Motors.

The biggest challenge for journalists is to learn how to filter, compress, digest, analyze, and respond to blog content. Journalists must not only report facts but also help shape conversations, put information into context, and remain independent in their thinking.

An Ongoing Blizzard of Change

On June 13, 2009, a shaky video of protesters being shot at in Iran during massive post-election protests was posted on YouTube and linked on Twitter. A full 98 percent of links circulated on Twitter that week were about Iran (Project for Excellence in Journalism 2009a). In media terms, the response by bloggers and microbloggers became known as the "Twitter Revolution."

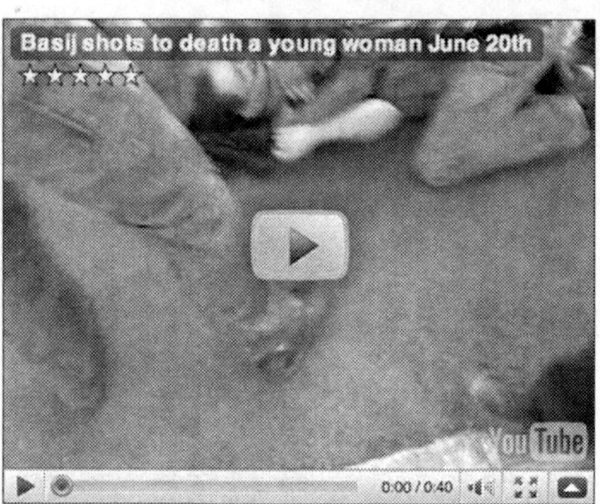

Figure 17.5 The death of Neda Agha-Soltan. The tragic death of a young Iranian woman, who instantly became known simply as "Neda," not only served to personalize for viewers worldwide the struggle for democracy in Iran, but is also considered a historic moment in the use of social media to break important news. The anonymous videographer was honoured with a 2009 George Polk Award in Journalism.

A week later, yet another YouTube video, depicting the graphic death of Neda Agha-Soltan, a young woman shot in the midst of the protests, caused a wave of tweets and an outpouring by bloggers (see Figure 17.5). In this case, despite harsh Internet censorship laws in Iran, Iranians led the news cycle with first-hand accounts from the streets. They communicated directly with journalists, fellow bloggers, and activists and sparked an intense international conversation about democracy in Iran.

Major news outlets demonstrated their ability to be flexible, open, and collaborative during their reporting of the Iranian election aftermath. The *New York Times*, officially shut out of covering protests in Tehran, said it was looking to "Iranians themselves" to "provide news, or at least the pictures" (Stelter and Stone 2009). CNN's Middle East correspondent Octavia Nasr (2009) noted the ability of bloggers to mobilize change: "Just give them a computer and an Internet connection and watch what they can do."

As marginalized voices gain access to expression, they resist images of themselves depicted by others and small but important societal transformations begin: Cristina Quisbert (2008), blogger from *Voces Bolivianas* (Bolivian Voices), a Global Voices project that trains underrepresented groups to use social media, said, "Our problem is the absence of visibility in the world. Our voices want to be heard, not just in Bolivia, but also outside Bolivia. Our reality was reflected by other people and not by ourselves. We are the ones familiar with our reality and we now reflect that reality."

As technology reaches more remote regions through projects like Global Voices, which invites many to join the global conversation online, the recognition of the need to hear multiple voices with a diversity of opinions takes root.

Blogging can be an empowering act for civil society. Bloggers have helped to bring down the one all-knowing voice from its pedestal and, instead, are communicating directly with one another to understand, learn, and spark action and reflection.

In *Domination and the Arts of Resistance*, James Scott (1992) explained that resistance in our society takes many forms and can come in ordinary, everyday acts. For many, blogging is one of these acts. As digital tools grow more accessible and cellphones continue to facilitate content delivery and creation, the numbers of bloggers, newsmakers, and storytellers will rise.

Blogging History Timeline

► 1998: A Blogger Breaks the Clinton/Lewinsky Story

Gift shop manager and "tip sheet publisher" Matt Drudge sparks a media frenzy after posting information from a killed *Newsweek* story about a sexual relationship between President Clinton and his intern, Monica Lewinsky (Allen 2006).

► 1999: Key Blogging Software Is Launched

LiveJournal and Blogger launch, but users must host their own blog.

► 2001: Online News Searches Spike

A healthy skepticism of mainstream press leads to a 30 percent spike in online news searches in the United States.

► 2003: Blogs Affect the Public's View of the Iraq War

"Guerrilla" reporting blogs appear from Iraq. Six weeks after, an anti-war movement through the Internet begins.

► 2004: CBS's Reporting Gaffes Are Uncovered Instantly Online

CBS's news anchor Dan Rather and producer Mary Mapes broadcast a story about George W. Bush's National Guard, and within minutes the conservative blogosphere mobilizes to discredit the research on which it was based. Both Rather and Mapes are forced to resign.

► 2004: Blogs Mobilize Around Indian Ocean Tsunami

Information on the tsunami is disseminated online, and aid for tsunami victims is collected online.

► 2005: YouTube Launches

In April, YouTube launches and makes eyewitness video accounts accessible. Cellphone videos and photos from the July 7 bombings in London are posted online.

► 2005: Hurricane Katrina Reports Are Made via MoJo (Mobile Journalism)

MSNBC, unsure how to report during Hurricane Katrina, decide to set up "virtual" newsrooms using Typepad blogging software so reporters can post from the field. The *Times-Picayune*, with flooded offices, took their entire operation online, allowing unprecedented reporter–citizen collaboration. See Poynter's News University (www.newsu.org/angel/content/ona_katrina06/course.php) for more information on this backstory.

► 2007: Bloggers Act as a Democratizing Force After Myanmar Clampdown

The Republic of Myanmar implements a press ban after widespread protests by monks defy a no-gathering rule. Outside bloggers continue to post text, photos, and videos sent by insiders.

► 2008: Twitter Changes the Game

Reports of the Mumbai attacks, the Chinese earthquake, and links to photos of US Airways Flight 1549 landing appear first on Twitter. Crowdsourcing is taken to a new level, with journalists asking Twitter users for their eyewitness accounts.

► 2008: Obama Leads the Way

Obama announces his choice for VP running mate to the press using a text message.

For additional key events in blogging history, see Paul Bradshaw's list at onlinejournalismblog .com/2008/11/20/are-these-the-biggest-moments-in-journalism-blogging-history/.

In China, 56 million citizens actively blog (OpenNet Initiative n.d.). Although we must wait to analyze the complicated long-term effects of the growing number of bloggers worldwide, evidence points to a shift toward a better-connected and a more democratic society with citizens as active producers instead of passive consumers. Professor Xiao Qiang of the University of California Berkeley School of Journalism said that the Internet in China empowers people "to effectively use information, and also to work together ... and even mobilize collective actions" (*PBS NewsHour* 2010).

Everyday resistance can lead to small but cumulative benefits. Blogging empowers people to act for a civil society: it nurtures local knowledge, it aids in the right to exercise the imagination, in the right to participate in the debate in society, and in the right to self-definition (Scott 1992; Appadurai 2003, 22). It contains "voice, agency and debate rather than ... mere reading, reception and interpellation" (Appadurai 2003, 22).

Urbanist Stephen Graham (2004) wrote, "We are experiencing a complex and infinitely diverse range of transformations where new and old practices and media technologies become mutually linked and fused in an ongoing blizzard of change." It's still too early to see clearly through the blizzard and into the future of digital media. But only by experimentation—and through some failure—will we learn what the next steps in journalism could look like.

Occasionally, a media outlet will get it right, with the right technology on the right day. The *New York Times*'s use of a Mood Tracker on Election Day in 2008 represents one of those moments. Readers were able to instantly share—in one word—how they were feeling at different times during election day, and the homepage of the *Times* grew into a cloud of popular words. By 11 p.m., the cloud read "elated," "inspired," and "optimistic." But other words scrolled across the screen as well: "scared," "cautious," and "amazed." Perhaps these words could also be used to describe the feelings of journalists as they look to the future of digital journalism.

NOTE

1. In this chapter, I use the term *bloggers* loosely: here it is used to refer to individuals and groups that use blog technology and other open source social media software to self-publish on the Web. For the most part, I discuss bloggers who intend to contribute to the news in some way. Bloggers fill in missing gaps using the endless "real estate" of the Internet and the relatively low cost of production; they mine copious links and information and share their findings with the world. The collective voice of bloggers affects journalists, news organizations, and public opinion.

DISCUSSION QUESTIONS

1. As readership of blogs increases and that of newspapers decreases, what is the role of journalism as "one voice" morphs into a million voices?
2. How should a journalist handle the overload of information with news sites, tweets, blogs, podcasts, YouTube videos, status updates, blog feeds, and news alerts? How might a journalist decide what is important news in the sea of information?
3. Given the sea of information in the blogosphere, what principles should guide journalism now?
4. Do you agree that blogging can be a tool for democracy?

SUGGESTED RESOURCES

Vinita's Recent Browser History

Boing Boing. http://www.boingboing.net.

Feministing. http://www.feministing.com.

Gawker. http://www.gawker.com.

Global Voices. http://globalvoicesonline.org.

the Hotness. http://thehotness.com.

The Huffington Post. http://www.huffingtonpost.com.

Ingram, Mathew. http://www.mathewingram.com.

The Lede. http://thelede.blogs.nytimes.com.

rabble blogs. http://www.rabble.ca/blogs.

REFERENCES

Allen, Stuart. 2006. *Online news*. New York: Open University Press.

Appadurai, Arjun. 2003. Archive and aspiration. In *Information is alive*, ed. Joke Brouwer and Arjen Mulder, 14–25. Rotterdam: V2_Publishing/NAI Publishers.

Arnett, Peter. 1998. State of the American newspaper: Goodbye, world. *American Journalism Review* (November): 50–67.

Barstow, David, and Robin Stein. 2005. Under Bush, a new age of prepackaged TV news. *New York Times*, March 13.

BBC. 2006. Reuters drops Beirut photographer. *BBC News*, August 8.

Bradshaw, Paul. 2008. Are these the biggest moments in journalism-blogging history? Online Journalism Blog, November 20. http://onlinejournalismblog.com/2008/11/20/are-these-the-biggest-moments-in-journalism-blogging-history/.

CBC Digital Archives. n.d. Concentration to convergence: Media ownership in Canada, 1960–2003. http://archives.cbc.ca/arts_entertainment/media/topics/790/.

Cohen, Noah. 2008. Blogger, sans pajamas, rakes muck and a prize. *New York Times*, February 25.

Cooper, Matthew. 2009. The crucifixion of Nico Pitney. *Atlantic*, June 24. http://politics.theatlantic.com/2009/06/the_crucifixtion_of_nico_pitney.php.

Gillmor, Dan. 2004. *We the media: Grassroots journalism by the people, for the people.* Sebastopol, CA: O'Reilly Media.

Goodman, Amy. 2006. UCLA police repeatedly Taser handcuffed student for refusal to show ID, university orders outside probe. Democracy Now! November 20. http://www.democracynow.org/2006/11/20/ucla_police_repeatedly_taser_handcuffed_student.

Graham, Stephen. 2004. Beyond the "dazzling light": From dreams of transcendence to the "remediation" of urban life. *New Media & Society* 16 (1): 16–25.

Green, Joshua. 2008. The amazing money machine. *Atlantic*, June. http://www.theatlantic.com/doc/200806/obama-finance/.

Grossman, Lev. 2006. Time's Person of the Year: You. *Time*, December 13. http://www.time.com/time/magazine/article/0,9171,1569514,00.html.

Ingram, Mathew. 2010. One door closes, another door opens. MathewIngram.com, January 9. http://www.mathewingram.com/work/2010/01/09/one-door-closes-another-door-opens/.

Jurkowitz, Mark. 2009. PEJ News Coverage Index: May 25–31, 2009—Sotomayor spin wars dominate the narrative. Journalism.org. http://www.journalism.org/index_report/pej_news_coverage_index_may_25_31_2009.

Lanier, Jaron. 2010. World wide mush. *Wall Street Journal*, January 8. http://online.wsj.com/article/SB10001424052748703481004574646402192953052.html.

Lenhart, Amanda, and Susannah Fox. 2006. *Bloggers*. Washington, DC: Pew Internet and American Life Project.

Leskovev, Jure, Lars Backstrom, and Jon Kleinberg. 2009. Meme-tracking and the dynamics of the news cycle. In *KDD '09: Proceedings of the 15th ACM SIGKDD international conference on knowledge discovery and data mining*. New York: ACM.

Luscome, Belinda. 2009. The HuffPo gets to question Obama—Making history. *Time*, February 10. http://www.time.com/time/nation/article/0,8599,1878625,00.html.

McDermott, Terry. 2007. Blogs can top the presses. *Los Angeles Times*, March 17. http://articles.latimes.com/2007/mar/17/nation/na-blogs17.

McIntosh, Neil. 2003. Google buys Blogger web service. *Guardian*, February 18. http://www.guardian.co.uk/business/2003/feb/18/digitalmedia.citynews.

Nasr, Octavia. 2009. Tear gas and Twitter: Iranians take their protests online. *CNN.com*, June 15. http://edition.cnn.com/2009/WORLD/meast/06/14/iran.protests.twitter/index.html.

New York Times. 2004. The Times and Iraq, May 26.

OpenNet Initiative. n.d. Country profiles: China. http://opennet.net/research/profiles.

O'Regan, Mick. 2002. Patriot games: American journalism post 9/11. Transcript. http://www.abc.net.au/rn/talks/8.30/mediarpt/stories/s659555.htm.

Padania, Sameer. 2006. USA: Video-sharing places L.A.'s police in the spotlight. Global Voices, November 17. http://globalvoicesonline.org/2006/11/17/usa-video-sharing-places-las-police-in-the-spotlight/.

PBS NewsHour. 2010. Google's threats to leave China renew censorship concerns. Transcript. January 13. http://www.pbs.org/newshour/bb/business/jan-june10/google_01-13.html.

The Poynter Institute. 2007. EyeTrack07. http://eyetrack.poynter.org/.

Project for Excellence in Journalism. 2009a. PEJ New Media Index: June 15–19, 2009—Iran and the "Twitter revolution." Journalism.org. http://www.journalism.org/index_report/iran_and_%E2%80%9Ctwitter_revolution%E2%80%9D.

Project for Excellence in Journalism. 2009b. *The state of the news media 2009.* http://www.stateofthemedia.org/2009/index.htm.

Project for Excellence in Journalism. 2010. PEJ New Media Index: December 28, 2009–January 1, 2010—Social and traditional media agree: Botched terror attack is big news. Journalism.org. http://www.journalism.org/index_report/december_28_2009january_1_2010.

Quisbert, Cristina. 2008. Lecture. We Media Conference, Miami, Florida, February.

Rainie, Lee. 2005. *The state of blogging.* Washington, DC: Pew Internet and American Life Project.

Rainie, Lee, Susannah Fox, and Mary Madden. 2002. *One year later: September 11 and the Internet.* Washington, DC: Pew Internet and American Life Project.

Rebick, Judy. 2001. Bringing democracy to the media. *rabble.ca,* November 1. http://rabble.ca/columnists/bringing-democracy-media.

Rich, Frank. 2004. Decision 2004: Fear fatigue vs. sheer fatigue. *New York Times,* October 31.

Riverbend [Girl Blogger]. 2003. Christmas in Baghdad … Baghdad Burning, December 26. http://riverbendblog.blogspot.com/2003_12_01_riverbendblog_archive.html.

Riverbend [Girl Blogger]. 2005. *Baghdad burning: Girl blog.* New York: First Feminist Press.

Rosen, Jay. 2005. Bloggers vs. journalists is over. PressThink. http://journalism.nyu.edu/pubzone/weblogs/pressthink/2005/01/21/berk_essy.html.

Scott, James C. 1992. *Domination and the arts of resistance: Hidden transcripts.* New Haven, CT: Yale University Press.

Shafer, Jack. 2009. Doubting Twitter. *Slate,* June 17. http://www.slate.com/id/2220736/.

Stelter, Brian, and Brad Stone. 2009. Stark images, uploaded to the world. *New York Times,* June 17. http://www.nytimes.com/2009/06/18/world/middleeast/18press.html.

Stephens, Mitchell. 2005. We're all postmodern now: Even Journalists have realized that facts don't always add up to the truth. *Columbia Journalism Review,* July 1.

Sullivan, Andrew. 2008. Why I blog. *Atlantic,* November.

Zeller, Tom, Jr. 2006. Passive resistance no match for Tasers. Lede, November 19. http://thelede.blogs.nytimes.com/2006/11/19/passive-resistance-no-match-for-tasers/.

IMAGE SOURCES

FIGURE 17.1: Doctorow, Cory. 2006. UCLA cops taser student who won't show ID. Boing Boing, November 16. http://boingboing.net/2006/11/16/ucla_cops_taser_stud.html.

FIGURE 17.2: Vinu. 2008. Bombay blast (photos). Flickr, November 26. http://www3.flickr.com/photos/vinu/sets/72157610144709049/. Reprinted by permission.

FIGURE 17.3: Krums, Janis. 2009. US Airways Flight 1549 in the Hudson River (photo). twitpic, January 15. http://twitpic.com/135xa. Reprinted by permission.

FIGURE 17.4: Riverbend [Girl Blogger]. 2003. Christmas in Baghdad … Baghdad Burning, December 26. http://riverbendblog.blogspot.com/2003_12_01_riverbendblog_archive.html.

FIGURE 17.5: Chang, Alex. 2009. Basij shots to death a young woman June 20th (video). YouTube. June 20. http://www.youtube.com/watch?v=OjQxq5N—Kc.

CHAPTER 18

Working with Photography and Video

Frank O'Connor and Tyler Anderson

CHAPTER OUTLINE

Introduction

The new journalist is, on any given day, expected to be not only a jack-of-all trades but also a master of all trades. The changing journalistic times we live in demand a skill set that is greater than ever before. The writer shoots pictures, the photographer writes stories, and, on any given day, both might record video and audio.

Photojournalism is, and always will be, about storytelling. Sometimes a story is simply told with one picture, and other times with ten. Add multimedia to the mix and the story may be told with a combination of photos, audio, and video.

Just as the new journalist uses words to tell stories in print or in voice, the new visual journalist uses the language of photography to tell visual stories. Mastering the language of photography as it applies to photojournalism is quite an undertaking and requires, as do all of the special skills in the new photojournalism, a focus of study all its own.

Getting Started with Still Digital Photography

Hardware and Software

For the beginner, learning the language of photography can be a daunting task. How well you learn that language may well determine what kind of gear you buy and how much you must rely on automation.

The camera equipment you use depends on a variety of factors. You might use employer-supplied equipment, which means that you must learn to master what is assigned to you. You might be a freelance photojournalist or a staffer with control over what equipment to buy, which leaves you with a myriad of purchase options.

Quality, capability, and cost are all considerations in the process of choosing camera equipment. Image capture on a budget may mean choosing one of the dozens of small point-and-shoot cameras that pervade the market today. Some are better than others, but all suffer from one or more drawbacks. Image quality may take a backseat to compactness and automation. Many models forgo a viewfinder, preferring to rely on a live-view screen to compose the image at arm's-length, which may be a drawback in bright light. Lens quality and speed may suffer due to compactness. The strength of these cameras is their portability and size, which can be a plus in many situations where a full-size digital single-lens reflex (SLR) is not an option. Canon's high-end G series cameras, for example, have earned a solid reputation for augmenting, but not replacing, a photojournalist's traditional SLR.

However, the traditional SLR still digital camera continues to be the standard for professional quality journalistic images. SLR cameras capture the lion's share of the images that form the daily record of our time. The new photojournalist may have a starting kit of a camera body and interchangeable lenses that allows him or her to shoot still digital images and, depending on the model, to shoot HD video as well. Full-frame sensor-equipped 35-mm cameras with double-digit file sizes may run into the thousands of dollars for the body alone, with lenses costing even more.

TOOLS & TIPS

Creating Slideshows

Slideshows are a popular format for storytelling and news presentation. While a simple gallery (that is, a series of images without audio) may suffice in some cases, the ability to add audio and captions means news photography's potential to help create true multimedia storytelling has been greatly expanded. Here are some key points to keep in mind when creating slideshows:

1. Start with a strong attention-getting first photo. Remember you are telling a specific visual story.
2. Edit your photos so that each photo has a purpose and says something that is important to the slideshow. On the Web, shorter is generally better.
3. Write captions that provide information beyond what the viewer can already see in the photo. Again, shorter is usually better, so avoid overly long captions. A sentence or two is usually enough.
4. Try for continuity of image quality. The images should have a similar look or aesthetic.
5. Finish off with a solid conclusion or culminating image.
6. Experiment with templated slideshow software (for example, see Soundslides.com) that offers the option of an audio track. If you do, ensure that the images match what the subject is talking about.

Less-expensive models with smaller sensors and file sizes are available in a cascading list of quality, capability, and cost. The camera gear of a photojournalist is like the toolbox of a mechanic: A real mechanic will have the necessary tools to do the job right. Those with a professional attitude never use a lack of gear as an excuse for image quality. Invest in a range of focal lengths that give you wide-angle capability as well as the magnifying capability of a long lens. Having the right gear is part of the overhead cost of doing business and will pay off in the end. Having the right gear is part of being professional. Being professional will help get you work.

Figure 18.1 Slideshows have added a new dimension to the craft of photojournalism.
SOURCE: TheMarkNews.com, accessed April 22, 2010.

One aspect of understanding the language of photography is learning the lexicon of light. As you become visually oriented to the world around you, the importance of the nuances of light, both natural and artificial, must become part of your dialect. Using supplementary lighting is often a requirement dictated as much by reproduction needs as it is by aesthetic considerations. Dedicated electronic flash systems are a big part of modern SLR digital camera systems. Nikon cameras, for example, allow you to control multiple flash setups directly from the camera.

Once you have captured those professional images, you must prepare them for use. Having the right computer hardware and software will help make your workflow faster and more efficient. You will need to be able to transfer images from the camera's flash memory card via a card reader to your computer so that they can be edited and prepared for publishing. The demands of your workflow and the capability of your computer will determine whether you choose to work in "camera raw" mode or in a compressed image mode such as a JPEG. Some photographers program their cameras to capture both simultaneously, depending on their needs and abilities. Raw files hold much more detail and information, but compressed files are much smaller, demand less processing power, and use less hard drive space.

Choose editing software that you are comfortable with and get to know it. Programs such as Photo Mechanic (by Camera Bits) and Photoshop (by Adobe) are industry-standard programs used in most shops. Develop an archive from the moment you begin. Save and name your image files so that they are easy to access for current use, secondary use, and sale down the road.

Tips on Hardware and Software

- Buy the right tools for the job. Don't cut corners on your gear.
- Quality image capture is essential. Garbage in … garbage out.
- Learn the language of photography. Don't rely on automation.
- Get organized. Archive your images from day one.

Remember: The quality of your work is your ticket and your reputation.

Content Is King

Staffer or freelancer? The new photojournalist is apt to be either. There are those who excel at promoting themselves, and who enjoy the freedom and variety of clients associated with freelancing. And there are those who prefer the security of a weekly salary, liberating themselves from the burden of running a small business.

But whether the new photojournalist works as a staffer with a news organization or as a freelancer, the pictures produced must be content-driven. Every picture must have a *purpose*, a reason for occupying our time and space. Every element within the frame of the camera should also have a purpose. The space allotted for individual images is at a premium now. The news "hole" in traditional media (newspapers) is often smaller, and the presentation options of the Internet dictate that an image's visual impact must be stronger within a smaller space. Although the Internet may be unlimited, the space allotted to an individual image for impact is not.

Aesthetic considerations are not enough in a journalistic photo. Context, relevance, and meaning all appear on the checklist of necessary considerations.

Control Your Light

To convey visual content effectively, the new photojournalist must master the controllers of light on a camera. That means turn off automatic settings and use manual control. The two primary controllers of light are the shutter speed and the aperture, or *f-stop* as it is often called. Success in emphasizing or de-emphasizing subject matter often hinges on the combined settings of these controllers of light. To achieve the correct exposure that produces the best image quality, those settings must allow the right amount of light to be exposed to the image sensor. A variety of combined settings will lead to correct exposure.

While we cannot explain the entire language of photography adequately in this chapter, we can say that understanding the basic relationship between aperture and shutter speed settings is the foundation of successful visual communication.

If you think of this relationship as one of time and space, you can begin to grasp how it all comes together. The "time" refers to the shutter speed and the "space" refers to the aperture setting.

Choosing the right shutter speed and aperture setting is comparable to the act of filling a bucket with water. In our comparison, the "correct exposure" is a volume given to us by the light meter of the camera. The aperture is the size of the tap opening, which, for our discussion, is adjustable. The shutter speed is the length of time we leave the tap open and fill the bucket. Carrying this idea forward, the larger the tap size (larger aperture setting), the less time is required to leave the tap open (faster shutter speed) to fill the bucket. On the other hand, the smaller the tap size (smaller aperture setting), the longer the time required to leave the tap open (slower shutter speed) and fill the bucket.

Controlling light gets more complicated: Each combination of aperture and shutter speed settings leads to specific results that affect successful visual communication.

A slow shutter speed may cause a fast-moving politician about to get a pie in the face to be blurred or a compelling portrait of an impoverished child to be blurred simply because the shutter speed was too slow to allow the photographer to hold the camera still.

A small aperture setting such as f/22 will create great depth of field (the area of the photo that is in acceptable focus). As a result, everything from foreground to background will be sharp. However, the photographer may not intend to produce this effect.

Conversely, a large aperture setting such as f/2.8 will create shallow depth of field that, depending on the focal length of the lens, will produce a sense of emphasis of one element or the exclusion of the background.

The Photojournalist on Assignment: Shooting the News, Features, and Sports

The craft of photojournalism involves a skill set that can be applied in a number of ways to a variety of situations. The skills of the new photojournalist are like the slices in a loaf of bread: Each is unique but similar and connected to the others. Whether the new photojournalist decides to work as a generalist and employ all of the skills to a variety of situations or as a specialist and employ some of the skills, it matters not. It's all the same loaf of bread.

Visual journalism assignments can be categorized in many ways, but perhaps the simplest way to understand how to approach them is to divide them into two main categories: managed and unmanaged.

In a perfect world, we have unlimited access with complete freedom of movement. The real world, sadly, is not perfect. Journalists must scramble for moments of access and live with the reality that they do the best job they can in the time allowed.

Shooting the News

News should not be managed. It must be accurately and fairly presented without malice. News may be of the breaking or "spot" variety, where fleeting moments come and go. Trauma, stress, danger, and confusion are often part of working conditions. The visual journalist may be exposed to these conditions at any time. Journalists who wish to work in this type of news reporting should be prepared for the accompanying emotional toll on both subject and photographer. Spot news is often best covered by simply showing the humanity in any given scenario. It is this humanity that will penetrate the hearts and minds of viewers, bringing understanding to the emotional effect of the moment.

News of the non-breaking variety is often referred to as "general news." This type of news involves routine planned events (such as press conferences, elections, court decisions) that are part of daily and weekly life. The challenge for the visual journalist is to find a creative way to cover general news without controlling it.

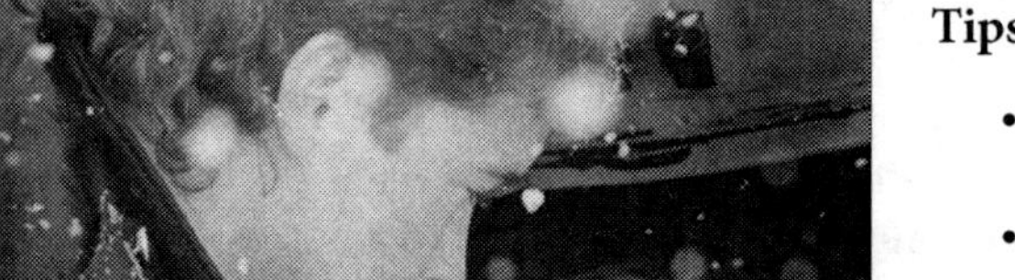

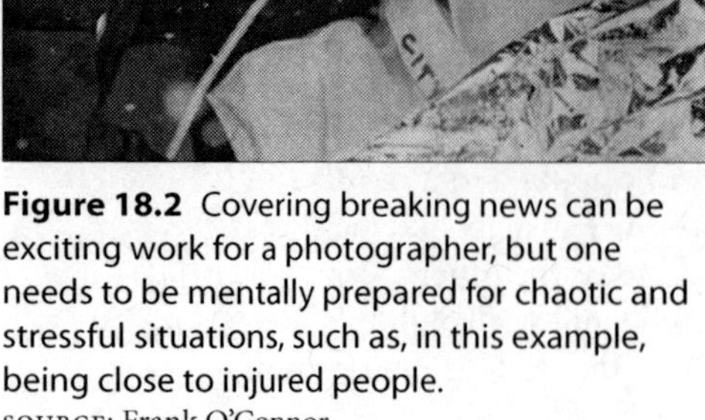

Figure 18.2 Covering breaking news can be exciting work for a photographer, but one needs to be mentally prepared for chaotic and stressful situations, such as, in this example, being close to injured people.
SOURCE: Frank O'Connor.

Tips on Shooting the News

- Work quickly at a scene to get what you can as the situation unfolds.
- Be as invisible as you can and don't get in the way of emergency crews.
- Show the humanity of the situation (people helping people).
- Keep your gear handy with fresh batteries and empty memory cards.
- Get accurate information, such as spelling of names and exact location.

Shooting Features

Feature photography is the most all-encompassing type of work performed by the new visual journalist. It is often defined as a "fresh view of the commonplace." Typically, it involves "slice of life" photos that make us smile, pull on our heartstrings, or grab our attention with their artistic or graphic impact. Sometimes we "featurize" the news with a compelling or informative portrait. Features are as likely to

Figure 18.3 Feature photography often takes the form of a unique perspective on commonplace situations, and can have an artistic dimension. It requires a keen eye for interesting situations, angles, and lighting, as well as an ability to get close to subjects without distracting them.
SOURCE: Frank O'Connor.

be "found" in self-assigned situations as they are in freelance or staff assignments. Observational and interpersonal skills and the ability to be a social chameleon are often as important as photographic skills when it comes to feature work. A strong feature photographer is invaluable to a news organization, as the skill set required extends to news and sports reporting.

Tips on Shooting Features

- Go where people are.
- Arrive early and stay late.
- Look for potential and anticipate the moment.
- Always carry your gear and be prepared.
- Jot down your ideas for future creativity.
- Use appropriate lenses to let the world unfold around you.

Shooting Sports

Sports photography is undeniably a specialty. More than any other genre or "slice of the loaf," sports photography requires specialty equipment. Long, fast lenses and cameras with a high frame rate are necessary to compete at a high level. That does

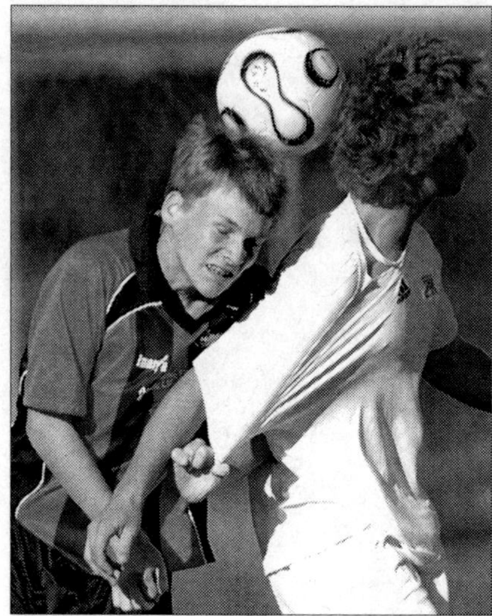

Figure 18.4 Photographers who know something about the sport being covered can anticipate situations and get great photos by finding the right vantage point, using proper lenses, and watching for the emotional as well as the athletic moments in a match.
SOURCE: Frank O'Connor.

not mean, however, that the generalist with less-suitable gear who covers sporting events from time to time cannot produce superior-quality images.

Photojournalists who cover sports are not required to know sports thoroughly, but a little knowledge is power. It's also unnecessary to be a sports fan or athlete to excel at covering sporting events. In a way, sports is theatre unscripted.

To best understand how to approach shooting sports, it's helpful to divide sports into categories. Some sports are territorial and involve variations on a theme of one team scoring on the other team's goal. Sports such as soccer, rugby, football, hockey, and lacrosse fall into this category. Because of the territorial nature of these sports, even a cursory understanding of the rules will dictate where to stand and when the most telling photos will happen. Soccer and rugby present the novice sports shooter with easy access up and down the field. Keep in mind that concentration and focus are essential in following the play. There are no second chances to capture the moment in sports photography.

Other sports are territorial but involve few players. Court sports such as tennis, badminton, and volleyball all have their own nuances and moments that typically define them.

Wrestling, boxing, and fencing are sports in close quarters that pit one competitor against another. Still other sports involve an individual competing against the clock or even themselves. All require a different approach.

Look for peak action moments in any sport. Some sports are more photogenic than others. Faces filled with emotion and the exertion of competition are more common in some sports than others. For example, the strain on the face of a soccer player reacting to the ball is much more visible than that of a football player, whose expressions are hidden underneath a helmet and a face mask.

Tips on Shooting Sports

- Buy the longest and fastest lenses you can afford.
- Learn as much as you can about the sport you are shooting.
- Fill the frame with the shot.
- Practise your sense of timing.

Getting Started with Video

The Internet has changed the way journalists do their job. Creative and adaptive journalists can now communicate in many new and exciting ways. Telling a great story is no longer as simple as putting the right words or pictures on a page. The ability to combine media including text, audio, video, photography, graphics, and web design allows journalists to immerse readers into the subject matter further than ever before.

A basic understanding of video is a valuable addition to the toolbox of any new journalist. The ability to unite audio and images offers the chance for a totally new form of communication. A capable visual journalist must couple the responsibility to inform with the audience's desire to be entertained.

The best way to entertain the audience is through high production value. Today's viewers expect strong narratives, imagery, sound, and editing. Given these expectations, the process of creating a good video can be broken down into four key parts:

1. The video interview
2. Video imaging
3. Natural sound
4. Video editing

The Video Interview

Great video journalism not only requires a clear understanding of the story but also a clear plan for how to tell it. Storytelling is an art form, and there are many proven techniques that can be used to keep the attention of viewers. Stories that include surprises, conflict, suspense, intriguing characters, and constantly evolving plots will ensure that your viewers stay interested.

Strong characters are at the core of most good video stories. Video journalism is at its best when these voices are allowed to tell their own stories in an unscripted manner. Unlike journalists in traditional television news, video journalists do not appear on camera and their voices are edited out of the final video. Therefore, it is the responsibility of video journalists to conduct interviews that allow their subjects to speak for themselves. Interviewees should be able to tell most of the details of their story, thereby avoiding the need for cumbersome text and additional narration.

TOOLS & TIPS

Your Silence Is Golden

A thorough discussion of interviewing techniques and considerations can be found in Chapter 14, "Interviewing in the Digital Age." But there are some differences between interviewing for video versus interviewing for print that one needs to keep in mind. One very important rule for video interviews is that once you have asked a question, it is time to be quiet. Your own voice should not interfere with your subject's responses. So, rather than respond with your voice, always use body language, such as head nods and hand gestures. Also, ask questions in ways that require full-sentence answers; try to avoid direct questions that are likely to lead to one-word responses. And always arrive prepared, with a plan for your interview. This doesn't mean you are trying to "script" the interview in advance, but you can steer the conversation in appropriate directions, and you should have all the important information you need in order to ask relevant questions that will help tell the story.

Factors to Consider When Choosing an Interview Location

- **Find a quiet spot.** Find the quietest place possible. Do your best to minimize sound interference by turning off loud appliances, moving clocks, turning off or unplugging phones, etcetera. Avoid places where there may be interruptions such as traffic sounds, animals, or other people. Avoid rooms that echo.
- **Ensure a proper light source.** It is extremely important that you choose a location with a consistent light source. At no point during the interview should the light change intensity or colour. The use of video lighting is very helpful for interviews. But if it is not an option, try finding a quiet outdoor spot in the shade. Always avoid fluorescent lighting and outdoor situations with inconsistent sunlight.
- **Choose the right background.** Try to find a simple background. Avoid busyness and clutter. Choose backgrounds that allow viewers to focus on the subject without distraction.

Figure 18.5 Your success in getting subjects to open up and express themselves can often be greatly determined by the location you select for an interview. In the video captured here, shot amid the chaotic aftermath of the January 2010 earthquake in Haiti, Tyler Anderson found a private place to interview a local pastor. Without the means to set up proper lighting, he made the decision to shoot the interview in a quiet, evenly lit spot in the shade.

SOURCE: Tyler Anderson/*National Post*.

Setting Up for a Video Interview

- Always use a tripod.
- Always use headphones.
- Be sure to have a secure power source (full battery or AC power supply).
- Adjust your microphone recording level manually, if possible, to ensure quality sound capture.
- Perform a manual white balance if possible (setting a manual white balance will ensure consistent colour throughout your interview).
- Whenever possible, use manual focus. Relying on the video camera to autofocus during an interview will often result in portions of your interview being out of focus.

Video Imaging

The foundation of all video storytelling is the video sequence. Video journalists can avoid long, boring clips by choosing to shoot a larger variety of smaller clips. When edited together, these clips can communicate a story in much less time and with less visual redundancy.

For example: Though it may take many hours for a carpenter to build a cabinet, video sequencing allows you to compress time by shooting and combining a series of relevant clips.

TOOLS & TIPS

Shooting Video

- Avoid pans and zoom. Although camera movement can sometimes be effective, it is a complicated process and should be avoided by beginners. Instead of following the action with the camera, simply allow it to enter and leave the frame.
- Learn to compose and hold pictures for at least ten seconds.
- Always hold your camera steady. Avoid unnecessary movement whenever possible by using a tripod or something to help you brace the camera.
- Shoot tight, medium, and wide shots. A large variety of shots makes editing easier and avoids visual redundancy.
- Anticipate action. Knowing what is about to happen will allow you to compose and capture the necessary parts of your sequence without interfering.
- Always pay attention to light. Light is the key element to good imagery. Low-lit situations do not look good on video. Learn to understand light and use it to your advantage.

Adding Stills to Video

Many journalists are comfortable working with still images. Strong photography can be an asset for video journalists. There are a few important things to remember if you are using still images as part of a video:

- Always shoot horizontal pictures. Video is always displayed in a horizontal frame; therefore, vertical pictures do not work nearly as well for video.
- When shooting and composing pictures, leave a little extra room for cropping. All pictures will need to be cropped in order to fit a traditional video frame.
- During the editing process, keep zooming to a minimum. Large, quick zooms on still images in a video are often dizzying and do not look good when displayed on the Internet.

Natural Sound

Natural sound is one of the best ways to immerse your viewers in a story. It allows viewers to hear the sounds of a place they have never been before and makes them feel more connected to the story. It also adds a layer of production and entertainment value to a video.

Strong natural sound is very valuable during the editing process. It is very useful for building effective transitions between video clips. It also allows editors to create breaks in the interview. This is often a useful tool in the storytelling process because it allows viewers to stop and think about what they've heard as well as what might come next.

Video Editing

It is essential for all video journalists to understand the editing process, regardless of whether they plan to edit their own videos or have them edited by others. An understanding of what is needed to successfully edit a video will make them more knowledgeable video journalists.

TOOLS & TIPS

Video Editing

- Learn the software. Video editing software is well designed. However, it is very powerful and includes many tools that can be complicated and confusing.
- Know your audience and edit accordingly. Tight editing is essential for Internet stories because in most cases the attention span of viewers is short. Television documentaries may allow for a slower pace, depending on the subject matter.
- Connect visuals with your narrative. Whenever possible, let viewers see the things they are hearing about. If a person is talking about her cat, viewers need to see the cat.
- Organize your media. Import all video, photos, graphics, music, and other media into your editing software at the beginning. Doing so will help you stay focused and avoid frustration during the editing process.

Video Gear

Video Cameras

The quality, functionality, and cost of video cameras vary immensely. However, there are a number of functions that are necessary for journalists interested in producing high-quality video and multimedia. The ability to control the image and sound manually is absolutely essential. Here are some important considerations:

1. Manual exposure control allows you to control both the iris (aperture) and shutter speed.
2. Manual white balance control allows you to capture accurate colour.
3. Manual audio controls allow you to adjust sensitivity of microphone for a high-quality sound recording.
4. Manual focus allows the operator, not the camera, to decide where and when to focus. This feature is essential because video cameras tend to focus on whatever is moving in your frame, which may not always be desirable.

Microphones

A good microphone is essential for recording high-quality sound. However, most video cameras do not come with a good built-in microphone. Therefore, a video camera that allows you to plug in an external microphone is often a necessity.

For most video purposes, a microphone that picks up the sound in front of the camera is desirable. Shotgun mics are the most directional and are designed to pick up sound in one direction, usually in front, which makes them the most useful microphone to attach to the top of a video camera.

A wireless microphone, or lavaliere, may also be an asset during interview situations or to record audio where it is not possible to have the camera close to the subject.

Software

Many video editing programs exist on the market. The two top software consumer applications are Adobe Premiere Elements and Final Cut Express (by Apple); they are also available as professional suites called Adobe Premiere and Final Cut Pro. In recent years, Final Cut Pro has become the choice of most professional video editors. It offers sound, video, and graphics editing tools simple enough for beginners and yet powerful enough for the most advanced professionals.

IN PRACTICE

The "Two-Way" Still Photographer/Videographer

Paul Darrow is contracted with Thomson-Reuters wire service as photographer for Canada's Atlantic region. He was the chief photographer at the Halifax Daily News *until 2006. He does work for the* Globe and Mail, Toronto Star, *and* New York Times. *His work has also appeared in* Time, National Geographic, *and* Rolling Stone.

When Paul Darrow started his career 25 years ago he says he chose still photography because he saw himself as an artistic purist.

That ideal is long gone.

Darrow is both a still photographer and videographer—a "two-way." He calls his career immensely satisfying, but says the journey to hybrid visual journalist has been an adventure.

"It didn't start as a love," he says. "It started as survival."

Darrow says the news agencies he works for now want stills first, video second. Usually, his clients want both. He is now expected to grab a sound clip or an interview after shooting stills.

"If you want to work for a national paper, the prerequisite now is to shoot stills and video," he says. "You're a multimedia photojournalist." He says there is still some work for dedicated still photographers and dedicated videographers, especially at large wire services. But tight budgets in most national and regional newsrooms mean assignment editors prefer to hire two-way shooters.

"The newspapers tend to go that way because of economy. If they can run a little clip on the Web, they're happy. We're not talking about full production here."

The key to succeeding in both functions, he says, is understanding what the client needs. "You've got to deal in peak moments ... You've got to really make the decision of what you're there for. What's your priority? If your client is principally for print pictures, then you shoot all the action that way. Then when the dust settles, you roll the video and then you gather the interview."

Hesitate for too long, he says, and "you'll get caught in the middle and you'll miss both."

Switching roles—and cameras—on the fly, he says, means making sacrifices. "There is a suffering of quality that goes on," he acknowledges. "Let's put it this way: you can do two things OK and you can do one thing extremely well."

He says there are new digital cameras on the market that allow the user to shoot stills and video simultaneously, but they are still expensive. When they come down in price, he says, "it'll be a fact of life that you will do both."

Right now, he says, the debate among still photographers over the need to remake themselves as videographers is heated. "There are people crying, 'There goes the end of an era. There goes photojournalism,'" he says. "But the idea of gathering news is always going to be there. Composition will always be an element of both. Some people may not like it because they are purists, but they'll be the people who are caught behind."

SOURCE: Telephone interview with Tim Currie, April 23, 2010.

DISCUSSION QUESTIONS

1. Why is it important for a photojournalist to be content-driven?
2. What are the two main controllers of light, and why is a solid understanding of them important?
3. What are the various ways to tell a visual story?
4. What is the role of a good visual journalist?
5. What are the three most important things to consider when choosing a video interview location?
6. What six things do you need to remember when setting up for a video interview?

SUGGESTED RESOURCES

The Loyalist College Photojournalism Program. http://www.loyalistcollegephotojournalism.ca.

Media Storm. http://mediastorm.org.

Multimedia Muse. http://www.multimediamuse.org.

MultimediaShooter. http://multimediashooter.com.

National Press Photographers Association. 2010. Best Of photojournalism: First winners picked in web categories. News release, March 22. http://nppa.org/news_and_events/news/2010/03/bop04.html.

News Photographers Association of Canada. http://npac.ca.

CHAPTER 19

Convergence Journalism: Audio

Karen Zypchyn

CHAPTER OUTLINE

Introduction

It's easy to take for granted, but sound plays a huge role in your life. Whether you are listening to music, watching a movie, walking through a crowded farmers' market, or having a conversation with someone, aural stimuli are sending lots of messages to your brain—messages that help you make sense of the world.

Both the human voice and natural sounds—such as the sound of traffic during morning rush hour or the sound of strong wind gusts on a winter's night—provide a rich source of information that journalists can weave into their storytelling. We are interested not only in what our sources say but also how they say it. And we're interested in where they say it: A minister defending her position on health-care cuts in front of a crowd of angry nurses facing layoffs will sound very different in a one-on-one interview on the same topic in her quiet office. The best storytellers—novelists, film directors, or journalists—place their characters in environments or scenes to bring them to life. Sound helps us do just that.

In this chapter, we'll explore how you can start to develop the skills to incorporate sound in your reporting and writing. From planning your story to recording audio, this chapter will get you ready to produce a variety of multimedia stories that will engage your audience with sound, be they radio stories, podcasts, audio slideshows, TV stories, or online video stories. (*Note:* An appendix to this chapter, which provides guidelines on audio editing using Audacity, is available for free on this book's website. See www.emp.ca/newjournalist.)

Audio as a Medium

Radio journalism has been bringing the world into people's living rooms and their vehicles for decades. And now podcasting can bring the world to just about anywhere

> **SIDEBAR**
>
> **Human Hearing**
>
> Sound enters the human ear at various frequencies, which are measured in hertz (Hz). A healthy young person can hear many frequencies as long as they fall within the range of 20 to 20,000 Hz. As we age, our ability to hear frequencies can diminish. But you can easily damage your hearing at any age by listening to loud music, for example, or by being repeatedly exposed to other loud sounds.

you are, as long as you have a portable digital device that can play audio files. Radio journalism relies on sound alone and thus can teach us a lot about how and when to use audio. Therefore, it will serve as our guide as we explore the role of audio in convergence journalism/multimedia reporting.

Listen to any CBC Radio program or a talk radio show on a private station, and you'll soon discover that the spoken word is powerful. And so is sound. The "golden days" of radio witnessed the rise of radio dramas and made stars of its actors. Those actors made characters come to life using a combination of their voices, music, and sound effects to tell stories. In 1938, Orson Welles's radio adaptation of the novel *The War of the Worlds* by H.G. Wells demonstrated the power of the medium and spurred public outrage at the use of its techniques to tell the story of an alien invasion. Welles interrupted music programming with frequent news bulletins about the invasion as a way to engage his audience, thereby mimicking radio programming of the day. Some people believed that the program was an authentic newscast. Whether the program actually caused real panic in the public is a matter of debate. However, it did fuel public discussion over regulations in the world of broadcasting and underscored the strength of audio storytelling.

Audio's Strengths and Uses

Audio has a number of strengths:

- It creates intimacy.
- It creates immediacy (something happening now).
- It reveals emotion and personality.
- It creates a sense of place.

Audio has a number of uses:

- It can offer explanations.
- It can relay conversation and debates.
- It can create ambience.

The same holds true for video stories. In fact, audio—instead of video—is the keystone of video stories. In fact, without audio, you wouldn't have a story: You would just have moving pictures, including visuals of people talking, and no sound. In short, audio matters.

BOX 19.1 News Values

News values include but are not limited to the following:

- proximity
- impact
- timeliness
- human interest
- conflict
- prominence

Reporting with Audio: Having a Plan

Audio will play a key role in some way in your reporting. Knowing how and when to use it, therefore, is essential in the early stages of researching your story. You will have to determine how audio will best be used to bring your story to life, and develop a plan to ensure you gather good sound.[1] In all cases, your decision to use audio must be anchored in good news judgment, which is applicable to all media, whether video, photo, text, or interactive multimedia. Specifically, you must consider how using audio will reflect news values such as impact, conflict, and human interest. Using audio for the sake of having audio in your story does not reflect good news judgment.

Depending on what format(s) you intend to use to tell your story, your choices will affect the following:

- how you conduct interviews
- what equipment you will use
- what audio you will capture

Some of the story formats that use audio are podcasts, audio slideshows, video, and interactive multimedia. As you read through this chapter, you'll begin to appreciate all the planning you must do to research, develop, write, and produce your story.

Conducting Audio Interviews

Interviewing is at the heart of newsgathering: It helps you to uncover the truth and ultimately enables you to tell a story. If you've never conducted an interview with a source with the intention of capturing an audio clip (also called an *actuality*) or a sound bite (see the sidebar for definitions), you may not have given much thought to the following:

- how you ask questions
- how you order the questions you want to ask

You must master these two key elements of interviewing if you want to obtain good audio clips for your stories. These elements are especially important if you want to post a significant portion of your interview online.

Key Terms Defined

- *Actuality:* An excerpt of an audio recording of someone talking.
- *Sound Bite:* A brief clip of both audio and video of someone talking.

Getting Basic Information

Always begin interviews by asking sources to say the following:

- their full name and title
- where they work/what they do

Ask sources to respond with, "My name is …" Then ask them to spell their full name. Why? That way, you'll know how to pronounce sources' names in the event you need to say them in your stories.

By having sources identify themselves, you have the option to let them introduce themselves in your audio clips, which is especially good for "streeters" (on-the-street interviews with members of the public). It also gives you the option during the editing phase to take yourself out of the story and include only audio clips from your sources.

Asking Good Questions: Wording Matters

When interviewing people for the purpose of capturing an audio clip, you must be careful how you ask questions in order to obtain complete sentences or thoughts. Partial responses from sources, such as "Sometimes scared" or "No, not really," are a reflection of poorly worded questions asked by the journalist. These types of responses will destroy the audio component of your story. Your story will lack emotion and human interest and leave you scrambling to fix the problem during editing. However, the problem is easy to prevent with some forethought and preparation.

Open-Ended and Closed-Ended Questions

In the preparatory phase of reporting, which includes research, write out the questions you want to ask your sources. Carefully word your questions so they are open-ended questions—questions that require sources to begin sentences with a subject followed by a verb. The five Ws of reporting (who, what, where, when, why, along with how) will serve as your best guide for framing questions correctly. Also, pay close attention to the words you choose: Use neutral language and avoid words with strong negative or emotional overtones.

Closed-ended questions, on the other hand, tend to encourage sources to provide you with yes/no responses or incomplete sentences. They include questions such as the following:

- "Do you agree with the police's response?" "Do you think the mayor made a good decision?"

Closed-ended questions can become leading questions, which are a problem because they imply an answer. The following example is a leading question:

- "Is the government's decision to slash housing making it harder for you to help the homeless?"

By correcting the wording, you arrive at an open-ended question:

- "What impact has the government's decision on housing had on your efforts to help the homeless?"

Ordering Questions: Strategy Matters

Not only do your questions need to be worded appropriately to get the best answers from your sources, they also need to be ordered strategically. For example, you would never begin an interview with the toughest question first. Keep in mind that your sources need to "warm up" during an interview. Also, your interview will flow more naturally if you structure questions in a logical progression, such as starting with questions that address *what* happened, followed by *how* it happened, and then *why* it happened. This is just one example of how to structure an interview. It is not the only way, of course.

There are many ways to structure interviews to help you obtain the best audio clips. However, the point is that you need a strategy, the very thing emphasized in the Sawatsky method of interviewing.[2] A strategy will keep you focused during the interview and help you avoid conducting an interview that jumps from question to question without any apparent structure or reason.

TOOLS & TIPS

The Sawatsky Method: Minimize Your Output, Maximize Your Source's Input

John Sawatsky, a renowned trainer in the art of interviewing and an award-winning former journalist, has made a business out of open-ended questions.

Simply put, he says these kinds of questions get you the most output from your sources. And he encourages you to keep those questions short. He says it's important that you minimize the amount of talking you do and let your sources do the bulk of it instead (Paterno 2000; Scanlan 2001).

A haphazard interview—one without a strategy—will make it difficult for you to produce stories to deadline because ideas contained in the interview won't be logically organized. Moreover, it will make it challenging for you to edit and select audio clips, especially if you want to post a portion of the interview online. If you conduct a haphazard interview, you will soon discover that you can't find a portion of the interview that sounds like a natural conversation in which ideas flow logically and are easily understood. And remember, you can't "fix" the problem during the editing phase by simply cutting and pasting portions of the interview in the order you'd like them to be arranged. Changing the original interview in such a fashion would violate the journalistic code of ethics concerning authenticity, which holds that journalists must not misrepresent reality or distort meaning through digital manipulation.

Audio Interviewing and Story Format

The types of questions you ask during an interview will depend on the format you've chosen to tell your story. A story format that relies on sound alone, such as an audio podcast, requires different interview questions than a story that contains visuals. For example, stories that use only audio must rely on the narrator and the people interviewed to describe things, such as the clothes someone is wearing or the room someone

> **BOX 19.2 Good Audio Clips**
>
> Good audio clips are *short* (10 to 20 seconds) and reveal
>
> - emotion
> - drama
> - colour/personality
>
> You need to listen closely for good audio clips during interviews with your sources. Remember: You can paraphrase portions of the interview that contain information.

is standing in, to create visual images for the listener. Remember, your listener cannot see physical images to interpret the story. In this case, the journalist must remember to ask questions that obtain descriptions of things that are relevant to the story. A video story doesn't require such questions to be asked because the video camera captures images that can be seen. In this case, the journalist can focus on other questions to obtain meaning and explanation for the story. So again, be sure that you have a plan in place for your story well in advance of conducting your interviews.

Interview Requirements for Stories That Use Audio

Whether you're creating a podcast, a video, or an audio slideshow with still photos, the audio will play a key role by providing a vehicle to hear people explain and describe things. Therefore, during interviews, ask your sources questions that require them to do the following:

- *Describe* people, places, things, or events to tell what's happening
  EXAMPLE: "Can you describe what we're looking at or what you're wearing?" (*Note:* Asking people such a question is particularly useful for stories that only rely on audio.)
- *Explain* their thoughts
  EXAMPLES: "What was your reaction when … ?" "What do you mean by that?"
- *Reveal* emotion, colour/personality, drama
  EXAMPLES: "How did you feel when … ?" "What happened after … ?"

For more on interviewing in the digital age, see Chapter 14.

Recording Audio

Equipment

With your story plan in place, research done, and interview questions sketched out, it's now time to go record audio for your story. You can capture audio using a variety of recording devices, including the following:

- digital audio recording devices, produced by companies such as EDIROL, Marantz, Sony, and Olympus (see Figure 19.1)
- digital video cameras, produced by companies such as Sony, Canon, and JVC
- mobile devices such as MP3 players and the iPhone (see Figure 19.2)

Higher-end recording devices provide *two* plug-ins (microphone and line in) that give you flexibility when recording.

Unfortunately, not all recording devices are equal: Some are better than others. Those that are better, of course, tend to cost more money. However, it is possible to find a device that meets both your budget and story needs. High-end audio recording devices from EDIROL and Marantz record broadcast-quality audio in stereo (which is the best quality) and are reasonably priced. High-end video cameras can also capture high-quality audio. The audio recording capability of mobile devices is improving, making it more convenient for reporters to file good audio quality from the field directly to the Internet.

What about consumer products, which tend to cost significantly less than broadcast-quality recording devices? In the past, consumer audio and video products were notorious for creating "cheap" quality audio and video clips. More recently, however, many consumer products have significantly improved recording capability that will generate adequate quality audio and video clips for use on the Internet. Some consumer products record in stereo, which is necessary to capture good sound quality, but many products record in mono only, which reduces the amount of audio captured on one channel. In short, shop around to find what suits your needs and your pocketbook.

Figure 19.1 Digital audio recording devices, such as this EDIROL model, record broadcast-quality audio.

Microphones

Good recording devices include a plug-in for a microphone, which is what you want to help improve the sound quality of your recordings. Like recording devices, mics can be one of the following:

- **Stereo.** The mic can record two channels of audio; these are best for capturing sound that conveys depth.
- **Mono.** The mic can record one channel of audio.

Mics can also be one of the following:

- **Omnidirectional.** The mic can record sound from any direction and pick up ambient sound. Using a wind sock with this type of mic helps reduce the sound of wind.
- **Unidirectional.** The mic can record sound only from the source it's pointed at. This mic is a good option when background sound is overwhelming.

Examples of quality mics:

- 635A, standard broadcast mic
- lavaliere mic (a.k.a. lapel mic; it can be clipped to a person's clothing)
- boom or shotgun mic (great for capturing sound at a distance)

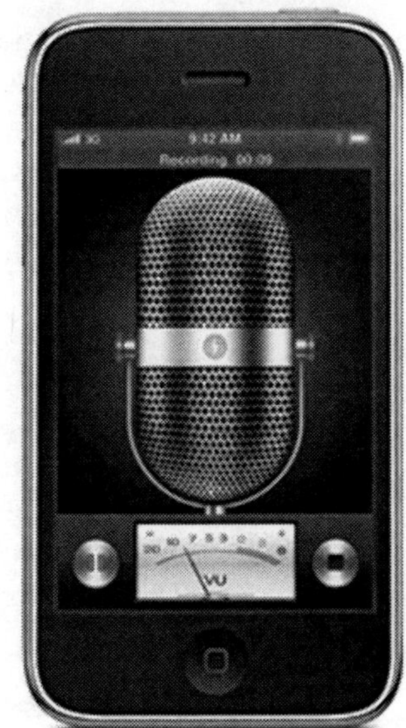

Figure 19.2 Mobile devices with recording capacity may be suitable for audio blogging.

Whatever device you decide to use, ensure that it can capture good audio quality: Without that quality, all the work put into gathering audio for your story will be wasted when it comes time to compressing the audio files for uploading to a website. Compression always degrades the quality of files. Therefore, poor-quality audio captured during the interviewing phase will only become poorer during the editing phase. Ultimately, a file with low audio quality will be difficult to hear when it is downloaded or streamed from the Internet.

Guidelines for Recording Audio

Regardless of the device you use, follow these guidelines to ensure you capture good audio quality:

- Do interviews *in person* as much as possible.
- Place the mic *close* to your interview subject.
- *Wear* your headphones during the interview so you can hear the audio while recording.
- Do a sound check to make sure your device works and is capturing good quality audio from where it and/or your microphone is positioned.
- Carry extra batteries for your equipment, and carry several types of cable cords that will permit you to plug in to sound systems if needed.
- Analyze the environment before you record; scope out places that are quiet enough so your source's voice records clearly and isn't drowned out by loud noises.
- Make sure you *hit record.*
- Play back and listen to your recorded interviews while in the field.

Recording Interviews Over the Phone: Legal Issues to Consider

As mentioned, when possible it's best to record your interviews in person in order to capture good audio quality. However, this type of interview is not always possible, and you may find it necessary to conduct an interview over the phone. Phone interviews fall under Canada's wiretapping laws in the Criminal Code, and you must ensure that you adhere to the law to avoid prosecution. By law, you must obtain consent from the person being interviewed to use his or her voice for the purpose of broadcast (as in radio or television) or for posting a story with audio to the Internet. For example, if you want to use all or part of an interview for a podcast, you must receive consent from your source to use the recording.

Follow this process to obtain consent:

1. Make sure you *hit record* on your recording device *before* you begin talking to your source over the phone.
2. Tell your source you intend to use the interview for the purpose of broadcast and/or for posting to the Internet.
3. Ask your source if you can proceed with the interview. If the source complies, his or her compliance is recorded on your device. This proof of consent will be required if your source ever challenges your journalistic practices, arguing that you did not obtain consent. The more sensitive the story you're working

on, the more critical it is to record the source's consent. Therefore, get into the habit of recording the consent part of the interview.

4. Continue conducting the interview, following the interviewing techniques discussed in this chapter.

When creating online stories, it's possible that you may change your mind on how best to use audio when it comes time to produce your story. While you may have intended to use a phone interview for an audio slideshow, for example, during the production phase you may decide it's best to post only a portion of the interview online as a downloadable element of the story. Therefore, when obtaining consent to use a recorded phone interview, simply identify the medium you're using to create the story. You don't have to provide specific details.[3]

Interviewing Guidelines Related to Recording and Editing

The following interviewing guidelines will further help you gather good audio clips for your stories and produce your stories to deadline. While conducting interviews, you want to take steps that will enable you to edit audio clips quickly while you're in the field or when you get back to your newsroom. You want to avoid having hours of recordings to review. Also, when you're recording an interview with a source, be mindful that your comments are being recorded too, so watch what you say.

- *Never interrupt* a source.
- *Never make comments* (such as, "I see," "uh-hum," "oh really").
- Make sure *you're on mic* when you ask questions so your voice gets recorded too.
- Permit moments of *silence* (they encourage your source to say something).
- *Listen* closely: You may have to re-ask a question to get a *shorter response* from your source.
- Keep interviews *short and focused* (approximately 10–15 minutes).

Recording Ambient Sound

The best audio and video stories include natural background sound, otherwise known as *ambient sound*, to help create scenes and a sense of place. When you conduct interviews in the field, you may notice ambient sound. It could be anything from the sound of children playing in a schoolyard to the sound of construction workers jackhammering a city road. Pay attention: Ambient sound will bring your storytelling to life in a way that writing about it couldn't possibly achieve. You'll need a plan to ensure not only that you have good quality ambient sound but also that you have enough sound to provide bridges between your story elements.[4] For example, if you want to create an audio slideshow, ambient sound can be an effective transition from one image to another. Or if you create an audio streeter, ambient sound can link the audio clips of the different voices of the people you interviewed. These sound bridges will serve as the glue that holds a story together, create dramatic effect, and provide you with creative flexibility in the editing phase.

Guidelines for Recording Ambient Sound

The following guidelines will help you record good ambient sound.

1. In the planning stage, determine as best as you can what kinds of ambient sounds your story will require.
2. Get out of the office to gather ambient sound. Avoid using sound effects. Recreating reality is journalistically problematic.
3. Scope out the environment to determine good sources of ambient sound and to position yourself appropriately to gather good levels of sound.
4. Use appropriate microphones to record ambient sound:
   - Omnidirectional mics should be used to pick up sound that is close at hand or surrounding you.
   - Boom mics should be used to pick up sound that is beyond your immediate reach or the proximity necessary to gather good sound.[5]
5. Wear your headphones while recording.
6. Adjust audio input levels to record good ambient sound (if your recording device has controls for input levels).
7. Keep quiet while you record.
8. Record ambient sounds on their own, separate from your interviews.
9. Record long enough portions of ambient sound to work with during the editing phase. It's always better to record more ambience than you'll need. But at minimum, record *one to two minutes* of ambient sound. *Note:* You may need longer-running ambient sound clips for the purpose of your story if you intend to let the sound carry the story.
10. Record a variety of different ambient sounds to help you create several scenes. Record sounds from different perspectives (close-up, medium, and long-range distances), as you would for video.[6]
11. Play back your audio recordings while in the field to ensure the following:
    - You actually recorded ambience.
    - You captured good sound quality.

Questions to Ask Sources Prior to Gathering Ambient Sound

It's important to ask sources questions about their environment *before* you go out to interview them. You need to do this to get a sense of the type of sounds you will be able to record while in the field. For example, let's say you want to tell the story of a creative local carpenter who makes statues out of wood. Before you interview him in person, call and ask him the following questions:

- "Do you have a project you're working on now?"
- "Where do you work on it?" (garage, et cetera)
- "What tools do you use to make a statue?"

Recording Speeches and News Conferences

When covering speeches and news conferences, you want to capture sound live from the microphone. To do that, you need to connect your recording device to the sound system provided by the organizers of the speech or conference. It's essential for you to carry various audio connectors to be prepared (see Figures 19.3, 19.4, and 19.5).[7]

Typical audio connectors:

- ⅛-inch connector (known as the "mini")
- ¼-inch connector
- XLR connector

One audio connector must plug into your recording device and the other into the sound system. As such, you may need a cable cord that has two different audio connectors. One end of the cable may be a ⅛-inch or mini phone plug to fit into your audio recording device's input jack, while the other end of the cable may be a ¼-inch phone plug to fit into the sound system's jack. You will likely need someone to help you create these various cables. Ask for assistance at audio stores or music specialty stores that sell microphones and recording devices.

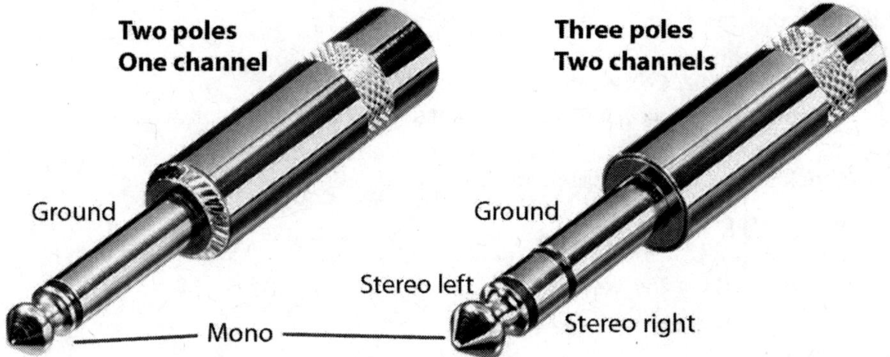

Figure 19.3 Audio connectors—stereo versus mono

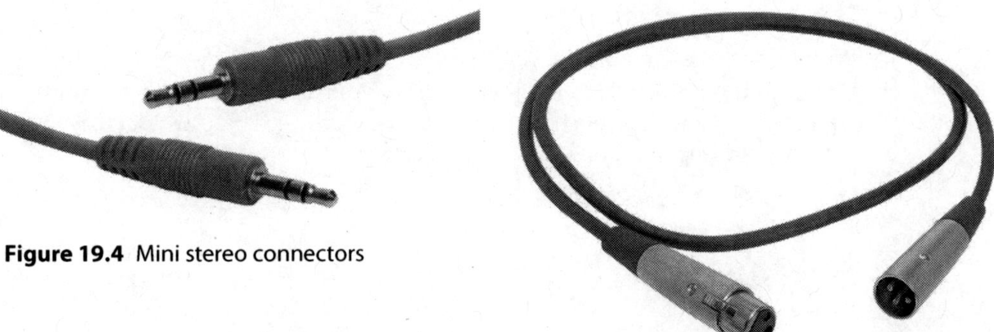

Figure 19.4 Mini stereo connectors

Figure 19.5 XLR female (left), male (right) connnectors

Guidelines on Recording Speeches and News Conferences

- Do a sound check and adjust input levels to make sure the sound isn't distorted.
- Wear your headphones while recording.
- Make sure your cable is plugged into the right *input jack* on your recording device. If you have both mic and line-in jacks, you want to plug the cable into the *line-in jack*. Listen for feedback or "hot sound," which indicates that you've used the wrong jack, and watch for sound levels if your device displays the levels. You know you have "hot sound" when you can see both digital recording meter bars bouncing far to the right into the maximum possible level, signalling distortion.

Writing for the Ear

Now that you've gathered the audio for your story, you may need to write lines of narration for yourself or for someone else, such as the host of a podcast. You should decide whether your story will be narrated by you or someone else in the planning stages of your story. Writing to be heard will be new to many of you. It takes a lot of practice to master, especially if you've been writing for print: You now have to write sentences that can easily be spoken.

Broadcast Writing Conventions

Broadcast journalists have mastered writing for the ear, so let's look at basic broadcast writing conventions.[8]

Write for immediate comprehension:

- Write short sentences.
- Write simply (avoid complex sentence structures).
- Write in the *active* voice.
- Minimize details.

TOOLS & TIPS

The Art of Omission

Writing for the ear means cutting back on the number of details in a story. But which details should you eliminate from your story? Although you must use fewer details, you must also choose the right ones. You wouldn't want your story to become unbalanced or inaccurate.

Keep the following facts to a minimum:

- names
- titles
- statistics

Round off large or complex numbers.

Keep it conversational:

- Use contractions.
- Use everyday speech.
- Write in the present tense.
- Read what you've written aloud.

Tell a story along a narrative line:

- It should have a beginning.
- It should have a middle.
- It should have an end.

Broadcast Writing: Attribution and Pronouncers

Writing stories for print and writing stories to be heard differ significantly in two areas: attribution and the pronunciation of words.

Attribution

If you don't attribute information at the right place, listeners will not be able to discern immediately whether the information they are hearing is fact or opinion. For that reason, and to avoid any possible confusion, attribution always comes first, *before* the information. It's important in audio stories to let listeners know *who* is saying the information. A lack of attribution in audio stories, as in print stories, means the information is to be taken as fact.[9]

Here is an example of attribution *after* the information, which is appropriate for print stories but not audio stories: "There's plenty of support in the classroom for children with learning disabilities, said Education Minister Eileen Smith."

Here is an example of attribution *before* the information, which is essential in audio stories: "Education minister Eileen Smith says there's plenty of support in the classroom for children with learning disabilities."

Pronouncers

If you use narration in a story, it's crucial to pronounce words correctly. Mispronounce a source's name or the name of a park, country, or river, and you may damage your credibility as a journalist. Identify correct pronunciation of words in your copy or script by using a pronouncer.[10] A *pronouncer* is a phonetic guide on how to say a name, place, object, or any other unfamiliar word correctly.

How to write a pronouncer:

1. Break the word into its separate syllables.
2. Identify the syllables that require emphasis by writing them in capitals; leave unstressed syllables in lower case.
3. Write the correct spelling of the word in your copy and, immediately following it, write the pronouncer in brackets. For example: "*Kim chi* [kim CHEE] is a spicy and sour pickled vegetable dish that is eaten with meals in Korea."

Music and Copyright Issues

While you're producing the audio part of your story, you may want to use music as a sound bed under narration or audio clips. Or, you may want to use music alone in an audio slideshow. You must be aware of copyright issues before you select music for use in your story to avoid legal fines for breaching copyright. Copyright clearance must be obtained if you are using music or sound effects created by musicians who have copyrighted their musical creations. You'll have to pay for clearance, which you may not be prepared to do financially. There are options, listed below, when considering the use of music in your stories.

The following guidelines will help you avoid copyright problems:

- At most, use only 20 seconds in total of copyrighted music in your story.
- Go to CreativeCommons.ca to download music free of charge. Credit the creator of the music or sound effect according to the attribution guidelines on the site.
- Use consumer musical software such as Apple's GarageBand to create your own music bridges or sound effects.

If you use only 20 seconds of copyrighted music in your story, you won't have officials calling you up to demand payment for use of a musician's creation. However, If you use 20 seconds here, there, and several places in a story, then you've arguably "borrowed" too much from a musician without paying to use his or her copyrighted creation. In this case, you could face legal problems.[11]

Ask yourself: Am I using a substantial, identifiable portion of music? If the answer is yes, you need copyright permission.

Ethical Issues in Audio Production

Editing

During the editing phase of producing your story, you may be tempted to cut and paste your interview recordings to change the original flow of the interview. Editing software programs make such changes easy and concealed: You can make it sound like your source said something in response to a particular question when, in fact, the source did not provide such a response. As with all journalistic endeavours, whether you are researching, gathering information, writing, or editing, you must uphold journalistic integrity and be committed to telling and presenting reality as accurately as possible. That means that during the editing phase of your story, you must maintain the authenticity of the original audio recordings you gathered and take extra care to avoid distorting or misrepresenting those audio files.[12]

Sound Effects

Let's say that you may want to add special sound effects to your story to augment a dramatic event. You find copyright-safe music and start creating a sound bed using audio editing software such as Audacity to lay the music under a gripping audio clip from a source. What's wrong with this picture?

You need to ask yourself the following questions:

- Am I distorting reality by doing this?
- Am I sensationalizing the story?
- Am I making an editorial comment by doing this?

If you can answer yes to any of these questions, you could be misrepresenting reality in some way and compromising journalistic integrity.[13] Journalists avoid the "Hollywoodification" of their stories, that is, making them more dramatic or sensational with the use of music or sound effects.

A word of advice: Always discuss your production ideas with your editor or producer before you spend hours editing audio for your story.

Case Study 1: Podcasting at CBC Radio

After several years spent in both radio and television, Dave Downey, manager of projects, planning and development at CBC National Radio News, is now in charge of podcasting the national broadcasters' radio news podcasts. He says podcasting will play an even larger role in the future of the CBC as the online world reaches into more facets of human behaviour, be it through smartphones or appliances such as refrigerators and toasters that become increasingly computerized. I interviewed him about the dos and don'ts of podcasting. Here's part of our conversation.[14]

KAREN ZYPCHYN: Is podcasting just good radio?

DAVE DOWNEY: Yes. If you put on a bad radio show, you won't get any audience. If you put on a bad podcast, you won't get any subscribers. Functionally, it's the same thing. All the qualities that go into radio programming have to be present in a podcast. The thing more [abstract] about podcasts, because they're recorded and not live to air, [is that] you do have more flexibility from a production point of view to do the kinds of things that you might want to do. If you want to do value-added content, if you want to add extra stuff, you can do that. You're not on a schedule. The radio schedule is pretty tight. Every program has its precise length and you can't exceed that. In a podcast, plus or minus five minutes doesn't matter as much particularly to your audience. And if you think it's a worthwhile five minutes, then absolutely you can put it up. It does give you that level of flexibility.

KAREN ZYPCHYN: What qualities make a podcast a "good" podcast?

DAVE DOWNEY: In terms of qualities, [they're] the things that I like, broadly speaking, about radio programs. It's the journeys to other places, it's the sound, it's the characters that I get to hear from, it's the people that I meet that I otherwise would never encounter. All of the things that make good radio make good podcasting. The vastness of the podcast universe is so great that really you have at your fingertips, in terms of audio, pretty much any kind of content that you want to grab. Because of the work that I do, I tend to listen more to news and current affairs, that kind of podcasting.

KAREN ZYPCHYN: What are some poor or bad things you've seen or heard in podcasting?

DAVE DOWNEY: I remember one time I was listening to a tech podcast, and it was a kind of panel discussion on some subject and people were doing all the things in radio you wouldn't want. They were talking on top of each other to the point where you couldn't understand the point that each one of them was making. They would sort of lean away, laugh off mic. In terms of production quality, it was awful. It was really amateurish and really difficult to listen to. As somebody who is in the business, when I hear that it just makes me kind of cringe. Those are things that are easily correctible and they're the basics of what you would say make good radio.

KAREN ZYPCHYN: What recording advice do you have for journalists who are gathering sound specifically for podcasting?

DAVE DOWNEY: A lot of the same advice I would give for radio:

1. You need to find a suitable place to do the recording.
2. You need to use decent equipment. Using a mic on your computer—the built in ones—won't be good; the audio quality isn't high.
3. And you need to practise and practise and playback. You need to listen to what you've done and make sure that you keep the same and consistent level around the volume that you're putting out, that you stay within the same distance range [when placing microphones near a person's mouth]—4 to 6 inches away from the microphone or even 8 inches depending on the mic you use.
4. Be consistent.

Case Study 2: Multimedia Production at the *Edmonton Journal*

Ryan Jackson was heading down the path of engineering and computer science when he decided to make an about turn and take up photojournalism. After studying at Loyalist College and working at several Canadian daily newspapers, he was hired at the Edmonton Journal *as a multimedia photojournalist. Ryan produces all kinds of multimedia stories for the paper, including stills, audio slideshows, and online video. Here is how he uses audio in his role as a multimedia photojournalist.*[15]

KAREN ZYPCHYN: What is the most challenging thing about using audio?

RYAN JACKSON: Being efficient with your time would have to be the most difficult thing. Anyone can hit record and let a recorder just go. When you're actually working and have to produce a story on deadline that's of high quality, that's when time constraints are your biggest challenge, so you have to find ways to make yourself more efficient; you have to take notes, you have to build a story in your head and do lots of little things that really add up to save yourself time and be efficient when it comes to editing and also so that you're not just recording ten hours of audio, and then getting home and listening to ten hours of audio and then cutting down that ten hours of audio. Instead, when you're recording, you are taking down notes and jotting down when the important quotes are so that when you get back to the office, you know to just jump to 4 minutes and 52 seconds and that's where the good audio clip is.

KAREN ZYPCHYN: In your opinion, what makes a good audio slideshow?

RYAN JACKSON: First, it should be a story that lends itself well to an audio slideshow, where strong still images and strong audio are arguably the best way to tell the story. And then it should be done in a way where the audio complements and strengthens the images. I always say that the best audio is where you don't think about the audio—where you just focus on the subject and focus on what's being said and what you're hearing, but you're not thinking about how it was recorded and the person recording it. And if the audio is of that quality and it strengthens the whole audio slideshow, then it's done well. it should have enough visuals to keep the viewer stimulated, and the audio should flow with the pictures and be relevant. You shouldn't be at the end of the slideshow, watch it, and think to yourself, what did that audio really have to do with those pictures? Other good things are you should have multiple voices, you know, more than just one person talking. And ambient audio is also very important. If you just have pictures and a person talking, that's good, it's OK, but if you have ambient sounds, you actually hear what's going on there, you actually hear the instruments and tools the person is using, then you get a better sense of placement and where you are.

KAREN ZYPCHYN: Thinking back on audio slideshow stories you've created, what's one that you particularly like best?

RYAN JACKSON: An audio slideshow that I really like, even though it's not the best one I've ever done, is called "Picking to Survive." (See punkoryan.com.) It was a story about a man who is an alcoholic, and he has back problems and he's unemployed and he can't work. He's prescribed drugs to help him deal with the pain from his back problems, but he doesn't like taking the drugs and he's an alcoholic. So every morning he wakes up early and he picks through garbage bins and he picks bottles. And every day he picks enough cans to get about $10 a day, which is enough for him to buy a six-pack of beer, and that's enough to feed his habit, helps him with the pain, and that's his life. I followed him for a couple of days, recorded his story. The audio slideshow is him telling his story, but you also get to hear the sound of him rummaging through the garbage bins, the sound of him crushing the cans, the sound of him excited when he gets enough money, and him going into the liquor store, bartering to try to get a little bit more beer, and finally the sound of him taking that first sip of beer every day, and him saying, "That's what it's all for."

KAREN ZYPCHYN: Looking to the future in journalism, what role do you see audio playing in the dissemination of news?

RYAN JACKSON: Audio is still a very popular medium, be it for radio or podcasting or using audio as a way to get your information or your news. For newspapers, audio will still be important in that the Web has to be more than just text, it has to be more than just the printed stories. It has to have that extra interactivity of added pictures, added audio, added video. Audio will still be important in the future because all those things, like multimedia and video and all that stuff, require audio. As the world gets more "webby," we're going to expect to have more multimedia and more rich, immersive media online.

NOTES

1. See Kern (2008), the subsection entitled "A Storytelling Sampler," on pages 64–72, which provides good examples of the type of planning required to use audio effectively in radio storytelling.
2. A must read and listen is Folkenflik (2006). Download the audio to hear interviews with Sawatsky. Also, download examples of great radio interviews by Sawatsky to hear his method in action.
3. Sean Ward (media lawyer, Reynolds Mirth Richards & Farmer LLP, Edmonton), in a telephone interview with Karen Zypchyn, October 19, 2009.
4. See Kern (2008), pages 80–81, for planning for use of sound.
5. See Foust (2009), pages 201–204, for details on microphones and recording devices.
6. See Kern (2008), pages 81–83, for a discussion on recording sound in the field.
7. See Foust (2009), pages 202–203, for a discussion on and images of audio connectors.
8. See Green (2001), Chapter 3 "Telling the News" and Chapter 4 "Broadcast Writing Conventions" for a good summary of broadcast writing style and conventions.
9. See Green (2001), pages 36–37, for further discussion on attribution.
10. See Green (2001), pages 112–113 for more tips on pronouncers; see also Kern (2008), pages 192–193, and Appendix II (Pronouncers).
11. Sean Ward (media lawyer, Reynolds Mirth Richards & Farmer LLP, Edmonton), in a telephone interview with Karen Zypchyn, October 19, 2009.
12. See also the CBC (2004) journalistic standards and practices guidelines.
13. See also McCombs (2009), CBC (2004, s. IV, B.2), RTNDA (n.d., Article 3), and Green (2001, 149).
14. Dave Downey (manager of projects, planning and development, CBC National Radio News), in a telephone interview with Karen Zypchyn, December 2, 2009. Downey's opinions on podcasting are shared by other radio journalists. Also see Kern (2008), pages 324–334, for a discussion on podcasting.
15. Ryan Jackson (multimedia photojournalist, *Edmonton Journal*), in an in-person interview with Karen Zypchyn, December 9, 2009.

DISCUSSION QUESTIONS

1. Story planning: Come up with a story idea that includes an audio component. Determine the best way to use audio, and develop a plan to write and produce your story. Who will you interview? What logistical matters must you consider to capture good sound? What kind of sound will your story require? Where will you capture your sound? What equipment will you require?
2. Effective interviewing: Using a story you are currently working on, let's assume that you intend to podcast a part of the interview with one of your sources. Write a list of good questions to ask that source and make sure you strategize the order of the questions. Then, conduct the interview and review it. Can

someone other than yourself listen to a portion of it and be engaged? Why or why not? Can you find a good portion of the interview that captures the essence of the interview without having to do major editing to make it flow better? Or do you have to make several edits? If so, why? Be critical of what happened during your interview so that you can learn to conduct effective interviews.

3. Podcasting: Go to the website of public radio stations—such as CBC Radio (www.cbc.ca/radio/), NPR (www.npr.org), and BBC Radio (www.bbc.co.uk/radio)—to listen to a variety of their podcasts. What do you notice about typical formats for podcasting? Why do you like some podcasts more than others? Come up with an idea for a podcast of your own and sketch out how you will produce it based on a format used in the podcasts you listened to. How will you start the podcast? What will you say? How long will it be? Who will be in it? How will you end it?

SUGGESTED RESOURCES

Audacity (free audio editing software): http://audacity.sourceforge.net/.
Note: An appendix to this chapter, which provides guidelines on audio editing using Audacity, is available for free on this book's website. See www.emp.ca/newjournalist.

CBC. 2004. Corporate policies—1.2 Journalistic standards and practices. CBC/Radio-Canada, September. http://cbc-radio-canada.ca/docs/policies/journalistic/.
This resource thoroughly addresses ethical issues in relation to editing both audio and video.

REFERENCES

CBC. 2004. Corporate policies—1.2 Journalistic standards and practices. CBC/Radio-Canada, September. http://cbc-radio-canada.ca/docs/policies/journalistic/.

Folkenflik, David. 2006. The art of the interview, ESPN-style. *NPR*, August 14. http://www.npr.org/templates/story/story.php?storyId=5625218.

Foust, James C. 2009. *Online journalism: Principles and practices of news for the Web.* Scottsdale, AZ: Holocomb Hathaway Publishers.

Green, Brian. 2001. *Canadian broadcast news: The basics*. Scarborough, ON: Nelson Thomson Learning.

Kern, Jonathan. 2008. *Sound reporting: The NPR guide to audio journalism and production.* Chicago: University of Chicago Press.

McCombs, Regina. 2009. Ethics policies regarding music use in news stories. *PoynterOnline*, April 1. http://www.poynter.org/content/content_view.asp?id=157862.

Paterno, Susan. 2000. The question man. *American Journalism Review*, October. http://www.ajr.org/article.asp?id=676.

RTNDA. n.d. Code of ethics. http://www.rtndacanada.com/Content.asp?PageID=10.

Scanlan, Chip. 2001. Tools of the trade: The question. *PoynterOnline*, October 23. http://www.poynter.org/content/content_view.asp?id=5075.

IMAGE SOURCES

FIGURE 19.1: http://www.rolandsystemsgroup.com/en/product-archives/332-r-09hr-high-resolution-wavemp3-recorder.

FIGURE 19.2: http://www.apple.com/ca/iphone/iphone-3gs/.

FIGURE 19.3: http://www.parts-express.com/pe/showdetl.cfm?Partnumber=092-130 and http://www.parts-express.com/pe/showdetl.cfm?Partnumber=092-132.

FIGURE 19.4: http://www.bhphotovideo.com/c/product/674004-REG/Gefen_CAB_AUDIO_6_1_8_Stereo_Mini_to.html. Image courtesy of B&H Photo-Video-ProAudio, New York.

FIGURE 19.5: http://www.bhphotovideo.com/c/product/158494-REG/Hosa_Technology_MCL_110_3_Pin_XLR_Male_to.html. Image courtesy of B&H Photo-Video-ProAudio, New York.

CHAPTER 20

Data Visualizations and Interactives

Tim Currie

Introduction

Smartphones, tablet PCs, and iPads are providing new platforms for journalism. But they also bring new challenges. As journalists, how can we tell complex stories on small screens? How can we keep mobile users engaged among competing distractions—in the real world and the virtual one?

New technologies bring innovative ways to tell stories and provide new career opportunities to those who grasp their potential. Journalists who understand the realm of new media recognize its fundamental nature as active, not passive. These journalists redefine the traditional journalistic function of storytelling as inviting story participation.

When American researcher Jakob Nielsen conducted his early studies into how people consume content on the Web, he came to a now-obvious conclusion: "The Web is a user-driven medium where users feel that they have to move on and click on things" (Nielsen 1997). As one participant in his 1997 usability studies said, "If I have to sit here and read the whole article, then I'm not productive."

CHAPTER OUTLINE

This idea holds true today, and it's an important consideration in creating journalism for distribution on the Internet. People want to feel engaged when they go online. On one level, they want to interact with people, comment on stories, vote in online polls, and participate in live chats. But even when they read stories or watch videos, they want to customize the experience. The Web isn't about reading long, grey passages of text. It's about "actionable content," as Nielsen (2008) puts it.

Apple Inc. CEO Steve Jobs may have been over the top in 2008 when he famously said "people don't read anymore" (Markoff 2008). But his comment, disparaging e-reader devices at the launch of Amazon's Kindle, holds an important observation for creators of online content. Small screens and ever-present distractions make it imperative that content be easily digestible and, if possible, interactive. And the best medium for this may not always be text.

Advances in technology have been coupled with a parallel development—an increase in the availability of structured data. Institutions have held their records in databases for many years. But journalists—and citizens—have prompted institutions to make these data more readily available. In 2009, the City of Vancouver became the largest city in Canada to commit to putting public municipal data online. The result in September 2009 was the launch of Vancouver's Open Data Catalogue, which contains information as diverse as municipal election results to data on the city's sewer network.

These kinds of public information portals are still in their infancy. Many levels of government—particularly in Canada—are still highly secretive with public records. This stance requires journalists to file freedom of information requests to obtain much of the most illuminating information.

Faced with new technology and greater access to structured data, journalists are asking: How can we make sense of these data for our online audience? How can we combine data to tell stories? The answer is data visualizations.

Data Visualizations

Print editors have used informational graphics for years to show static representations of what numbers mean or how an event happened. But the Internet offers the benefits of interactivity and personalization. It also offers the potential to visualize data in real time, as it is being acquired.

Data visualizations show a story in the numbers. They help audiences make sense of vast amounts of information, showing aspects to the story that might not be apparent otherwise. Data by itself is cold and not that interesting. Visualizations help bring it alive. Visualizations can be as simple as a chart or as complicated as a multimedia-enhanced tour in Google Earth.

The best visualizations do two things:

- They offer a simple, compelling snapshot of data.
- They provide a way to explore deeper meaning contained in that data.

Visualizations should always have a point. They should support the narrative and show a meaningful aspect of the story that isn't presented elsewhere in the content. They should never be gimmicky or be an end unto themselves.

Visualizations are especially valuable in helping to tell the stories of real people. An intensity map might show hot spots around the country where high proportions of homeowners are defaulting on their mortgages (see Figure 20.1). A timeline might show how seemingly minor discoveries by individual researchers culminated years later in a major scientific breakthrough.

A table of figures shows exact values, but a visualization shows the big picture. Memorable visualizations make us go "Wow! I never saw the story that way."

The New York Times: The Life and Death of Movies

Every week entertainment reporters announce revenue figures showing how new movies either blow past box office expectations or tank on opening weekend. But

Figure 20.1 NPR.org published this intensity map of foreclosure rates in January 2010.

what does an opening-weekend draw of $3.3 million really mean? The *New York Times* (2008) looked at box office receipts for hundreds of movies from 1986 to 2008 with a Flash-based interactive graphic called "The Ebb and Flow of Movies" (see Figure 20.2). The visualization, called a *stream graph*, shows movie revenues as water-like waves, making a big splash on opening weekend, and then subsiding over time. The height of the wave represents revenue peaks, but the roll of the wave shows its longevity in theatres. The result offers amazing insight into how some movies embed themselves in popular consciousness.

Scroll through the timeline and the visualization shows two movies opening within weeks of each other in the summer of 1994: *Forrest Gump* and *Clear and Present Danger*. The latter, an action movie starring Harrison Ford and Willem Dafoe, beat *Forrest Gump*'s opening-week revenues, but the splash was short-lived. In contrast, the "wave" representing Tom Hanks's comedic drama rolls on and on persistently for months, finally subsiding from theatres nearly a year later.

Users can click on each movie to read a short synopsis or click on a link to a *New York Times* review. They can search for their favourite movie or browse by year. The resulting interactive portrays the life and death of first-run movies in a way that has never been shown before.

TOOLS & TIPS

Reporting with Visuals

"While reporting, ask yourself whether there might be angles to the story which would lend themselves to being stored as rows and columns which can later be analyzed, assessed, and displayed as charts and graphs," says Scot Hacker (2009), webmaster for the Knight Digital Media Center.

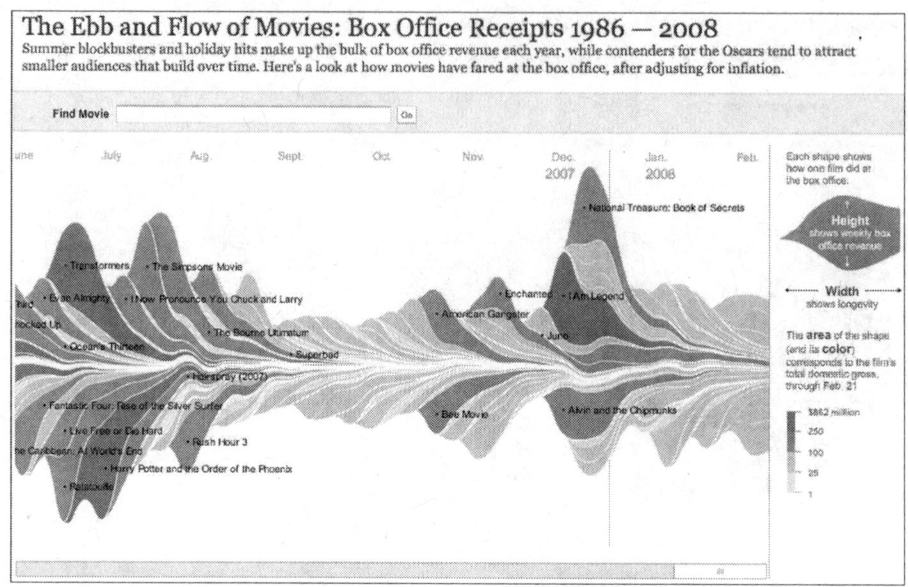

Figure 20.2 The *New York Times* published this interactive stream graph to show how movies fared at the box office from 1986 to 2008, adjusting for inflation. © 2008 New York Times Graphics.

Types of Data Visualizations

The data visualization tools at your disposal range from simple to complex—from static to highly interactive. A discussion of a few of the most popular ones follows.

Word Clouds

Word clouds—sometimes called *wordles*—extract recurring words from a document and show the most common ones in larger type. The result is a map that shows the relative prominence of each word in a document. In speeches, word clouds can reveal the specific words a speaker emphasizes and can highlight key points of a message, which might not be apparent otherwise.

The *National Post* used word clouds in December 2009 to visualize speeches delivered by US presidents Barack Obama and George W. Bush (NP Editor 2009). On December 1, 2009, Obama delivered a speech committing an additional 30,000 soldiers to Afghanistan. On January 10, 2007, Bush made a speech committing 20,000 additional troops to fight in Iraq. The two word clouds offer insight into how each president made his case to the American people (see Figure 20.3 for the word cloud of Obama's speech).

You need to be careful about how you interpret word clouds. This visualization groups words rather than concepts or themes, which the speaker might phrase differently each time he or she refers to them. But even though this tool is static, it provides a visually interesting and insightful means of telling a story.

Figure 20.3 On December 1, 2009, the *National Post* published word clouds to compare a speech by US President Barack Obama on military efforts in Afghanistan with a speech in 2007 by former US president George W. Bush on military efforts in Iraq. This word cloud represents Obama's speech.

Charts

Figures in a table show us exact values. But a column of numbers to three decimal places often fails to show meaning. Charts sacrifice numeric detail to highlight trends and comparisons visually.

Pie chart: It presents data as a proportion of a whole. It's a simple visualization best used for displaying relative values at a glance. It can be used to show how many people voted for each option on a ballot or how a total budget is distributed across the divisions in a company. Be sure to include detailed labels in a pie chart because the size of sections other than halves, quarters, or thirds can be difficult to judge. (See Figure 20.4.)

Bar chart: It provides a simple means of showing relative sizes, usually between things you can count using whole numbers. Bar charts show data as stepped, not continuous, values. For example, a bar chart could show the number of Honda SUVs sold each month. It could also show multiple sets of data such as sales of Honda, Ford, and GM SUVs each month. Keep them simple—25 bars look crowded—and, if you use multiple data sets, make sure you're using the same units. (See Figure 20.5.)

Bubble chart: It uses circles to show the orders of magnitude among values in a data set. It can be used to show the relative size of sectors in an economy or the popularity of religions worldwide. It's best used to present data sets with many values in a wide range. (See Figure 20.6.)

Line chart: It connects values to show trends, usually over time. It's often used to show changes in the value of a currency or stock. An *area chart* shows the area below the line as a coloured block to allow the display of multiple sets of data. (See Figure 20.7.)

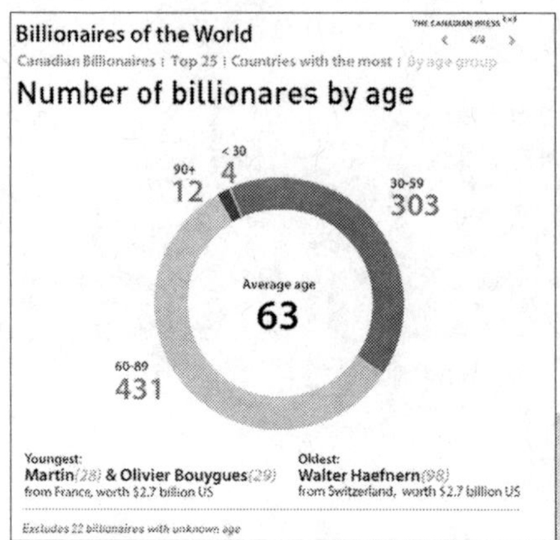

Figure 20.4

Figure 20.5

Figure 20.6

CBC.ca published a Canadian Press visualization in 2009 using a pie chart (Figure 20.4), a bar chart (Figure 20.5), and a bubble map (Figure 20.6) to show the relative wealth of Canada's billionaires.

Figure 20.7 *USA TODAY* used line charts and pie charts to visualize presidential approval ratings.

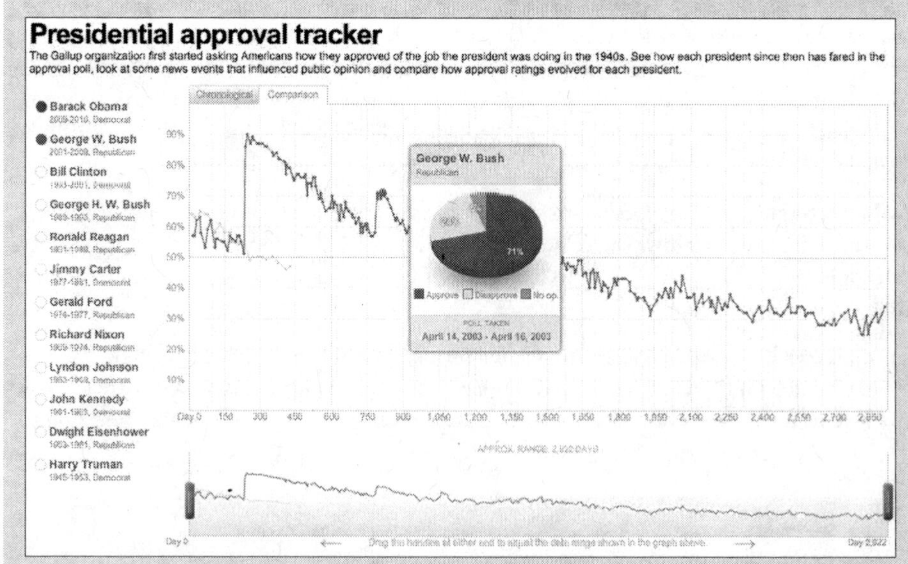

IN PRACTICE

Using a Network Diagram to Show Corporate Structures

John Bowman is an associate producer at CBC.ca and author of "Network Map of Media Ownership in Canada" (2009). The author spoke with him about his experience in using a network diagram—a bubble chart with connector lines—to show the corporate relationships among media properties.[1]

In June 2009, John Bowman was thinking about how he could explain to his readers the intricacies of media ownership in Canada.

He thought first about a simple interactive graphic: Click on the logo of a parent company, such as Torstar or Canwest, to see a description of the company and a list of the media outlets it owns. But that didn't seem like the best way to show the hierarchy of companies or the relationships among them.

He remembers thinking, "We really need to see how this plays out as a web—who owns what in a visual way. Because just showing and clicking doesn't really tell you that story."

So he turned to a site called Many Eyes (manyeyes.alphaworks.ibm.com), which was developed by IBM in 2007. It's a data visualization tool that aims to harness "the power of human visual intelligence to find patterns" in complex sets of data.

Visualizations, he says, allow journalists to display information in a way they can't with simple lists or a narrative.

"You can write that TorStar is one of the five corporate owners of CTV Globemedia, along with Bell Canada Enterprises. But to actually see all the relationships that happen there ... it tells a story that you can't tell with just a chart or a table."

Bowman settled on a map template called a *network diagram* that was built to show computer networks or social relationships among people. It wasn't exactly what he needed, but he figured it could accurately describe corporate relationships too. Users could zoom in on particular bubbles of information and click on them to show coloured lines highlighting how they relate to other bubbles.

So he created a data set in a spreadsheet that was essentially a two-column table showing what each company owned—and who owned it. He uploaded it to the site and Many Eyes produced a basic visualization. Bowman then had to tinker with the table to "tease out" the finer relationships. (See Figure 20.8.)

The result, he said, revealed some surprises.

"I already knew the broad strokes of who owned what. But it was interesting to see three different companies owning a particular cable channel or the fact that one company can own one CBC affiliate and one CTV affiliate. Those little branching lines are shown in the visualization. If you knew what you

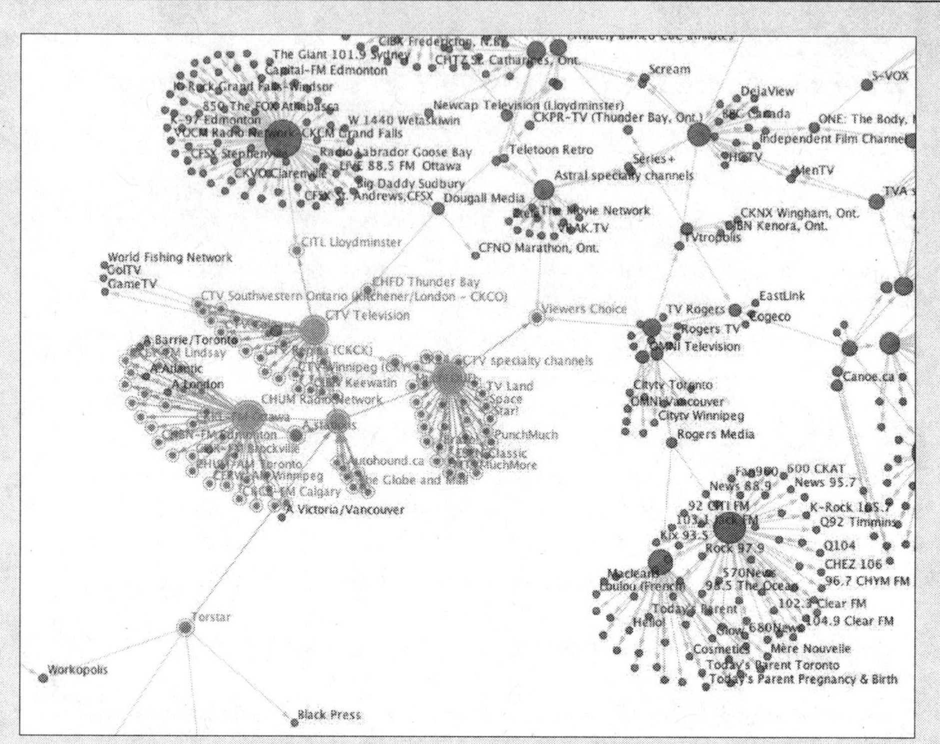

Figure 20.8 CBC.ca used an interactive network diagram to show media ownership in Canada in 2009.

were looking for, you could see how in one town there would be one company that owns all three of the TV stations and a couple of the papers. Things like that pop out."

However, the tool was far from perfect. Bowman said the project required a lot of work and, ultimately, it didn't do an ideal job of showing the hierarchy of ownership.

"The big dots are things like Canwest community papers, where there are a hundred papers under that. So they dominate visually," he says. But the number of publications a company owns doesn't accurately represent the numbers of people who read it or its influence. The visualization was good at showing relationships, he says, but it didn't reveal the full dominance exercised by a few companies in Canada's media landscape.

Still, Bowman says the tools available to journalists get better each year. He sees an evolving breed of programmer-journalists who use object-oriented programming languages such as Python or more specific ones geared to data visualizations such as Processing.

How do you get started? Become proficient with a spreadsheet program such as Excel, he says, keep abreast of what news organizations are using by following blogs and Twitter streams and "find out what free tools are out there."

Timelines

Mention a bunch of dates in audio and you may as well invite people to tune out. Even in text, long lists of dates and events attract only information diggers and can muddy a narrative. However, interactive timelines can layer text and multimedia for users to explore, exposing the arc of history in a simple but rich storyline (see Figure 20.9). Timelines are among the most simple and effective ways to enhance an online story.

When creating a timeline, the temptation can be to pack in events. The result can be clutter and confusion. Don't set the stage for disorder by picking a topic that's too broad—make sure you have a tight focus.

Figure 20.9 The *Globe and Mail* tackled the issue of detainee transfers in Afghanistan in this interactive multimedia timeline from 2005 to 2009. Some events have audio clips embedded.

Maps

Location-based data is almost certainly going to be a huge part of journalism's future. On the supply side, the amount of geographically tagged content is exploding as more people use GPS-enabled devices, such as cameras that record the exact location where a photo was taken. On the demand side, people increasingly want stories that show them how events affect not just their city, but also their neighbourhood and their street. Both of these trends highlight the importance of maps. Data in maps can show patterns that occur in geographic space. Maps can take a few different forms.

Country or region maps: These maps include political boundaries. A colour-coded map is a simple visualization that can indicate which countries share similar attributes. An *intensity map*, a more complex variation, highlights geographic regions with gradations of colour that represent different intensities of particular numeric values. Darker colours show higher values, whereas lighter values show lower values. You might use a geographic intensity map to show income levels by postal code or life expectancy by country. Be careful when using these maps—the relative importance of large regions that dominate visually can be overstated.

IN PRACTICE

Using Maps to Show Patterns Related to Geography

Patrick Cain is a web editor at TheStar.com and editor of Map of the Week, an ongoing series of interactive maps at thestar.blogs.com/maps/. The author spoke with him about his experience in using maps as stand-alone features.[2]

One of the most popular maps Patrick Cain created for the *Toronto Star* is one showing incidences of impaired driving in Toronto.

Cain obtained the data from Ontario's Ministry of Transportation by filing an access-to-information request. He then mapped the ratio of driver's licence suspensions for impaired driving in 2007 by postal code in the Toronto metropolitan area. The results were remarkable (see Figure 20.10).

While there was an "extremely consistent pattern" of rural suburbs having higher rates than urban centres, he says, the effect of available public transit was stark.

"If you superimpose the subway lines on the map, the 'low' area is visually striking. There's no instance of a Toronto subway station being in a high postal code for impaired driving," he says. "There does seem to be a relationship between impaired driving and urban form."

Cain began Map of the Week in spring 2008. Since then, the site has mapped street racing, bike accidents, university admissions, and dog ownership. The goal is to "reflect the city through as many lenses as possible," he says. "To show data that has never been seen before."

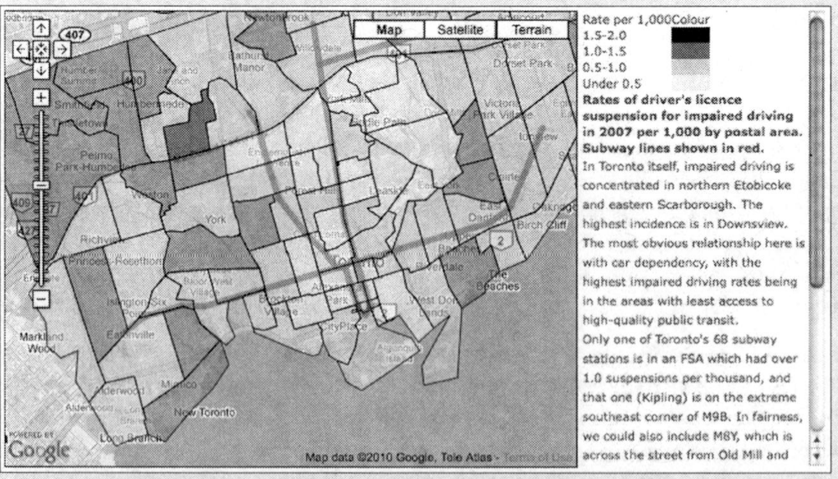

Figure 20.10 The *Toronto Star* published a Map of the Week on driver's licence suspensions for impaired driving in the Toronto metropolitan area in 2007.

He argues he's simply allowing the data to tell the story—and traditional storytelling forms aren't well suited to that.

"Some things don't lend themselves to the traditional article format. The project actually started with this article I kept pitching about where people's dogs are. It became clear that it just worked better as an interactive graphic than as a traditional story with a pyramid lede and three people and an authorized knower."

Cain says he doesn't tackle the "why" aspect to the story. It's an entirely different area of investigation. As well, in many cases, he says, the person he'd put the question to would likely have never heard of the data until he introduced it.

Unlike stories, which have a short life in terms of popularity, the maps have proven consistently popular over time, no matter when they were created, Cain says. Part of the reason for their continued popularity is that Cain links to them again and again as issues resurface in news coverage.

Another map that has proven popular is the map of homicides in the Greater Toronto Area. "Homicide maps show a very striking pattern, especially if you look at homicides of male victims. They are very, very tied to geography. Something happens across the face of the city. They happen in one place. They don't happen in other places."

Similarly, a map of postal codes containing high numbers of births to single mothers shows a stark band beginning in the northwest of the city, cutting across downtown and spreading east into Scarborough.

"[This] is exactly the low-income Toronto map. Period. That is what it looks like," he says. "The male victim homicide map is exactly that pattern. Sometimes you look at that and think 'Oh yeah, that's familiar.'"

Cain merges spreadsheets to apply geographic coordinates to the data. He then creates the visualization by using Keyhole Markup Language (KML) and an enterprise version of Google Maps. Picking up the technology is not difficult, given a range of books and web resources on the subject, he says. "You can always figure out the technology," he says. "What you need to learn are basic journalism question-asking skills. If I were to file a freedom of information request, what would I get from it? What am I expecting to see? What might I want to show and how might I get the information? The big thing is having an idea. What do you want to show and why."

Map of the Week was a 2009 Notable Entry in the Knight-Batten Awards for Innovations in Journalism.

Google Maps: These popular, easy-to-create maps are a category unto themselves. Describing a location in text just doesn't compare to seeing it from the sky or on a map. Stories about natural disasters, parade routes, zoning, or park land can usually benefit from an interactive Google Map. See the sidebar "In Practice: Using Maps to Show Patterns Related to Geography" to grasp the potential of Google Maps.

Google Earth: This geographic information program is more than a mapping service. It's part multimedia and part data visualization. Journalists are still experimenting with its capacity to tell stories. See the sidebar "In Practice: Using Google Earth to Profile a Country" to understand some of its possibilities.

Finally, we can combine types of data visualization to communicate complex ideas. The stream graph in the *New York Times*'s movie-revenue visualization, for example, is the combination of an area graph and a timeline. A *bubble map*, shown in Figure 20.6, is a combination of a map and a bubble chart. For more on this type of hybrid visualization, see the sidebar "In Practice: Using a Network Diagram to Show Corporate Structures" on page 301.

IN PRACTICE

Using Google Earth to Profile a Country

Ruby Buiza is a web producer at CBC.ca and the producer of "A Narrated Google Earth Tour of Afghanistan" (CBC 2009b). The author spoke with her about using Google Earth in a multimedia story about Canada's military effort in Afghanistan.[3]

By August 2009, producers at CBC.ca had been looking for a way to use Google Earth as a storytelling tool. The 3D map and geographic information program was well known for its "flyover" effect that virtually transports users across the globe before plunking them down at a precise location. A cool effect, to be sure. But they hadn't yet found a narrative that made good use of the application.

"Tools are great," says web producer Ruby Buiza. "But I've always believed that content is key. Having a fancy-schmancy tool doesn't do much if the content isn't there."

That summer, the news unit had been working on Crossroads Afghanistan, a special multimedia section of the site focusing on Canada's military effort (CBC 2009a). The producers' usual practice was to put together a Quick Facts page—a mix of text and photos that gives readers a brief summary of an issue, including links to previous coverage. But Google Earth seemed like a better fit. "Even though our troops are in Afghanistan, I think a lot of people don't know much about the actual country itself. Letting them see the main points of interest as well as the basic background information—population, what the possible problems are—helps give the user a better understanding of what's actually going on." Buiza hadn't used Google Earth before, so she spent about two weeks putting together the feature—while working on her other editing duties. The work included gathering images and text, recording an audio narrative, and creating a text file structured in Keyhole Markup Language (KML) that specified geographic coordinates.

The result was "A Narrated Google Earth Tour of Afghanistan." At its heart, it was an audio tour of Afghanistan illustrated with photos. But the Google Earth interface gave users the ability to travel—to zoom, change perspectives, and move in 3D. Clickable place marks popped up facts about certain cities and offered links to videos and text. The overall package offered users an in-depth, interactive look at the geography, economy, and people that shape Canada's involvement there.

"It's multimedia the way people would like to use it," says Buiza. "It's like a movie. You're hoping to be able to take your user and get them inside that movie with you."

She says the strength of the interactive tool is its non-linear structure for storytelling. Users can follow their own interest. "I think that freedom is one thing a lot of people really like about the tool," she says. "If they don't want to listen to the narration, they can stop at any point and click on any marker you've left for them so they can investigate it at their own pace."

Buiza says a major downside to the tool is that users have to install the Google Earth browser plug-in before they launch the tour. Plug-ins are a barrier for audiences. An installation forces users to take a minute or so out of their surfing experience, and plug-ins require a restart of the browser. Some users also worry about security and performance issues associated with plug-ins.

"If I have to install something it had better be worth it. There has to be real content in there," she says. Overall, Buiza says audience feedback suggested people were more engaged using the tour than if they had just read a regular Quick Facts page. So, should journalists be clamouring for courses in KML? Buiza says no—the most important thing for journalists is to understand the capabilities of their visualization tool so they can find the right content for it.

"Journalism is the most important thing," she says. "Get the story right first. The tools you can always learn."

Choosing the Right Format

There is no one data structure or technology for data visualizations. Many different file formats exist, and a number of tools are available to create them. You simply need to try them out on your own to see how they work. An interactive visualization may achieve ease of use, but there are downsides. Many visualizations require a browser plug-in—usually Adobe's Flash. Almost all desktop computers come with Flash preinstalled. But Flash doesn't work on all mobile devices, and many Flash graphics do not scale well on the small screens of mobile and tablet PCs. Further, using a plug-in usually keeps the content from being indexed by search engines. So search engines such as Bing or Google will index words in a text-based timeline on a standard web page. But usually only the title and description of a Flash interactive will appear in the results of a search query.

Career Opportunities

Interactive editors are a new breed of journalists. They straddle the production and newsgathering departments of the newsroom. An editor is part data-wizard, part coder, all storyteller.

The career opportunities for interactive editors are bright and getting brighter all the time. At large media outlets, journalists work with designers and programmers to create highly detailed, graphically rich, and customizable visualizations. The *New York Times*, for example, is a leader in interactive content. Visit global.nytimes.com frequently to see how complex visualizations add depth to stories.

If you're working at a smaller news outlet, or if you're on your own, you'll need knowledge of spreadsheets, databases, and markup languages such as Keyhole Markup Language. If you do in-depth work, you will need to learn skills that involve manipulating data to show patterns—sometimes called *computer-assisted reporting* (see Chapter 10, "Practical Research and Web Navigation Skills"). These skills may sound intimidating, but a little interest goes a long way. Many of the leading interactive editors today don't consider themselves technical experts. Visualization tools—many of them free—are evolving constantly, becoming more intuitive and easier to use by those with no background in programming at all. These free tools—by Google and others—won't give you the flexibility to create highly customizable visualizations, but they will allow you to create professional-looking content.

No matter where you work, the key skill you need is a journalistic mindset—curiosity to identify a story, persistence to find data, skepticism to understand data's limits, and dedication to put all the pieces together.

NOTES

1. John Bowman (associate producer, *CBC.ca*), in a telephone interview with Tim Currie, October 2, 2009.
2. Patrick Cain (web editor, *TheStar.com*), in a telephone interview with Tim Currie, September 25, 2009.
3. Ruby Buiza (web producer, *CBC.ca*), in a telephone interview with Tim Currie, October 27, 2009.

DISCUSSION QUESTIONS

1. How would you use data visualization tools to cover an earthquake? An election campaign?
2. Should data visualization skills be taught in journalism school? Why or why not?
3. What are the advantages/disadvantages to telling stories interactively?

SUGGESTED RESOURCES

Data Visualization

FlowingData. http://flowingdata.com.

Hacker, Scot. 2009. Data visualization for non-programmers. Knight Digital Media Center. http://multimedia.journalism.berkeley.edu/tutorials/intro-dataviz/.

New York Times Visualization Lab. http://vizlab.nytimes.com.

Vancouver's Open Data Catalogue. http://data.vancouver.ca.

Word Clouds

Wordle. http://wordle.net.

Charts

Google Charts API. http://code.google.com/apis/chart/image_charts.html.

Google Visualization Gadgets. http://code.google.com/apis/visualization/documentation/usinggadgets.html.

Many Eyes. http://manyeyes.alphaworks.ibm.com.

Timelines

Dipity. http://dipity.com.

Timetoast. http://www.timetoast.com.

Maps

Google Chart Tools/Image Charts (aka Chart API). http://code.google.com/apis/chart/docs/gallery/map_charts.html.

Google Earth. http://earth.google.com.

Google Maps. http://maps.google.com.

Map of the Week. http://thestar.blogs.com/maps/.

REFERENCES

Bowman, John. 2009. Network map of media ownership in Canada. *CBC.ca*, June 10. http://www.cbc.ca/money/story/2009/06/05/f-canada-media-ownership-network-map.html.

CBC. 2009a. Crossroads Afghanistan. *CBC.ca*. http://www.cbc.ca/crossroads-afghanistan/.

CBC. 2009b. A narrated Google Earth tour of Afghanistan. *CBC.ca*, August 19. http://www.cbc.ca/crossroads-afghanistan/story/2009/08/19/f-afghan-googleearthtour.html.

Hacker, Scot. 2009. Data visualization for non-programmers. Knight Digital Media Center. http://multimedia.journalism.berkeley.edu/tutorials/intro-dataviz/.

Markoff, John. 2008. The passion of Steve Jobs. *New York Times* Bits, January 15. http://bits.blogs.nytimes.com/2008/01/15/the-passion-of-steve-jobs/.

New York Times. 2008. The ebb and flow of movies: Box office receipts 1986—2008. February 23. http://www.nytimes.com/interactive/2008/02/23/movies/20080223_REVENUE_GRAPHIC.html.

Nielsen, Jakob. 1997. Alertbox: Why web users scan instead of read. Useit.com. http://www.useit.com/alertbox/whyscanning.html.

Nielsen, Jakob. 2008. Alertbox: Writing style for print vs. web. Useit.com, June 9. http://www.useit.com/alertbox/print-vs-online-content.html.

NP Editor. 2009. Graphic: Bush vs. Obama, two speeches on war. *National Post*, December 1. http://network.nationalpost.com/np/blogs/posted/archive/2009/12/01/graphic-bush-vs-obama-two-speeches-on-war.aspx.

IMAGE SOURCES

FIGURE 20.1: NPR. 2010. Interactive map: The economy where you live. January. http://www.npr.org/templates/story/story.php?storyId=111494514.

FIGURE 20.2: *New York Times*. 2008. The ebb and flow of movies: Box office receipts 1986–2008. February 23. http://www.nytimes.com/interactive/2008/02/23/movies/20080223_REVENUE_GRAPHIC.html. Reprinted by permission.

FIGURE 20.3: NP Editor. 2009. Graphic: Bush vs. Obama, two speeches on war. *National Post*, December 1. http://network.nationalpost.com/np/blogs/posted/archive/2009/12/01/graphic-bush-vs-obama-two-speeches-on-war.aspx.

FIGURES 20.4, 20.5, 20.6: Canadian Press. 2009. Billionaires of the world. *CBC.ca*. http://www.cbc.ca/news/interactives/cp-billionaires/. Reprinted by permission of The Canadian Press.

FIGURE 20.7: Couch, William, Kristen Novak, Michelle Price, and Joshua Hatch. 2009. Presidential approval tracker. *USA TODAY*, July 20. http://www.usatoday.com/news/washington/presidential-approval-tracker.htm.

FIGURE 20.8: Bowman, John. 2009. Network map of media ownership in Canada. *CBC.ca*, June 10. http://www.cbc.ca/money/story/2009/06/05/f-canada-media-ownership-network-map.html.

FIGURE 20.9: *Globe and Mail*. 2009. Tracking Afghan detainee transfers. December. http://www.theglobeandmail.com/news/politics/tracking-afghan-detainee-transfers/article1393402/. Reprinted by permission.

FIGURE 20.10: *Toronto Star*. 2010. The Toronto impaired driving map. Map of the Week. http://www3.thestar.com/static/googlemaps/starmaps.html?xml=081201_impairedweek2_toronto.xml.

PART FOUR
Responsibilities

CHAPTER 21

Ethics for the New Mainstream

Stephen J.A. Ward

CHAPTER OUTLINE

Introduction

A media revolution is transforming, fundamentally and irrevocably, the nature of journalism and its ethics.

Our media ecology is a chaotic landscape evolving at a furious pace. Professional journalists share the journalistic sphere with tweeters, bloggers, citizen journalists, and social media users. Amid every revolution, new possibilities emerge while old practices are threatened. Today is no exception. The economics of professional journalism struggles as audiences migrate online. Shrinkage of newsrooms creates concern for the future of journalism. Yet these fears also prompt experiments in journalism, such as non-profit centres of investigative journalism.

These changes challenge the foundations of journalism ethics. The challenge runs deeper than debates about one or another principle, such as objectivity. It is greater than specific problems, such as how to verify content from citizens (Friend and Singer 2007). The revolution requires us to rethink assumptions. What can ethics *mean* for a profession that must provide instant news and analysis, where everyone with a modem is a publisher?

Journalism ethics is troubled by a tension among values on two levels. The first level is online journalism. The culture of traditional journalism, which emphasizes accuracy, pre-publication verification, balance, impartiality, and gatekeeping, rubs up against the culture of online journalism, which emphasizes immediacy, transparency, partiality, non-professional journalists, and post-publication correction. The second level is global journalism. If journalism has global impact, what are its global responsibilities (Ward and Wasserman 2010)? When international issues arise, should journalists be patriotic and promote the interests of their own country, or should they report as global citizens who promote fair responses to global issues?

Whither ethics in a world of multimedia, global journalism?

Journalism ethics must do more than point out tensions. Theoretically, it must untangle the conflicts between values. It must decide which principles should be preserved or invented. Practically, it should provide new standards to guide online and offline journalism.

This chapter proposes a framework for understanding the current revolution in journalism. I explain the status of journalism ethics today according to my theory of ethical revolutions. I argue that we are moving toward what I call an ethics for a new mainstream media, an ethics for multiple media platforms. The old mainstream consisted of professionals working for large newspapers and broadcasters. The new mainstream is a hybrid of professionals and amateurs working for media outlets that integrate both old and new forms of journalism. I conclude by showing how an ecumenical ethics is one approach to constructing a new ethics.

Ethical Revolutions

From Conflict to Integration

Journalism ethics is applied ethics. It is the articulation and analysis of the aims and principles of responsible journalism and their application to situations. Journalism ethics attempts to answer the practical question: What should journalists do in general, and in situations *x*, *y*, and *z*? For example, should a photojournalist invade the privacy of a politician? How graphic should images of war be? How much verification does a damaging story need? Do journalists best serve democracy by being objective or partisan?

Over the centuries, journalism values have been articulated by codes of ethics, editors' statements on controversial stories, and ethics textbooks. Journalists also have helped to construct entire theories (or systems) of journalism ethics, from the liberal theory of the press in the 19th century to the ethics of professional journalism in the 20th century.

What is a revolution in journalism ethics? A revolution is "any fundamental change or reversal of conditions."[1] During political revolutions, a system of governance is replaced by another. In scientific revolutions, a conceptual system is superseded by another; for example, Newtonian physics gave way to the relativistic physics of Einstein. In an ethical revolution, a system of norms replaces another. A revolution in journalism ethics, then, is a fundamental change in the prevailing ethical system. Principles are reinterpreted or they give way to new principles. Value change does not occur *ex nihilo*. It is caused by changes in the socio-economic, technological, and political environment. For example, the 1960s' social revolution, which stressed peace and equality—not to mention "sex, drugs, and rock and roll"—was prompted by a growing economy and education system, communication technology, the civil rights movement, and resistance to the Vietnam War. Revolutions create new opportunities, new attitudes, and new problems. Existing norms may fail to express the spirit of the times and seem irrelevant. This shift in values is captured by slogans, from the 1960s' "Make Love, Not War" to today's "Broadcast Yourself." Yet, the far-reaching implications of this shift may go unrecognized.

By analogy, revolutions in journalism ethics are caused by changes in the socio-economic, technological, and political environment that create new opportunities, new attitudes, and new problems. The far-reaching consequences of the shift for journalism are difficult to ascertain.

Revolutions are exceptional events. Therefore, we should distinguish between what Kuhn (1962) called (with respect to science) revolutionary and normal periods. During normal periods, scientists share a paradigm of methods, assumptions, and theories. During revolutionary periods, the paradigm comes under attack and new conceptual schemes are put forward. A crisis occurs. Confusion reigns until a new paradigm is constructed and signals a new normal period. Adapting Kuhn's ideas to journalism, we can say that during normal periods, such as the dominance of objective reporting in the early 1900s, journalists share a common understanding of their aims, values, and methods. Ethical issues are discussed by reference to this paradigm. However, over time, the paradigm comes under criticism and new forms of journalism emerge. A crisis occurs. Journalism in this century has followed a similar pattern, moving from a period of consensus on professional, objective reporting to a period of non-consensus on the ethics of journalism as objectivity is questioned. It has entered a revolutionary phase of conflicting values, methods, and practices. Eventually, a new consensus will be established around a new paradigm, a new normative system. Journalism ethics will return to a normal phase.

The normal-revolutionary scheme provides an abstract framework for understanding some forms of revolution. We can deepen our understanding of the revolution in journalism ethics by noting two other features: One, in a revolution, the relationship between journalists and their public changes fundamentally. Two, the revolution typically passes through three stages: conflict, rapprochement, and integration. Let's consider each of these two points.

What is this relationship between journalists and the public, and why is it important to journalism ethics? The relationship is defined by the manner in which journalists communicate with, and serve, their public. The journalist–public relationship has three elements: (1) journalists, (2) the public, and (3) how the two groups communicate, such as the technology used by journalists to deliver the news. For brevity's sake, let's call this relationship the "j-c-p" (journalists–communication methods–public).

Across journalism history, new forms of journalism have created new relationships. The relationship between the 17th-century London editor and his readers is vastly different from the relationship of 20th-century professional journalists and their mass audience. Embedded in the j-c-p is a set of expectations that constitutes a social contract. The public recognizes the freedom of the press. In return, they expect journalists to perform certain information functions according to certain norms. Like any successful relationship, there must be trust and credibility on both sides.

Historically, journalism ethics grew out of journalists' need to maintain a healthy j-c-p. Editors claimed to reliably report the truth or to be objective to maintain public confidence in their publications, to explain new practices, and to defend controversial decisions. Journalism ethics in any given era is the norms that define the journalist–public relationship. A revolution in journalism ethics occurs when technological and social changes alter journalism and the journalist–public relationship.

A revolution in journalism ethics tends to follow the three-step process of conflict, rapprochement, and integration. During a period of conflict, social and technological trends prompt new forms of journalism. But not just any new forms will do. The new forms need to be so different as to alter substantially the j-c-p and create a crisis—a clash of values.[2] The conflict destroys the ethical consensus of the previous normal period. Many journalists divide into two camps—the mainstream versus the non-mainstream. A war of rhetoric ensues between the practitioners of the old and the new journalism. Traditionalists accuse the new journalism of being irresponsible or of not being journalism at all. The new journalists claim that traditional journalism is doomed. They are the "real" journalists of a new, bold era. Meanwhile, citizens change their media habits. They become accustomed to the new media and use journalism in new ways. The j-c-p begins to change, and the public itself debates the ethics of the old and the new media.

As the ideological battle runs its course, economic and other realities encourage a rapprochement between traditional and new media. Mainstream media do not disappear. They evolve, if slowly and awkwardly, by incorporating new forms of media and their editorial and publishing techniques. Journalists, who now use both old and new media, begin to seek common ground. The conflict between old and new media abates, the hot rhetoric cools, the line between old and new media blurs.

Eventually, rapprochement leads to integration across the media system. What emerges after a difficult transition is journalism that is a synthesis of old and new practices, guided by a new system of ethics that is a synthesis of old and new norms.

From Partisan to Objective Journalists

Examples of ethical revolutions can be found across the 400-year history of modern journalism. In this section, I examine only one—the creation of a professional ethics for the mass commercial press of the late 1800s and early 1900s. I selected this revolution because it created the ethics currently challenged by new media.

The creation of mass commercial newspapers at the end of the 19th century was a radical change in journalism, the prevailing j-c-p, and journalism ethics. In the 19th century, prior to mass commercial newspapers, the press in Europe and Canada fought a long battle to secure the right to publish free from undue restraint by law and censor. A liberal press, with its emphasis on a free marketplace of ideas, was established. By the end of the century, the small liberal newspaper, based on subscriptions and political support, gave way to a large mass commercial newspaper, based on mass circulation and mass advertising. Yet no sooner was the mass commercial newspaper—published by Pulitzer, Hearst, and others—ascendant on both sides of the Atlantic than doubts were raised about its ethics. The commercial press was accused of being sensational, irresponsible, and controlled by press barons and business interests. A rhetorical war ensued between the old elite journalism and the new "yellow" journalism.

By the turn of the 20th century, conflict began to give way to rapprochement and integration. Journalists formed associations that created a new ethics calling for accuracy, balance, and "just the facts." These demanding norms were thought necessary to reduce the blatant bias and lack of independence of journalists. The partisan libertarian approach to journalism was replaced by a professional model that stressed objectivity and impartiality. More and more newsrooms practised the new objective journalism until it became the new mainstream. The professional ethics was a synthesis of old and new. Freedom of the press became part of an ethics that called for verification, independence, and minimizing harm.[3]

The new journalism changed the j-c-p fundamentally. Journalists became powerful gatekeepers within large profit-seeking ventures. The public came to rely on newspapers as sources of information on most areas of society, from the legislature to the sports arena. Reporters were asked to provide accurate news for a public that demanded less partisan journalism. The j-c-p became a one-to-many, hierarchical form of mass communication.

Where Are We Today?

Normal and Revolutionary Periods

The ideas of normal and revolutionary periods, the j-c-p, and the principle of integration are tools for understanding revolutions in journalism. They tell us that we know we are entering a revolutionary phase when a consensus on the existing ethical paradigm starts to break down, and changes in technology and other factors radically alter the relationship between journalists and the public.

What do these ideas say about journalism today? They tells us that we are indeed in the middle of an ethical revolution. In fact, we are in the middle of the fifth revolution in journalism ethics since modern journalism began in the 17th century.[4] The rise of Internet-based media is a revolutionary event because it substantially alters the prevailing professional model of the j-c-p. The journalistic element of this relationship is transformed to include, for the first time, ordinary citizens in great numbers. It becomes a sphere of professionals and non-professionals of varying ability, training, and motivations. The communication element has been revolutionized by interactive and global media. The public term of the relationship is altered almost beyond recognition. Citizens are no longer the passive, dependent consumers of professional media. They have the technology to be active members of the j-c-p by creating content and using media tools to evaluate reports. Increasingly, citizens *are* the media.

Journalism occupies a progressively smaller portion of the public sphere, which is being enlarged by a chaotic and expanding media universe. This media universe has contributed to a period of conflict—a clash of values between the professional and new media models.

The professional model recognizes the worth of well-trained journalists who make sure their stories are accurate, verified, and well researched before publication. The story is the end product of an editorial process. Its authority depends mainly on the capabilities and character of the individual professional journalist. The ethical mantra is, "Filter, then publish," or "Get it [news] first, but first get it right." In contrast, new media value the speedy posting of information by anyone, even if there is uncertainty about its source or accuracy. The slogan is, "Publish, then filter." As a correction to inaccurate or bogus stories posted in haste, new media journalism recommends prepublication warnings about the uncertain verity of material. New media ethics emphasizes the remedial function of post-publication assessments of stories by a "community of interest"—the people who regularly visit a website or blog. The posted story is not the end of a process. It is the start of an online dialogue whereby everyone is free to critique the story and to enrich its sources, facts, and perspectives. Ideally, the authority of a new media story is not individual but communal. It must pass the scrutiny of online readers and experts around the world.

In the professional model, the public's role is to be an audience—to receive the completed story. In the new media model, journalism is considered to be a more cooperative project of citizens and journalists. The professional and new media models also differ on what sort of journalism democracy needs. The professional model thinks objective news reporting and well-informed analysis are essential for informed public decisions. The new media model favours a participatory model of democracy that is libertarian in spirit. A free and many-voiced marketplace of ideas, using the interactive medium of the Internet, is sufficient for democracy. What is crucial is the free expression and sharing of voices. New media communication is inclined toward opinion journalism and is suspicious of the ideal of objectivity. Rather than maintain an objective stance, new media journalists are transparent about their biases.

Signs of Rapprochement

This clash of values has received extensive comment in the media. What has received less attention is the fact that journalism ethics is emerging from this conflict. It is entering a stage of rapprochement.

One sign of rapprochement is the sense that new media are no longer new. They are part of our daily lives. At the same time, the line between new and old media blurs. Newspapers and major broadcasters are online and their websites are popular. They have their own bloggers, citizen journalists, podcasts, websites, Twitter feeds, Facebook pages, and interactive online forums. New media journalists write for traditional media. Successful bloggers attract large numbers of readers, resembling the influential newspaper columnists of a previous era. The distinction between big mainstream media and small, iconoclastic new media is fading as the leaders of the new mainstream become large, corporate, online enterprises, such as Google. Citizen journalism sites have become a permanent part of the media landscape. Partnerships between citizens and newsrooms are increasingly common with the advent of CNN iReport and the BBC's Your News. Citizens provide story ideas, video, eyewitness accounts, and other information. Non-profit centres for investigative journalism such as the Wisconsin Center for Investigative Journalism (WisconsinWatch.org) are collaborative in nature. Their newsrooms combine the talents of many types of journalists.

A rapprochement in ethics is also under way. We are moving toward a new system of ethics, a mixed-media ethics that defines responsible public journalism across media platforms. Recently, traditional news media such as the *Wall Street Journal*, *New York Times*, the BBC, the Associated Press, and the *Washington Post* have developed guidelines on how their journalists can responsibly use social media. Their guidelines encourage journalists to use social media, such as Facebook, but also to respect traditional values such as avoiding conflicts of interest. Bloggers and online journalists form associations and construct codes of ethics, engaging in the same ethics-creating exercise that occupied newspaper journalists a century ago.[5] The online codes are an interesting synthesis of old and new elements, reinterpreting—not rejecting—many of the major principles of professional journalism, such as truth seeking and independence.

The motivations for rapprochement are the same as in previous revolutions. Traditional media need to adapt to survive, and to serve the changing media habits of the public. Everyone wants to figure out how to make money from the public's appetite for online content and love of interactivity. Also, journalists and citizens grow increasingly critical of the rumours and misinformation on the Internet. They seek to carve out a media sphere where journalists can work according to appropriate standards.

Finally, integration appears as a worthy goal because no one form of journalism has all the virtues and the other all the vices. The virtue of the professional model is that, ideally, it supports reliable, professionally trained journalists dedicated to the public, thus maximizing accurate, unbiased news while reducing misinformation. The vice is that it places enormous influence in the hands of a privileged class of citizens (journalists) who work for powerful news organizations that may not care about ethics. The virtue of the new media model is that it places the freedom to publish in the hands of countless citizens. This freedom reduces the power of mainstream journalists and media owners. The vice is that new media cause both misinformation and information overload. The power of journalism can be exercised by anyone with any ethics and any motivation. Good journalism and reliable information become lost in a sea of unreliable voices. Weakening the economics of mainstream journalism results in layoffs for experienced journalists, reducing journalism's ability to act as watchdog on power.

For these reasons, the ethical task is to construct an ethics for the new mainstream that combines the virtues of both models.

The Future Shape of Journalism Ethics

Layered Journalism

What would an integrated ethics look like?

It will be the ethics of the integrated newsroom, a newsroom that practises layered journalism. Layered journalism brings together different forms of journalism and different types of journalists to produce a multimedia offering of professional-styled news and analysis combined with citizen journalism and interactive chat.

The newsroom will be layered vertically and horizontally. Vertically, there will be many layers of editorial positions. There will be citizen journalists and bloggers in the newsroom, or closely associated with the newsroom. Many contributors will work from countries around the world. Some will write for free, some will be equivalent to paid freelancers, others will be regular commentators. In addition, there will be different types of editors. Some editors will work with these new journalists, while other editors will deal with unsolicited images and text sent by citizens via email, websites, and Twitter. There will be editors or "community producers" charged with going out to neighbourhoods to help citizens use media to produce their own stories.

Horizontally, the future newsroom will be layered in terms of the types of journalism it produces, from print and broadcast sections to online production centres.

To be sure, newsrooms in the past have had vertical and horizontal layers. Newspaper newsrooms have ranged vertically from the editor-in-chief at the top to the cub

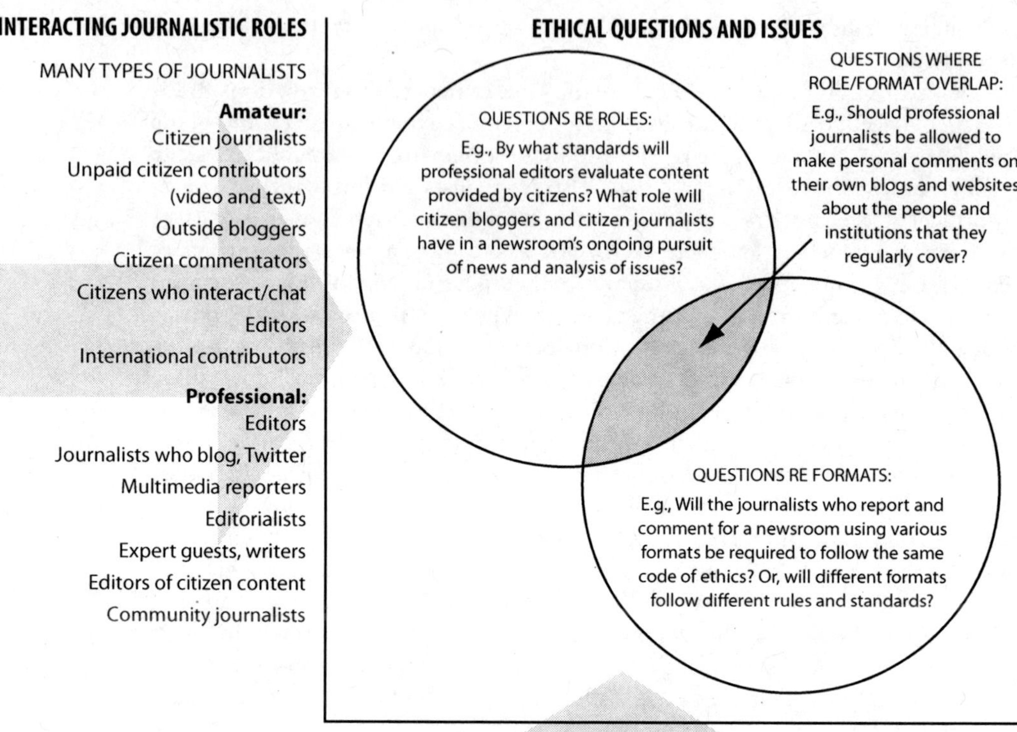

Figure 21.1 Ethics in the layered newsroom

reporter at the bottom. Horizontally, large mainstream newsrooms have produced several types of journalism, both print and broadcast. However, future newsrooms will have additional and different layers. Some news sites will continue to be operated by a few people dedicated only to one format, such as blogging. But a substantial portion of the new mainstream will consist of these complex, layered organizations (see Figure 21.1).

Layered journalism will confront two types of problems: vertical and horizontal. First, there will be "vertical" ethical questions about how the different layers of the newsroom, from professional editors to citizen freelancers, should interact to produce responsible journalism. For example, by what standards will professional editors evaluate the contributions of citizen journalists? Second, there will be "horizontal" questions about the norms for the various newsroom sections.

Ecumenical Ethics

The layered newsroom calls for an ecumenical approach to ethics. I borrow "ecumenical" from its original Christian context, which is a desire to find unity among the sects of Christianity. Ecumenicalism does not seek to impose a unity that ignores (or is intolerant of) differences. It recognizes differences within a common framework of values.

By analogy, ecumenicalism in journalism is the search for a unifying set of values that are realized in different ways by varying forms of journalism. Ecumenical ethics has two parts: (1) general aims and principles for all forms of journalism, and (2) specific standards and rules of practice for particular forms of journalism. Different forms of journalism will have different practices and express different values. However, these distinct practices and specific rules must be consistent with the general aim and principles of (1).

What aims and principles might form the ethical basis of a new ethics? An ecumenical ethics must provide a unifying conception of the aims of democratic journalism. I believe the unifying aim is this: All participants in the new journalism should promote a free and just democracy in which citizens flourish.[6] A new ethics must explain journalism's role in a media-linked global world. It needs to update well-worn phrases such as "journalism in the public interest." It should explain how serving the public interest now includes facilitating online deliberation, empowering citizens to participate in media and in civic life, and building bridges of understanding among groups in pluralistic democracies.

The aim of democratic journalism implies several fundamental beliefs. One belief is that a healthy public sphere should be as free as possible, and populated by many forms of communication and a diversity of communicators. Different forms of journalism fulfill different public functions. Differences in practices and values are expected, given the different aims and methods of communication.

Ecumenical ethics affirms the continuing need for, and central role of, journalism ethics. Ethics provides the aims and principles that restrain and channel the freedom to publish. Ecumenicalism is liberal but not libertarian. It believes that a free marketplace of ideas is a necessary but not sufficient condition for good journalism. It is not enough for democracy to have "many voices" linked by a sophisticated media system. Democracy depends on the quality of information exchanged, the manner in which citizens speak to each other, the knowledge and skills of their journalists, and media "spaces" where reasonable citizens can deliberate. Journalism ethics is about how journalists should use their freedom to publish to maximize reliable public information, informed commentary, and reasoned debate.

The aim of ecumenical ethics is to articulate a number of principles that all integrated newsrooms should embrace to promote the aforementioned aims. What might those principles be? Despite the current conflict of values, there is substantial common ground. I believe that reconstruction in ethics begins with a reaffirmation of truth and objectivity in journalism, although our conceptions of truth and objectivity must be recast to apply to layered journalism. Mainstream and new media journalists both agree on the goal of truth and its two parts—truth seeking and truth telling. Online and traditional journalists may disagree on how journalists should seek truth.

But few journalists would claim to not care about the truth. The principle of objectivity is more contentious. For objectivity to apply to mixed media, the traditional idea of news objectivity as a strictly neutral reporting of just the facts must be abandoned and replaced by pragmatic objectivity. Journalists practise pragmatic objectivity when they adopt a critical stance toward their own beliefs, and evaluate their stories for empirical validity, coherence, and other virtues of good journalism.[7] Objectivity as testing of interpretations is a flexible method that can apply in various ways and in various degrees to a wide range of journalism online and offline. Without a reaffirmation of truth and objectivity, journalism will lack the critical, independent, and non-partisan character that constitutes good public journalism.[8]

Beyond truth and objectivity, there are other areas of common ground to explore. The strong professional emphasis on editorial independence and the avoidance of conflicts of interest is not far from the ubiquitous stress on transparency among online writers. There is a good chance that rules for revealing and minimizing conflicts can be formulated that apply across media platforms. By integrating the values of professional independence and online transparency, journalists will advance another common value—media accountability.

These principles are not new. What is new is how they are to be understood and applied in the integrated newsroom. In the end, there may be deep differences over other principles, such as objectivity or restraining one's reporting to minimize harm. However, this overlap in major principles is a good start for the construction of a new ethics.

Ethics of Difference

Agreement on general aims and principles would not solve all problems. Integrated journalists would still face perplexing questions caused by different practices. Recall the vertical and horizontal issues of the layered newsroom. Even if all journalists subscribed to common principles such as truth seeking, should they cover stories in a similar manner, according to the same protocols? Should online journalists be allowed to publish stories before print reporters because of the speed of the Internet? Should a newspaper allow anonymous commentators on its website but refuse anonymity in its letters to the editor in the printed paper? When news reporters "tweet," can they be more opinionated than when they report for their paper?

These difficulties raise the following question: Is it ethically permissible for sections of layered newsrooms to operate according to different guidelines because of the distinct nature of their media platforms?

The answer to this question, in general, is yes, as long as: (1) the protocols reflect the nature of the medium; (2) it is clear to the public what form of journalism is being practised, including an understanding of its aim and its limits; and (3) the protocols do not violate the general aims and principles mentioned above. If conditions (1) to (3) are honoured, then ecumenical ethics allows different rules for distinct areas of journalism.

Why do I qualify my answer by insisting on conditions (1) to (3)? I qualify the answer because the question is difficult and there are dangers. One doesn't want to say that any practice is valid just because the medium makes the practice possible.

For example, I do not see how the reckless online posting of a false and damaging rumour could ever be ethically justified, even if the Internet makes possible the instantaneous circulation of rumours. A new media ethics should not tolerate the negative consequences of rumour journalism, such as the "fraudulent" posting to CNN iReport by a blogger that Apple founder, Steve Jobs, had suffered a severe heart attack (Blodget 2008). As we develop ecumenical ethics, we will have to work carefully, going from case to case, until we reach a deeper understanding of how the new mainstream ethics should allow diversity within unity.

There are cases where conditions (1) to (3) are satisfied, and old and new practices are integrated. Consider the vexing question of how newsrooms should use information supplied by citizens. It might appear that there can be no rapprochement between the practice of traditional journalism to not publish without verification and the practice of new media to post unverified video and text from little-known sources. Yet, rules for responsibly integrating these different practices can evolve.

For example, mainstream news coverage of demonstrations in Iran after the June 2009 presidential election indicate how it is possible to develop protocols for using unverified information from citizens. In Iran, professional foreign journalists were forbidden to cover "unauthorized" demonstrations. Meanwhile, Iranian citizens used Twitter, YouTube, cellphones, and text messaging to circulate pictures and commentary around the world. Major broadcasters, such as the BBC and CNN, used the information carefully. News anchors repeatedly explained to the public the limitations on their own journalists and why they were using citizen-generated information. They warned viewers that they could not verify the veracity of many of the images, or the identity of the sources. Although bogus and erroneous information was circulated by these means, vital information was also made public. The Iran coverage shows that the ecumenical search for combining old and new forms of journalism is possible and developing.

On what principle is ecumenical tolerance toward differences in editorial rules based? It is what I call the "principle of communicative intention": The norms of practice for any specific form of communication, including forms of journalism, are influenced by the nature and intent of the communication, as well as by what the public expects of this form of communication. So we should seek to shape the ethics of journalism to fit the communication form.

The validity of this principle was recognized, if implicitly, by traditional journalism ethics. Even at the height of news objectivity in the 1940s and 1950s, newspapers recognized the difference between reporting and column writing, between satirical journalism and news analysis, between investigative journalism and fashion reporting, and between feature writing and hard news reporting. Mainstream codes of ethics recognize these differences. For example, the codes for broadcasters contain protocols for approaching certain types of stories, such as broadcasting live from hostage takings, that are not found in newspaper codes of ethics. Nothing is amiss as long as readers are alerted to different forms of journalism by labelling them "analysis" or "opinion" and the protocols do not violate basic principles, such as truth telling. Similarly, we can argue that nothing is amiss if new media journalism follows different practices so long as the forms of journalism are clearly labelled, the public understands the communicative intent of the journalism, and the forms of journalism do not violate basic principles.

The ecumenical approach is inevitable, given the direction of journalism. It is unlikely that the vertical and horizontal questions of the layered newsroom will be resolved by insisting that the blogger, the tweeter, or the citizen journalist adhere completely to the more restrictive norms of practice that guide other forms of journalism, such as straight professional news reporting. Conversely, more traditional modes of journalism, such as verified reporting in high-quality papers, should not abandon the values that have long defined their medium. They should not simply opt for the more freewheeling practices of the Internet. The challenge is to maintain common values while showing how norms of practice can vary according to the medium.

Conclusion

This chapter has interpreted the direction of journalism ethics according to a three-step theory of ethical revolutions. It concluded that journalism ethics is entering a stage of rapprochement that will lead to an ethics for a new mainstream media, characterized by layered newsrooms. The chapter suggests that ecumenical ethics is one possible approach to the construction of a new ethics for multiple platforms.

In the end, what is the future of ethical journalism in an expanding media world? What can we reasonably hope for? What should we work toward? The future of ethical journalism depends on the creation of a core of public informers across all media platforms who are dedicated to responsible journalism in the public interest. This group will be an ethical anchor for a media system in danger of drifting further out into that sea of misinformation and partisan propaganda. This core must provide deliberative spaces where in-depth, unbiased, important journalism is produced by all forms of news media.

It is unrealistic to assume that all communicators will use their chosen medium in an ethical manner, especially not in an age where the number of citizen journalists and media producers grows exponentially. But if deliberative democracy is to be possible, a substantial group of practitioners across media platforms must remain committed to ethics and, in particular, committed to the creation of an ethics for the new mainstream.

NOTES

1. This is the ordinary dictionary definition of *revolution* (Barber 2004).
2. This is why I do not think the advent of radio and television news prompted a revolution in journalism ethics. It extended the professional model. Broadcast news followed the main principles of existing codes of ethics created by the newspapers a few decades before.
3. The classical example of this professional synthesis is the influential code of the Society of Professional Journalists, which emphasized truth telling, objectivity, independence, and the news–opinion distinction. A revision of the code in the 1990s added accountability.
4. In Ward (2005), I identified five ethical revolutions: the invention of journalism ethics in the 17th century, the "public ethic" of the Enlightenment press, the

liberal theory of the press in the 19th century, a professional ethics for the mass commercial press of the late 1800s, and the current mixed-media ethics.

5. Increasingly, there are attempts to systematically discuss and codify the practices of online media, through the creation of associations such as the Media Bloggers Association (www.mediabloggers.org) and the Online News Association (journalists.org). A well-known code by Jonathan Dube (2003) extends the principles of the Society of Professional Journalists to online journalism.
6. In Ward (forthcoming, Ch. 3), I argued that the type of democracy needed is deliberative democracy, promoted by a deliberative journalism.
7. In Ward (2005, Ch. 7) I presented the idea of pragmatic objectivity.
8. For my views on the reaffirmation of truth and objectivity, see "Reaffirming Truth and Objectivity" in Ward (forthcoming, Ch. 4).

DISCUSSION QUESTIONS

1. Do you think the trends in journalism, offline and online, are leading to a new mainstream media? What trends support this view? What trends don't support it?
2. What values do online and offline journalists share? Do you agree that they have enough in common to agree on a code of ethics?
3. If citizens are increasingly the media, what ethical principles should apply to their use of media?

SUGGESTED RESOURCES

Center for Journalism Ethics at the School of Journalism and Mass Communication, University of Wisconsin-Madison. http://www.journalismethics.info.

J-Source.ca, The Canadian Journalism Project. http://www.j-source.ca. See the "Rights & Wrongs" section for information on ethics and law.

PoynterOnline. http://www.poynter.org. A website on journalism, journalism trends, and ethics from the Poynter Institute.

REFERENCES

Barber, Katherine, ed. 2004. *Canadian Oxford dictionary*. 2nd ed. Don Mills, ON: Oxford University Press.

Blodget, Henry. 2008. Apple denies Steve Jobs heart attack report: "It is not true." *Business Insider*, October 3. http://www.businessinsider.com/2008/10/apple-s-steve-jobs-rushed-to-er-after-heart-attack-says-cnn-citizen-journalist.

Dube, Jonathan. 2003. A blogger's code of ethics. CyberJournalist.net, April 27. http://www.cyberjournalist.net/news/000215.php.

Friend, Cecilia, and Jane Singer. 2007. *Online journalism ethics: Traditions and transitions*. Armonk, NY: M.E. Sharpe.

Kuhn, Thomas. 1962. *The structure of scientific revolutions*. Chicago: University of Chicago Press.

Ward, Stephen J.A. 2005. *The invention of journalism ethics: The path to objectivity and beyond.* Montreal: McGill-Queen's University Press.

Ward, Stephen J.A. Forthcoming. *Media ethics: An introduction.* Cambridge: Cambridge University Press.

Ward, Stephen J.A., and Herman Wasserman, eds. 2010. *Media ethics beyond borders: A global perspective.* New York: Routledge.

CHAPTER 22

Libel, Journalists, and the Online World

Dean Jobb

CHAPTER OUTLINE

Libel 101

Imagine turning on the television news or clicking a headline on a newspaper website and finding a story that a prominent journalist lies to sources, does shoddy research, and rarely gets the facts right. It would destroy the journalist's reputation and career. No one would believe what she wrote and no employer would publish her work. This all assumes, of course, that the allegations made in the story are true. If there's no evidence to support the attack on the journalist's reputation, she would have the legal right to sue for defamation—and a court could order any media outlet that ran the story or any website or blogger that re-posted the allegations to compensate her with thousands of dollars in damages.

The law of defamation—or *libel*, as it's better known—protects a person's reputation from unfair and unjustified attacks. In the words of the Supreme Court of Canada, a good reputation "enhances an individual's sense of worth and value," and unfounded allegations can "very quickly and completely destroy a good reputation. A reputation tarnished by libel can seldom regain its former lustre" (*Hill v. Church of Scientology of Toronto* 1995). The law is not concerned with insults, name-calling, or abusive comments—while they may be offensive and hurtful, they are not necessarily defamatory. Language that is "simply crude, offensive and in bad taste," says a leading expert on defamation law, is unlikely to be considered libelous unless it also damages someone's reputation (Brown 2003, 26). One Canadian judge ruled that it is not libelous to call someone a "son of a bitch," for instance. "One has sympathy for a poor son of a bitch, admiration for a brave son of a bitch, affection for

This chapter is adapted from Dean Jobb, *Media Law for Canadian Journalists*, 2nd ed. (Toronto: Emond Montgomery, 2011).

a good son of a bitch, envy for a rich son of a bitch," the judge noted, but these terms are not libelous. Adding the adjective "sick," however, crosses the line, and describing someone as a "sick son of a bitch" is defamatory (*Lawyers Weekly* 1992).

A defamatory statement strikes at the heart of someone's reputation as an honest, law-abiding, decent person. The classic legal definition of a defamatory statement is one "which tends to lower a person in the estimation of right-thinking members of society generally, or to cause him to be shunned and avoided, or to expose him to hatred, contempt or ridicule" (Bruser and MacLeod Rogers 1985, 51). The following examples would fall into this category: any allegation of misconduct, corruption, wrongdoing, or criminal behaviour; an attack on someone's ethics, motives, competence, trustworthiness, or morality; calling a person a crook, a liar, or a racist; accusing someone of corruption, sexual impropriety, or professional incompetence. *Innuendo*—what a reader or listener can read between the lines of a news report—also may be defamatory. A news report exploring a municipal politician's lavish lifestyle and ties to a successful developer may never use the words "corruption" or "kickback," but this is the defamatory conclusion a reader would likely draw.

A note of caution: There is no magic in using the word *alleged*. Describing someone charged with fraud as an "alleged con man" is likely fine, but a media outlet that used these words to describe a suspect who never faces charges might have to prove in court that the fraud occurred.

Media law scholar Robert Martin (2003) suggests a common-sense definition: A defamatory statement "is simply something you would not like to see said in public about yourself." Imagine that *you* are the journalist described as inaccurate and untrustworthy. You would expect that those making such damaging accusations should be required to back them up with evidence.

Who Can Be Sued?

A lawsuit for libel will target the author or creator of an offending item—the reporter, columnist, editorial cartoonist, reviewer, or the citizen who submitted a letter to the editor. The editor or producer who handled the copy or authorized it to be published or broadcast can also be named as a defendant in the lawsuit. The news organization will also be sued. Media companies are responsible for all information they circulate and for this reason, usually carry libel insurance to cover any damages awarded.

Journalists cannot escape a lawsuit by claiming that they merely passed along the statements of a source quoted in a story. The source makes the defamatory statement to a single person—the journalist—but the media makes it public, causing the real damage to reputation. News outlets can also be sued if they reproduce defamatory information provided by a wire service or made public by another media organization.

A libel suit can target any element of a newspaper, magazine, or website: news stories, articles on sports and entertainment, editorials and columns, letters to the editor, cartoons, advertisements, and reviews of movies, music, books, and restaurants. The same goes for radio and television newscasts, from the lead story to commentaries, on-screen graphics, and audience feedback. Poorly or harshly worded headlines and photo captions can also defame, even if the accompanying stories do not.

SIDEBAR

Who Can (and Can't) Be Defamed?

Defamation law protects the reputations of *identifiable individuals*. For a claim to succeed, the plaintiff must establish that he or she is the person portrayed in a bad light in a media report. The person need not be named in the story, if his or her identity is clear from the context of the story or the facts reported.

- **Living persons.** The person must be alive. A reputation may survive long after death, but the legal right to defend that reputation does not. Relatives and descendants cannot pursue a libel action on behalf of a deceased person unless the defamatory comment reflects on them in some fashion. For example, a news report that a family's wealth was generated through the illegal acts of a deceased ancestor could damage the reputation of descendants.
- **Corporations.** Corporations are considered "persons" in the legal sense, giving them the right to sue for defamation. Allegations must relate to the way the company conducts its affairs; for example, accusations of defrauding customers or violating environmental laws. Other bodies incorporated or created by law, such as unions, school boards, non-profit organizations, and associations can also sue.
- **Group members.** It is difficult for members of a group to sue over allegations made against the group as a whole. A writer could not be sued for asserting that "all engineers are incompetent," even though the statement is clearly false, because individual engineers could not establish that the statement refers to them. Toronto's police union lost a bid to sue the *Toronto Star* over stories that alleged a pattern of racial profiling in arrests because the stories did not single out specific officers as racists.
  - *The size of the group matters*: the smaller the group and the more specific the reference, the greater the risk that one or more individuals can establish that they have been defamed. After a prostitute claimed in an interview that two members of a narcotics squad who were "high up—right up on top—take payoffs," a judge ruled that the squad's two senior officers could sue. Seven other members of the squad were barred from taking legal action because the allegation referred to only the "top" officers. Journalists must ensure that allegations against unnamed members of a group do not tar the entire group with the same brush. An Alberta court allowed 25 prison guards to sue over a story describing guards at a particular jail as "goons" and "not having the brains to be Nazis." No guards were named, but the criticism applied to the facility's entire staff.
- **Politicians and public figures.** In Canada, unlike the United States, politicians and public figures have the same right as other citizens to sue for libel.

Former prime minister Brian Mulroney sued the federal government over a letter linking him to allegations of kickbacks on a contract to purchase Airbus passenger jets, and received an out-of-court settlement of $2 million to cover his legal costs. The Supreme Court of Canada has rejected the American approach, which prevents public figures from suing for libel unless a media outlet or journalist has acted with malice. In a 1995 judgment, the court said, "it is not requiring too much of individuals that they ascertain the truth of the allegations they publish."

- **Governments.** Governments cannot sue for libel. To protect the right of freedom of expression, an Ontario judge ruled in 2006 that citizens must be able to question and criticize government actions and policies without fear of being sued. Individual politicians and government officials, however, have the right to sue to protect their personal reputations.

SOURCES: Brown 1994, 54, 79–83, 298–299; *Gauthier v. Toronto Star* 2003; *Booth et al. v. BCTV* 1983; *A.U.P.E. v. Edmonton Sun* 1986; Tu Thanh Ha 1997; *New York Times Co. v. Sullivan* 1964; *Hill v. Church of Scientology of Toronto* 1995; *Montague [Township] v. Page* 2006.

Good Journalism: The Best Defence

The law of defamation fosters and promotes good journalism. If journalists simply passed along rumours or allegations without separating fact from fiction, the news media would have no credibility. "If no one had any redress for libel," British journalist Paul Foot once noted, "no one would ever believe a word we wrote" (Martin 1992). The law protects news stories, columns, and opinion pieces that are factually correct, balanced, and fair in an effort to defend the media's role as public informer and government critic. "Libel chill"—the fear of being sued—may force media outlets to avoid or water down controversial stories. But if journalists conduct themselves professionally and responsibly, the risk of being successfully sued is greatly reduced.

Several defences can be made in response to a libel claim.

Truth or Justification

If there is proof a person lies or steals, that person cannot win a defamation suit over media reports that brand him a liar or a crook. But proving that information is true may not be easy. Allegations must be established using evidence admissible in court. Witnesses must be produced and they must be believable; a progression of shady characters with criminal records may have little credibility. *Hearsay*—what witnesses say other people heard or saw—is generally inadmissible in court. And witnesses are needed to verify that documents are genuine.

Consent

Like truth or justification, consent is a complete defence. If someone agrees to the publication or broadcast of defamatory information about himself or her company, the person cannot blame others for the resulting damage to reputation. People rarely give journalists permission to sully their names, of course, so this defence rarely comes into play. If a politician scoffed at concerns about his expense claims, for instance, he could not sue the media later if his own comments provoked a public backlash over such a cavalier attitude toward spending public money. By simply agreeing to an interview or to appear on an open-line show, however, a person does not consent to being subjected to defamatory questions or comments (*Syms v. Warren* 1976).

Qualified Privilege

Defamatory statements may be made in many public forums and in official documents—and, in turn, publicized through the media—without fear of attracting a libel action. Qualified privilege is a defence that protects the free flow of information and opinion, which is vital to our democratic system of government and the administration of justice (Gatley 1998, 327). Politicians can accuse their opponents of wrongdoing in Parliament or in a provincial legislature, even though the same statement made outside the chamber could trigger a libel suit. The same protection is granted to witnesses testifying at a trial, who must be free to implicate a suspect in a crime without fear of being sued. Other examples of forums protected by privilege include city and municipal councils, school boards, as well as their committees. There must be some element of public control over the proceedings for privilege to apply, so press conferences, lectures, political rallies, and church sermons are not subject to privilege (Crawford 2002, 40).

The person making statements in these protected forums enjoys absolute privilege, or complete immunity from being sued. The privilege granted to journalists to report such statements is "qualified"—subject to certain conditions. A news report must be a "fair and accurate" reflection of what was said. While this condition does not require a verbatim account of what occurred, the story must be accurate, precise, and reflect any conflicting facts or points of view (Canadian Newspaper Association 2002). The report must not be motivated by malice—there must be no evidence the journalist reported privileged material out of spite or as part of a vendetta against the person whose reputation has been tarnished. And the privilege ends at the door of the courtroom or meeting room. If allegations are repeated outside the protected forum, media outlets that report the comments can be sued.

Qualified privilege also applies to news reports based on the reports and records of privileged bodies, including transcripts of political debates and the rulings of courts, tribunals, public inquiries, and royal commissions. Information in documents used as evidence at a court hearing or discussed in a privileged forum is also privileged. Information in these documents must be reported fairly, accurately, and without malice. Qualified privilege also applies to news reports of pleadings filed in civil actions, as long as journalists make it clear allegations made in these documents have not been proven in court (*Hill v. Church of Scientology of Toronto* 1995).

Fair Comment

Journalists may argue that a defamatory statement is "fair comment"—a statement of opinion based on fact. The defence applies to editorials, columns, op-ed pieces, reviews, and other forms of comment, as well as media reports that express opinions. Like qualified privilege, fair comment is designed to promote free expression in our democratic society (Brown 2003, 169). Canada's highest court says the law must protect the right to debate and criticize. "We live in a free country where people have as much right to express outrageous and ridiculous opinions as moderate ones," Justice Ian Binnie of the Supreme Court said in 2008, ruling that a radio host's comparison of an anti-abortion activist to Adolf Hitler was harsh criticism, but fair comment (*WIC Radio Ltd. v. Simpson* 2008).

To be considered fair comment, a statement must meet four criteria. It must deal with a matter of *public interest*, which means a subject of public importance, not something trivial that happens to capture the public's attention. The opinion must be based on *established facts*, and these facts must be set out in the story or commentary. It must be an *honest expression* of what the writer or speaker believes, even if that person is "prejudiced, exaggerated or obstinate in his views." Finally, the opinion must be published or broadcast *without malice* (*WIC Radio Ltd. v. Simpson* 2008).

Responsible Communication in the Public Interest

The Supreme Court of Canada created this defence in a pair of 2009 rulings that overturned large damage awards against the *Toronto Star* and the *Ottawa Citizen* (*Grant v. Torstar Corp.* 2009; *Quan v. Cusson* 2009). It shifts the focus from what was published or broadcast—Are the facts true? Were comments made in a privileged forum?—to whether journalists acted responsibly in producing the story. It grants journalists reporting on issues of public importance the right to be wrong if, despite their best efforts, some facts or allegations turn out to be wrong or false. "Productive debate is dependent on the free flow of information," the court noted, and demanding perfection leads to an "inevitable silencing of critical comment" (*Grant v. Torstar Corp.* 2009).

To be protected by this defence, a media report must deal with an issue of public interest; this can be a story of either national or local importance, as long as "some segment of the community would have a genuine interest in receiving information on the subject." Stories can be about government, politics, or subjects "ranging from science and the arts to the environment, religion, and morality." A court will then assess whether reasonable steps were taken to verify the story before it appeared. The research done, the reliability of the sources used, and the efforts made to interview the person defamed and to get the other side of the story will be reviewed by the court. The defence also creates a class of news story called "reportage," which refers to stories where the debate itself, or the fact an allegation has been made, is of public interest even if the facts or allegations themselves cannot be proven. This defence may be a boon to reporters when they cover heated exchanges between politicians or when it is difficult to determine who's telling the truth. How this defence will be interpreted remains to be seen, but the Supreme Court says it may apply if statements are attributed to their source, the story makes it clear the statements have not been verified, and both sides of the dispute are reported fairly (*Grant v. Torstar Corp.* 2009).

Apologies and Retractions

If a media outlet discovers its report is false or inaccurate, it may promptly publish or broadcast a correction that sets the record straight and apologizes for the error. The wording of an apology or retraction is usually worked out in advance with the person defamed, as part of a settlement to prevent the filing of a libel suit. If no agreement can be reached and the person insists on filing a lawsuit, an apology or retraction reduces the damage to reputation as well as the amount of money a court will award if the libel action is successful.

TOOLS & TIPS

How to Libel-Proof Your Story

How a journalist has reported and written a story will likely determine whether a libel case is won and lost. Here are some steps to take to ward off "libel chill" and avoid a lawsuit:

- **Be accurate.** Double-check every fact and seek multiple sources to verify information. Where possible, base the story on documents protected by qualified privilege, such as court records and transcripts of political debates.
- **Avoid speculation.** Report the facts without speculating on motives. Is the politician who misled the public a liar, or was she mistaken or poorly briefed when the statement was made? The member of a visible minority denied a bank loan may be a poor credit risk and not the victim of racism.
- **Be wary.** Sources may have their own agendas or an axe to grind, so check out what they say before accepting it as gospel. Ask tough questions and be skeptical of any source who objects to being challenged or second-guessed. Leaked documents may be bogus and must be checked against other records and sources.
- **Be hesitant.** Mistakes may be made in the rush to make deadline or to avoid being scooped by a competitor. If the allegations made against someone are serious, it may be prudent to take an extra day or two to make further inquiries and seek more evidence to back up the story.
- **Aim for fair and balanced reporting.** Strive for a balanced report that portrays all sides of an issue or controversy. Good-guy/bad-guy stories are easy to produce; the truth is usually found in the grey areas between these extremes. Make a genuine effort to contact anyone who is being criticized in a story, even if the result is only a terse "no comment."
- **Be restrained.** Avoid sensational writing and headlines, and don't use words that are overly harsh or judgmental. Terms such as *conflict of interest, corruption*, and *negligence* refer to serious acts of misconduct and should not be used lightly. Let the facts speak for themselves; viewers and readers can draw their own conclusions.

Online Defamation

The Internet's global reach and easy access have created new challenges for journalists—and a new, rapidly evolving field of online defamation law. A defamatory statement is considered published if it is available to others, and posting information on the Internet is akin to displaying it on a global billboard that invites everyone to take a look. The Internet has been dubbed "the supreme mechanism for perpetuating libelous statements"—anyone with online access and a complaint or grudge can create a website or post a message for the world to see (Takach 1998, 388).

Publishing a libel to the Internet's vast audience has the potential to cause more damage to reputation than a report in the traditional media. Court-ordered damage awards reflect this. In 1998, in one of the largest defamation awards in Canada, a judge awarded Vancouver journalist David Baines $875,000 after a Florida-based writer launched a smear campaign accusing him of manipulating stock prices. A large portion of the award—$350,000—was compensation for information disseminated to "a worldwide audience" on the Internet (*Southam Inc. v. Chelekis* 1998).

The proliferation of news websites means that most journalists report and write for the Web, or soon will. Newspapers and broadcast outlets re-post material and original content to their sites, new sites devoted to news and commentary are popping up, and blogs give journalists and ordinary Canadians alike a chance to report and comment on events. The courts are recognizing this shift in the way news is published and received, and defamation law is evolving to keep pace. The new libel defence of responsible communication in the public interest is a forward-thinking example. The Supreme Court of Canada deliberately used the term "responsible communication" rather than "responsible journalism" to signal that the defence is available to anyone "publishing material of public interest in any medium." As the court noted, "the traditional media are rapidly being complemented by new ways of communicating on matters of public interest, many of them online, which do not involve journalists. These new disseminators of news and information should … be subject to the same laws as established media outlets." Citizen journalists will be held to the same standards as professional journalists, the court added, but these standards "will necessarily evolve to keep pace with the norms of new communications media" (*Grant v. Torstar Corp.* 2009).

Online Publishing and Libel Risk

Websites and Blogs

A journalist's blog posts denounced an Ontario businessman as a "huckster," a "two-bit shyster" and a "professional nuisance." In response, the businessman sued for $2 million, claiming damage to his character and reputation. The 2007 lawsuit, which was settled out of court after the blogger posted an apology, is one of many launched against Canadian bloggers (Cohen 2007; Canadian Press 2007; Ingram 2007). Posting libelous information on a website or blog is no different from publishing it in a newspaper or broadcasting it on radio or television.

All those who maintain a website or blog—media outlets, companies, and individuals alike—are considered publishers, making them legally responsible for their personal posts as well as the comments or responses others post to their sites. Webmasters should screen comments posted by others to weed out those that could be defamatory. Promptly removing comments that draw complaints or threats of legal action should be sufficient to stave off a libel action. In such cases, the website operator should be protected from liability as an "innocent disseminator" of a libel, but a word of caution: Canadian courts are only beginning to consider this aspect of the law and may hold media websites responsible for posted comments (Wong and Fischer 2008).

What if a website gets few visitors? One judge has ruled that the number of "hits" or visitors to a website is irrelevant. When a political party posted potentially defamatory statements on its website under the heading "Senate scandals," the judge ruled the party had published the material by making it available to a vast audience without restriction (Sutherland 1999).

Social Media

A Canadian poll conducted in 2009 found that more than one-quarter of respondents were unaware that they were legally responsible for libelous material distributed through social network sites such as Facebook, MySpace, and Twitter (Tong 2009). Rock star Courtney Love appears to be the first Twitter user sued for libel, accused in March 2009 of defaming a designer in a tweet (Marr 2009). In another well-publicized case, a Chicago woman was sued in 2009 for $50,000 by her landlord after posting a tweet that complained her apartment was mouldy. A judge dismissed the suit, ruling that the tenant's comments were too vague to be considered libelous (Sloan 2010). Libel law also applies to YouTube—in 2007 a judge ordered a London, Ontario man to remove a video posted to the site in which he attacked his former lawyer (Oakes 2007).

Hypertext Links

A website operator, blogger, or tweeter who provides a hypertext link to defamatory statements on another website may risk legal action. A British Columbia court has ruled that simply posting a link to a libelous article or website does not expose the person posting the link to a defamation suit. But those who post such links could be sued if they duplicate the libelous statements, endorse them, or encourage others to click on the link to view the offensive material (*Crookes v. Newton* 2009; Crerar and Skene 2009).

Newsgroups and LISTSERVs

Electronic bulletin boards, newsgroups, and LISTSERVs enable people with shared interests to exchange information. Although these services restrict their audiences, an Australian court has ruled that comments posted in these forums are published. In this case, a professor was awarded damages after an American colleague posted an inflammatory message about him on a LISTSERV, aimed at anthropologists, with 23,000 subscribers at universities around the world (*Reform Party of Canada v. Western Union Insurance Co.* 1999). A Canadian man who posted messages to a number of bulletin boards and message groups used by investors, accusing a mining company of theft, stock fraud, and genocide, was ordered to pay $125,000 in damages (*Barrick Gold Corp. v. Lophandia* 2004). In 2004 an Iqaluit woman threatened to sue a local online forum, Rantin' and Raven, after users posted abusive comments about her (CBC 2004).

Journalists and researchers often use these forums—which bring together people who share an interest in everything from antiques to zoology—to post appeals for information. When such requests deal with the reputation of an individual or a company, they must be drafted with the same care as if they were destined for a traditional form of publication.

Anonymous Postings

Posting information anonymously or using a pseudonym is no protection against a libel action. Courts in Canada and other countries have ordered companies that provide Internet access to disclose the names of account holders, so they can be sued for defamation (Geist 2001, 178–179).

Email

A derogatory statement made in a private email could become the subject of a defamation action. If the email is circulated to at least one person other than the recipient, it has been published in the eyes of the law (*Rindos v. Hardwick* 1994). Because email can be forwarded with ease, the person who wrote and sent the initial message could be held responsible if it is retransmitted by others—a court would likely take the view that the writer should have anticipated that his words could be disseminated to a wider audience (*Egerton v. Finucan* 1995). In 2008 an Ontario man paid a settlement of almost $8,000 for sending a defamatory email that was distributed to only three people (Powell 2008).

A writer or researcher who contacts a source via email must guard against posing questions or making comments that attack someone's reputation. Internet law expert Jeffrey Schelling's advice to writers is blunt: "Do not send any messages that you would not otherwise send in a letter." The ease and brevity of communicating by email, he adds, may leave a terse or poorly worded message open to misinterpretation. "What might sound reasonable in ordinary speech could be interpreted as aggressive, abrupt, or rude" in an email (Schelling 1998, 20).

A deliberate attempt to use an email message to defame someone is likely to result in a substantial award of damages. An Ontario man who falsely accused an archaeologist of being a "grave robber" in a widely circulated email—he urged recipients to forward the message to as many people and LISTSERVs as possible—was ordered to pay the archaeologist $125,000 in damages. In making the award, the judge said email messages are "far more powerful than … hard-copy letters" as a tool to defame (Freeze 2004).

Responding to a Complaint of Online Libel

If someone threatens to sue, an online publisher should seek legal advice on ways to reduce the damages a court could award if a lawsuit is filed. Online publications have the flexibility to remove an offending item almost instantly and can promptly post a correction, retraction, or apology. Steps also should be taken to remove erroneous or defamatory material from databases or archives that are accessible online. If someone retrieves or downloads the item, a court could consider this to be a fresh publication of the libel. If the story has gone viral and bloggers or other websites have re-posted the information, each of them risks being sued unless they take similar action to remove the defamatory material. The Canadian Press wire service, which offers a database of past news stories to its clients, has a policy of removing items that contain errors or have become the subject of a legal challenge, and replacing them with corrected versions (Tasko 2002, 178).

Conclusion

Journalists seek the truth and strive for accuracy. Their tools are an open mind and thorough research; their watchwords are fairness and balance; their criticism is based on fact, not conjecture. These are the elements of good journalism, and they are also a journalist's best defence against a libel action. The law of defamation is complex and evolving, but what it demands of journalists is simple: Get the facts right, report all sides of the story, be independent and even-handed when expressing opinions, and ensure allegations can be proven or defended. Journalists should demand nothing less of themselves.

DISCUSSION QUESTIONS

1. How do defamation laws encourage and protect good journalism?
2. A journalist receives a brown envelope containing documents that suggest a politician has been reimbursed for expenses she was not entitled to claim. The sender is unknown. What steps must the journalist take to verify the information before reporting the allegation in a story?
3. Which of the following statements could lead to a libel lawsuit? Why or why not?
   a. Professor James Smith is the best teacher in the world.
   b. Constable Jane Doe is a racist—she arrested a Middle Eastern man for the crime.
   c. ABC International Corp.'s forced removal of villagers to build its mine is an act of genocide.
   d. Mayor Jones bought a mansion and an expensive car soon after he voted in favour of developer Smith's condominium project.
   e. The top officials at city hall take bribes to fix parking tickets.
   f. The minister of justice lied when he told reporters no incidents of abuse had occurred at the jail.
   g. Many Canadians cheat on their taxes.
   h. The federal government is abusing its powers and violating the Constitution.
   i. The unnamed policeman, the only one in the city ever awarded the medal of bravery, allegedly beat up the suspect but has not been charged.

SUGGESTED RESOURCES

Grant, Torstar Corp. v. 2009. [2009] SCC 61.

This ruling established the "responsible communication in the public interest" defence. It is available at http://csc.lexum.umontreal.ca/en/2009/2009scc61/2009scc61.html.

Jobb, Dean. 2011. *Media law for Canadian journalists.* 2nd ed. Toronto: Emond Montgomery, Chapter 4 (Defamation).

J-Source.ca, The Canadian Journalism Project. http://www.j-source.ca.

See the "Law" section for updates on libel trends and other aspects of media law.

REFERENCES

A.U.P.E. v. Edmonton Sun. 1986. [1986] AJ No. 1147 (QB).

Barrick Gold Corp. v. Lopehandia. 2004. 2004 CanLII 12938 (ONCA).

Booth et al. v. BCTV. 1983. 139 DLR (3d) 88 (BCCA).

Brown, Raymond E. 1994. *The law of defamation in Canada.* 2nd ed. Scarborough, ON: Carswell.

Brown, Raymond E. 2003. *Defamation law: A primer.* Toronto: Carswell.

Bruser, Robert S., and Brian MacLeod Rogers. 1985. *Journalists and the law: How to get the story without getting sued or put in jail.* Ottawa: Canadian Bar Foundation.

Canadian Newspaper Association. 2002. Fair and accurate reports aren't necessarily complete, judge rules. *The Press and the Courts* 21 (1).

Canadian Press. 2007. Steelback Brewery president drops libel lawsuit. *Toronto Star*, July 3.

CBC. 2004. Web comments prompt threats of legal action. *CBC.ca*, August 2.

Cohen, Tobi. 2007. Steelback president files suit against Ottawa blogger. *Globe and Mail*, June 11.

Crawford, Michael G. 2002. *The journalist's legal guide.* 4th ed. Toronto: Carswell.

Crerar, David, and Michael Skene. 2009. Hyperlinks to defamatory material: Avoiding liability. *Lawyers Weekly*, November 20.

Crookes v. Newton. 2009. [2009] BCJ 1832.

Egerton v. Finucan. 1995. [1995] OJ 1653 (Gen. Div.).

Freeze, Colin. 2004. Scientist awarded cyberlibel damages. *Globe and Mail*, November 13.

Gatley, Clement. 1998. *Gatley on libel and slander.* 9th ed. London: Sweet & Maxwell.

Gauthier v. Toronto Star. 2003. [2003] OJ No. 2622 (SC).

Geist, Michael. 2001. *Internet law in Canada.* Toronto: Captus Press.

Grant v. Torstar Corp. 2009. 2009 SCC 61.

Hill v. Church of Scientology of Toronto. 1995. [1995] 2 SCR 1130.

Ingram, Mathew. 2007. Media stardom is pricey. *Globe and Mail*, June 16.

Lawyers Weekly. 1992. Calling B.C. alderman a "son of a bitch" isn't libel, but adding "sick" is libel [reporting on the ruling in *Ralston v. Fomich*]. March 27.

Marr, Garry. 2009. Tweet this: You're being sued. *Financial Post*, May 2.

Martin, Robert. 1992. Ont. paper's coverage shows why we need law of libel. *Lawyers Weekly*, March 27.

Martin, Robert. 2003. *Media law.* 2nd ed. Toronto: Irwin Law.

Montague (Township) v. Page. 2006. 2006 CanLII 2192 (Ont. SC).

New York Times Co. v. Sullivan. 1964. 376 US 254.

Oakes, Gary. 2007. Rant against lawyer on YouTube ordered removed. *Lawyers Weekly*, September 28.

Powell, Betsy. 2008. Defamatory email costs sender $7,800. *Toronto Star*, September 4.

Quan v. Cusson. 2009. 2009 SCC 62.

Reform Party of Canada v. Western Union Insurance Co. 1999. [1999] BCJ 2794 (SC).

Rindos v. Hardwick. 1994. [1994] ACL Rep. 145 WA 4 (Sup. Ct.).

Schelling, Jeffrey M. 1998. *Cyberlaw Canada: The computer user's legal guide*. North Vancouver, BC: Self-Counsel Press.

Sloan, Karen. 2010. Dismissal in early test of Twitter libel liability. *National Law Journal*, January 25. http://www.law.com/jsp/nlj/PubArticleNLJ.jsp?id=1202439486524&rss=nlj&slreturn=1&hbxlogin=1.

Southam Inc. v. Chelekis. 1998. [1998] BCJ 848 (SC).

Sutherland, David F. 1999. Defamation on the Internet. Paper prepared for Advocates in Defence of Expression in the Media (Ad IDEM). http://www.adidem.org/Defamation_on_the_Internet.

Syms v. Warren. 1976. 71 DLR (3d) 558 (Man. QB).

Takach, George S. 1998. *Computer law*. Toronto: Irwin Law.

Tasko, Patti, ed. 2002. *The Canadian Press stylebook: A guide for writers and editors*. 12th ed. Toronto: Canadian Press.

Tong, Tracey. 2009. Why the Internet can trap talkers. *Metro Halifax*, October 8.

Tu Thanh Ha. 1997. Mulroney, Ottawa settle libel suit. *Globe and Mail*, January 6.

WIC Radio Ltd. v. Simpson. 2008. 2008 SCC 40.

Wong, Tony, and Iris Fischer. 2008. Media must tread cautiously with defamatory web postings. *Lawyers Weekly*, March 21.

CHAPTER 23

Surviving and Thriving in Journalism

David Beers

Introduction

I used to believe I was teaching my students to be journalists. Now I tell them, and myself, that I simply share various ways to practise journalism. The Internet is so quickly and profoundly changing how journalism is done, paid for, and distributed that I no longer in good conscience can promise students that I'm training them for a lasting, well-defined job. And if Internet journalism is to blame for the shift, then so am I, because when I'm not teaching at the UBC School of Journalism, I'm editor of *The Tyee*, an online news and culture magazine in Vancouver, British Columbia. For people inside traditional newsrooms looking out, *The Tyee* probably seems the adversary, because we help nibble away at newspaper audiences and provide very few well-paying jobs in the process. We are part of the tide sucking away the sand beneath their feet.

CHAPTER OUTLINE

This does pain me, having spent a number of enjoyable years collaborating with excellent colleagues in two big city newsrooms, but the digital revolution is not to be thwarted—and so the question becomes: How can a young person (who has learned various ways to practise journalism) survive and even thrive producing for the Internet?

Launching Yourself into the World of Journalism

Begin with the Realization That the Internet Is, at Least for Now, a Lousy Money Economy—But an Amazingly Open and Efficient Reputation *Economy*

Twenty years ago, had you decided that you wanted to become a non-fiction writer recognized for your distinctive voice or insightful grasp of issues, you would have had to impress some of maybe two dozen editors at magazines or top newspapers in North

America, the gatekeepers who lunched with their favourites and had assistants sift through "slush piles" of unsolicited manuscripts and story pitches. That flow chart—with its vertical structure feeding into a few editor chokepoints—is much less relevant today, because the Internet is a far flatter, wider landscape. The Internet provides myriad places to be published, along with buzzing social media networks that will find and promote the journalistic voices they find relevant.

Especially when starting out, therefore, be clear in your aim to build your reputation on the Internet. You will need to build it consciously, strategically (about which more later). For some time, doing so may require you to find other ways to pay the bills. Until, that is, you have figured out a way to convert your reputation into money. Many people who write for *The Tyee* also teach or write books or edit reports or research others' books or consult with organizations—and all the journalism they produce enhances the reputation that allows them to command fees for what they do away from journalism.

Before the Internet, such people were looked upon with suspicion by those in newsrooms. But the world of newsroom denizens, after all, was holistically complete. Their reputation was earned and rewarded in the same realm where they made their pay. The Internet has proven a great force for pulling apart that world. Classified ads, stock prices, gossip, political opinions, funny pages—what used to be packaged all in one publication, now is fragmented into various sources online. Similarly, the Internet is pulling apart and refashioning the definition of who is a journalist. Some websites want bits and bytes and fast turnaround. But others, like *The Tyee*, are hungry to share the best, the smartest, the most capable voices with our readers, because that journalism is what "virals" outward, building our own reputation and traffic. Which brings me to …

Read the Best, Write Long, and Submit on Spec

You might think that succeeding at Internet journalism means mastering being succinct and even simplistic, the better to spare eyes weary of the screen. I would say the opposite. On the screen, as on a page, compelling storytelling is always a "faster read" than dull writing of fewer words. The journalism that enhances its creator's reputation often is the definitive piece on a subject—and that is rarely a short piece. So go ahead, give in to the pleasure of reading poetry, novels, the great journalistic stylists born of print's heyday. Then, inspired, report and write ambitiously, taking the room you think you need to tell the story in a way that is distinctive and powerful and memorable. Write the argument that everyone will use for ammunition on their blogs and Facebook pages. Write the first-person essay that everyone will want to email a friend. Craft the explanation that will cause everyone to say *ah-ha!* and hit "forward."

Don't be afraid to write without an agreement from an editor to publish your work. If this sounds like self-exploitation, you might also see it as liberation—the freedom to do it your way first. And consider this: Internet editors live in a sped-up world of emails and tweets and hearing their phone say "your voicemail is full." If I don't know a writer, I am much more inclined to invest time in reading an email that summarizes the gist of a piece, and then attaches a complete version. In a few minutes I can get a good sense of the person's talent, depth of expertise, and whether I might have something to run on Thursday after all. And if a good digital photo or two accompany the piece, I will be all the more motivated.

Of course, you don't want to be pushing poorly done finished pieces at that impatient editor, so ...

Learn to Edit

They say the best way to know a subject is to teach it. The corollary in journalism might be the best way to write well is to know how to analyze any piece of writing and, if need be, tear it apart and put it back together better than it was originally. In other words, to write well, learn to edit. And by edit I don't mean simply copy-editing for typos and homonym errors. The term "substantive editing" means being able to sense where a piece is going off the rails—Too dense? Too confusing? Voice a poor match for the topic?—and make improvements to its structure as well as the line-by-line prose. Volunteer to edit colleagues' pieces, and pay attention to the logic behind any good editing you receive from seasoned instructors or journalists. Doing so will make you more valuable and beloved when you ...

Build a Circle of Supportive, Serious Journalists (in the Real World)

Editors are good for some things: fast (often brutal) feedback, access to audiences, hopefully a cheque. But they aren't to be confused with mentors or colleagues. You need regular camaraderie with people in roughly the same situation as you, there to

David Beers with some of his staff at *The Tyee*. Building one's professional reputation and list of connections in the world of Internet journalism requires a clear strategy and focus, but aspiring journalists should also seek out a more informal "real world" community of friendly, supportive peers. (PHOTO: Justin Langille.)

share a laugh and also a frank appraisal of your work before you send it off to your dream publication. Finding freelancers to commiserate with is pretty easy. Seeking out and building a communal culture of friendly, supportive mutual criticism is harder—and far more essential to your success. Years later, in fact, this cohort may be instrumental in your ongoing success as they refer you to editors they know, or even become gatekeepers themselves. For now, as you assemble your circle and begin communing, a good way to avoid jealousy and overly competitive feelings is to share a dedication to craft, while each member pursues different routes of inquiry. This idea brings me to the need to …

Develop Your Own Set of Interlocking Areas of Expertise

The Internet is voracious for content, and the person starting out is tempted to be cheerfully up for any assignment. That's doubly true if the goal is to pay your bills solely through the freelance journalism you land. The problem with this strategy is that if each assignment isn't much related to the last one, the learning curve is steep each time. Contacts, research materials, and a sense of the next, best story to tell have to be acquired from scratch. And the sum of all your work, when you step back and look at it a year on, might seem without coherence. That won't help your reputation grow as a freelancer.

Here's one way to think about it. In the corporate newsroom, a strategy for being happy, needed, and productive is to be versatile, willing to take on any assignment. As you complete each assignment, your reputation as a team player within the organization grows, and your name comes up positively several times a week in the newsroom's editorial meetings, leading to rising status within the organization. The game is different for a freelancer. You'd like your name to come up now and again within the editorial suites of many different publications at different moments over the course of a year. One way to make that happen is to become known as one of the best writers in one or two or three areas. Whether it is water conservation or child psychology or fusion pop culture, the goal is to be clearly identified with the subject—the go-to person who is already up to speed. Consider maintaining your own blog as a way to demonstrate your expertise in one or just a few areas—as long as you keep your blog focused on those specialties, building your persona online as a serious person with focus rather than as an impulsive spouter of feelings and attitudes.

In deciding where to invest your journalistic energies, if you can choose subjects that overlap like the Venn diagram you learned in math class, all the better, as researching one area sparks story ideas and sources in another. When I was starting out, for example, I happened to live in a city with a fast-growing high-tech economy. I became interested in the temporary workforce model that was evolving there. Researching and writing about such labour trends led me to learn about and cover the boom in suburban development, which led to an intensive self-education about urban planning. And what were a lot of the high-tech companies in my region making? Weapons. Which led me to write about artificially intelligent weaponry and the ethics of working on such projects. Within a year I had developed a cluster of expertise loosely centred on the social implications of the vaunted high-tech economy, including labour, real estate, and military concerns. These subjects were fertile ground for good local stories, but, more important, they were of national and even global interest, broadening my chances for publication immensely. Most important, these issues really mattered to me and fired my intellect. I had been raised in suburbia in a family whose father was employed by a military contractor. My journalism was fused to an exploration of who I was and my hopes and fears for where our society was headed. That made it a lot easier to get up every day and go to work as a freelancer without a boss telling me what to do. Which raises the necessary caution …

Make It Fun, and Nip Self-Defeating Behaviour in the Bud

The Internet—with its lower pay rates and endless room for content—seems designed to accelerate burnout, already a too common occurrence among freelancers. Check your pulse regularly. If it's at a crawl because you are bored, ask yourself whether you are spending too much time alone in front of a screen. The best stories I've found arise out of face-to-face conversations, and journalism provides you a carte blanche to arrange coffees and lunches with the most interesting acquaintances and strangers, so take advantage of that. If your pulse is racing too often for the wrong reasons—anxiety or self-doubt—change your expectations and work rhythm. Avoid spiralling into procrastination and the limbo of self-loathing for missing deadlines that procrastination can produce. Learn to compartmentalize so that when you are doing journalism you are fully into it, and when you are not, you are fully there for friends and family, and yourself.

By all means, curse the Internet on the days it refuses to help you pay your rent with your journalism. Just don't forget that its creative destruction of the old order also opens up chances that were closed off to many in the generation that preceded you. Thanks to the Internet, there are many more paths to becoming a public person who contributes regularly and substantively to the democratic conversation. Such a person was, to me, the very definition of what it meant to be a journalist, when I first realized I wanted to become one. By that measure, at least, I have no doubt that the digital era is a better time than when I was coming up, sans Internet.

The well-resourced but walled world of the newsroom is passing, and the old road maps that would have taken you there are fading as they become obsolete. What lies ahead is an uncharted landscape that I believe will offer more freedom and opportunity to people who, while they may not *all* be journalists, are strategically and passionately good at practising journalism.

DISCUSSION QUESTIONS

1. Why do you want to practise journalism? Make a list of at least five reasons and rank the motivations in order of importance. (Examples: celebrity, being "in the know," making a positive difference in society, satisfying my craving for new experiences, et cetera …)
2. It's three years from today. You are spending the day doing exactly what you hoped to be doing, which involves (to some degree at least) journalism. What does that day look like, morning, midday, evening?
3. Seek out others who are currently doing what you hope to be doing. Ask them what strategies got them there, how they make ends meet, and how they define happiness.
4. Is the Internet eroding or increasing the power of journalism to inform the citizenry?
5. If the Internet is an ecology of information gatherers and sharers, what kinds of creatures do you wish to associate with and help flourish?

SUGGESTED RESOURCES

Benton, Joshua. 2009. Clay Shirky: Let a thousand flowers bloom to replace newspapers; don't build a paywall around a public good. Nieman Journalism Lab, September 23. http://www.niemanlab.org/2009/09/clay-shirky-let-a-thousand-flowers-bloom-to-replace-newspapers-dont-build-a-paywall-around-a-public-good/.

A video and transcript of NYU professor Clay Shirky's talk at the Nieman Journalism Lab, introduced by Joshua Benton.

Froomkin, Dan. 2009. Shout truth from the rooftops; passion is part of our job. Nieman Journalism Lab, May 27. http://www.niemanlab.org/2009/05/dan-froomkin-shout-truth-from-the-rooftops-passion-is-part-of-our-job/.

According to Dan Froomkin, "Our job is to expose and combat lies and propaganda, not pass them along for fear of appearing partisan." Read his entire series on news' future here: http://www.niemanlab.org/category/themes/danfroomkin/?=sidelink.

Gaulin, Jeff. n.d. Gaulin's Job Board lists opportunities in the journalism, media and communication industry. http://www.jeffgaulin.com.

Rosen, Jay. 2009. Rosen's flying seminar in the future of news. PressThink, March 26. http://journalism.nyu.edu/pubzone/weblogs/pressthink/2009/03/26/flying_seminar.html.

NYU professor Jay Rosen surveys a range of provocative thinking about where the Internet is taking journalism.

Tierney, John. 2010. The madness of crowds and an Internet delusion. *New York Times*, January 11. http://www.nytimes.com/2010/01/12/science/12tier.html.

New York Times writer John Tierney and the web culture critics he cites question "the glorification of open-source software, free information and collective work at the expense of individual creativity."

Index